Learning to Teach History in the Secondary School

In some hands, history can be an inspirational and rewarding subject, yet in others it can seem dry and of little relevance. The aim of this textbook is to enable student teachers to learn to teach history in a way that pupils will find interesting, enjoyable and purposeful. It incorporates a wide range of ideas about the teaching of history with practical suggestions for classroom practice.

This is the third edition of a textbook that has established itself as the leading text for student teachers of history. It has been thoroughly updated, with a revised chapter on the use of ICT in history teaching and major new sections in the areas of inclusion, resources, assessment and professional development. It provides an array of references and materials that give a sound theoretical foundation for the teaching of history, including weblinks to further resources. A range of tasks enable students to put their learning into practice in the classroom.

The book also provides reference and access to a wide range of recent and relevant research in the field of history education, which will be of use to student teachers pursuing courses that have a Master's level component. In all, it is an invaluable resource for student and beginning history teachers.

'This book is without question the standard text for the history PGCE market.' – Dr Ian Davies, University of York, on the first edition.

Terry Haydn is a Reader in Education at the University of East Anglia, UK. He was formerly Course Director of the Secondary PGCE course at UEA. **James Arthur** is Professor of Education at Canterbury Christ Church University, UK. **Martin Hunt** was formerly Principal Lecturer in Education at Manchester Metropolitan University, UK. **Alison Stephen** is Head of Humanities at Abraham Moss School Manchester, UK.

Learning to Teach Subjects in the Secondary School Series

Series Editors
Susan Capel, Marilyn Leask and Tony Turner

Designed for all students learning to teach in secondary schools, and particularly those on school-based initial teacher training courses, the books in this series complement *Learning to Teach in the Secondary School* and its companion, *Starting to Teach in the Secondary School*. Each book in the series applies underpinning theory and addresses practical issues to support students in school and in the training institution in learning how to teach a particular subject.

Learning to Teach History in the Secondary School

Third edition

A companion to school experience

Edited by Terry Haydn, James Arthur, Martin Hunt and Alison Stephen

Routledge
Taylor & Francis Group

LONDON AND NEW YORK

First published 1997 by RoutledgeFalmer
Second edition published 2001 by RoutledgeFalmer
Third edition published 2008
by Routledge
2 Park Square, Milton Park, Abingdon, Oxon, OX14 4RN

Simultaneously published in the USA and Canada
by Routledge
270 Madison Avenue, New York NY 10016

Routledge is an imprint of the Taylor and Francis Group, an informa business

© 1997, 2001, 2008 Terry Haydn, James Arthur, Martin Hunt and Alison Stephen

Typeset in Bembo and Frutiger by RefineCatch Limited, Bungay, Suffolk
Printed and bound in Great Britain
by TJ International, Padstow, Cornwall

British Library Cataloguing in Publication Data
A catalogue record for this book is available from the British Library

Library of Congress Cataloging in Publication Data
A catalog record for this book has been requested

ISBN 10: 0–415–43785–7
ISBN 13: 978–0–415–43785–1

This book is dedicated to the memory of Martin Hunt who inspired several generations of history teachers.

Contents

Illustrations

TASKS

Acknowledgements

The authors would like to acknowledge with thanks the contributions of Joe and Mark Haydn who did the illustrations for the book.

Introduction to the series

The third edition of *Learning to Teach History in the Secondary School* is one of a series of books entitled *Learning to Teach Subjects in the Secondary School* covering most subjects in the secondary-school curriculum. The books in this series support and complement *Learning to Teach in the Secondary School: A Companion to School Experience*, 4th edition (Capel, Leask and Turner, 2005), which was first published in 1995. These books are designed for student teachers learning to teach on different types of initial teacher education courses and in different places. However, it is hoped that they will be equally useful to tutors and mentors in their work with student teachers. A complementary book entitled *Starting to Teach in the Secondary School: A Companion for the Newly Qualified Teacher*, 2nd edition (Capel, Leask and Turner 2004) is designed to support newly qualified teachers in their first post and covered aspects of teaching which are likely to be of concern in the first year of teaching.

The information in the subject books does not repeat that in *Learning to Teach*; rather, the content of that book is adapted and extended to address the needs of student teachers learning to teach a specific subject. In each of the subject books, therefore, reference is made to *Learning to Teach*, where appropriate. It is recommended that you have both books so that you can cross-reference when needed.

The positive feedback on *Learning to Teach*, particularly the way it has supported the learning of student teachers in their development into effective, reflective teachers, has encouraged us to retain the main features of that book in the subject series. Thus, the subject books are designed so that elements of appropriate theory introduce each behaviour or issue. Recent research into teaching and learning is incorporated into this. This material is interwoven with tasks designed to help you identify key features of the behaviour or issue and apply these to your own practice.

Although the basic content of each subject book is similar, each book is designed to address the unique nature of each subject. In this book, for example, consideration is given to the importance of pupils' perceptions of history as a school subject. How can we teach history in a way which convinces puplis that it is interesting, important, useful and relevant to their lives? This will influence not only whether they will go on to take history after Key Stage 3, but will also have a bearing on their achievement in history.

The book also focuses on the ways in which student teachers of history should interpret the statutory requirements pertaining to school history. Above all, it attempts to bring together theories (or ideas) about the teaching of history with practical classroom approaches and examples. The third edition takes account of changes to the National Curriculum in England and Wales and to the way teachers are trained.

We, as editors, have found this project to be exciting. We hope that, whatever the type of initial teacher education course you are following and wherever you may be following that course, you find that this book is useful and supports your development into an effective, reflective history teacher.

Susan Capel, Marilyn Leask and Tony Turner
November 2007

1 Introduction

Almost every person who reads this book has studied history as a school subject in some shape or form. Most have encountered more than one history teacher and are aware of the difference the teacher can make to the experience of school history.

In some hands, school history can seem a desiccated and stultifying subject, of dubious relevance and little clear purpose; in others it can seem inspirational, important and rewarding. It can change pupils' lives, not just in terms of which direction they take at Key Stage 4 and beyond, but in terms of what they will be like as adults. The aim of this book is to provide practical guidance in preparing to become a history teacher, and insight into the factors which enable you to teach history effectively, and in a way which elicits the interest and enthusiasm of pupils.

Most people acknowledge that although subject knowledge is important, it is not the only factor involved in being a good history teacher. There is no *necessary* correlation between how well you did in your history exams and how good you will be at teaching history to children, although it is difficult to envisage how to teach history without a reasonable base of subject knowledge. Good subject knowledge is a necessary, but not sufficient prerequisite for effective teaching. Having degree level knowledge of the English Civil War does not in itself guarantee that you will be able to teach it in a way that makes sense to 12 year olds.

What are the other factors involved in teaching history, and how are the skills involved best acquired? The aim of this book is to provide practical guidance on these questions, and on how to bring together theory (ideas about teaching) and classroom practice.

FRAMEWORKS

It is important to remember that although you have a substantial degree of latitude in the way in which you approach the teaching of history in the secondary school, you are not a completely free agent, and that there are frameworks in place which you must take account of if you are teaching history in a state school in England or Wales. Perhaps the most important of these is the National Curriculum (NC) for history. In spite of concerns that a NC would significantly erode the professional autonomy of history teachers (Phillips, 1991; Thatcher, 1993), it should be remembered that the NC is a framework for the teaching of history, not a straitjacket (see Jenkins and Brickley, 1992; Bennett and Steele, 1995; Riley, 2000; Byrom and Riley, 2003). It requires initiative, imagination and interpretation, in order to teach it effectively.

We are aware that you are preparing to be a history teacher in different situations and contexts. We have tried to make the content of this book relevant to all student teachers of history, but when talking about the statutory requirements for history have, for ease of reference, referred to the NC for England. Those of you who are subject to other regulations should still find that much of what is said is of relevance.

Another essential document in your initial teacher education (ITE) course if you are learning to teach in England is the framework of teaching standards laid down by the Teacher Development Agency (TDA, 2007). Unless you have developed to competence in all strands of the three key areas of teaching expertise specified by this document, it will not be considered appropriate to unleash you on future generations of pupils. The statements of competence stipulated by the Standards for Qualified Teacher Status (TDA, 2007) are at the heart of the development of teaching capability, and you should refer to them regularly throughout your course, remembering that in terms of all these areas of competence, there is a continuum between complete ignorance and inadequacy on the one hand, and the (in practice unattainable) mastery of a teaching competence on the other. Part of your professionalism should be to aspire to the highest levels of competence possible in all aspects of history teaching, and to make as much progress as possible towards expert levels of competence, as a student teacher, and throughout your professional career.

Other important frameworks involved in your development as a history teacher are the schools and the history departments which you work with. History departments are organic and co-operative enterprises, which have a collective responsibility for delivering the history curriculum effectively, and for contributing to whole school policies. You have to harness your own talents and ideas to those of the department you work in so as to optimise the quality of experience for you, the department, and the pupils in your care. At its best, it can be a mutually enriching and positive experience for both the department and for the student teacher, but it is not invariably thus, and you need to deploy personal and professional qualities in addition to technical competence in the classroom.

PERSONAL AND PROFESSIONAL QUALITIES AND THE DEVELOPMENT OF TEACHING COMPETENCE

Very few student history teachers start their course with expert levels of proficiency and knowledge of all aspects of their subject, and in all aspects of teaching. Most student teachers will have some knowledge and experience in certain areas, but are novices in other aspects of subject knowledge and teaching expertise. Acquiring expertise and teaching proficiency is not just a matter of being instructed into a body of professional knowledge. It requires the application of personal qualities, such as perseverance, resilience, initiative, determination, and perhaps above all, willingness and ability to learn from experience, observation and advice (see Standards Q7–9, TDA, 2007: 4). In addition to the obvious attributes of professional integrity, reliability, conscientiousness and commitment to the welfare of the pupils in your care, you need to exercise qualities of adaptability, tact, and a willingness to make the best of whatever situation and circumstances you find yourself in. As a student teacher, you should always work within the aims, policies and practices of the department and the school you are a guest in. An important part of preparing to be a teacher is learning to work as part of a team, and 'fitting in' so that you are in effect a member of the history department, doing your best to make a full contribution to the work of the department in exchange for the time, care and guidance you receive (see Standards Q3–Q6, TDA, 2007: 4). The relationship should be a symbiotic one, where the student teacher contributes time, energy, imagination and initiative, in terms of developing resources, helping with visits, field work, schemes of work, and display work, in exchange for the support and advice which the history department provides. There are many difficult continuums involved in mentoring – the changing balance between pressure and support, encouragement and criticism, direction and freedom to experiment – as your competence and confidence develops. Your task, as a student teacher, is to make best use of all the resources and support available. This sometimes means reconciling conflicting views and advice as to best practice, and tests your skills of tact and diplomacy, as well as your ability to be 'a good learner'.

HOW DO YOU GET BETTER AT TEACHING HISTORY?

The following activities (Figure 1.1) are all areas of experience which you will encounter in the course of your ITE. Which do you feel will be most influential in enabling you to develop your teaching competences?

---

a **'Doing it'** – your own experience of teaching history in the classroom.
b **'Observing it'** – watching experienced and accomplished teachers teaching their history lessons.
c **Advice** – comments from, and conversations with your school tutor, and/or course tutors.
d **Teaching sessions** – formal seminars, lectures or workshops either in school or at your Institute of Higher Education (IHE).
e **Reading** – either prescribed reading, reading books like this, reading for assignments or casual reading of the *Times Educational Supplement* or articles in the newspapers.
f **Talking about it** – with fellow student teachers, in school, at your IHE institution or socially.

Figure 1.1 How do you get better at teaching history?

All of these experiences *might* make a contribution to the development of your competence as a classroom teacher, but the extent to which they are helpful depends on your response to them. It is important to consider that the process of becoming a history teacher is not purely aggregative, in that the more you do of all the above things, the better you become. Some student teachers are dismissive of 'theory' and tend to believe that it is mainly about 'doing it' in the classroom, and learning from 'seasoned combat veterans'. They may well miss out on some of the ways in which teachers improve their practice (see Figure 1.1). Others do lots of reading, talking and reflecting, but do not necessarily use these experiences to change the way they do things. It is about getting the most out of the range of experiences listed in Figure 1.1 by being open minded, being prepared to 'take things on board', trying things out and experimenting, and cultivating a good sense of self awareness of your developing strengths and weaknesses as a teacher.

There is explicit mention of the need to cultivate and develop these attributes in Standards 7 to 9 of the QTS Standards, particularly in Standard Q9, which states that student teachers must be able to 'act upon advice and feedback and be open to coaching and mentoring' (TDA, 2007: 4).

One theory which has been influential in teacher education in recent years is that of the 'reflective practitioner' (Schon, 1983). This rests on the proposition that gains in competence and understanding are at least to some extent influenced by the quality of thinking and learning which accompanies the activities undertaken by the student teacher. At its most simple, this encompasses the cliché that 'a mistake is not a mistake as long as you learn from it', and the idea that you must develop the skill of profiting from experiences by reflecting on them and attempting to distill the benefits which might be derived from them into what Labbett has termed, 'Principles of Procedure' (Labbett, 1996) for future occasions: what have I learnt from this, what would I do differently next time, how will this affect the way I operate in future? In Labbett's words, 'How have I transformed these experiences into practical suggestions to myself, when planning my teaching during first teaching practice?' It is possible that the comparative utility of these experiences will fluctuate in the course of your development as a history teacher, and that reading about teaching history, for instance, is more helpful when you can place the ideas and suggestions it contains in the context of classroom experience. What is crucial, however, is Labbett's contention that you need to be able to transform reading about educational matters into proposals to inform and test out in your subsequent teaching.

It should be stressed that the idea of the 'reflective practitioner' is only one model about how to develop competence as a teacher, albeit one which has been influential in recent years (for more development on this theme, see Moore, 2004). Others maintain that the craft of the history teacher is best acquired by the apprenticeship model, of learning it 'on the job', or that academic historians are best placed to deliver the enthusiasm for subject, and expert subject knowledge which are at the heart of good history teaching (Lawlor, 1996).

As with all theories concerned with education, it is important to be aware that there are usually differing theories and schools of thought as to how education is most effectively delivered, and that these theories need to be tested against your own experience to see which ones appear to be most valid or helpful. Teaching is not like bricklaying, plumbing or learning to play a technically correct backhand drop shot on a squash court; there is no single way of doing it which will work best for all pupils, for all classes, in all schools. There are different views on why history should be taught in schools, and how to teach it most effectively, and although teachers retain the ultimate control of how history is taught in the classroom, it is part of their responsibility to be aware of the range of views on why and how history might be taught.

HOW TO USE THIS BOOK

The book is set out in a way which attempts to provide a pragmatic introduction to teaching history in the secondary classroom. An important element of this is the bringing together of theory and practice, so that you are aware of some of the current thinking, problems and differing views on aspects of history teaching and can relate them to the situations you encounter in your classroom practice, and become aware of ideas about history teaching which you might *not* encounter directly in your school experience. The text is also interspersed with tasks or suggestions for points to discuss or reflect on with tutors or fellow student teachers. Where the tasks ask you to engage in activities which impinge upon other people, whether it be structured observation, or asking for information, it is important that you first seek the permission of the staff concerned, and that you exercise tact, sensitivity and good judgement in the timing of such requests.

In some sections of the book, there are also links to material on the internet, which provide further examples, references and ideas. The book provides examples of the sort of activities which might be attempted in your practical teaching. They do not come with a guarantee that they will work perfectly with all teaching groups, and you may well want to amend, adapt or discard them from your teaching repertoire in the light of your experience. Whilst you should feel free to experiment with some of these suggestions, or variations on them, you must remember that in the long term, you have got to develop your own ideas for planning for learning in history. Student teachers often find that it takes an inordinate amount of time to plan lessons in the early stages of school experience. There is an understandable temptation to use the resources which have already been developed by the department you are working in, or some of the ideas in this book. There is nothing wrong with this in the short term, and in a sense, all history teachers have to be 'scavengers' for ideas, materials and activities.

What is important is that you progress towards using your own ideas, or adapting some of the ideas you encounter in this book to other historical contexts, or developing extensions and variations to these suggestions and examples. Your short term 'want' is sometimes anything that will get you through Friday afternoon with 9Z; your long term 'need' is to be able to function autonomously, in generating your own ideas for effective teaching and learning in history – not just in terms of individual lessons, but in terms of planning your own route through topics, and into medium and long term planning for learning in history.

WHAT DO WE MEAN BY EFFECTIVE LEARNING IN HISTORY?

If you are reading this book, it is presumably your intention to devote at least some of your professional life to teaching history. If you have made this decision, you clearly want to do it well, in a way that is of maximum benefit to the pupils in your care. The following propositions underpin the content of this book:

There is more to teaching history than simply possessing expert levels of subject content knowledge

One of the main challenges of ITE is developing the art of transforming your subject knowledge into effective learning experiences for pupils. There is such a thing as 'pedagogy' – the science of teaching, and it is as important to develop expertise in this as to possess and develop your subject knowledge of the NC for history. In the words of Jacqui Dean, 'pedagogical content knowledge includes knowledge both of how children learn and of a range of teaching strategies; in short, the teacher's craft knowledge of how to teach . . . History teaching thus involves craft knowledge which is underpinned by academic subject knowledge and shaped by the teacher's concept of the nature of the discipline' (Dean, 1995: 4).

It is helpful for both teacher and pupils to have an understanding of history as a discipline, as well as a body of knowledge

If the study of history is to be of maximum benefit to pupils, it is important that there is a shared understanding of what 'history' is. If pupils are to make sense of the past it would be helpful if they understand why history is important and what are we dealing with when we study the past – what is the nature and status of the body of 'knowledge' which is the raw material of history lessons? Although many undergraduate history courses now include elements of historiography, not all history graduates can confidently answer the question, 'What is a fact?', or are familiar with the distinction which is sometimes made between 'substantive' and 'second order' concepts (see Lee and Ashby, 2000: 199–200, for a succinct explanation of this distinction). If the history teacher is quite clear in her own mind about the nature of the discipline, there is more chance that the pupils will have a sound understanding of what they are working with in the history classroom. Although there are those who argue that there has been a tendency to undervalue the importance of pupils' acquiring knowledge of the past, it would seem reasonable to suggest that they should also become acquainted with some of the rules of procedure of the discipline of history.

There are differing views on why and how history should be taught to children

It is your responsibility to be aware of the NC (or other appropriate) documentation pertaining to history, and the general debate over the purposes of school history over the past decade or so. It can be immensely helpful to keep this debate in mind as you teach history in the classroom. As the non-statutory guidance to the original NC for history stated, 'a strong sense of *why* history is being taught should pervade all curriculum planning, influencing the selection of content and methods of teaching' (NCC, 1991). One of the most common mistakes made by student teachers when faced with unfamiliar or intractable areas of content is to resort to treating the topic as a slab of the past to be transmitted to pupils 'neat' or in simplistic form, without thinking about what questions it poses, or why it might be helpful to pupils to know about this morsel of the past.

It is helpful to know something about how children learn

Just because you've taught it doesn't mean that they've learnt it. The *QED* documentary 'Simple Minds' (BBC2, 19 September 1994) demonstrated that in many cases, fewer pupils understood a topic after the teacher had taught it than before it was taught – teaching can actually damage pupils' minds. If we decide that something is worth teaching, it is worth spending some time thinking about how to teach it effectively. There is a body of research evidence which gives us some ideas and suggestions about achieving this. It would be churlish to disregard this source of help. Pupils arrive at your lessons with strongly rooted ideas and preconceptions about many aspects of how the world (including the past) operates. It is important that you try to understand and take account of pupils' preconceptions and ways of thinking if you are to move them on to more sophisticated and powerful ways of understanding both the past and the present. Without taking their understandings into account in your teaching, you may well leave their misconceptions undisturbed (see Lee, 1994: 141–8 and Lee and Ashby, 2000: 199–222, for further development of this point).

An important element of preparing to become a history teacher is the attempt to bring together theory and practice

'Theory', might equally be regarded as *ideas* about history teaching. Isaac Newton once said, 'If I have been able to see further than others, it is because I have been able to stand on the shoulders of giants.' Even the most creative and imaginative history teachers have augmented their teaching repertoire with things they have read about, as well as things that have evolved out of their own practice. Theories about how to teach history effectively constitute a potentially important resource in your development as a history teacher. The trouble with theories is that there are different ones which don't always work, and sometimes they contradict each other. This doesn't mean that they are not worth bothering with. Millions of words have been written about teaching history. Some of them will be helpful and give you insight, understanding and ideas to improve your teaching. Theories that do not seem to be of use can be discarded.

It is helpful if pupils can be engaged in the process of learning

It has been claimed that the attempt to engage pupils in 'active learning' has been at the expense of academic rigour, and has led to meretricious activities which children might find enjoyable, (for instance poster work) but which do little to enhance their understanding of the past. Whilst accepting that there might be times when this is true, as a general rule, there is more chance of real gains in learning where pupils are interested and motivated to learn. Successful history teaching depends in part on the ability of the teacher to present the past in a way which makes the pupils want to find out about the past. In the words of Burston and Green, 'The problem for historians and the history teacher, is how to demonstrate the relevance of history to the present in a sufficiently convincing manner to gain the interest of the pupils' (Burston, 1972: 3).

This is not to suggest that history needs to be reduced to constant game playing, poster drawing and group work. 'Engagement' in the process of learning history can be simply listening to the teacher's exposition, and thinking about the past. James Schick claims that in the United States, students often express a preference for lectures over other types of class, 'They want the teacher to tell them what's important, to select appropriate facts, to focus on the important issues. They want the teacher to provide all the answers . . . This low-stress arrangement puts as much burden as possible on the teacher and demands little intellectual growth by students. As teachers of history, we must not only revere truth, honour courage, and smash icons, we must require our students to do the same. We must not abet students' intellectual passivity . . . In education, the vital interaction should take place in the student's mind. Without this the potential for learning diminishes significantly. No teaching has occurred if students do not understand' (Schick, 1995: 11–12). It is not about making learning easy, but about making it interesting and challenging. But one of the 'bottom lines' is that it helps if you can get them to want to learn. In the words of Sue Hallam (1997), 'If you lose that, you lose just about everything.'

You need to develop a clear grasp of *progression* in history

What does it mean 'To get better at history?' There is more to it than just 'learning more stuff' – aggregating more information about what happened in the past. If you are to help pupils towards achieving their 'personal best' in the subject, you need to have a clear understanding of what progression entails in history, and what it means to be 'historically literate'. (See Chapters 2 and 10 for further information on progression.)

History in school can be a dispiriting and seemingly pointless experience for the pupils on whom it is inflicted. A survey of 10,000 pupils by Barber found that 70 per cent regularly counted the minutes to the end of the lesson (Barber, 1994). How many of us have not done this at some point? But history can also be taught to pupils in a way which gives them knowledge and understanding of the past, insight into some of the most important and difficult questions of human existence, and in addition, gives them other educational skills and an enthusiasm to pursue the subject beyond year 9. The aim of this book is to provide practical guidance, structure and ideas for your induction into the profession, and help towards teaching history in a way which is rewarding and fulfilling for you and your pupils. Effective teaching is not just 'common sense', and to regard it as such is to undervalue the skill and professional expertise of experienced teachers; teaching is a complex and difficult activity. It is because it is so difficult that it is also interesting, rewarding and worthwhile. Much of the job satisfaction of being a teacher derives from getting better at what you do (it can be helpful for student teachers to reflect on how much better they are in the latter stages of their education compared to their early efforts in the classroom). You will be exceptional if you manage to develop to expert levels of competence in all facets of history teaching in the course of your education, but you will hopefully witness expert levels of practice which will make you aware of levels to aspire to. We hope that this book will serve as a useful foundation for your development as a history teacher. The Board of Education Report for 1910–11 advised that 'in the long run, success or failure in history teaching, perhaps more than in any other subject, depends on the ability and interest of the individual teacher' (quoted in Aldrich, 1991: 97). We believe that this advice still applies.

Task 1.1 Learning from your own experiences in a history classroom

It is important not to make the assumption that because you probably enjoyed studying history at school, all pupils find history interesting and enjoyable. Several surveys over the past 50 years have found that many pupils think that school history is boring and useless (see Figures 1.2 and 1.3). You will have been 'the victim' of many history teachers. What were the characteristics and approaches which evinced your enthusiasm for the subject and made you want to learn and do well in history? And what were the activities and teacher characteristics which you found boring or pointless in history lessons? (It is perhaps important to remember that this might be partly about what the teacher was like as a person, not just their peda-gogical skills and teaching repertoire).

Survey and date	Useful	Not very useful
Schools Council Survey (1967)	29%	71%
Hargreaves Report (1984)	53%	47%
2005 QCA Survey	69.3%	30.7%

Figure 1.2 Pupils' views on the usefulness of history

Survey and date	'Enjoyable'	'Not enjoyable'
Schools Council Survey (1967)	41%	59%
Hargreaves Report (1984)	61%	39%
2005 QCA Survey	69.8%	30.2%

Figure 1.3 Pupils' views on enjoyment of history

(for further detail on these surveys, see Aldrich, R., 1987 and the Qualifications and Curriculum Authority (QCA) report, 'Pupil perceptions of history at Key Stage 3', online at http://www.qca.org.uk/qca_6391.aspx.

Task 1.2 Learning from recent research on pupils' attitudes to history in school

There is now a body of research evidence on pupil perceptions of history as a school subject. If you explore it you can gain some insight into what puts pupils off doing history, and what they enjoy about the subject. Below are five recent pieces of research in this area. Access at least some of these sources and draw up a brief list of some of the things which either deter or enthuse pupils in history. You may wish to consider how these relate to your own experiences of history in schools.

Adey, K. and Biddulph, M. (2001) 'The influence of pupil perceptions on subject choice at 14+ in geography and history', *Educational Studies*, Vol. 27, No. 4: 439–47.
Biddulph, M. and Adey, K. (2003) 'Perceptions v. reality: pupils' experiences of learning in history and geography at Key Stage 4', *The Curriculum Journal*, Vol. 14, No. 3, 292–303.
Harris, R. and Haydn, T. (2007) 'Pupils' enjoyment of history – what lessons can teachers learn from their pupils?', *Curriculum Studies*, Vol. 17, No. 4: 315–33.
Norwich Area Schools Consortium (NASC) (2002) 'Teachers researching disaffection', online at: http://www.uea.ac.uk/~m242/nasc/cross/cman/histfav.htm, http://www.uea.ac.uk/~m242/nasc/cross/cman/histworst.htm, accessed 9 October 2007.
QCA (2005) 'Pupil perceptions of history at Key Stage 3', online at http://www.qca.org.uk/qca_6391.aspx, accessed 9 October 2007.

Task 1.3 What can you usefully do before the start of the course?

- It is important that before the course starts, you try to address gaps in your content subject knowledge, particularly that relating to British History 1066 to 1900, which still forms a substantial part of the history curriculum at Key Stage 3. Student teachers often don't know which GCSE and GCE A Level courses they will be teaching until they are allocated to their placement schools, but you will almost certainly be teaching Key Stage 3 classes so you should ensure that you familiarise yourself with the NC for history at Key Stage 3 (http://curriculum.qca.org.uk/ subjects/history/).
- Try to gain as much experience as possible of working or observing in a secondary history department. This is invaluable in terms of developing your 'situational under-standing' (Elliott, 1991) of the context in which history curriculum specifications are turned into practice, and the wide range of factors that influence teaching and learning in the history classroom.
- Start reading about teaching history *in addition to* developing your subject content knowledge. You should read at least one book about teaching history (it doesn't have to be this one), and perhaps most importantly, you should subscribe to the main professional journal for history teachers, *Teaching History*. This now gives you electronic access to many back issues of the journal and to the Historical Association's website, which is becoming an increasingly valuable resource for history teachers (see www.history.org.uk). You may also wish to look at or subscribe to some of the many History magazines which are available, such as the *BBC History Magazine*, or *History Today*.
- You should find time to familiarise yourself with some of the many websites which are designed to support history teachers (see Chapter 8). The internet is now an invaluable resource for history teachers, and the sooner you learn to 'tap in' to this resource, the better.

- It can be helpful to read a book about classroom management and learning before starting the course. There are few schools where pupil behaviour is not an issue (see Haydn, 2007), where you can just walk in to any teaching group and just teach, without having to think of control issues. Some further guidance and suggestions for reading are given in the class management section of the website (www.uea.ac.uk/~m242/historypgce).
- You should register and do a preliminary exploration of the TDA's Professional Resource Networks for student teachers (IPRNs). These are major web resources which support student teachers by reviewing the knowledge base related to aspects of initial teacher education, identifying and developing effective practices, and providing relevant support and examples for student teachers. The sites also provide links to many sources and articles which are available electronically. Given that many student teachers will now be following 'M' level routes into teaching, these networks provide a very useful supplement to the resources available in libraries and course booklets. The web addresses for these IPRNs are given below:
- 'Behaviour for Learning': http://www.behaviour4learning.ac.uk/
- 'Multiverse': http://www.multiverse.ac.uk/
- 'Teacher Training Resource Bank': http://www.ttrb.ac.uk/

Task 1.4 The overarching importance of your professional attitude and approach to learning to teach history

It is impossible to overstate the importance of this area of the Standards for QTS (see Section 1 of TDA, 2007: 4). Two questions you might ask yourself, one at the end of your first visit to your placement school, and one at the end of the whole placement experience:

> *After your first visit:* 'To what extent did I make a good general impression on the colleagues I will be working with (to what extent are they looking forward to working with me, feeling confident that I will be highly professional and a pleasure to work with)?'

> *At the end of your placement:* 'If there was a job going in the department, how strongly would the department want me to apply for and get the job, even though they know there are a lot of very good student history teachers out there?'

Many teachers would argue that it is as important to be a good colleague as to be a good classroom teacher. One of the main concerns that a head of history has when interviewing for a new history teacher is whether that person will 'fit in' and work well within the department. Yes, they expect that teacher to be 'good with the kids', and a good classroom practitioner, able to teach the subject in a way that motivates and engages pupils. But if you are not accomplished in terms of the professional atributes listed in Section 1 of the Standards for QTS (TDA, 2007: 4), you may well struggle to find employment even if you are strong in other areas of the standards. Read through the sections on the website relating to mistakes that some history student teachers have made, as reported by history tutors (www.uea.ac.uk/~m242/historypgce/mistakes).

Some of these relate to 'technical' issues related to history teaching, but most refer to flaws in student teachers' overall professional attitude and approach.

If you have been working with a group of other student history teachers, towards the end of the course, (discreetly) think about which of your peers you would want to have working in your department if you were a head of history. What are the personal and professional qualities which makes some people attactive or congenial to work with?

Task 1.5 Dealing with difficulties

Part of learning to teach, and 'being professional', is learning how to handle things when they are not perfect or as they should be. There will be a vast *dramatis personae* in your education – tutors, pupils, year heads, colleagues, peers. It will be unusual if everything is perfect and unproblematic in your dealings with all these people. Think of a problem that has occurred in the course of your education, and discuss with a fellow student teacher what the options were for dealing with the problem and acting professionally.

SUMMARY AND KEY POINTS

If you are to be an effective teacher, you must be well prepared and well informed. You must quickly acquire a sound grasp of the requirements of the Standards for Qualified Teacher Status (for teachers in England, see TDA, 2007), the curriculum specifications for your subject, and the schemes of work of the history department you are working in. Your overall professional attitude and approach to the challenges of becoming a teacher are of overarching importance in making progress.

REFERENCES

Aldrich, R. (ed.) (1991) *History in the NC*, London: Kogan Page.

Barber, M. (1994) *Guardian* 23 August.

Bennett, S. and Steele, I. (1995) 'The revised history order', *Teaching History*, No. 79: 5–8.

Burston, W.H. (1972) 'The place of history in education', in W.H. Burston and C.W. Green (eds) *Handbook for History Teachers*, London: Methuen.

Byrom, J. and Riley, M. (2003) 'Professional wrestling in the history department: a case study in planning and teaching the British Empire at Key Stage 3', *Teaching History*, No. 112: 6–14.

Dean, J. (1995) *Teaching History at Key Stage 2*, Cambridge: Chris Kington.

Elliott, J. (1991) *Action Research for Educational Change*, Buckingham: Open University Press.

Hallam, S. (1997) Unpublished lecture on differentiation, Institute of Education, University of London, January.

Haydn, T. (2007) *Managing Pupil Behaviour: Key Issues in Teaching and Learning*, Oxon: Routledge.

Jenkins, K. and Brickley, P. (1991) 'Always historicise: unintended opportunities in NC History', *Teaching History*, No. 62, January: 9–14.

Labbett, B. (1996) 'Principles of procedure and the expert teacher'. Online at: http://www.enquirylearning.net/ELU/Issues/Education/Ed4.html. Accessed 9 October 2007.

Lawlor, S. (1996) *Times Educational Supplement*, 6 September.

Lee, P. (1994) 'Historical knowledge and the NC', in H. Bourdillon (ed.), *Teaching History*, London: Routledge.

Lee, P. and Ashby, R. (2000) 'Progression in historical understanding among students ages 7–14', in P. Stearns, P. Seixas and S. Wineburg (eds) *Knowing, Teaching and Learning History*, New York: New York University Press.

Moore, A. (2004) *The Good Teacher: Dominant Discourses in Teaching and Teacher Education*, London: RoutledgeFalmer.

NCC (1991) *History: Non-statutory Guidance*, London: National Curriculum Council, see section B1.

Phillips, R. (1991) 'National Curriculum history and teacher autonomy, the major challenge', *Teaching History*, No. 65: 21–4.

Riley, M. (2000) 'Into the key stage 3 history garden: choosing and planting your enquiry questions', *Teaching History*, No. 99: 8–13.

Schick (1995) 'On being interactive: rethinking the learning equation', *History Microcomputer Review*, Vol. 11, No. 1, 9–25.

Schon, D. (1983) *The Reflective Practitioner*, New York: Basic Books.

TDA (2007) *Professional Standards for Teachers: Qualified Teacher Status*, London: TDA.

Thatcher, M. (1993) *The Downing Street Years*, London: Harper Collins.

Remember, not all pupils share your love of the subject.

 Using this book: we have inserted many web references in the book, as this can often provide easy access to relevant resources, but web addresses can change, so you may find in some places you have to search within the relevant website to locate the relevant page where the website has been revised or updated.

2 The place of history in the school curriculum

From a transcript of a lesson on the Munich Crisis of 1938 (one of the aims of the lesson was to help pupils understand the concept of appeasement):

Tentative question from an intelligent, well motivated and polite pupil:

I'm sorry Miss . . . I'm not meaning to be rude . . . please don't take this personally, and I'm not meaning to get at history teachers . . . but why are we doing this?

Figure 2.1 Why are we doing this?

INTRODUCTION

One of the most common causes of poor history teaching is that student teachers have not thought through clearly the purposes of school history, and do not have a sound grasp of the full breadth of benefits that young people can derive from the study of the past. If you are going to dedicate your professional life to becoming a history teacher, you ought to be able to justify the worth of your subject's place on the school timetable, and understand why the study of history will be of use to your students.

As noted in Chapter 1, several surveys of pupils' views about studying history in schools have revealed that substantial numbers of them feel that the subject is boring and useless. One of the reasons that some pupils do not do well in the subject is that they are not committed to learning history. One of your responsibilities is to ensure that pupils feel that history is relevant, important and essential – it is one of the tests of your ability as a teacher. As Burston and Green noted in 1962, 'The problem for historians and the history teacher is how to demonstrate the relevance of history to the present in a sufficiently convincing manner to gain the interest of the pupils' (Burston and Green, 1962: 34). This is as true today as it was in 1962. You must look for opportunities to relate the past to the present and the future so that pupils can 'see the point' of learning about the past.

Although some challenges for the history teacher are perennial or longstanding ones, new ones are emerging. There have been a number of innovations and changes in the areas of teaching methods, ideas about 'learning styles', curriculum specifications and educational technologies, all of which have impacted on pupils' learning in the history classroom, as have 'public' and political ideas about school history. It is an important part of your subject knowledge that you are aware of these issues and developments, and that you keep 'up to date' with your subject.

Task 2.1 Developing your understanding of the range of views about why pupils should study history at school

You should try to read widely on the recent history of the history curriculum and the 'history wars' of the past few decades. This should help you to acquire a clear and well developed sense of *why* you are teaching history, and an awareness that there are very different views about why young people should study history.

 The webpage below will give you suggestions for further reading on the recent history of the history curriculum, and a number of quotes from prominent politicians, historians and educationalists on the purposes of school history: www.uea.ac.uk/~m242/historypgce/purposes.

OBJECTIVES

At the end of this chapter you should:

- be aware of the on-going debate about the place of history in the school curriculum and have a sound grasp of the evolution of the present NC for history;
- be aware that there are differing views as to why and how history should be taught in schools;

- be familiar with the rationales for the teaching and learning of history which have been advanced in recent years, providing a justification which you could articulate to others for its continuing place in schools;
- have a critical perspective on the teaching and learning of history within current developments, policies, practices and debates.

DIFFERING VIEWS ON THE PURPOSES OF SCHOOL HISTORY

(The list is not an exhaustive one, and in some cases, it could be argued that they are 'phoney' arguments, or false dichotomies; it is a question of balance, rather than 'either-or'.)	
School history should be about cultural transmission, passing on the best of what has been written and said, giving pupils a sense of identity, and developing the values and attitudes that will make them good citizens.	School history should be about teaching pupils to handle information critically and intelligently; it should be about helping pupils to think for themselves, rather than teaching them what to think.
There needs to be more emphasis on British history, as this is the country that pupils grow up in.	We need to move away from a narrow, Anglocentric model of school history.
Political and constitutional history – great events, great men and women – should be at the heart of school history.	There should be more to school history than 'the great tradition'. School history should reflect changes in academic history and the moves towards 'histories'.
Modern/contemporary history is most relevant and useful for pupils.	There is a worrying trend towards pupils receiving a diet of 'Hitler, Stalin and the World Wars' – and repeating the same topics at Key Stage 3, GCSE and 'A' level.
There should be a clear separation between history and current affairs – history teaching has become too 'political'.	It is important to link the past to the present if it is to be relevant and helpful to pupils.
School history should be about providing pupils with a body of knowledge about the past. Pupils need to be told what happened, and learn facts and dates. Recent trends, such as analysing 'dismembered gobbets' of history, have meant that pupils don't really know 'what happened'.	Pupils also need to understand the nature of historical knowledge, and history as a discipline, if they are to make sense of these facts and dates.
History teachers should tell pupils what happened in the past.	History teachers need to teach pupils about 'interpretations' of the past.

Figure 2.2 A 'thumbnail' summary of some of the recent arguments about school history

Task 2.2 Developing an understanding of the breadth of ideas about why young people should learn history in school

Look at the list of quotations about the purposes of school history at: www.uea.ac.uk/~m242/historypgce/purposes/purpquotes.htm. The purpose of this sub-collection of quotes is to make student history teachers aware of the range of views which are held about the purposes and benefits of the study of history. Is it possible to classify them into 'schools of thought'? Can you draw up a concise list of the benefits bestowed by the study of history by reading through the quotes, avoiding repetition? Do views on the purposes of school history depend on one's perspective? Do politicians tend to want history to develop loyal, patriotic and compliant citizens, and educationalists want school history to develop independence of mind, informed scepticism and good judgement? Could you make an intelligent guess whether the quotes were uttered by politicians, historians or educationalists? Does the study of history give people the ability to make inferential judgements of this nature?

The URL www.uea.ac.uk/~m242/historypgce/purposes/welcome.htm also contains a link to a longer list of quotations about the purposes of school history which may be of interest or use when writing assignments in this area.

The decision to implement a NC for history brought about several attempts to summarise the aims of school history (DES,1988; NCC,1991; DfEE/QCA,1999; Haydn, 2004). At one level, these lists were generally uncontroversial, and gained tacit acceptance at least within the teaching profession. The public debate which was unleashed by the decision to introduce a NC for history did however make it clear that once one got beyond very general statements of aims, there were very differing views on what historical content should be taught, and which of the aims of school history were most important. Successive Prime Ministers and Secretaries of State for Education made pronouncements on school history, and there were hundreds of newspaper articles about school history. The national debate on school history helped to raise the profile of the subject. At least it seemed that there was a consensus that history was very important, and that the way in which it was taught would have a significant bearing on the sort of citizens who would emerge from schools.

The debate also raised the question of the connection between the uses of history in general, and history in schools. One view of the purpose of history is to record those things which have been selected as important in giving us a sense of identity and context.

Task 2.3 Developing an understanding of the issues of 'identity' and 'Britishness' in the context of the history classroom

a   The issue of 'identity' has become politically high-profile in recent years, particularly in the context of 'Britishness', and what it means to be British in the twenty-first century. How would you approach a lesson on 'Britishness' in a lesson with Key Stage 3 pupils? A list of readings and resources on the issue of school history and identity can be accessed at www.uea.ac.uk/~m242/historypgce/purposes/welcome.htm.

b   What other forms of identity do people have, and to what extent should school history address forms of identity other than 'national' ones? (It can be interesting to ask pupils to make a list of loyalties, affiliations and 'identities' and then ask them to put them in order of importance, although this idea often needs to be 'modelled' by the teacher so that pupils get a clear idea of the full breadth of 'identities' that people have.)

Issues such as 'identity' and 'Britishness' help to explain the controversial and contested nature of school history. In the words of Tate, 'A fundamental purpose of the school curriculum is to transmit an appreciation of and commitment to the best of the culture we have inherited' (Tate, 1996). Implicit in this statement is the reality that as the record of the human past is so vast, we cannot learn everything about it, and we must therefore make a selection from the past.

It is at this point, when the business of school history is seen to be one of cultural transmission, that the difficulties in achieving consensus on school history becomes more apparent. Who selects? What are their motives? Are they promoting any particular ideology, explicitly or covertly? Is there any significance in those topics which are not selected? What criteria are used for the selection of content? You need to be continually aware of the different rationales for the selection of history content and also remind yourself of the content of a discussion paper on 'History from 5–16' which suggests that the content of history courses needs to be continually re-assessed and recast (HMI, 1988). Slater has argued that until recently, the selection from the culture that formed the basis of school history was 'an inherited consensus, based largely on hidden assumptions, rarely identified, let alone publicly debated.' He parodied (but with a degree of accuracy) school history as:

> largely British, or rather Southern English; Celts looked in to starve, emigrate or rebel, the North to invent looms or work in mills; abroad was of interest once it was part of the Empire; foreigners were either, sensibly, allies, or, rightly, defeated. Skills – did we even use the word? – were mainly those of recalling accepted facts about famous dead Englishmen, and communicated in a very eccentric literary form, the examination-length essay.
>
> (Slater, 1989: 1)

In addition to these concerns, developments in academic history also percolated through to school level, with the idea of a range of histories, rather than one grand historical narrative, including 'history from below', women's history, and the history of minority cultures. Discussion of what should be essential elements of a NC for history produced very different ideas as to essential content.

An idea of the scale of these differences can be gained from comparing Pankhania's suggestions in *Liberating the National Curriculum* (Pankhania, 1994), featuring the oppression of Ireland, the oppression of the Palestinians, the oppression of the native peoples of North America, the oppression of slaves, oppression by the British Empire . . . with the more classical canon stipulated by Robert Conquest:

> an educated man must have a certain minimum of general knowledge. Even if he knows very little about science and cannot add or subtract, he must have heard of Mendel and Kepler. Even if he is tone deaf, he must know something about Debussy and Verdi, even if he is a pure sociologist, he must be aware of Circe and the Minotaur, of Kant and Montaigne, of Titus Oates and Tiberius Gracchus.
>
> (Conquest, 1969: 3)

Somewhere between these views was the concern that it would be helpful to those who had to teach history in the secondary classroom (sometimes to pupils who were not devoted scholars or persuaded of the utility or relevance of school history) if the content could bear in mind the extent to which it would be likely to engage pupils in the enthusiastic and committed pursuit of history. It was pointed out that 'many pupils in comprehensive schools have a pragmatic and instrumental approach to education and a degree of resistance or indifference to some of the more arcane aspects of history . . . interest, relevance and accessibility are the *sine qua non* of teaching history in ordinary schools' (Haydn, 1992a: 9). This echoes the concerns expressed in an HMI discussion paper which stated that 'skills are unlikely to be acquired . . . unless they are related to content that has some inherent interest and appears to relate to the lives of the pupils' (HMI, 1985: 12).

For much of the time that history has been on the school curriculum, its prime aim was seen as providing moral examplars. In the words of Willis Bund:

> to bring before the children the lives and work of English people who served God in church and state, to show that they did this by courage, endurance and self-sacrifice, that as a result the British Empire was founded and extended, and that it behoved every child to emulate them.
>
> (Willis Bund, 1908)

Such ideas about school history have not disappeared, and as recently as 1990, one MP asked 'Why cannot we go back to the good old days when we learnt by heart the names of the kings and queens of England, the feats of our warriors and our battles and the glorious deeds of our past?' (Stokes, 1990).

But by the 1980s, there were also different ideas about the ways in which school history might be used as a sort of 'social cement', to bind the population together (Aldrich and Dean, 1991: 102). Although some commentators still believed that school history should be about persuading pupils that 'to be born British is to draw first prize in the lottery of life', some metropolitan education authorities wanted to use school history to promote appreciation of cultural diversity, celebrate cultural pluralism, and combat racism (Haydn, 1992b, 1996). Others expressed reservations about the use of school history to 'demonstrate' any of these claims or values, arguing that school history was more useful in terms of helping pupils' understanding of the world and their place in it: 'the reason for teaching history is not that it changes society, but that it changes pupils, it changes what they see in the world, and how they see it' (Lee et al., 1992: 23). Whether school history should concern itself with the affective domain of values and attitudes is another contested area. Is school history to tell pupils what to think or to teach them to think for themselves?

It is tempting to be seduced by Christopher Hill's dictum that 'history properly taught can help men to become critical and humane, just as wrongly taught, it can turn them into bigots and fanatics' (Hill, 1953: 8), but as soon as we start to enter the realm of values and attitudes, and what constitutes history 'properly taught', we encounter problems of consensus as to which values and attitudes should be inculcated through the study of history.

Another important point to note is the relation between history for academic purposes, and history in schools. An explanation of some of the differences between academic and school history is provided by Husbands:

> Where historians are engaged in an interpretative activity relating the current state of the discipline to new research findings, history teachers are largely concerned with their pupils' intellectual and personal development . . . There is an academic discipline called 'history', a school subject called 'history', and a widespread popular interest in 'history'. There is no reason why all these pursuits should have the same label, nor why the label should have the same meaning in different contexts.
>
> (Husbands, 1996: 5)

Keeping in mind these distinctions is an important part of learning to teach history effectively. We teach it not simply as a preparation for the study of history at university – many of your pupils will not go to university – but because some aspects of the subject are useful to pupils in their lives after school. History is both a body of knowledge, and a form of knowledge, and some of the historian's rules of procedure may aid intelligent decision making in life beyond the classroom. Some aspects of the discipline help pupils to cope with the 'spin' which has become a pervasive part of modern life. In the words of HMI, 'A subject that insists on the critical evaluation of evidence . . . and encourages the analysis of problems and the communication of ideas, not only contributes to pupils' general education, but develops skills and perceptions that increase the employability of young people' (HMI, 1985: 12).

As history teachers, how do we handle the lack of consensus about the purposes of school history, and about which (if any) values and attitudes should be promoted through school history? One way forward is to consider Slater's suggestion that school history is where values and attitudes are *examined, discussed and debated*, rather than simply transmitted:

> [History] not only helps us to understand the identity of our communities, cultures, nations, by knowing something of their past, but also enables our loyalties to them to be moderated by informed and responsible scepticism. But we cannot expect too much. It cannot guarantee tolerance, though it can give it some intellectual weapons. It cannot keep open closed minds, although it may sometimes leave a nagging grain of doubt in them. Historical thinking is *primarily* mind-opening, *not* socialising.
>
> (Slater, 1989: 12)

Examining competing claims about the past, and making comparisons between the past and the present is a way of making history powerful, rigorous, relevant and interesting to pupils. As Arnold notes,

> If the past came without gaps and problems, there would be no task for the historian to complete. And if the past always spoke plainly, truthfully and clearly to us, not only would historians have no work to do. We would have no opportunity to argue with each other. History is above all else an argument.
>
> (Arnold, 2000: 13)

There continues to be much debate about the aims of school history; the 'wars' of school history are not over. It is therefore important that you are aware of the differing views about the purposes of school history, and that in the light of this knowledge, you consider carefully what you are trying to achieve in your history lessons. With any area of historical content, and with regard to the discipline of history as a whole, you should be able to justify why it is worthwhile teaching it to young people.

Task 2.4 Relating what we are trying to achieve in the history classroom to the values aims and purposes of the National Curriculum

to think about...

Another way of handling the range of views about the purposes of school history is to look at the official 'definition' of the aims, purposes and values which the school curriculum aims to imbue in young people. This is a comparatively neglected component of the NC, and yet it is clearly very important. Read the section on values, aims and purposes at: http://www.nc.uk.net/nc_resources/html/valuesAimsPurposes.shtml.

What are the implications of these statements for teachers of history? You may wish to print off the section and underline the statements which clearly have implications for the way in which you teach history.

This section can be in a sense, your 'warrant' for how you teach your subject. (You may also wish to think about the extent to which these values, aims and purposes are reflected in current practice.)

During school experience you should discuss with your tutor the department's policy and documentation which attempts to interpret the NC for history, and identify how the key aims in learning/teaching history are reflected in that documentation. You generally find that history teachers do have views on the purposes of school history which influence the ways in which they teach their subject. Different teachers and departments see some purposes as more important than others.

Task 2.5 The aims of teaching history

As part of your school experience you are given a history departmental handbook which contains the stated aims of the history teaching in your school. You also have a number of opportunities to observe history teaching by qualified teachers in your subject prior to you being responsible for planning and teaching history yourself. To what extent do the following aims feature in the practice and documentation of history teaching in your school? Use the four questions below to frame your answers.

- History taught 'for its own sake', because it is interesting.
- History taught to expand pupils' knowledge and understanding of their local, national, and international communities.
- History taught as a means of socialisation through the transmission of cultural norms and values to the next generation.
- History taught to introduce pupils to their heritage through monuments, historic buildings and towns, architecture, museums, and written sources which chronicle the events of the past.
- History taught to develop some of the skills of the historian, in a way which enriches the pupils' intellectual development.
- History taught to instil civic pride and patriotism.
- History taught to promote virtue and awareness of what is right and wrong.
- History to help people to handle information critically and intelligently.
- History to provide a sense of identity.

1   Which of these aims do you find in the department handbook?
2   Which of these aims did you observe being implemented in practice?

> 3   Which of these aims is your current teaching concerned with?
> 4   Which, if any, of the above aims of teaching history are problematic for your teaching of history to pupils and why would this be the case?
>
> Describe any difficulty you might have with any of these aims; discuss these issues with your tutor.

THE RECENT HISTORY OF THE HISTORY CURRICULUM: HOW DID WE GET TO WHERE WE ARE NOW?

Concern about the nature and state of health of history as a school subject could be dated from Mary Price's influential paper, 'History in danger' (Price, 1968). History in schools, Price suggested, was unpopular, in decline, and often taught with pupils adopting a mainly passive role absorbing a body of knowledge or facts from the teacher. Change came slowly, but grew partly out of a perception of danger for the survival of the subject. There was real concern that the subject could be marginalised as just one component in an 'integrated' humanities/social studies model. Partly in response to these concerns, the Schools Council History Project was established in the early 1970s and promoted new teaching methods in order to generate more active learning among pupils and placed greater emphasis on the use of resources in the classroom. The project was designed to encourage understanding of the nature of history and its fundamental concepts. This process of change was controversial for it entailed making history less exclusively a body of knowledge to be learnt, and placed more emphasis on pupils' understanding of history as a form of knowledge, with its particular procedures and conventions. The 'New History', as it came to be called, focused on concepts such as evidence, empathy and cause and used primary sources as evidence in a pupil centred approach. Former HMI for history John Slater described the Schools History Project as 'the most significant and beneficent influence on the learning of history to emerge this century', arguing that this form of school history could give young people 'not just knowledge, but the tools to reflect on, critically to evaluate, and to *apply* that knowledge. It proclaims the crucial distinction between knowing the past and thinking historically' (1989: 2–3).

The project was not without its critics. Williams (1986) commented that whilst history had been liberated from 'the transmission of a corpus of information in a linear and chronological framework' it was also true that 'a sense of chronology had been sacrificed' and that this was something that traditional history did much better. Even defenders of the project such as Slater acknowledged that there was a price to be paid in terms of the breadth of content which could be covered if time was also to be given to providing pupils with more insight into the nature of historical knowledge, and in terms of coherence, continuity and focus (Slater, 1989: 2).

Criticism began to emerge that history had gone full circle, from an excessive emphasis on content to an excessive emphasis on process or skills. Beattie high-lighted two main criticisms from the political right. First, an increase in what was seen as corrosive and insidious moral relativism, and the contention that there were no 'facts' in history any more since empathy, evidence and imagination were to take on greater importance as the pupils themselves were asked to analyse and interpret the past. Second, that the demand for relevance in history was reducing history to current affairs.

The fact that the new GCSE examination in 1988 appeared to adopt many aspects of 'new' history served to polarise the debate still further. Other than the stipulation that each examination board should offer at least one examination based on the history of the United Kingdom, and that syllabuses must be of sufficient length, range and depth, deal with key issues and be 'coherent and balanced', there was no requirement to teach any particular areas of historical content. It seemed to many to be a denial of the existence or desirability of a historical 'canon' which all pupils should be taught. To some, it seemed tantamount to saying that the content of school history didn't matter – that it was acceptable for pupils to learn GCSE history through content that had little or nothing to do with British history.

Another important contribution to the debate on school history was made by Secretary of State for Education, Sir Keith Joseph. He strongly advocated the teaching of history to all up to the age of 16 and his speech remains a benchmark for the place of history in the school curriculum. Joseph pointed to a key difference between the processes of reasoning which might be used in history as opposed to science, when he noted that one of the purposes of school history was to help pupils to 'use their reason as well as their memories, and to develop skills of analysis and criticism in a situation where there cannot be a right answer' (Joseph, 1984). In 1985 Her Majesty's Inspectorate (HMI) produced a framework in which secondary schools might develop history schemes of work, detailing targeted aims, objectives and principles (HMI, 1985). Their aims of history varied from the general, 'to understand the values of our society', to the more focused, 'to look for explanations of change in terms of human intentions, beliefs and motives as well as of environmental factors'. It is helpful to understand these developments because the NC for history that you have to teach is an uneasy mixture of 'new' and 'old' history (and the 'history wars' which have accompanied its development continue).

Task 2.6 Thinking about teaching approaches and what pupils are learning

Over a period of one week during your school experience make a list of the range of teaching approaches used in the history classroom, either by you or other teachers. They might include some of the following:

dictation   discussion   use of textbooks   use of worksheets   reading round the class   copying from the board   group work   use of original sources as evidence   teacher exposition/storytelling   pupils watch video/DVD extract   use of interactive whiteboard   roleplay   pupils read   pupils work on computers   pupil presentations or poster work

What is the relationship between the pupils' knowledge, skills and understanding while these activities were taking place?
In what parts of the lessons did pupils gain knowledge?
In what parts of the lessons did pupils gain 'skills'?
In what parts of the lessons did pupils gain in understanding of aspects of the past?
In what ways do teaching methods influence the balance between knowledge, skills and understanding?
What are history teachers trying to get their pupils to learn *as well as* knowledge and understanding of some of the things that happened in the past?

What proportion of the pupils seemed to be committed to learning in the various activities?

(See Counsell, C. (2000) 'Historical knowledge and historical skills: a distracting dichotomy', in Arthur, J. and Phillips, R. (eds) (2000) *Issues in History Teaching*, London, Routledge, for more detailed discussion of some of these issues.)

THE EVOLUTION OF THE NC FOR HISTORY

The NC for England and Wales was first taught in schools in 1991. It had initially been envisaged that history would be compulsory to the age of 16, but the KS4 history curriculum, due to start in 1994, was never implemented due to the Dearing Review (Dearing, 1993).

In terms of the purposes of school history, the NC Working Group which formulated the original NC for history identified nine purposes of school history:

1   To help understand the present in the context of the past.
2   To arouse interest in the past.
3   To help to give pupils a sense of identity.
4   To help give pupils an understanding of their own cultural roots and shared inheritance.
5   To contribute to the pupils' knowledge and understanding of other countries and other cultures in the modern world.
6   To train the mind by means of disciplined study.
7   To introduce pupils to the distinctive methodology of historians.
8   To enrich other areas of the curriculum.
9   To prepare pupils for adult life.

(DES, 1990)

The original stipulation that the study of political history should end 20 years before the present, was quietly discarded in the first revision, which also significantly slimmed down the content which had to be studied, and attempted to simplify assessment arrangements. Significantly, the 1995 revision confirmed that the study of history would be optional after the age of 14, and this remained the case with 'Curriculum 2000', the outcome of the second revision, (DfEE/QCA, 1999), although there was a substantial amount of continuity between the 1995 and 2000 history curricula. The five aspects or 'components' of history, originally termed 'Key Elements' (DfE, 1995) were now referred to as five areas of knowledge, skills and understanding, but the written descriptions of these areas was very similar. Content was now referred to as 'Breadth of Study' rather than 'Programmes of Study, but the broad areas of content to be studied were almost identical, and there was almost no change to the attainment Targets. There were more substantial changes to the General Teaching Requirements, formerly known as Common requirements, with guidance on principles for inclusion, and on the use of language and Information and Communications Technology (ICT).

There have been three revisions to the NC for history since its inception in 1991, in 1995 and 1999, and the most recent revision, introduced in September 2008, so when you qualify to teach, you will be working with the 'Mark 4' version of the NC for history.

Access the current Key Stage 3 Curriculum for history is at: http://curriculum.qca.org.uk/subjects/history/. (Web addresses sometimes change. If this link does not work, search for it in the history section of the QCA website, www.qca.org.uk.)

1   What curriculum aims are stipulated in the new NC for history? (To what extent are they being delivered in your lessons? What skills do you need as a teacher to achieve these aims? Are they just 'history teaching skills' or are there some 'generic' teaching skills that are relevant here?)
2   What were the five 'key elements' and then the five 'areas of knowledge, skills and understanding' have been changed to six 'Key Concepts' and three 'Key Processes'. In what ways are these a continuation of the 'Key elements/K, S, Us' and in what ways are there departures/differences from the 1999 version of the NC for history?
3   Look at the section on 'Range and content': to what extent is there continuity with the 1999 NC for history, and what has changed?
4   Similarly, how does the 'Curriculum opportunities' section of the document differ from the 1999 version?
5   Why do you think they have put in a section on 'The importance of history' in the new version of the NC for history?

Your placement school is organising a year 9 options evening for pupils and parents, and you have been asked to help with a display which points out the benefits of taking history. How would you present the case for school history to a parent whose child 'enjoyed history but didn't think it would be very useful'.

You have urged on a year 10 class the importance of arguing and debating issues in history in class. A pupil states that 'history is a waste of time because it won't help to get you a job when you leave'. What would you say in response to this question? Would you use the same arguments as with the parent or present a different justification for taking history beyond Key Stage 3?

HISTORY AND THE CHANGING CURRICULUM

Although the basic subject structure of the NC has remained unchanged, there have been changes in the underlying rationale for school subjects. The original (fairly vague) notion of all subjects contributing to 'cross-curricular themes', such as careers, environment, health education and citizenship, has been replaced by a much more strongly defined stipulation that all subjects should contribute to the development of 'key skills'. These include communication, numbers, ICT, problem solving, 'learning to learn', and learning to work with others. All these skills are considered important by employers. The 1995 revision of the NC also placed a much stronger emphasis on vocational education post-14. The requirement for schools to provide spiritual, moral, social and cultural guidance for pupils also has implications for the ways in which history is taught.

Curriculum 2000 also required citizenship to be a statutory part of children's education – an area with rich opportunities for history teachers (DfEE/QCA, 1999). The development of 'thinking skills' is another area which history teachers need to consider.

Although some schools continue to require pupils to choose a humanities option post 14, history teachers need to be able to provide convincing arguments about history's contribution to the whole curriculum in the face of these 'curriculum shifts'. Carol White argued that history must fit into the school's principles and aims – and if these aims include 'the development of tolerance, understanding of other cultures and societies, the promotion of citizenship and understanding of social responsibility then the place of history cannot be denied' (White, 1996: 25). It is important that you develop the ability to make clear *to pupils* the purposes of school history, and to persuade them that the study of history is useful, worthwhile and interesting. Some history teachers are able to convince pupils that in studying history, they are addressing some of the most important and difficult questions of human existence; like philosophy, history has its 'big questions' (see Swain, 2005). If you can ensure that you keep the purposes of school history clearly in mind in your teaching, and be explicit about them with your pupils, you are more likely to secure the positive engagement in learning that makes teaching a pleasure rather than a chore.

Task 2.9 History's contribution to cross-curricular, 'key' skills, and the wider curriculum

In your lesson planning, look for an opportunity to incorporate an activity which attempts to address one of the 'key skills', or aspects of history's contribution to the wider curriculum.

Look through the NC for history at Key Stage 3, and the schemes of work which your department uses, and look for areas where it might be appropriate to address citizenship issues, spiritual or moral education, ICT, inclusion, equal opportunities, literacy, creativity, thinking skills or any other 'general' aim of the school or the curriculum.

For further information on some of these strands, see: http://www.qca.org.uk/history/innovating/key3/wider_curriculum/index.htm.

It should be apparent that history can make a contribution to the school curriculum in several ways, including the development of 'key' or general educational skills. The study of history could be a vehicle to develop such skills, but the question arises, why do this through the study of history? In assessing and evaluating the record of human activity and thought through time, history provides insight into many of the situations and decisions which pupils will confront in their lives after school. In the words of HMI, 'Their effectiveness as citizens will depend above all on the crucial historical skill of assessing and evaluating the record of human behaviour. Without an understanding of history, young people will enter the worlds of work, citizenship and leisure, blinkered and partly uncomprehending' (HMI, 1985: 2).

Contrary to the assertions of the tabloid press, there are few history teachers who do not believe that it is important for pupils to develop knowledge and understanding of the past. Many also believe that it can be helpful if this is complemented by an understanding of the nature of history as a form of knowledge, and an academic discipline. If you think about the events of the twentieth century, the era of spin doctors, media manipulation, soundbite politics and information overload, 'it does require some little imagination to realise what the consequences will be of not educating our children to sort out the differences between essential and non-essential information, raw fact, prejudice, half-truth and untruth, so that they know when they are being manipulated, by whom, and for what purpose' (Longworth, 1981:19). It is difficult to think of another school subject which offers the potential to address this important issue as directly.

THE NATURE OF HISTORICAL KNOWLEDGE

If we are going to teach children history, shouldn't they know something about what history is – what they are dealing with, as well as information about what happened in the past? Pupils need to develop an understanding that history is not 'what you are told about the past' (information = what happened); history is a construct. It has been 'put together' by someone. As Lee and Ashby point out, if we are taking 'knowledge' seriously, shouldn't pupils understand the nature of historical knowledge, as something that has to be 'understood and grounded?' If pupils have some grasp of the nature of the relationship between facts, claims and accounts, 'as well as acquiring knowledge of the past, students develop more powerful understandings of the nature of the discipline, which in turn legitimate the claim that what they acquire is indeed knowledge' (Lee and Ashby, 2000: 200).

The statement that history is 'an account of what happened in the past' (Thatcher, 1995: 595) does not equip pupils to deal with the fact that there are *differing* accounts of the past. As Lee and Ashby point out, 'Many stories are told, and they may contradict, compete with or complement one another, but this means that students should be equipped to deal with such relationships, not that any old story will do . . . Students who understand sources as *information* are helpless when confronted by contradictory sources' (Lee and Ashby, 2000: 200).

Arnold reminds us that 'the Greek word which has become "history" originally meant "to enquire", and more specifically, indicated a person who was able to choose wisely between conflicting accounts' (2000: 18). Postman, and Weingartner have less elegantly described history as a 'crap-detecting' subject (quoted in MacBeath, 1998). It is precisely this facet of history as a discipline which can be helpful in persuading pupils of its utility and relevance.

It is therefore important that you understand and are able to explain to pupils what historians do, and why they do it; what 'facts' are, the difference between 'sources' and 'evidence', and why it is in the nature of accounts to differ. It is important to be aware of the difference between substantive and second order concepts in history. If you are not clear about these things, what chance have your pupils got of making sense of history?

If you are want to reinforce or refresh your understanding of the nature of historical knowledge, and consider some of the questions noted above, further information and suggestions for wider reading are provided at www.uea.ac.uk/~m242/historypgce.

Another important consideration in persuading pupils that the study of the past is of relevance to their lives is to clarify the relationship between historical knowledge and the present. There are many definitions of history, but Aldrich's is particularly helpful to the history teacher. 'History is about human activity with particular reference to the whole dimension of time – past, present and future' (Aldrich, 1997: 3). It is important to be explicit about the idea of historical perspectives as *one of the ways* of understanding how things are today, and how they might be in the future. Is there any present day problem or question where it might not be possible to glean some degree of further insight into that problem or question by considering what has gone before? Don't forget to look for opportunities to relate the past to the present and the future, in order to persuade pupils of the importance and relevance of history. HMI state that student teachers should demonstrate 'an ability to relate the present to the past' (Baker *et al.*, 2000: 219). Remember that not all your pupils have a clear idea about why historians bother 'to do history'. When asked to explain the success of a recent adaptation of *Vanity Fair*, Lisa Jardine commented, 'You need to generate a connection with today. That's how I teach' (*Observer*, 8 October 1998). When you think about the starting point for your lessons, remember that often the present, rather than the past, can be the best option.

Task 2.10 Handling the 'so what?' question

Why do historians bother to 'do' history? Is it just a hobby, like stamp collecting or trainspotting? In addition to trying to establish what happened in the past, historians research into the past to see what insights historical perspectives might shed on the present and the future. Teachers of history must remember to do the same, if pupils are not to ask the 'so what?' question after studying a particular morsel of the past.

One student history teacher wrote in the evaluation of a lesson (honestly but worryingly) 'I have no idea why I am teaching this'. If the grown ups don't have a clue about why they are inflicting morsels of the past on their pupils, what hope is there that the pupils will commit themselves enthusiastically to learning about it? Whether or not a pupil puts their hand up and asks why you are doing a topic, it can be helpful to think through the answer to this question before you start planning how you are going to approach the topic.

Spend a few minutes thinking about why pupils should have to learn about the following:

castles (no one's build one for hundreds of years);
peasants (we don't have them any more);
life in a medieval village;
roads and canals in the seventeenth century;
Hargreaves' Spinning Jenny;
the agrarian revolution.

(See Chapter 3 for some suggestions for approaching such topics. Some guidance is also given in Hunt, 2007.)

A third point for consideration in terms of historical knowledge is to focus on the sorts of questions that historians ask. As Lee points out, 'even questions have their standards – some are uninteresting, and some merely foolish' (Lee, 1994: 44). To some extent, the quality of your history teaching is a function of the quality of the questions you ask. One of the common early difficulties which student teachers encounter is in devising questions which go beyond recall and comprehension, and which focus on historical understanding. Even a topic as important as the Holocaust can be rendered sterile and meretricious if time and thought is not given to the quality of questions to be posed (see Chapter 3).

Part of becoming an effective history teacher is to have a sound structural understanding of the discipline of history, and the nature of historical knowledge. There is more to subject knowledge than just 'knowing your stuff' in terms of content knowledge, important though that is.

DEVELOPING YOUR SUBJECT KNOWLEDGE

At all stages, the subject expertise of the teacher is the most important factor determining the work of the teacher in the classroom.

(OFSTED, 1995)

Research shows that there is a close relationship between teachers' subject knowledge and the quality and range of learning experiences in their classrooms. The message is, if you don't know it, you can't teach it.

(Dean, 1995: 4)

A decade or so ago there was perhaps a tendency for courses of initial teacher education to 'take as read' student teachers' subject knowledge, and to assume that as most student teachers had to at least some extent, a degree background in history, attention could be focused on other issues, such as pedagogy, theories of learning, and classroom management.

Since then, research evidence and inspection findings have suggested that there is a close relationship between teachers' subject knowledge and the quality of pupils' learning, and that without secure knowledge and understanding of the concepts and skills in their specialist subject, 'the quality of teaching and learning in the classroom suffers' (Baker et al., 2000: 211).

Even single honours history graduates are unlikely to possess graduate level knowledge of every period and topic which is taught in secondary schools. Most of you have some 'black holes' in terms of subject content knowledge. As soon as you have been offered a place on a course of initial teacher education, you should work on addressing gaps in your subject knowledge; once you are on teaching placement, you are unlikely to have time to read weighty tomes and biographies. This does not mean that there are not other useful strategies for acquiring subject knowledge. You are unlikely to inspire confidence in your pupils if you do not possess subject knowledge which is substantially beyond that which is available to them in text books. Although there are several facets to subject knowledge, discussions amongst one group of history tutors concluded that in making judgements on student teachers' subject knowledge, the most important consideration was 'the degree to which student teachers had used their initiative, intelligence and energy to prepare effectively for the classes they had been assigned to teach' (Minutes of UEA history tutors' meeting, May 1998).

Task 2.11 How will you develop and audit your subject knowledge?

If someone asked you what you had done on the course to develop your subject knowledge, what would you say?

Conduct a brief audit of your subject knowledge, reviewing it against the NC for history at Key Stage 3, and noting down any areas of weakness. Keep a record of the steps you make to develop your subject knowledge. This need not be reading and/or note taking, and might include familiarisation with history CD-ROMs, films, audio tapes and television programmes such as *Timewatch* and *The People's Century*. Try to be systematic about this monitoring process and keep a record in such a way as to be able to demonstrate to an external examiner or interview panel that you have been taking action to develop, enhance and update your subject knowledge. How can you do this in a way that is 'time effective' and not just a pointless administrative chore?

Some suggestions for strategies for addressing gaps in subject knowledge are available at: http://www.uea.ac.uk/~m242/historypgce.

It is important to remember that there is more to subject knowledge than depth and breadth of substantive content knowledge. HMI feedback from the most recent round of Initial Teacher Education (ITE) inspection stresses the importance of student teachers possessing 'a clear understanding of the nature of the subject and its guiding principles . . . key concepts, key questions . . . key words' (Baker *et al.*, 2000: 212, 216). The standards for achieving QTS are quite explicit in this area: Standard Q14 is explicit in requiring you to possess 'a secure knowledge and understanding of your subjects/curriculum areas *and related pedagogy*' (TDA, 2007: 5). So it is not just about having a sound grasp of the substantive past. It should include an understanding of the nature of history as a form of knowledge, with its rules, conventions and procedures, awareness of pupil misconceptions and areas of difficulty in history, familiarity with recent inspection and research findings, and a sound grasp of curriculum arrangements, for the NC for history, and GCSE and GCE A level exam specifications.

Suggestions for further reading in this area can be found at: www.uea.ac.uk/~m242/historypgce.

Another important aspect of subject knowledge is an understanding of what it means 'to get better' at history. There is more to getting better in history than simply acquiring a greater depth and breadth of subject content knowledge. How can you help to move pupils forward in the subject if you are not clear about what it means 'to get better' at history?

Task 2.12 Developing your understanding of progression (what it means to get better at history)

In addition to a careful study of the Attainment Targets for history (DfEE/ QCA, 1999: 38–9) and the criteria for GCSE and post-16 specifications, the following weblink provides some suggestions for reading which enhances your understanding of progression in history: www.uea.ac.uk/~m242/ historypgce/sk.

The standards for QTS specify 12 areas of knowledge and understanding related to your overall professional knowledge and understanding (TDA, 2007: 5–6). You need to keep in mind the full breadth of the standards in the course of your initial teacher education. They might be considered as 'many of the things which you need to keep in mind if you are to develop into a fully effective teacher'. It might be helpful to classify them into five main areas:

Subject content knowledge

When you go in to teach a class, do you always have a sound grasp of the topic you are going to teach, so that you can teach it effectively, answer pupils' questions confidently, and retain the confidence of the pupils?

Are you developing a sound basis of subject content knowledge across the compulsory elements of the NC, and in the examination syllabuses which the department enters pupils for?

NC and history syllabus knowledge

As well as knowledge of Key Stage 3 and examination syllabuses, you should be familiar with what pupils have done at Key Stage 2, and with safety issues in areas such as field trips (see DfEE, 1999; ATL, 2000).

You should be aware of the various *components* of the NC for History. (See below.)

A developing knowledge of research and inspection findings relevant to school history, and an understanding of history as a discipline

Knowing what pupils find difficult in history, what misconceptions and gaps they have in their understanding of the past, what sort of ideas they are 'operating with', and what sort of ideas are suggested for helping them to progress in history.

This comes from reading about research in history education, accessing inspection evidence, and considering it against your own teaching experience.

Knowledge of the cross-curricular, and 'key skills' implications of history teaching

You are able to teach history in a way that takes advantages of opportunities to develop pupils' 'key skills', their spiritual, moral, social and cultural development, and education for citizenship.

Knowledge of safety regulations and recommendations when working with pupils inside and outside the classroom

Figure 2.3 Facets of subject knowledge

Task 2.13 Developing your breadth of subject knowledge

How would you respond if someone asked you . . .

- What history are pupils likely to have encountered before secondary school?
- What else is there in the NC for history besides the specified areas of content to be studied – what are the other 'components'?
- What are 'key skills' – and what can history do to help pupils make progress in them?
- Can you think of anything you have read about teaching history which has had an influence on your thinking about how children learn in history?
- What do you understand by the term 'new history', and what are some of its advantages and disadvantages compared to the 'old' history?

What would you say in response to these questions? By the end of your course of ITE, you should be able to give a cogent and well informed answer to these questions.

Task 2.14 Developing your awareness of recent inspection findings about history

Access the OFSTED website (www.ofsted.gov.uk) and search for the report 'History in the balance', which provides a summary of recent OFSTED findings on history teaching in English schools. Read pages 11–14 and 16–20 which focus on history in secondary schools and note the main findings in terms of 'areas of strength' and 'things that need to be worked on'. What are the implications for your own development as a teacher?

Task 2.15 What are pupils' ideas about why they do history in school?

Throughout the lesson, the teacher stressed to the pupils that the skills they were learning would be of use in the wider world when they left school.
(Extract from a student teacher's notes from observing an experienced teacher)

Recent surveys have revealed that many pupils do not have a well-developed understanding of why they are doing history in school, or the ways in which might be helpful to them in their lives after school (see, for example, Adey and Biddulph, 2001; QCA, 2005).

Go to www.uea.ac.uk/~m242/historypgce/purposes and click on the link to 'Pupil perceptions'. Read the summary of what pupils said when asked to explain why they thought the government made it compulsory for them to do history at school. What implications does this research have for your practice as a history teacher? Pick out 2–3 lessons which you will be teaching and think how you incorporate some component which establishes or clarifies some of the ways in which the study of the past is useful to young people.

It is important not to *assume* that pupils understand why they are doing history, or particular aspects of it. There is a degree of paradox here – often at the 'micro' level, the learning objectives for the lesson are written up on the board in every lesson, but at the 'macro' level ('why do we have to learn about the Stuarts?'), the understanding is not there and we have to be explicit about getting ideas about 'purposes' and 'benefits' across to pupils. It can also be helpful to keep in mind the idea of 'historical perspectives': the idea of the discipline of history providing one way of developing our understanding of the world we live in (see Aldrich, 1997). Everything has a history: food, jobs, transport, clothes, weapons, schools, television. Part of our job is convincing pupils that many of the things that have happened in the past have an effect on their lives when they leave school, and that it can be helpful for them to have an understanding of some of these changes and developments. It is a question of persuading them that in the words of William Faulkner, 'the past is not dead, it is not even past'.

SUMMARY AND KEY POINTS

It is possible to have a first class honours degree in history, and yet not be an effective and accomplished teacher of the subject. As *well as* being a good academic historian, you need to have a clear grasp of the rationale for teaching history to young people (including an awareness that there are differing views on this).

You need to be able to relate your subject knowledge to the demands of the NC for history, and the criteria for GCSE and post 16 specifications.

It helps to know something about how children learn in history; what they find difficult, what mistakes they commonly make, and about some of the ideas which have emerged for helping them through these difficulties. You should therefore develop an awareness of relevant literature in these areas, by reading *Teaching History*, the professional journal for history teachers and student teachers, and other books, journal articles and OFSTED findings.

Above all, you must also keep in mind the full breadth of benefits which pupils can derive from the study of the past. History can make a profound difference to the sort of citizens who emerge from our schools. It can contribute to their ability to handle information critically and intelligently, to their spiritual and moral development, their self-esteem and ability to work well with others, their ability with language, numbers, and ICT, and other 'key skills' which are valued by employers, and which can also contribute to your pupils' chances of living happy, worthwhile and fulfilled lives. But it will not necessarily do all or any of these things. It depends how thoughtfully and skilfully the subject is taught. (Remember: some pupils have considered school history to be 'useless and boring'.) In the end it is your commitment, expertise and persuasiveness as a history teacher, together with your grasp of the nature and purpose of school history, that influences pupils to value and commit themselves to the subject. Without a clear grasp of the purposes and benefits of school history, the best you can hope for from pupils is desultory compliance with things they neither care about or understand. As well as the benefits for the pupils in your care, a clear sense of purpose enables you to feel confident that what you are doing is important and worthwhile, so that you enjoy your teaching, and find it rewarding.

Further resources and suggestions for further reading in this field, can be accessed at: www.uea.ac.uk/~m242/historypgce/purposes/welcome.htm.

REFERENCES

Adey, K. and Biddulph, M. (2001) 'The influence of pupil perceptions on subject choice at 14+ in geography and history, *Educational Studies*, Vol. 27, No. 4: 439–51.

Aldrich, R. (ed.) (1991) *History in the National Curriculum*, London: Kogan Page.

Aldrich, R. (1997) *The End of History and the Beginning of Education*, London: Institute of Education.

Aldrich, R. and Dean, D. (1991) 'The historical dimension', in R. Aldrich (ed.) *History in the National Curriculum*, London: Kogan Page: 99–113.

Arnold, J. (2000) *History: A Very Short Introduction*, Oxford: Oxford University Press.

Arthur, J. and Phillips, R. (eds) (2000) *Issues in History Teaching*, London: Routledge.

ATL (Association of Teachers and Lecturers) (2000) *Taking Students Off Site*, London: ATL.

Baker, L., Cohn, T. and McLaughlin, M. (2000) 'Inspecting subject knowledge', in J. Arthur, and R. Phillips (eds) *Issues in History Teaching*, London: Routledge.

Beattie, A. (1987) *History in Peril: May Parents Preserve It*, London: Centre for Policy Studies.

Burston, W.H. and Green, C.W. (ed.) (1962) *Handbook for History Teachers*, London: Methuen.

Conquest, R. (1969) in C. Cox and A. Dyson 'Fight for education: a black paper', in *Critical Quarterly*, quoted in M. Ballard (ed.) (1970) *New Movements in the Study and Teaching of History*, London: Maurice Temple Smith.

Dean, J. (1995) *Teaching History at Key Stage 2*, Cambridge: Chris Kington.

Dearing, R. (1993) *The National Curriculum and its Assessment: Final Report*, London: SCAA.

DES (1988) *History from 5–16*, London: HMSO.

DES (1989) *Interim Report of the National Curriculum History Working Group*, London: HMSO.

DES (1990) *Final Report of the National Curriculum History Working Group*, London: HMSO.

DfE (1995) *History in the National Curriculum*, London: DfE.

DfEE (1999) *Health and Safety of Pupils on Educational Visits*, London: Department for Education and Employment.

DfEE (2000) Safety. Online at http://www.funandgames.org/resources_safety.htm

DfEE/QCA (1999) *History: The National Curriculum for England*, London: DfEE/QCA.

Haydn, T. (1992a) 'History for ordinary children', *Teaching History*, No. 67, April, 8–11.

Haydn, T. (1992b) 'History reprieved?', *Teaching History*, No. 66, January, 17–20.

Haydn, T. (1996) 'Nationalism begins at home; the impact of national curriculum history on perceptions of national identity in Britain, 1987–1994', *History of Education Bulletin*, No. 57, 51–61.

Haydn, T. (2004) 'History', in J. White (ed.) *Rethinking the School Curriculum*, London: RoutledgeFalmer.

Hill, C. (1953) *Suggestions on the Teaching of History*, Paris: UNESCO.

HMI (1985) *History in the Primary and Secondary Years*, London: HMSO.

HMI (1988) *History 5–16*, London: HMSO.

Husbands, C. (1996) *What is History Teaching: Language, Ideas and Meaning in Learning about the Past.* Buckingham: Open University Press.

Johnson, P. (1994) *Daily Mail*, 30 April.

Joseph, K. (1984) 'Why teach history in school?', *The Historian*, No. 2, Insert.

Lee, P. (1994) 'Historical knowledge and the National Curriculum', in H. Bourdillon (ed.), *Teaching History*, London: Routledge: 41–48.

Lee, P. and Ashby, R. (2000) 'Progression in historical understanding 7–14', in P. Seixas, P. Stearns and S. Wineburg (eds) *Teaching, Knowing and Learning History*, New York: New York University Press: 195–220.

Lee, P., Slater, J., Walsh, P. and White, J. (1992) 'The aims of social history', *The National Curriculum and Beyond*, London: Tufnell Press.

Longworth, N. (1981) 'We're moving into the information society – what shall we tell the children?', *Computer Education*, June, 17–19.

MacBeath, J. (1998) *Observer*, 22 February.

NCC (1991) *History: Non-Statutory Guidance*, York: NCC.

OFSTED (1995) *History: A Review of Inspection Findings 1993/4*, London: HMSO.

Pankhania, J. (1994) *Liberating the National History Curriculum*, Lewes: Falmer.

Phillips, R. (1997) *History Teaching, Nationhood and the State: A Study in Educational Politics*, London: Cassell.

Price, M. (1968) 'History in danger', *History*, Vol. 53: 342–7.

QCA (2005) Pupil Perceptions of history at key stage 3, London QCA. Online at http://www.qca.org.uk/qca_6391aspx. Last accessed 3 January 2008.

Slater, J. (1984) 'The case for history in school', *The Historian*, No. 2.

Slater, J. (1989) *The Politics of History Teaching, a Humanity Dehumanised?*, London: ULIE.

Slater, J. (1991) 'History in the National Curriculum: the final report of the history working group', in R. Aldrich (ed.) *History in the National Curriculum*, London: Kogan Page: 8–38.

Stokes, J. (1990) Speech in the House of Commons, quoted in *Sunday Telegraph*, 1 April.

Swain, H. (2005) *Big Questions in History*, London: Jonathan Cape.

Tate, N. (1996) Address to the SCAA Conference on Curriculum, Culture and Society, held at the Kensington Hilton Hotel, 7 February 1996, School Curriculum and Assessment Authority.

TDA (2007) *Professional Standards for Teachers: Qualified Teacher Status*, London: TDA.

White, C. (1996) 'History 14–19 challenges and opportunities', *Teaching History*, No. 82, January: 23–6.

Williams, N. (1986) 'The Schools Council Project: History 13–16, the first ten years of examinations', *Teaching History*, No. 46: 8–12.

Willis Bund, J., quoted in G. Batho, (1986) 'From a test of memory to a training for life', in M. Price (ed.) *The Development of the Secondary Curriculum*, London: Croom Helm: 212–26.

3 Planning for learning

My problem Miss, is how the different bits fit together.

(Quoted in Ward, 2007)

Figure 3.1 The history jigsaw

INTRODUCTION

Do you have a clear idea, or plan, of what you are trying to achieve, both within a lesson, and in the longer term, over a series of lessons? Why are you telling these children about something that happened hundreds of years ago, what good will it do them?

Given the pressures on you in your first weeks of teaching (will they behave, will I remember my script, have I enough to get through the lesson?), it is easy to lose sight of why we are teaching children about aspects of the past (exactly what *do* you want them to 'get' from learning about the Industrial Revolution?). Along with lack of clarity about the purposes of school history, one of the most common causes of indifferent or unsatisfactory teaching by student teachers is the absence of precise, clearly thought out and appropriate learning objectives for pupils. There is also a tendency to think of lessons as 'free-standing', rather than being related to a planned programme for progression in learning, linked to previous lessons, and future lessons. There is an understandable tendency for student teachers to think of lessons one at a time, especially in the early stages of teaching experience. An important element of progression in your planning skills is the extent to which you can 'think long-term', refer back to previous lessons, and have a coherent plan for developing pupils' knowledge, skills and understanding in history. If you don't recap, reinforce, check, make connections, and link 'depth' studies with 'overviews' of history, there is a danger that pupils forget what they have learnt, not have a sound grasp of what happened in the past, and not really understand what history is about.

If you can manage to maintain a clear sense of direction and purpose to your lesson planning, and an awareness of the breadth of factors involved in planning, this can have a positive influence on many of the other preoccupations which dwell in the minds of student teachers. Most pupils are more likely to behave and respond well if the lessons have been well planned and 'make sense' to the pupils.

If you explain (for instance), the causes of the outbreak of Civil War in 1642 in the same way that you acquired your knowledge of it at GCE A level, or at university, you may as well explain it in a foreign language for all the sense it makes to many 12 year olds. Subject application – being able to teach effectively – is as important as subject knowledge. The non-statutory guidance for the original NC for history stated that 'A strong sense of *why* history is being taught should pervade all curriculum planning, influencing the selection of content and methods of teaching' (NCC, 1991: B1). In spite of the subsequent revisions of the history curriculum, this is still an essential element of planning for learning in history. It is also important to keep in mind that just because pupils are 'on task' and well behaved, it does not guarantee that valuable learning is taking place. You have to beware that you do not 'fill up their days with dull, repetitive tasks that make little or no claim on their intelligence' (Holt, 1982: 119). A clear grasp of the full range of learning objectives which might be relevant to school history can help you to minimise this danger.

OBJECTIVES

At the end of this chapter, you should be able to:

- identify how the purposes of school history might interact with the process of lesson planning;
- understand the relationship between short, medium and long-term planning;
- use the NC for history to structure learning;
- understand the range of learning objectives which can be relevant to the study of history in the secondary school;
- formulate precise and appropriate learning objectives;
- use the idea of a 'planning loop', where teaching, assessment and evaluation inform your further planning and teaching.

CONNECTING LEARNING OBJECTIVES TO THE PURPOSES OF SCHOOL HISTORY

As Chapter 2 demonstrated, there are very different views on the purposes of school history, and no universally accepted consensus on either why or how it should be taught. How are you to reconcile this divergence of opinion with the suggestion that what you attempt to achieve in your history lessons should bear in mind the purposes of school history? One helpful way forward is to make sure that you have a secure grasp of the NC for history: this is the current official 'warrant' for teaching history in schools. The NC documentation translates the accepted purposes of school history into 'what this means when you teach pupils in school', in a way that tries to ensure that you give pupils a broad and balanced 'diet' of history, which reflects *the full range* of ways in which being in your history classroom can be of benefit to your pupils. This means keeping in mind not just all the components of the NC for history, but agendas such as 'key skills', citizenship, inclusion, every child matters and the general values, aims and purposes of the NC (see DfEE/QCA, 1999: 10–13, 21–5).

There are two things of overarching importance which you should keep in mind when planning for learning:

- Although developing pupils' knowledge of the past is an essential part of school history, it is possible to teach it in such a way that it is also helpful to pupils in other ways. There is more to it than just getting them to know 'more stuff' about what happened.
- Although developing pupils' historical knowledge and understanding of the past should be central to planning for learning, more general educational object-ives should also be considered if pupils are to derive maximum benefit from the study of history in your classroom.

> **Task 3.1 Keeping in mind the full breadth of learning objectives in history**
>
> When you are at a stage of your school experience where you have had at least several weeks of planning, teaching and evaluating lessons, look through your teaching experience file together with the NC for history at Key Stage 3. To what extent have you addressed the full breadth of Key Concepts and Processes detailed in the NC for history? (QCA, 2007). There is a tendency for student teachers to concentrate mainly on the transmission of knowledge of the topic in the early stages of their school experience.
>
> Is it clear from your lesson evaluations that they are *history* lessons, with history specific comment, rather than largely general comment on task and class management?

 One of the difficulties which student teachers encounter in the early stages of school experience is formulating precise and appropriate learning objectives. Many students have found Martin Hunt's work 'Thinking it through' (Hunt, 1997) useful in helping them through this problem. Extracts and examples from the paper, and other resources on objectives and evaluations can be found at http://www.uea.ac.uk/~m242/historypgce/planning/.

Hunt makes the point that student teachers need to 'think through' objectives into lesson activities and their evaluations – if your objectives are meaningful, it should be possible to make connections and 'track through' objectives through the various components of the lesson plan, from where you detail the learning objectives, through to the timings of activities and then in the evaluation of the lesson.

Figure 3.2 'Thinking it through'

There may be some lessons where the principal aim is to transmit to pupils information about what happened in the past, but if *every lesson* were to have this objective, and this objective alone, this would limit the benefits which might accrue from the study of the past (they are not all going to go on to take history at university) and there is a danger that it may be difficult to elicit and sustain pupils' enthusiasm, interest and desire to learn if attention is limited to this objective.

So what other objectives might there be? What should student teachers keep in mind when planning schemes of work and individual lessons?

Figure 3.4 attempts to make the point that there is more to think about than simply subject knowledge in putting together a history lesson. The generally accepted purposes of school history enumerated in the non statutory guidance (NCC, 1991: B1), and by the Historical Association (Historical Association, 1988), embrace both the development of knowledge and understanding of the past, and the development of pupils' understanding of the discipline of history – what history is, and its rules and conventions. This stems from the belief that some aspects of historical method might imbue pupils with 'transferable skills', which will be of use to them in life after school. Thus at the core of the teacher's aims are the twin pillars of knowledge and understanding of the past, and understanding of the nature of history – what history is, and what the rules and conventions of the discipline are. These are considered in detail in subsequent chapters.

Then there are more general educational objectives; you are not just teaching pupils history, you are attempting to develop oral skills, writing skills, listening skills; the ability to record and recall information and deploy it appropriately. In the section on 'General

Teaching Requirements', the NC for history stipulates that every history teacher is also contributing to children's language skills, and should also provide opportunities for pupils to develop and apply their information technology capability in their study of history. Your planning also needs to consider 'inclusion' – the provision of accessible and challenging learning opportunities for all pupils (DfEE/QCA, 1999: 26–36). There are also the 'cross curricular' areas which obtrude into the study of history; there are times when the study of history sheds light on pupils' economic and industrial awareness, or provides insight into moral and ethical issues, citizenship, and links into geography or philosophy. All school subjects also have a responsibility to contribute to pupils' 'spiritual, moral, social and cultural development', to their 'thinking skills', their 'financial capability' and 'education for sustainable development' (DfEE/QCA, 1999: 24–5). During history lessons, pupils might also develop some of the 'Key Skills' which the Dearing Report noted as being essential elements of education for all pupils – numeracy, problem solving, communication skills, ICT, team working and 'learning to learn' (Dearing, 1994). Remember, you can't do *all* this in every lesson, or even every study unit, but you should be aware of opportunities which might present themselves in these areas.

In planning lessons, there are also pragmatic considerations, which must take into account the nature of the pupils who are to be taught. One is the question of *differentiation* – how the lesson can be structured so as to maximise access to learning, and meaningful gains in learning, for all pupils in the teaching group. Another is *progression* – giving thought to moving pupils forward in history, to higher levels of understanding, increased knowledge of the past, and more expert levels of accomplishment in skills of analysis, synthesis, selection and evaluation.

There are also what might be termed 'tacit' considerations or objectives, and although even the most accomplished and experienced history teachers have to take account of them, they loom particularly large in the planning of student teachers. They include considerations such as classroom management. How do I settle the class down? How can I draw the lesson to a conclusion in an orderly and effective way? How can I reduce the chances of child X messing around and disrupting the learning of others?

Some of these 'tacit' objectives are a function of the comparative inexperience and limited repertoire of the student teacher. Because you do not as yet possess a vast archive of successful and proven teaching techniques and ideas on all aspects of the NC for history, there are times when pupil learning has to be balanced against classroom management and 'survival' strategies in your planning. Student teachers and NQTs have at times to devise 'coping strategies', in order to get through lessons as best they can. If student teachers are honest with themselves, there are times when some of the learning activities are designed more for classroom management purposes than to advancing learning in history. If you have 'the class from hell' on Friday afternoon, a video extract which the class might enjoy, followed by a worksheet which 'keeps their heads down', and 'keeps them occupied', might seem an enticing option, and make for a more controlled and effective lesson than a roleplay on the Battle of Hastings. Such strategies may well have diminishing returns in terms of their effectiveness. If you become over-reliant on 'anaesthetic', 'this will pass the time' strategies, pupils may well grasp that child minding is taking the place of learning, and their behaviour and respect for you as a teacher will deteriorate accordingly. One of the central challenges of your education is to progress as rapidly as possible towards consistently purposeful learning for pupils, as your expertise as a history teacher develops, whilst making appropriate use of 'coping strategies' where necessary. There way well be legitimate reasons for not always placing the development of historical knowledge, skills and understanding at the centre of your planning for the whole lesson or series of lessons. Some pupils may be reluctant scholars, who need to be lured into learning history, and will be 'biddable' to learning history if it is presented in an interesting and accessible manner. A common strategy is to try to ensure that lessons have a good 'starter' or 'initial stimulus material': some form of intriguing or entertaining prologue to the 'serious' history which will follow (Phillips, 2001). If your control of the class you are teaching is not secure, you may have to think carefully about what is attempted, and opt for 'settling activities' (such as setting written tasks, or taking notes from a video extract), which are more conducive to a quiet working atmosphere, rather than 'stirring' activities (such as drama, 'hotseating' or roleplay), which are more suited to eliciting the enthusiasm and commitment of pupils to actively engaging in 'doing' history. (For a fuller explanation of stirring and settling activities, see MacLennan, 1987.) There are times when you may need to concentrate on developing a calm and purposeful working atmosphere in the classroom, and history learning objectives are influenced (and limited) by this imperative.

There is also sometimes a difficult tension between the long term need to do interesting and stimulating work which wins the pupils over to the study of history, and the short term agenda of staying within 'the comfort zone', and sticking to a tried and tested 'survival agenda' which is comfortably within your compass. Tempting though this may be at times, you must remember that by the end of your course, you want to have as full a repertoire of teaching experience and methods as possible. Progression in learning is just as important for student teachers as for pupils, and one of the reservations about teacher education is the tendency of some student teachers to 'plateau' in their learning (Baker *et al.*, 2000: 199).

In addition to there being many things to consider in planning for learning in history, there are also tensions between some of the factors involved. It is important that you think about these tensions, and discuss them with your tutor, if you are to make maximum progress in the course of your initial teacher education. 'Tacit' lesson objectives rarely feature in student teachers' lesson plans; it might be helpful to acknowledge them if you are to gain insight into the full range of factors influencing planning for learning. The way forward is not to pretend that they don't exist, but to think, talk and discuss how to get beyond tacit lesson objectives.

'I hate teaching this class and have major discipline problems with them. Forget the history, I just want to get to the end of the lesson without feeling shattered. I'll show an episode of *Blackadder* and then give them a War and Peace scale worksheet with lots of drawing work and copying little stick men cartoons, that should do the trick.'

Figure 3.3 Tacit lesson objectives

Tempting though some aspects of these strategies might be, they do not offer a long term way forward. Not only is such an outlook ethically indefensible – you shouldn't be teaching history if you don't believe in it – but it is likely that pupils will become aware that you are merely passing (or wasting) time rather than teaching anything of value. As one student teacher noted in her observation of such a lesson, 'A number of pupils expressed frustration at being given yet another drawing and colouring in exercise' (extract from student teacher assignment, January 1997).

A popular series of history text books pre-National Curriculum, the 'History Alive' series by Peter Moss contained many pages of easy to copy cartoon diagrams (Moss, 1970). If used imaginatively, the books could be very useful; if they were used to get pupils to copy the diagrams and cartoons on a regular basis, they would do little to develop children's historical understanding. There may be a justification for using 'low value' activities which entice reluctant scholars into learning, but only if something educationally worthwhile is to follow. Your aim should be to build up an archive of worthwhile activities, information, questions and problems on an increasingly broad range of historical topics. You cannot construct a comprehensive archive in the first few weeks of teaching practice, and may at times have to resort to 'low value' activities as a coping strategy because of classroom management or other concerns, but these should be kept to a minimum, and reduced, as your competence and confidence develops.

LOW AND HIGH VALUE ACTIVITIES IN THE HISTORY CLASSROOM

Heafford's typology of tasks in modern language teaching illustrates the idea that some pupil activities might be of more value than others in planning for learning (Heafford, 1990: 88). Word searches, copying from the board and reading round the class are regarded as low value activities, dialogue in the target language, reading silently and 'doing written work of an error-avoiding nature' are cited as activities of high value.

Task 3.2 Considering the value of classroom activities

1   Reading can be done in different ways in the classroom. If you want your pupils to read something, it can be done by either:

    a   Pupils taking it in turn to read aloud.
    b   You read the passage or extract to the whole class.
    c   You ask the pupils to read the passage in silence.
    d   The pupils read the passage to each other in pairs or small groups.
        What might be the advantages and disadvantages of these options, for the teacher, and for the pupils?

2   Drawing on your experiences and observations in history lessons (both as a pupil and a student teacher), draw up a list of other activities which might occur in a history classroom, and consider what they lend themselves to in terms of usefulness (for the teacher) and value (for the pupils). If possible discuss your views with other student teachers. It might also be helpful to test out your views on the advantages and disadvantages of the various activities in your teaching, to see if 'theory' accords with practice.

Why do teachers not always use high value activities? In some instances, it may be due to limitations in teacher competence – no history teacher has a *comprehensive* archive of high value scripts, questions, problems and tasks for every historical topic, although good history teachers are constantly extending their repertoire of purposeful and valuable activities or explanations. A key point here is that some activities are valuable because they help to develop pupils' knowledge and understanding of the past, and others are useful for other reasons; for settling a boisterous class down, for instance, or devising an 'enabling' task, which introduces a difficult historical concept in an accessible or striking manner. Although it should be central to planning for learning, developing historical understanding is not the only factor which you have to consider when putting together a lesson or series of lessons (see Figure 3.4). It is important to remember that good teachers often use strategies which might be considered 'low value' very adroitly, and in a way that leads on to positive learning outcomes.

In thinking in terms of 'high' and 'low' value activities it is important to keep in mind that 'fitness for purpose' is equally important to effective planning and teaching. You must beware of the danger of thinking that 'active' learning (such as roleplay, groupwork, drama) is a priori better than 'chalk and talk'. There are times when talking to pupils to explain aspects of the past to them is the most efficient way of teaching the class. Sometimes student teachers quote the Chinese proverb, 'I am told, and I forget, I am shown, and I remember, I do, and I understand'. Less quoted, but equally valid is Lawton's reminder that it all depends who you're teaching and what you're trying to achieve; 'There are important distinctions to be made between memorisation without understanding, acquiring knowledge by traditional didactic methods but with a grasp of its significance, and learning experientially. Because learning experientially is excellent for some aspects of the curriculum however, it does not follow that all learning must be active and experiental' (Lawton, 1985: 84–5).

TENSIONS IN PLANNING FOR LEARNING

In addition to the awareness that there are many factors involved in planning for learning, there is the complication that there is sometimes a tension between them. For instance, your needs as a student teacher attempting to broaden your teaching repertoire by experimenting with new teaching methods might conflict with the reality that you are faced with a teaching group over which your control is tenuous – you might need to 'play safe' and consolidate your control and confidence with this group rather than take risks and end up with a lesson which drifts out of control. If your relationship with the group is poor because they are sick to death of worksheets, drawing pictures, and other 'low value' containment activities, trying something different may be the way forward. You need to develop skills of judgement, in order to find the best way through these tensions. Hopefully, your 'percentages', and sureness of touch will improve with experience and reflection. There are many such continuums in planning for learning, and you need to deploy perceptiveness, professional integrity and determination to find the right point on them.

Another important tension in planning for learning is reconciling long and short term planning. Teachers sometimes think about what would constitute a good next lesson, given the resources available, the teacher's ideas and knowledge for that topic, and the nature of the pupils to be taught. But they also need to think about planning for learning in the longer term: over a topic, a study unit, a whole key stage. What do the pupils need for a comprehensive and coherent education in history? If you were to teach a class right through from the start of year 7 to the end of year 9, what benefits would they have

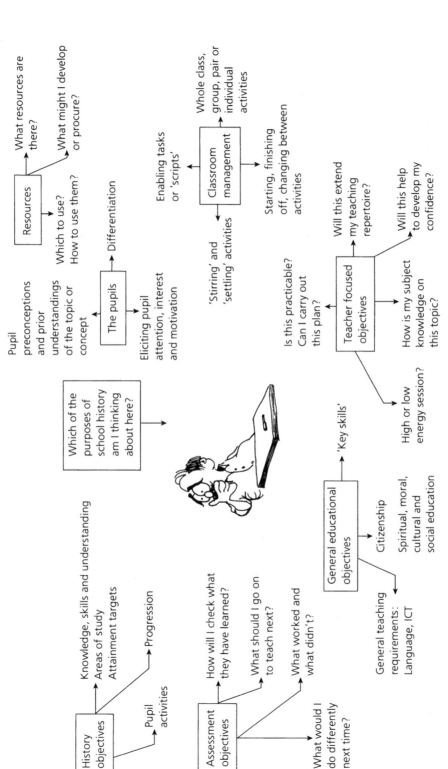

Figure 3.4 Things to think about when putting together a lesson

derived from your teaching, in terms of knowledge, understanding, skills and experiences? If teachers do not give some thought to 'curriculum mapping', pupils might receive many high quality individual lessons, but have studied history in a way which has only bestowed a fraction of the potential benefits which might accrue from the study of the past. One of the reasons behind the formulation of the NC was the belief that pupils needed a broad and balanced diet of history teaching, rather than one which was driven by the particular talents, specialisms, idiosyncrasies (and limitations) of individual history teachers. The six key concepts and three key processes identified in the NC for Key Stage 3 history are designed to help ensure that pupils receive a broad and balanced 'diet' of history (QCA, 2007). You *must* keep in mind all the key concepts and processes in your planning. Breadth and balance is also assured by planning to cover the breadth of the 'range and content' identified in the NC for history for Key Stage 3, and that over the course of the key stage, pupils get the chance to access all the 'curriculum opportunities' identified in the most recent version of the NC for history (QCA, 2007).

(See http://curriculum.qca.org.uk/subjects/history/ for details, or search the history section of the QCA website, www.qca.org.uk if this link changes.)

Your school department is responsible for constructing a programme to teach the NC for history in an effective way. Long term departmental planning encompasses issues such as progression, differentiation, coherence, continuity, assessment, and the provision of a wide range of learning experiences. Short term planning, including the planning of individual lessons, is still generally in the hands of individual class teachers, who decide on resources and teaching methods within the framework of school policies and the department's scheme of work. You have to work within these parameters and guidelines, whilst developing the range and levels of your teaching competence.

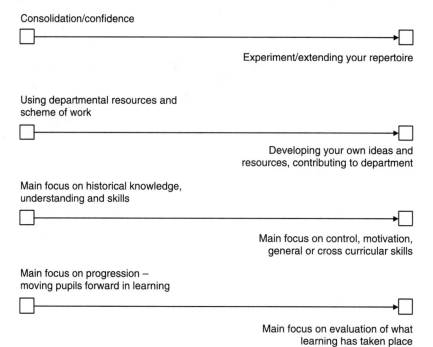

Figure 3.5 Some tensions in planning for learning

The list above is not a comprehensive one, but gives an indication of some of the processes involved in planning for learning.

STARTING POINTS FOR PLANNING FOR LEARNING

There is often a difference in the degree of latitude accorded to student teachers in terms of what and how they teach – some departments give you a fairly free hand in terms of *how* you deliver the topics you have been assigned – in others, you have to teach closely to the schemes of work which have been devised by the department.

Given that you are not a free agent in the classroom, and must adhere to school and departmental policies, and be guided by the framework of the NC for history, there are some factors which might be helpful to consider in putting together history lessons.

Some 'morsels' of the past might lend themselves to particular approaches

When you first consider the historical topic, event or question you have been asked to teach, think about which purpose of school history it lends itself to. To many experienced teachers, issues such as the Norman Conquest, the Glorious Revolution, Hargreaves' Spinning Jenny and the Holocaust immediately suggest ways into the topic in terms of what questions to ask, and what teaching approaches might be most appropriate. All of these topics pose very important questions, but very different ones. This is not to say that there is one definitive, best way of translating the topic into classroom experience, but that the topic might lend itself to, or easily relate to, a particular second order concept or teaching approach. A history topic might even be considered as a piece of raw meat – you have to think what you are going to do with it to make best use of it.

It is important to think about what questions or problems are posed by the topic

What important and/or interesting questions does the topic pose? How can you problematise the topic in a way which presents 'thinking problems' for pupils? When we present pupils with information about the past, the purpose is to get them to think about what questions one might usefully ask of that information, in a way which develops their historical understanding. It is not until questions are asked that the information can be thought of as 'evidence'. A helpful way forward for lesson planning can be to think what questions you pose for the pupils to work on and attempt to resolve, and for you to present and discuss some of the answers which have been suggested. In the long term, we want the pupils to be able to work out for themselves what are the intelligent and important questions to ask of the past. (See 'asking and answering historical questions', later in this chapter for further development of this issue.)

You should keep in mind and sometimes draw on, the pupils' ideas about why and how things have happened in the past

It is important to take account of the understanding and ideas that pupils bring with them to the lesson. They may not know a great deal about the topic itself, but they will have their own ideas about how and why things happen, and if you are to help them to progress to more powerful and effective ideas about why and how things have come to be are as they are, you need to be sure that you are talking to pupils in a way that engages with their ideas rather than passes over their heads.

A useful starting point for thinking how to approach the topic can be the present rather than the past

One of the commonly cited purposes of school history is 'to understand the present in the light of the past'. There are few topics in the NC which do not have in some way a relation to questions and problems which pertain to the present. Making links between the present and the past can be an effective tool for persuading pupils of the importance and relevance of history. In the words of Ministry of Education pamphlet No. 23:

> The divorce between current affairs and history so that they are regarded as separate subjects gravely weakens both. It accentuates the natural tendency of children to see history as something remote and irrelevant, instead of something which has formed the world around them and which is continuously being formed by that world. And it accentuates equally the tendency to look at contemporary questions as though they had no context in time, no parallels or precedents.
>
> (Ministry of Education, 1952: 32)

Making comparisons with the present also helps to clarify concepts and ideas about the past. Husbands makes the point that

> learning about the concept of kingship frequently involves two sets of simultaneous learning: learning about power and its distribution in past societies, and learning about power and its distribution in modern society. The former cannot be given any real meaning until pupils have some more contemporary knowledge against which to calibrate their historical understandings.
>
> (Husbands, 1996: 34)

In some cases, this means trying to explain how the present is explained by the past – how the Bill of Rights was an important step towards our present mode of government, why there is conflict in some areas between Catholics and Protestants. In other cases, it may be a question of pointing out that many of the major problems and questions of human existence remain the same, but ways of resolving them are affected by changes which have taken place. How do rulers control their citizens, and how do dissidents oppose them? 'Work' is still an important part of the way societies are organised, but the way in which people work, how work is distributed and problems relating to work have changed over time. The place where we draw the line between what is the state's concern and what is private has changed over time; why and to what effect? In essence, a doctor does the same job now as 2,000 years ago, but the problems which confront doctors have changed. In the words of Bowen it can be helpful to 'work from the known to the unknown'; to start from the present, and work back to the past (Bowen, 1993: 19). Robbins (2004) provides some useful suggestions and strategies for linking the past to the present.

Sometimes it can be helpful to approach the topic in an oblique or eclectic manner in order to draw pupils into learning

You do not have to confine yourself to the historical narrative, and the 'straight' history which is in text and topic books. Sometimes points can be made very powerfully and effectively by the use of analogy, anecdote, cartoon, newspaper article or video extract, before concentrating on the more formal historical record. These are sometimes referred to as enabling or engaging strategies. Their purpose is to secure the interest and commitment to learning of the pupils, or to put over an important idea or concept in an arresting or striking manner. The concept of appeasement might be understood more readily by pupils if it was explained that teachers and parents often use it as a strategy, instead of explaining its use in the Belgian crisis of 1831–2 or at Munich in 1938. A common strategy for introducing the idea of long term and short term causation and 'trigger causes' (frequently used to explain the outbreak of wars and revolutions) is a short paragraph about a car crash:

> Mr Jones drove home to watch the football match. He was late setting off and so drove faster than usual. His car skidded on an icy corner as he swerved to avoid a dog which had run across the road. He had not slowed down approaching the corner as there was no street lighting on that stretch of road. One of the car tyres was worn, and Mr Jones had drunk 8 pints of lager before setting off.

The teacher might at this point describe events leading to the First World War, the Franco-Prussian War, or other crises which lend themselves to this form of analysis or comparison.

Lawlor (1989) has pointed out that teachers might go too far towards turning learning into meretricious 'fun and games', which remove intellectual rigour from learning, and avoid the reality that sometimes worthwhile learning can require patience and determination. School history has at times been brought into disrepute by the use of drawing and copying work, wordsearches and low value 'pass the time' type activities. However, you face the reality that not all your pupils are driven by a burning desire to do well in history, and that one of the first steps in putting together a history lesson is to try to engage the attention and commitment of the pupils to the learning activities which are planned, and to ensure that they *understand* what you are talking about. If they are not listening, or if they do not understand, no learning can take place. Initiative, imagination and an awareness of your pupils' abilities and prior understandings are as important as your subject knowledge in planning for effective learning. All history teachers find that some topics offer more obvious opportunities for learning activities than others; many would feel that the Second World War is perhaps a more 'user friendly' topic than 'Roads in the seventeenth century' or 'The wool trade in the fourteenth century', but by adopting an imaginative and eclectic approach to seemingly intractable topics, and thinking carefully about what questions to ask, experienced teachers can often render them just as intriguing and valuable to pupils. Some topics need to be 'opened out', and interpreted in a broader context. 'Roads in the seventeenth century' could be taught in a way which concentrates on transmitting to pupils knowledge of the improvements wrought by Telford and Macadam, or it could examine the question of transport in a broader sense, by considering in what ways transport problems have changed over time. 'Historical perspectives' can help to shed some light on transport problems today – same issue, different problems – why, and what are the implications of these differences for the future?

Sometimes, the starting point for putting together a history lesson can be a resource rather than a lesson plan

Although the traditional 'theory' of lesson construction tends to place the resources to be used after the 'ideas' which are to be addressed in the lesson, there are times when history teachers read a newpaper article, see a cartoon, watch something on the news, or *Timewatch*, or visit a museum, which gives them an idea for a successful lesson, or a component of one. They then have to think carefully about how to make best use of the resource, and how to incorporate it into their teaching. Part of planning for learning is being alert to possibilities, scavenging for good resources, and displaying initiative in building up an archive of materials and ideas which can be used to augment the department's reserves.

Task 3.3 Initiative with resources

Part 1

Sometimes lessons can be to at least some extent, 'resources led', rather than 'ideas led'. Good teachers are continually on the look out for resources which might help to teach something more effectively.

For a period of about a week, make a conscious effort to scan newspapers, magazines, television schedules, and spend some time browsing the internet, to look for resources on topics you may encounter in your teaching. Cut out, bookmark, or record them. At the end of the week, compare your collection with fellow student history teachers. Hopefully, this will lead to the realisation of how many 'gems' there are which can help you in your planning if you keep your eyes open for things.

Part 2

Look at the specimen schemes of work which have been commissioned by QCA and the DfEE at www.standards.dfee.gov.uk/schemes, and see if you can find something useful to incorporate into your own planning.

In general, try to get into the habit of keeping an eye out for resources, and gathering together 'collections' or resources on particular historical topics.

The following is an example of how the topic of the Industrial Revolution might be approached in terms of 'first thoughts' in planning for learning.

At the end of this topic, I would hope that the pupils would have a better understanding of questions such as:

What do we mean by 'industrial revolution'?

Why was Britain the first country to have one?

In what ways did the Industrial Revolution change what Britain was like? (The difference between feudal/agrarian societies and industrial ones, how and where people lived and worked, changing role of land and commerce and industry on wealth and power in Britain.)

What effect did the Industrial Revolution have on Britain's position in the world in relation to other countries? (What part did the Industrial Revolution play in making Britain a great power?)

What factors make countries 'great' and do those factors change over time?

What happened when other countries had industrial revolutions?

How does all this affect us in Britain today?

What are the connections between industrialisation and the environment and how have they changed over time?

What are the important questions to ask about industrialisation today?

At the end of this topic, I hope pupils will have a better understanding of the following concepts and vocabulary:

resources	colony	capital
feudal system	domestic industry	factory system
technology	privatisation	manufactured goods
the class system	division of labour	alienation
supply and demand	monopoly	profit
Luddism	laisser-faire	protection
free market	mixed economy	nationalisation
regulation	deregulation	balance of payments
labour	trade unionism	trade

Whilst addressing these questions and ideas, in addition to developing the range and depth of the pupils' historical knowledge and understanding, I hope that pupils develop their understanding of the nature of history as a discipline (in particular that there are differing interpretations of these events), their ability to structure their enquiries into the past and work things out for themselves, and their ability to organise and communicate the results of their enquiries, both orally and in writing.

In order to derive these benefits from the study of the Industrial Revolution, pupils will engage in a variety of activities which will develop their historical knowledge and understanding, and also some more general educational skills (such as oracy, proficiency in information technology and writing skills). In the course of the unit they might work with artefacts, visit a site, do a group presentation to the class on an aspect of the Industrial Revolution, do an extended piece of writing, study written sources, read, listen to teacher exposition, do a data handling exercise and in groups, produce a newspaper front page on an aspect of the Industrial Revolution in order to demonstrate their understanding of some of the concepts or questions above.

Figure 3.6 Thinking about how to approach the treatment of the Industrial Revolution in Study Unit 3, Britain, 1750–1900

Task 3.4 Thinking how to make your teaching of a topic coherent and worthwhile

Read Byrom and Riley's article about planning to teach the British Empire at Key Stage 3 (*Teaching History*, No. 112: 6–14). The article shows very powerfully what difficult choices history teachers have to make when planning for learning in particular topics. Think of another fairly substantial topic (The First World War, the English Civil War, the Norman Conquest of Britain, the French Revolution . . .) and draw up an outline plan of how you would teach six to eight lessons on the topic. How would you divide it up? What would be the main focus within the topic? What would be the main learning outcomes you would hope for? How would you build in plans to assess the extent to which the learning outcomes will be achieved? You may find it helpful to consider the information in Figure 3.6.

Task 3.5 'Opening topics up': approaching challenging aspects of the history curriculum

Although in theory, outstanding history teachers should be able to render all aspects of the past intriguing and accessible to pupils, the reality is that some topics might offer more obvious opportunities, ideas and resources than others. As Byrom and Riley point out, some topics are 'important but boring' (Byrom and Riley, 2003: 6). The following suggestions may be your favourite bits of history, but some student teachers have mentioned them as topics that they feel they are comparatively intractable in terms of being able to transform them into interesting and enjoyable experiences for their pupils.

life in a medieval village   factories/textile machinery   the Agrarian Revolution
the Chartists   roads and canals in the C17/18   the League of Nations

How might you 'open up' these topics so that the pupils might find the topics powerful, interesting and relevant?
   Ask the history teachers you work with, and fellow student teachers, how they approach less propitious topics, and what engaging and enabling strategies and tasks they use to try and draw pupils into learning.

Some suggestions on 'opening up' topics can be found in the web section on planning: www.uea.ac.uk/~m242/historypgce/planning.

Task 3.6 Working out what key enquiry questions might be used to explore particular historical topics

One of the major changes on planning for learning in history over the past decade has been a tendency to move away from planning 'grids' and towards the use of 'enquiry questions' (see, for example, Riley, 2000). Care in getting your enquiry questions right in the first instance can make the detail of subsequent planning much easier. Remember that often you will have an overarching enquiry question, and some 'sub-questions' arising from the main enquiry question.
   The questions posed by study of the Industrial Revolution, (and the concepts involved), might be very different from those which arise from a consideration of other historical events.

In the form of a spider diagram, draw up a list of possible 'key questions' and concepts which might provide a basis for teaching a series of lessons on

a   The Norman Conquest
b   The outbreak of civil war in England in 1642
c   'The Glorious Revolution' of 1688
d   The Holocaust
e   Propaganda in Nazi Germany
f   Slavery.

Examine some fairly recent history textbooks and explore how they often use enquiry questions to structure learning around particular topics. Some examples of recent texts are given in Chapter 9.

There are some things that all these topics have in common; in teaching all of them we are considering information about what happened in the past, we are developing children's knowledge and understanding of the past, and there are some recurrent themes or questions which pertain to the study of many historical topics, such as 'Why did this happen?', 'What effect did this have?', 'How do we know about this?', and 'How reliable is this information?'

However, different topics offer different *opportunities* to the history teacher, can suggest different 'key questions', and offer insights into very differing sorts of ideas and concepts. Study of the Industrial Revolution generally enriches the pupils' grasp of economic concepts and the cross-curricular theme of economic and industrial awareness. Study of the events of 1688 might prove an excellent opportunity to develop *political* concepts, and be the point at which to give an *overview* of how government has developed in this country, from 1066 to the present day, culminating in an examination of pupils' understanding of the present system of government, and the way in which the events of 1688 relate to this. The events of 1066 might not throw as much light as 1688, or 1867, on how Britain is governed today, and so instead of focusing on the purpose of 'explaining the present in the light of the past', the main focus might be developing pupils' understanding of evidence, the nature of history, how we know about the events of 1066, and what criteria we use to assign significance to events. Although their are several approaches to the Holocaust (including evidence and the Holocaust), many history teachers use the topic to focus on moral and ethical questions.

Guidance on teaching sensitive and controversial issues in history can be found from the following sources:

Carrington, B. and Troyna, B. (1988) *Children and Controversial Issues*, London, Routledge.

Arthur, J., Davies, I., Wrenn, A., Haydn, T. and Kerr, D. (2001) 'History, citizenship and diversity', in *Citizenship through Secondary History*, London, RoutledgeFalmer: 101–13.

Historical Association (2007) 'Teaching emotive and controversial history 3–19', London, HA, online at: www.dfes.gov.uk/research/data/uploadfiles/RW100.pdf.

Stradling, R. Noctor, M. and Baives, B. (1984) *Teaching Controversial Issues*, London, Hodder Arnold.

Figure 3.7 Teaching controversial issues in history

THE IMPORTANCE OF CONCEPTS IN SCHOOL HISTORY

'Historical knowledge includes an understanding of certain ideas and concepts. These are more than glossaries of historical terms; they are aids to categorising, organising, analysing and applying historical information. They can only be understood when they are used in illustrating a variety of different historical circumstances. "Revolution", for example, is a historical idea. But a simple definition does not help pupils to understand why the word is applied equally to events in France after 1789, in Russia in 1917, or to the history of industry in later eighteenth-century England, or whether it can equally usefully describe events in seventeenth-century England. Ideas such as "left wing" or "right wing" have their value, but only if pupils begin to appreciate their limitations and the oversimplifications they sometimes suggest' (HMI, 1985: 14).

Understanding concepts helps pupils make sense of the world they are living in, and in order to make sense of the past, pupils need to understand the ideas and concepts which emanate from the study of a historical topic as well as the factual details they are presented with, if they are to 'transform' the learning experience into knowledge and understanding. The HMI document, 'History in the primary and secondary years', provides a useful, but not comprehensive list of the concepts which pupils studying history should develop an understanding of in their study of the past (HMI, 1985: 15).

In terms of organising planning for learning, many history teachers have found it helpful to make a distinction between 'substantive', concepts, such as 'liberal', 'capital', 'propaganda' and 'reactionary', and 'second order' concepts such as 'change', 'cause' and 'evidence'. Lee and Ashby provide a lucid and succinct explanation of the difference between substantive and second order concepts in history (Lee and Ashby, 2000: 199–200).

Part of a study of the Russian Revolution of 1905 is an understanding of the groups opposing the Tsar. The aim of the exercise is to extend the pupils' understanding of the different ways in which the state can be opposed, as well as their grasp of the continuum between terrorism and peaceful protest which can be adopted by opposition groups, both in Russia in 1905, and at other points in history, including the present day. This could lead on to a consideration of which methods of opposition are 'justifiable', which methods were available to the protesters of 1905, whether what is justifiable varies according to the way in which the state exercises its power and control, and what the advantages and disadvantages are of the various forms of opposition.

1   Pupils are given an explanation of the events leading up to the 1905 revolution, including the actions and motives of factions opposing or criticising the Tsar's regime.
2   Pupils are asked to brainstorm a list of ways in which citizens oppose governments today in different parts of the world, including Britain.
3   Pupils are given two quotes about opposition which are written on the board at either end, with a line drawn across the width of the board to represent a continuum between the two statements.

   Quote A: 'Nothing is ever done in this world until men are prepared to kill one another if it is not done.' (George Bernard Shaw)

   Quote B: 'No revolution is worth the effusion of a single drop of human blood.' (Daniel O'Connell)

3   Pupils are asked to place the methods of opposition which they have thought of in order, from those which accord with Shaw's view, to those which accord with O' Connell's, or given cards

which outline methods of opposition and asked to place them in a continuum between the two positions.

Voting against government in elections	Threats of poisoning of water/food supplies	Hunger strikes	Bomb/sniper attacks on government security forces
Placing anti-government advertisements in newspapers	Damage to public/ government property (slashing paintings, setting fire to post boxes)	Drawing up petitions and presenting them to government	Sit-down protests/ blocking public highways
Peaceful protest marches	Hijacking of aeroplanes	Kidnapping and ransom threats	Assassination of government agents
Random bomb attacks in cities	Graffiti/poster campaigns against government	Non-payment of taxes	Public suicides

4   Pupils are asked to categorise types of opposition. (Some classes or pupils within classes could be given categories, i.e. peaceful/nuisance/violence against self/damage-violence to property/ violence against government agents/random violence.

5   Pupils are asked to position the groups opposing the Tsar along the continuum between Shaw's position and O'Connell's, to state which methods of opposition were available to them in Tsarist Russia in 1905, and why different opposition groups used different methods of opposition.

The idea of continuums of opposition can obviously be applied in other historical contexts, (for example, discontent in Britain after the Napoleonic Wars), and can encompass understanding of the concept of radicalism – including the fact that there can be conservative as well as progressive radicalism.

Figure 3.8 An example of the integration of concepts into learning about the past

Task 3.7 Linking content to concepts

Think of a topic which you expect to teach to a class, and a concept which might arise in the course of covering that topic. How can you structure the work in a way which develops pupils' understanding of the concept, as well as developing their knowledge of the historical content involved. (The concept might, for example, be appeasement, in the course of covering Hitler's foreign policy; imperialism, in the course of covering Britain in the nineteenth century; trade, in covering the Roman Empire, or propaganda, in covering Nazi Germany.)

For further discussion of the use of concepts in history teaching, see Haenan and Schrijnemakers, 2000, 2003; Chapman, 2003; and van Drie and Van Boxtel, 2003.

PLANNING TO DEVELOP USEFUL FRAMEWORKS OF THE PAST FOR PUPILS

Not all commentators on school history are convinced of the utility and importance of concepts in the study of history. Several pamphlets from the Centre for Policy Studies argued that the centrality of a coherent historical narrative and sound grasp of the record of the past had been undervalued at the expense of themes, concepts and skills (see, for example, Deuchar, 1987; McGovern, 1994). More recently OFSTED (2005) and QCA (2005) reported that many pupils lack a general overview or 'mental map' of the past. As the pupil testimony at the start of the chapter suggested, one of the problems which many pupils have is how the different bits that they do in lessons fit together. For many pupils, history is just 'one damn thing after another'. This is why you should give some thought to long term planning in history. What will pupils end up with at 14 or 16 in terms of a general understanding of the past?

Lee, P. (2004) 'Walking backwards into tomorrow: historical consciousness and understanding history', online at: http://k1.ioe.ac.uk/schools/ah/HistoryInEducation/walkingbackwardsinto tomorrow.pdf.

Lee, P. and Howson, J. (2006) 'Two out of five did not know that Henry VIII had six wives', online at: http://k1.ioe.ac.uk/schools/ah/HistoryInEducation/twooutoffive.pdf.

Shemilt, D. (2000) 'The Caliph's coin: the currency of narrative frameworks in history teaching', in P. Stearns, P. Seixas and S. Wineburg (eds) *Knowing, Teaching and Learning History*, New York: New York University Press: 83–101.

Shemilt, D. (2006) 'The future of the past: how adolescents make sense of past, present and future, online at: http://k1.ioe.ac.uk/schools/ah/HistoryInEducation/Thefutureofthepast.pdf.

Wineburg, S. (2001) 'Making historical sense in the new millennium', in *Historical Thinking and Other Unnatural Acts*, Philadelphia, Temple University Press: 232–55.

Figure 3.9 Further reading on frameworks of the past

USING THE NATIONAL CURRICULUM TO PLAN FOR LEARNING IN HISTORY

It is essential to keep in mind that the NC for history is more than a list of content to be covered.

The section on 'Range and content' indicates that pupils should be taught 'through a combination of overview, thematic and depth studies' and that pupils can identify and understand 'the major events, changes and developments in British, European and world history covering at least the medieval, early modern, industrial and twentieth-century periods. The new Key Stage 3 curriculum also stipulates that all pupils should be taught a range of what it terms 'aspects' of history: including political developments, and social and economic stands of the national past, such as 'the movement and settlement of diverse peoples', 'changing ideas, beliefs and attitudes' in Britain, and developments in trade, empire, industrialisation and technology. Teachers also need to ensure that they plan for inclusion in history, so that their lessons provide access and challenge for all pupils (QCA, 2007).

Here we see the tension between simply thinking about what would make a good lesson, and planning for a 'balanced diet' of school history which incorporates a broad range of learning objectives. There is also the question of the time allocation for covering a study unit. You have to think about how a broad and balanced programme of learning in history can be delivered in the teaching time available (the exact amount of which will vary from school to school).

At times you are linking together work which has been done over the course of the year or key stage, in order to help pupils to see 'the broad sweep' of history, and aid progression in key areas of the subject, whilst at other times, you will be studying a particular event in considerable detail. This will clearly influence your teaching methods, and the resources you choose. When teaching GCSE and post-16 specifications, make sure that you are familiar with the objectives of the examination.

In order to guard against the risk of thinking too much about 'What would make a good lesson?', at the expense of 'How can I ensure that pupils receive a broad and balanced "diet" of school history?', many departments use planning grids, so that it is easy to check whether and where the different key concepts and processes of the NC are being taught. Figure 3.10 shows an example of a planning grid for a scheme of work for a series of several lessons on the Norman Conquest.

Although planning grids can be helpful in checking breadth of coverage, variety of focus, and range of teaching methods, Tim Lomas makes the point that 'the matrix approach can obscure much that is significant and critical in pupils' learning – the links, echoes and threads and 'the spontaneous responses of pupils' (Lomas, 2000: 3). Make sure that your lesson plans, evaluations, and schemes of work do not become mechanistic, cosmetic, and divorced from the reality of your pupils' experiences. HMI observe that although nearly all student teachers keep records to meet their professional obligations, some of them 'failed to reflect on why they kept the records, or whether keeping them in this or that particular form was either the most efficient means or helped them and their pupils achieve their ultimate teaching and learning objectives respectively' (Baker *et al.* 2000: 200). In the words of Counsell, are you converting the curriculum 'into something that *means something* to the students' (Counsell, 2000: 2)?

ASKING AND ANSWERING HISTORICAL QUESTIONS

One of the things which student teachers of history sometimes find difficult is how to ask questions of the past which go beyond recall and comprehension, and which develop pupils' understanding of history as a body of knowledge, and as a form of knowledge. If we are to develop the 'thinking skills' referred to in Chapter 1, we must attempt to get beyond questions which simply ask pupils to locate information and write it down, or reiterate what we have just told them.

One way of doing this is to think of the six Key Concepts and three Key Processes outlined in the NC for history at Key Stage 3 when constructing lessons. Second order concepts such as chronology, time, change, cause, evidence, interpretation and motive can often be a way of leading pupils into the problems and difficulties which historians face, and which require discussion, debate and thought, rather than pupils consistently being asked to do no more than write down or repeat what they are told.

Key Questions	Concepts, vocabulary	Historical content	Resources	Pupil activities	Teaching objectives	Assessment opportunities
Why did the Normans invade England?	invasion, heredity, power, resources	The quarrel for the throne, England before the invasion	Briefing sheet on claims, Medieval Realms, pp15–19	Listen to story, groupwork preparing claims for court, presentations	Understanding of motives for invasion and nature of govmt pre-invasion	Oral presentations on claims to throne
What happened at the Battle of Hastings, how do we know, why did William win?	evidence, accounts and chronicles	The military campaigns of 1066	Video extract of battle, worksheet on death of Harold miniature of Bayeux Tapestery	Sequencing exercise, extended writing, "How and why Harold lost"	Understanding nature of hist. record-interpretations	Extended writing exercise on 1066 campaigns
How did William gain control of England with only a few thousand men?	power, authority, administration, deterrence	From Hastings to 1086; castles,The Domesday Book	Maps from Medieval Realms, pp.21-2. "The Normans" software	Mapwork, sourcework exercise from Medieval Realms, p. 22, IT suite	Accounts and explanations, taxation, role of individual in history	Sourcework exercise on interpretations
Why were these events important, what difference did it make to life in England?	kingdom, feudal system, heirarchy	The changed social and political order	Visit to museum, Normans film strip, Medieval Realms, pp. 24-6	Construct timeline, newspaper front pages and obituary for class display	Significance, notion of "turning points", factual grasp of main events and changes	Recap test on main events and key vocabulary

Figure 3.10 An example of a planning grid for a series of lessons on the Norman Conquest

What are historians trying to do when they investigate the past? Why do they bother?

What happened?

Events, time periods, time lines, story lines, chronology, accounts, sequencing.

Why did it happen?

Explaining things, actions, events, developments, causes, motives, ideas, beliefs.

What changed? What stayed the same?

Patterns in/of the past, looking for similarities and differences, charting change.

How did what happened and what changed affect things?

Consequences and significance for people at the time, for us now.

How do we find out what we want to know? What problems are there in finding out and being sure? What claims can we make?

Looking at sources, asking them questions, deciding whether they can be used as evidence for a particular question or what they can be used as evidence for, sources, evidence, relevant, reliable.

Why might we get different answers to our questions?

Purposes, interests, concerns for reconstructing the past, *why* was this produced? Problems of available evidence, issues of interpretation.

(Ros Ashby, 'An introduction to school history', Workshop, Institute of Education, University of London 11 February 1995)

Figure 3.11 Things we want to know about the past

Sources are not evidence until we start to ask questions of them. It is the asking of questions which renders the study of the past meaningful, and which can help to explain to pupils why historians bother to do what they do, and why it might be helpful to understand these processes. So having thought of the questions we wish to pose of the historical content we are teaching, the next stage is to look for sources, stories or ideas which problematise those questions, in a form which your pupils can engage with. Although the questions relating to second order concepts permeate the history curriculum, there are times when you are also addressing substantive concepts, and trying to develop pupils' understanding of ideas such as *government, democracy, collectivism, oligarchy*, etc. Keeping in mind substantive and second order concepts can be a way of ensuring that you are asking historical questions, rather than comprehension ones. The following is a small selection of the type of historical questions you may find helpful suggested by Tim Lomas, in his Historical Association pamphlet, 'Teaching and assessing historical understanding' (Lomas, 1990).

Cause and consequence
- What was the importance of economic factors in causing the Russian civil war?
- What influence did Robespierre have on the outcome of the French Revolution?
- Why were the children evacuated from this town but not that town?
- Who would be most upset/pleased when the law said that children could not work in the mine anymore?
- What long-term factors may have led to the decision to send the Spanish Armada?

Time/change
- What difference might a cotton worker have noticed about conditions at work between 1750 and 1850?
- Look at the picture of the Victorian school. What has changed in most schools, since the time of that picture?
- Why did the Renaissance happen at the time that it did?
- The events in this story about the murder of Thomas Becket are jumbled up. Put them in the order which you think makes the most sense.
- Why did it take 20 years before Germany took revenge for the Treaty of Versailles?

Evidence
- What do you think this artefact would be used for?
- Look at the two sources about the Second World War. Where do they not agree with each other?
- Which parts of this newspaper account are just the opinions of the person who wrote it?
- How reliable do you think the author is even though she was an eye witness?
- Why might the Bayeux Tapestry have been compiled?

Significance
- Why can 1485 be described as a 'turning point'?
- Did the legislation of 1918 solve all the problems of inequality which British women faced?
- Which of these do you think an ordinary villager in the Middle Ages would have felt was more important in her life?
- What might have happened if the Jacobites had not been defeated at Culloden?
- Put the following sixteenth-century events in what you consider to be their order of importance giving reasons for your choice.

Similarity and difference
- Compare the peace treaties and agreements after the First and Second World Wars.
- Why might France have felt differently about Germany in 1918, 1940 and 1980?
- Could the events which caused the French Revolution have produced a similar effect in Britain?
- What differences can you find in the way these two battles were fought?
- How typical was this of Richard the Lionheart's policies?

Figure 3.12 Examples of questions relating to second order concepts

THE LINK BETWEEN PLANNING AND EVALUATION OF PUPIL LEARNING

Another important aspect of planning for learning is to consider how you assess what pupils have learnt, in order to think of what elements need to be gone over again or reinforced, what pupils might go on to learn next, and what might be done differently, the next time you teach the lesson. There should be a 'planning loop' of planning teaching → assessing → evaluating → revised planning and teaching. It is important to keep in mind that effective learning requires you to think carefully about two questions. How much that you have taught has been learnt? Once the pupils have learnt something, what should you teach next?

Holt makes the point that these two questions are not always asked:

> I assumed for a long time that my students knew when they did, or did not understand something. I was always urging them to tell me when they did, or did not, understand, so that with one of my 'clever explanations', I could clear up everything. But they would never tell me. I came to know by painful experience that not a child in a hundred knows whether or not he understands something, much less, if he does not, why not. The child who knows, we don't have to worry about, he will be an 'A' student. How do we find out when, and what, the others don't understand?
>
> (Holt, 1982: 276)

Holt goes on to attempt to provide possible ways of exploring the problem of understanding. A key element is that pupils are not simply regurgitating information in exactly the same form as it was given, but are asked to manipulate or analyse the information in some way to demonstrate that they have assimilated it into other, contingent areas of knowledge and understanding. In Counsell's phrase, they need to move from being 'knowledge tellers' to knowledge transformers' (Counsell, 1996).

Holt gives the following descriptors of situations where understanding has taken place:

'It may help to have in our minds a picture of what we mean by understanding. I feel I understand things if I can do some, at least, of the following:

1   state it in my own words;
2   give examples of it;
3   recognise it in various guises and circumstances;
4   see connections between it and other facts or ideas;
5   make use of it in various ways;
6   foresee some of its consequences;
7   state its opposite or converse.

This list is only a beginning; but it may help us in the future to find out what our pupils really know as opposed to what they can give the appearance of knowing, their real learning as opposed to their apparent learning' (Holt, 1982: 177).

Figure 3.13 Assessing for understanding

The following table is an attempt to assess how well pupils have grasped the relations between the major powers of Europe in 1914. They are asked to give a mark out of 10 to each relationship, with 10 out of 10 representing the most solid and committed of alliances, and 0 out of 10 representing countries which were intensely hostile to each other. In addition to shedding light on their understanding of the two main camps (the Triple Alliance and the Triple Entente), it tests their understanding of the comparative strength of the different alliances and relationships.

Relations between the great powers of Europe, June 1914

	Great Britain	France	Germany	Italy	Russia	Austria-Hungary
Great Britain						
France						
Germany						
Italy						
Russia						
Austria-Hungary						

Figure 3.14 Assessing for understanding, an example

Another example of a format for assessing whether pupils have understood relationships is provided in the National Curriculum Council's booklet, 'Teaching History at Key Stage 3' (NCC, 1993).

The following 0–5 scale is about how much power different groups or people had in the country at a particular time.

0	-	1	-	2	-	3	-	4	-	5
No power				Some power				All power		

Fill in this table and then stick it in your book.

In a group, put the number from the scale which you think applies to that person or group of people in that particular year on the table, e.g., if you think the King had all the power in 1649 put 5 under 1649 in the first line across. Discuss your group's findings with another group.

	1640	1649	1701
The King			
The House of Lords			
The House of Commons			
The Church of England			
The Army			
The Common People			

Figure 3.15 Worksheet designed to help pupils understand changes in the distribution of power, 1640–1701 (from NCC, 1993)

A further example of assessment for understanding can be found on the 'School History' website, see the 'What did Hitler believe in?' homework exercise at: www. schoolhistory.co.uk/gcselinks/indepth/germany/resources/hitlerbeliefs.pdf.

In many lessons, you will have what Battersby calls a 'golden nugget', a key idea or fact that you hope all pupils have grasped, to take away from the lesson with them (Battersby, 1996). In a lesson on propaganda in Nazi Germany, an example of this might be that all pupils understand that propaganda is not something that only happened in Nazi Germany; its use is widespread and it still exists today, particularly in time of war. It addition to 'the golden nugget', it is also helpful to try to have at least one resource or component of each lesson which (hopefully) elicits the interest or engagement of the pupils.

As your assurance and competence develops, your lesson evaluations should increasingly focus on the central issue of pupil learning, rather than simply evaluating your own teaching performance. They should move from 'Was I OK?', to 'How was it for them?', by considering questions such as:

- How many of the pupils grasped the main points I was trying to make?
- Which aspects did they understand and which aspects do I need to return to?
- How can I try and put this across in another way for those who did not grasp the key points of the lesson?
- How can I reinforce and consolidate what they have learnt?
- What points should I move on to for those pupils who have grasped the 'golden nugget' which was the key point of the lesson?
- In what ways might I teach this more effectively next time – what would I change, what would I retain?
- Were they listening to what I was saying or looking out of the window, bored stiff and inattentive?

Teaching is a very creative activity. Don't be surprised if you find planning difficult and time consuming at first. As a teacher, you have to in effect 'put on' 15 to 20 'shows' a week. You are the director, the producer, the props manager, the casting manager. But you are not the star. At the centre of your planning is concern for the quality of pupils' learning, progress and performance. Most teachers get better at the 'technical' aspects of teaching. As intelligent graduates, it would be surprising if they did not improve with practice. But what marks out the teachers who go on to be inspirational and exceptional is the quality of thinking and preparation that goes into their lessons.

SUMMARY AND KEY POINTS

- Planning goes on after the lesson has finished: reflect on how you might teach the lesson more effectively next time.
- Don't forget to make connections to pupils' prior learning, so that they develop a coherent overview of the past.
- Try to formulate precise and appropriate learning objectives for history in your lessons, and 'track them through' in the lesson activities and your evaluation of the lesson. This can make the written aspect of lesson planning seem purposeful and worthwhile, instead of seeming like pointless paperwork.

- Keep in mind the full breadth of the NC for history; it's not just about covering subject content.
- As well as moving pupils forward in history, you are also responsible for the development of their general educational skills, whether in terms of language, ICT capability or other 'key' skills. Make sure that your lesson planning incorporates these factors.
- You also need to consider your own learning needs, departmental policies and classroom management concerns. You have to balance these as adroitly as possible – this can require skills and qualities of tact, perseverance, insight and determination.
- Initiative and imagination are also important attributes in planning; sometimes it may be necessary to adopt an eclectic 'way in' to the topic.
- Give some thought to the interplay of high and low value activities to maximise pupil engagement and learning.

Cross curricular (handwritten annotation)

More information on planning, lesson objectives and evaluations and suggestions for further reading can be found at http://www.uea.ac.uk/~m242/historypgce/planning.

REFERENCES

Baker, C., Cohn, T. and McLaughlin, M. (2000) 'Current issues in the training of secondary history teachers: an HMI perspective', in J. Arthur and R. Phillips, (eds), *Issues in History Teaching*, London: Routledge: 191–202.

Battersby, J. (1996) 'Discipline and control', unpublished lecture, University of East Anglia, 4 November.

Bowen, P. (1993) 'Work from the known to the unknown', *Welsh Historian*, No. 20, Autumn, 19–22.

Chapman, A. (2003) 'Conceptual awareness through categorising: using ICT to get Year 13 reading', *Teaching History*, No. 111: 38–43.

Counsell, C. (1996) 'Progression at key stage 3: what does "getting better at history" mean?', Address to Historical Association Conference, York, 14 September.

Counsell, C. (2000) 'Editorial', *Teaching History*, No. 99, May, 2.

Dearing, R. (1994) *The National Curriculum and its Assessment*, London: SCAA.

DES (1985) *History in the Primary and Secondary Years*, London: Department for Education and Employment/Qualifications and Curriculum Authority.

DfEE (1998) *Teaching: High Status, High Standards Requirements for Courses of Initial Teacher Training*, London: Department for Education and Employment.

DfEE/QCA (1999) *History: The National Curriculum for England*, London: DfEE/QCA.

Deuchar, S. (1982) *History on the Brink*, York: Campaign for Real Education.

Deuchar, S. (1987) *History and GCSE History*, London: Centre for Policy Studies.

Haenen, J. and Schrijnmakers. H. (2000) 'Suffrage, feudal, democracy, treaty . . . history's building blocks: learning to teach historical concepts', *Teaching History*, No. 98: 22–9.

Haenen, J., Schrijnmakers. H. and Stufkens, J. (2003) 'Transforming year 7's understanding of the concept of imperialism: a case study on the Roman Empire', *Teaching History*, No. 112: 28–34.

Hallam, S. (1996) 'Differentiation', unpublished lecture, Institute of Education, University of London, January.

Heafford, D. (1990), 'Teachers teach but do learners learn?', in C. Wringe (ed.), *Language Learning*, Journal 1, quoted in N. Pachler and C. Field (1997) *Learning to Teach Modern Foreign Languages in the Secondary School*, London: Routledge.

Historical Association (1988) *History in the National Curriculum*, London: Historical Association.

HMI (1985) *History in the Primary and Secondary Years*, London: HMSO.

Holt, J. (1982) *How Children Fail*, New York: Delacorte/Seymour Lawrence.

Hunt, M. (1997) 'Thinking it through', unpublished paper, Manchester Metropolitan University.

Husbands, C. (1996) *What is History Teaching?*, Buckingham: Open University Press.

Lawlor, S. (1989) 'Correct core', in B. Moon, P. Murphy and J. Raynor (eds), *Policies for the Curriculum*, Milton Keynes: Open University Press.

Lawton, D. (1985) *Education, Culture and the Curriculum*, London: Hodder and Stoughton.

Lee, P. and Ashby, R. (2000) 'Progression in historical understanding 7–14, in P. Seixas, P. Stearns, and S. Wineburg (eds) *Teaching Knowing and Learning History*, New York: New York University Press: 195–220.

Lomas, T. (1990) *Teaching and Assessing Historical understanding*, London: Historical Association.

Lomas, T. (2000) 'Letters', *Teaching History*, No. 99, May 3.

McGovern, C. (1994) *The SCAA Review of National Curriculum History: A Minority Report*, York: Campaign for Real Education.

MacLennan, S. (1987) 'Integrating lesson planning and classroom management', *ELT Journal*, Vol. 41, No. 3: 193–6.

Ministry of Education (1952) *Teaching History*, Pamphlet 23, London: HMSO.

Moss, P. (1970) *History Alive 55 BC–1485*, London: Hart-Davis.

National Curriculum Council (NCC) (1991) *Non-Statutory Guidance for History*, York: NCC.

National Curriculum Council (NCC) (1993) *Teaching History at Key Stage 3*, York: NCC.

OFSTED (2005) *Annual Report of Her Majesty's Inspector for Schools*, London: OFSTED.

Phillips, R. (2001) 'Making history curious: using initial stimulus material to promote enquiry, thinking and literacy', *Teaching History*, No. 105: 19–25.

QCA (2005) *History 2004–5 Annual Report on Curriculum and Assessment*, London: QCA.

QCA (2007) The National Curriculum: History Key Stage 3. Online at http://curriculum. qca.org.uk/subjects/. Last accessed 3 January 2008.

Riley, M. (2000) 'Into the Key Stage 3 history garden: choosing and planting your enquiry questions', *Teaching History*, No. 99: 8–13.

Robbins, D. (2004) 'Learning about an 800 year old fight can't be all that bad can it?' *Teaching History*, No. 117: 44–8.

Van Drie, J. and van Boxtel, C. (2003) 'Developing conceptual understanding through talk and mapping', *Teaching History*, No. 110: 27–31.

Ward, R. (2007) 'Creating a curriculum that will help all young people in Britain understand the world in which they live', paper presented at the Why History Matters Conference, Institute of Historical Research, 13 February.

It helps if you can somehow get them interested. In the words of Hallam (1996) 'They must want to learn, if you lose that you lose everything.'

4 Learning strategies and the use of language

INTRODUCTION

One of the many skills you need to develop as a history teacher is the ability to select teaching methods which are appropriate for the particular pupils you teach and for the achievement of the objectives of the lesson. The choice of method usually resides with the class teacher for, although the NC for history identifies the key concepts and key processes which pupils should be addressing, the methods by which the NC is delivered are left for the teacher to decide.

Most methods have their strengths and their weaknesses. Your skill as a teacher is knowing which approaches are most likely to maximise the learning achieved by the pupils. Different methods suit different circumstances, so you need to be competent in the use of a range of styles and methods, sometimes within the same lesson. *Over-reliance on one approach limits the learning potential of the pupils*. OFSTED reports have noted a narrow range of teaching styles as a weakness in school history (see, for example, OFSTED, 2005). Exploration of the National Strategy approaches for Key Stage 3 will encourage you to consider how different pupils respond to different styles of learning. Some will have a strength in auditory learning, others respond well to visual stimulus and still others benefit from a kinaesthetic approach, which allows greater physical involvement in their learning by touching, feeling and doing. Additionally you will find some pupils are more likely to benefit from collaborative working, while others prefer individual learning programmes.

A range of factors may inhibit your choice of method, particularly in the early weeks of your school experience. There may be times when it is unwise to move away too abruptly from the methods the pupils have usually experienced. There may be classes where the choice of methods is influenced by issues of control and discipline (see Chapter 3). Above all, remember that there is no hard and fast rule which guarantees success: teaching is a context dependent activity. Sometimes adopting a different approach with reluctant learners is just what is needed – but it won't always work, you need to be pragmatic and adaptable.

Whatever style you chose to employ, how you make use of language is often the key to successful learning. This chapter will also address the ways in which use of languages is one of the key issues in effective history teaching.

OBJECTIVES

At the end of this chapter you should be able to:

- examine the subject specific nature of some teaching methods and skills;
- discuss the strengths and limitations of various strategies;
- consider the linguistic demands and the potential difficulties which the learning of history makes on pupils.

LEARNING STRATEGIES

Because you may eventually be teaching the same group of pupils for a whole year or even over several years, you need to make a conscious effort to build up an 'archive' of teaching ideas and resources, some of which may be adaptable to differing topic areas.

As you grow more confident in the classroom, you begin to think more about the quality of learning you are providing and to evaluate the methods and the materials you are using. With that growth of confidence also comes the opportunity to try out new approaches and to take a few risks. Be prepared to experiment even though you may not have seen an approach before. Although your course provides you with experience in more than one school, you would be very fortunate if the amount of observation of experienced teachers you can manage covers the breadth of methods available to the history teacher (this is why *reading* about teaching history is so essential). If you are trying out a method for the first time and it does not work particularly well, try to work out why this was the case but do not dismiss it forever. Try it again perhaps with a different class and a different topic. Variety of method is often a key ingredient for a successful scheme of work. The Key Concepts and Processes which underpin the NC for history are themselves very varied in their demands and emphasis and you need to have a range of teaching styles and approaches if all these major 'domains' of history are to be successfully developed (see QCA, 2007 for details of these Key Concepts and Processes).

Task 4.1 The application of different learning styles to the teaching of history

1 Look at a history scheme of work to identify the extent to which different styles are met. Does any one style predominate?
2 Consider what changes might be made to increase the variety of styles used.
3 Discuss with your tutor examples of different pupils responding to different approaches.

PROBLEMS IN THE USE OF LANGUAGE FOR THE HISTORY TEACHER

Concern over pupils' literacy skills can be traced back to at least as far as the Bullock Report (*A Language for Life*, 1975), which gave an impetus towards a greater concern for the use of language in the teaching of all subjects across the secondary curriculum. The report was followed by a range of publications, which sought to apply its thinking at subject specific level. An outstanding example of these is that of Nick Levine's contribution for the teaching of history to M. Torbé's series on Language, Teaching and Learning (Levine, 1981).

It has long been established that history is well-placed to make a significant contribution to pupil literacy. Burson (1963) asserted that 'history, more than any other school subject, depends upon literacy in its pupils as a prerequisite to success and increased literacy is perhaps its most important by-product.' More recently, history's contribution to the development of pupils' literacy has been used to defend its place on the school curriculum. There may well be times when you may find it useful to be able to articulate these claims. One way of doing this is to seek to apply advice of publications such as *Literacy Across the Curriculum* (DfEE, 2001) to the specific requirements of learning history. Rudham sees the challenge presented by the National Literacy Strategy as for all history teachers to consider and to adopt their planning and delivery of direct literacy teaching not by the creation of new and 'artificial' literacy lessons but by refocusing the objectives of existing activities (Rudham, 2003).

As a student teacher, you will soon appreciate how much the ability (or lack of it) of your pupils to read, write and generally communicate their knowledge and understanding will influence the planning and execution of your lessons. History has much to offer in the development of language capability, and history teachers must be constantly alert to opportunities to enrich this aspect of pupils' learning.

In this chapter we consider four aspects of the role of language in history teaching: teacher talk, reading, pupil talk and pupils' written work. These four activities, which form an essential part of your classroom teaching, are all dependent on the effective use of language for their success. You need to be aware of both the problems and the opportunities which you will encounter in the use of language in your teaching.

The limited understanding often experienced by pupils in history lessons suggests that the learning of history makes considerable linguistic demands on pupils. Language issues can be deceptive. Edwards (1978) noted the 'frequently occurring paradox' that history teachers can experience. On one hand the subject would seem to lack extensive 'technical' language and is often dependent on everyday language and yet on the other hand the subject has been identified as one presenting 'unusual linguistic difficulties'.

Consider first the *dependency on ordinary language*. It is easy to make too many assumptions about what is everyday language. What may seem ordinary to a graduate will not necessarily be so to pupils. In your search for words to aid description and explanation it is easy to be over-reliant on phrases that have become familiar to you. Gunning (1978) used the term 'weasel words'. He said that such words had certain characteristics; they do not always seem difficult and probably are not in some contexts, but can be very confusing in others. In some cases such as the use of the word 'church', 'state' or 'party', teacher and pupil could be using these words differently. To the teacher the 'Church' is describing the institution, to the pupil, a building. Pupils usually apply the concrete meaning of a term rather than its more abstract or generic use. Gunning also noted the danger of using words, which seem straightforward enough but really cover vague or partial understanding. A good example he quotes is 'There was discontent with the Republic', but what does 'discontent' really mean? If pupils are to understand such words they need to be more explicit. 'Ordinary language' can also provide problems to pupils when some apparently familiar words had different meanings in the past. For example, 'enthusiasm' was not always viewed as positively as today.

The study of history also requires the use of a host of *abstract terms* and, although the subject cannot claim a monopoly of such terms, because subjects such as economics, policies, sociology and perhaps, theology are usually studied after the age of 16, it is often through their study of history that pupils have their first acquaintance with concepts such as 'revolution', 'democracy', 'colonialism', 'representation', 'taxation', 'inflation', and so on.

In addition to the vast array of names of people and events, pupils are faced with *subject specific labels*, often implying interpretations, such as the 'Glorious Revolution' and the 'Peterloo Massacre'. Furthermore they need to understand and use a range of terms to help them achieve another of the activities of the historian, to categorise and classify. For example, words which help to group together ideas or events to help structure understanding – like 'The Eleven Years' Tyranny' 'The Interregnum' – or words needed to classify causes and consequences such as 'social', 'technical' and 'economic'. The nature of history, with its abundance of abstract ideas such as 'sovereignty', 'revolution' and 'appeasement', means that the successful use of language is particularly important for history teachers. Husbands (1996) emphasised the need for history teachers to be aware of the 'fuzzy' and problematic nature of the historical language they use. He showed the distinction between language used as a labelling system, where words are used in a clear unambiguous way to communicate factual information and language used as an interpretative system, in which the meaning of words varies according to the context and their use. Hence you need to be constantly aware of the problems presented by your language in your teaching for example of historical evidence and historical interpretations. Similarly the DfES publication, *Literacy in History* aims to demonstrate how focused literacy teaching can enhance historical understanding with due attention to the way the history teacher approaches speaking and listening, reading and writing (DfES, 2004).

All present real problems for pupils unless they are anticipated by the teacher and adequately explained. This means we have to give particular thought and attention to the needs of pupils with very limited or low levels of literacy (see Chapter 7). Pupils need to be encouraged to use such terms in a way that shows they do understand them and are not repeating other people's language without fully understanding it.

Cowie (1979) noted a further difficulty, which the use of language can create for pupils. She noted that history requires the use of a full range of past tenses (perfect, past perfect, past continuous as well as the simple past), which are not often used by pupils in their usual speech. Such *difficulties with tenses* help to explain why the pupils usually feel more comfortable with more creative and imaginative tasks than those requiring a more academic exposition.

Task 4.2 Language problems in history teaching

Acquire three or four history textbooks that have been produced at different times in the last 30 years. Select from each book a paragraph and try to identify those words and phrases which you think might prove to be problematic for the pupils for whom they are intended. If the opportunity arises, talk to pupils about their understanding of such extracts. Consider the difficulties that might arise from the conciseness of the text, the style and the use of metaphorical language, the use of abstract concepts, of vague descriptive words, of words related to time and place and the use of quotations from sources.

Select one of the passages and try to rewrite the content so that the potential problems have been eliminated. There will be some occasions when you have to rewrite material to make it accessible to your pupils.

TEACHING METHODS INVOLVING THE DIFFERING USE OF LANGUAGE IN HISTORY

Teacher talk: developing your skills of exposition

As a history teacher it is difficult to avoid the use of teacher talk as a significant element of your lessons. The reason for this is the fact that history is one of those subjects which involves a vast amount of content, so there can be a great deal to talk about. There is and always will be an important place for teacher talk whether it be questioning or exposition and the subject offers plenty of topics, which can be described in a stimulating way. The development of your skills both in exposition and in questioning is an essential feature of your competence as a history teacher. Such teaching figured highly in the traditional approach and there is little doubt it can be overdone. Yet, however accomplished you become at devising purposeful and worthwhile learning activities for pupils, you must at some point be able to use the skills of exposition and questioning to explain the past to pupils in an engaging and effective manner.

An important part of your role as a history teacher is to be able to sell the subject, to transmit your enthusiasm for the topic to the pupils. Reluctance to develop exposition skills can encourage the uninspiring use of the textbook or an over-reliance on duplicated handouts. At times you can call on the assistance of a video to stimulate interest in the topic, but there are times when you are dependent on yourself, your knowledge and classroom personality. You need to have a good command of the topic and to have selected from it the significant points you want to stress and the kind of detail appropriate to the age and ability of your class. It is useful to have your notes at hand but try to remember as much as you can. If you appear to be tied to your notes, this serves only to reinforce your inexperience and limits your movement about the class. One of the ways of avoiding frequent reference to notes is to use visual aids, be it the board, the overhead projector (OHP), PowerPoint, pictures or your own creations. These not only serve as an aid to your memory, they help the pupils follow your exposition and also focus their attention away from you. They can also help in reinforcing and recapping key points. Some teachers have found it useful to practise exposition skills at home, not exactly declaiming from the top of the stairs, but possibly using a tape-recorder to help them reflect on their use of language, about any assumptions they may be making about the pupils' understanding and about how they use their voices. If you feel you have a problem with the way you use your voice, most courses have a specialist available to help you.

> **Task 4.3 Developing your skills of exposition**
>
> Make notes on the topic you wish to transmit to the class. Then identify those details, which will benefit from the use of visual aids and how you use the board or whiteboard. Underline those *key* points that you consider to be the ones that need emphasis and which are related most clearly to your lesson objectives.
>
> Record about ten minutes of your exposition and on listening to the play-back, assess the extent to which you have used your voice to make the topic interesting, relevant and stimulating for your pupils.
>
> In at least one of your lessons, make a conscious attempt to undertake a piece of teacher exposition which, *above all other considerations*, interests and engages pupils.
>
> For further guidance read Chapter 3 of Capel *et al.* (2005) to help you develop this important skill of communicating historical content.

You should find that your worries about exposition skills recede as you teach more lessons. Whereas in the early stages of school experience, a ten-minute explanation can appear a daunting prospect, after a while the use of teacher talk can present a different challenge – that is, *how to avoid talking for too long* (with most classes 15 to 20 minutes is a maximum). Effective teacher talk is better measured by quality rather than by quantity.

You will find that there are times when there is a place for self-denial. You must learn to judge how long to talk for, and when to stop. That is, to be aware of what has been termed, 'discursive intrusiveness' – the belief that if the teacher 'bangs on about it' for long enough pupils will understand. At times there may be a negative correlation between the quantity of teacher talk and pupil understanding. Although you might be tempted to display your knowledge ('I know it, therefore I will tell them about it . . .'), such loquacity may not be in the best interests of your pupils. You need to develop a sense of when you may have 'lost' your audience, and need to move quickly on to something else.

A dataset giving pupils' views about what they do and don't like about being in classrooms, and the factors which they think either help or hinder their learning is accessible at: www.uea.ac.uk/~m242/nasc/welcome.htm. Excessive teacher exposition and teachers 'not explaining things well' are two of the most commonly cited things that put pupils off learning.

'He's not my sort of teacher, he's like a Duracell battery, he just goes on and on' (Pupil describing his history teacher).

Your competence in talking to pupils should include an awareness of the disadvantages and advantages of this approach:

1 *The disadvantages.* This style of teaching does invite questions about the quality of learning that might be involved, particularly if overused or used with content for which this 'transmission mode' is not really appropriate. Criticisms of this mode are most valid when its use may be seen to reflect an attitude towards the learning of history, which places the teacher too exclusively in the role of the 'expert', the fount of all knowledge to be covered and the pupil in the role of the receiver, who sits like an empty receptacle waiting for 'knowledge' to be poured in. Teaching through teacher exposition raises fundamental questions about how pupils learn and specifically acquire language in a way they can understand and make use of it.

2 *The advantages.* Advocates of the value of teacher exposition usually emphasise its efficient use of time, a precious commodity for a subject often restricted to two or even one lesson per week. The material can be thought through ready for presentation, given a logical structure and pared down to the essentials so that due emphasis can be given to key points. Any subject-specific words can be explained as the talk proceeds.

The material can be presented with a style and organisation suitable for meeting the needs of assessment, particularly external examination syllabuses. There is little doubt that, with an accomplished practitioner, there are times when this approach can be an effective learning experience, perhaps even the highlight of the lesson, and it is perhaps significant that OFSTED (2005) have commented critically about the lack of input by the teacher. Part of that input should be the development of your narrative skills.

THE NARRATIVE ART OF THE HISTORY TEACHER

It has become evident that there has been a re-appraisal of the role of exposition within the context of a curriculum that emphasises skills as well as knowledge and understanding. Story has long been used as a means of addressing wider complex, abstract ideas. An early example of this was Longman's 'Then and There' series. Lacey's series 'Great Tales from English History' is an attempt to revive this tradition (Lacey, 2006). Husbands welcomes this 'reshaped' narrative tradition as a means of stimulating ways of thinking about the past and about the ways the past was experienced (Husbands, 1996). He is mindful of the obligations of the teacher adopting a narrative approach, stressing the importance of factual accuracy, consistent with historical evidence, the need for authenticity to period and character and the need to ensure the pupils realise that this is not the only story. It is also important to think through how you engage the pupils in the course of the narrative. Given a dilemma, what could be done about it?

The success of the narrative approach often lies in the detail and the nature of the details. Wilkinson questions the capacity of the double-page spread of a typical textbook to be of real use in understanding a topic or the arguments being explored. He advocates a narrative skill that gives 'the opportunity to flesh out people, figures and events and to add some of the colour, sights and smells that children love but often miss out on' (Wilkinson, 2006: 17). To succeed with the narrative approach you need to acquire the sort of detail that makes a story. Such information you accumulate over time as you select to read more detailed books on topics you think likely to benefit from the narrative approach. Wilkinson (2006) and Goodwin (2006) offer the following advice for the successful use of narrative, the latter particularly with beginning teachers in mind.

GUIDANCE FOR SUCCESSFUL USE OF NARRATIVE

Wilkinson		Goodwin	
1	Learn the plot and revise in the light of the response.	1	Move around the room to emphasise the movement of the story but stand absolutely still to emphasise key events.
2	Vary your voice – do not keep the same flat tone and do not be afraid to repeat things to emphasise them.	2	Lowering the classroom lights will help to focus the pupils' attention on you and any visual material you use to support your narrative. This will signify a different type of activity.

3	Entertain – act it up even more than usual.	3	Vary the volume of your voice for emphasis. Once you have the pupils' attention try lowering your voice so they strain just a little to hear you.
4	Plan. Consider carefully how you are going to follow-up the story – what aspects you are going to focus on and build on in the follow-up.	4	Beginners may find there is reassurance in giving the pupils a written version for reference if you are losing the thread.

The most practical answer is that there are times when teacher exposition is the most appropriate teaching method, and the art of the teacher is to judge when this or is not the case. What is essential is that you give the pupils plenty of opportunity to use what they have learnt from your exposition. Bullock (1975) stressed that 'what is known' must be brought to life afresh by the pupils' own efforts. Similarly in stating that 'learning is a matter of personally engaged struggle rather than detached acquiescence', Levine (1981) emphasises the paramount importance of the way you follow–up your narrative. Be aware of the dangers of the pupils merely repeating what the teacher has said and try to use activities by which pupils can rework the new content and make the knowledge and concepts their own.

To think about...

How good are your skills of exposition?

a   I'm fairly confident about this aspect of my teaching; when talking to my teaching groups, I think I can generally interest them and hold their attention, whatever the topic. Question, answer and discussion activities are usually lively and stimulating.

b   I'm OK; I feel relaxed and confident in talking to my teaching groups, and talk quite fluently and effectively to them most of the time. I think I explain things quite well. Sometimes they are interested in what I say, and they enjoy the bit of the lesson where I am talking to them. I can think on my feet fairly well and feel comfortable with QUAD activities with most groups.

c   Reasonable, but it's an aspect of my teaching that I will need to work on whilst on second placement. Sometimes I suspect that they do not find my exposition helpful or interesting, and I don't relay enjoy this bit of the lesson. I find QUAD activities quite difficult and sometimes they don't really take off.

d   Definitely a weakness; I am aware that pupils are frequently bored and restless when I try to talk to them at any length, even on topics where my subject knowledge is quite good. I don't feel confident or relaxed when doing QUAD activities with them.

e   I'm so bad at this that I avoid doing it as much as possible, I talk for about 10 seconds and then set them some written work or a group work task.

USE OF QUESTIONING

A common classroom strategy is that of exposition interspersed with questioning. Questioning is an important skill for any teacher. It has been calculated that teachers spend about 30 per cent of their time asking questions. However, the rate and the nature of oral questioning vary from subject to subject. How you formulate questions and use them is a good indicator of what you think the pupils are gaining from your history lessons. Much has been written since the 1950s about the type of questions used in lessons, which demonstrates the link between objectives and questions. Bloom made an early contribution to the classification of types of questions and since then there have been many variants to his original attempt to place the questions in a hierarchical order, from the easiest to the most difficult (Bloom, 1956). A common list would be recall, comprehension, translation (e.g. transfer from one medium to another such as writing a description of a picture), analysis, comparison, interpretation, synthesis, hypothetical (invention), evaluation. Opinions vary about the order for it is important to stress that some comprehension questions can be very difficult as will be very clear from a glance at some historical sources and some interpretations can be relatively straightforward. The following taxonomy with particular reference to the use of evidence in history teaching can be helpful:

1   Recall questions: give details of events, people, places mentioned in the source.
2   Comprehension questions: What does the evidence say? Do I understand it? Can I picture to myself the scene that it represents?
3   Interpretation questions: How does the evidence compare with my knowledge of the historical context? What was the writer's purpose in writing?
4   Extrapolation questions: Does it contradict other evidence? What new light does it shed?
5   Invention questions: If you had been there questions. 'What if' questions.
6   Evaluation questions: What is the value of the evidence? Is it trustworthy? What is your opinion about the course of action taken? (Garvey and Krug, 1977)

Such lists give you a useful basis for an analysis of the type of questions to use in your lessons. A familiar criticism of lessons is that too much emphasis is given to what are thought to be the undemanding questions; that is an overuse of what may be called the 'lower order' questions involving recall, comprehension and translation with only a limited use of the 'higher order' questions which encourage the pupils to think, such as interpretation and evaluation. Of course, the difficulty of a question depends on the context and materials being used, even so your aim is to encourage your pupils to think for themselves and to try and use the 'higher order' questions as much as the situation allows. It should be noted that there is also the skill of listening and responding to questions in a way, which encourages pupils to volunteer answers.

Task 4.4 Using 'thinking' questions

1   Using the hierarchy of questions presented above, analyse a selection of worksheets and try to identify the types of questions that have been asked. What is the distribution of 'lower' and 'higher' order questions? If there are few 'higher' order questions, try to formulate some that might be added.
2   Use the same method with questions on two or three topics in a textbook.
3   When you are planning a question and answer session within your lesson, write out the principal questions you will be asking. McCully (1997) has shown how there are times when the whole lesson can be structured around a set of key questions. Think about the sequencing and how you might include some 'thinking' questions. After the lesson reflect on how you used such questions and on how the techniques you used might differ from the asking of recall questions.

Questioning should not all be one-way, that is the teacher questions, the pupil responds. Pupils should be encouraged to ask questions both of the teacher and of each other. Much can be learnt about pupils' historical understanding or lack of understanding from the questions they ask. There is a connection here with your own subject knowledge, because you are more likely to wish to monopolise the questioning if you feel insecure about your knowledge of the topic. OFSTED (2005) noted how, in circumstances that indicated good practice, pupils raised their own questions, developed and tested hypotheses and undertook investigations. A methodology, in which the pupils undertake their own historical enquiries, gives you the opportunity to encourage them to ask questions about the topic and the sources of information they are using.

There are also interesting issues arising out of 'wait time': how long do you give pupils to think about an answer before providing it, or asking someone else or moving on? You can give pupils, individually or in pairs, some time to come up with an answer, in order to get them to think in a bit more depth.

Task 4.5 Encouraging pupils' questioning

1　When you have taught some lessons, look back on your lesson plans and consider whether there might have been some opportunities for the pupils to have done some questioning.

2　Try to list the range of situations that could generate pupils asking questions of yourself, of each other or for interrogating sources. Here is a list to get you started: asking questions of you as Oliver Cromwell; mock trial of Charles I; questioning group reports on a decision-making exercise; questioning the producer/author of a costume drama seen on video; researching family history; questioning a group presentation. Now try to add to these.

3　Think of, and experiment with, strategies for dealing with problems such as:
　a　the reluctance of some pupils to answers questions;
　b　how to deal with 'wrong' or inappropriate answers;
　c　overenthusiastic or attention-seeking pupils wanting to answer all the questions.

READING

It is possible to argue that the role of reading in the teaching and learning of history has paradoxically been one of both great concern and yet of considerable neglect. Concern has been expressed about its suitability for stimulating interest and its accessibility to younger and slower readers. Neglect has resulted in pupils' limited ability to engage upon more extended reading and to use texts effectively higher up the school. Cottingham and Daborn (1999) identified reading, rather than writing as being the biggest literacy problem in our history classrooms and found that teachers felt that history placed greater demands on the reading skills of pupils than any other subject. Recent findings of Key Stage 3 tests at 14 placed attainment in reading below that for writing (*The Guardian*, 14 September 2006).

This paradox may be associated with the changing fashions in the use of the textbook. What lessons can be learnt from thinking about your own use of textbooks when you were at school? (Do you remember it as an exciting bit of history in school?) Over a generation ago the typical textbook of the time had little attraction for many pupils.

With its lack of illustrations, its terse and concise style, such books attempted to cover a vast range of content. When such books were allied to methods such as 'reading round the class' or the silent reading of a whole chapter followed by a factual test, there is little wonder that the memories of many adults of their school history lessons is one of unmitigated boredom. Many teachers of that era decided it was better to disregard the textbook and rely on resources of their own. Hence by the 1970s it was significant that the Schools Council 'Effective Reading Project' (1978) found that the textbook played a relatively minor supporting role in many classrooms. Teachers had more faith in the spoken word and teacher exposition. The project found that on average only four minutes of a forty-minute lesson was spent on reading and Lunzer and Gardiner (1979) found that in approximately half of all classrooms reading occured in bursts of less than fifteen seconds in any one minute. Explanations of such limited use ranged from the cost of the books, the complexity of the language, the pupils' limited attention and the inappropriateness of much of the content at a time when the content was not prescribed by statute. Thus, with the emergence of the Schools Council History Project materials it was not surprising that many teachers had difficulties in coming to terms with the extensive reading which those materials provided, particularly the wealth of source material.

The introduction of the NC has brought with it a new wave of textbooks, written for the prescribed units. These are a vast improvement on the books of a generation ago, reflecting not only the technical advances in publishing but also some of the issues of accessibility and pupils' reading ability. In addition the books are much more task-orientated. With such resources available, the textbook has once more become an important resource for the teacher and can, *when used selectively and in association with other approaches*, be an effective resource. More recently, aware of history's contribution to literacy, textbooks have been published which include more extensive reading. However, textbooks, no matter how attractive, will not increase the quality of the pupils' learning if they re-introduce the 'bad habits' of the past, namely 'reading round the class', copying, and comprehension exercises which have little or nothing to do with developing pupils' historical understanding. OFSTED (2005) noted that the excessive dependence in some schools on a single textbook is also a cause for concern because it can so often result in a narrow teaching style. If you decide to use a textbook, you must give some thought to how to ensure that it is an engaging and effective contribution to pupils' learning, rather than something that is just passing the time until the bell goes.

STRATEGIES FOR THE USE OF READING

1   Seek to establish the role of reading in history by taking steps *to build up the pupils' confidence*, taking measures to ensure success. These could include making sure the pupils have sufficient background knowledge so that the reading makes sense; identifying beforehand the words and phrases that could stop the reader's progress, both subject-specific and non-technical language; and, where significant, the use in the text of structure words such as 'if', 'although', 'nevertheless'; giving them an overview of what the reading involves by summarising the arrangement of the paragraphs. Encourage the pupils to appreciate the value of re-reading. ('A quick reader is not necessarily a good one.') Make a point of

praising pupils' reading and emphasise that a good effort at reading is comparable with a good effort at writing.

2   Make sure the pupils' can see *the purpose of the activity* (e.g. questions to be answered), diagrams or charts to be completed. Try to ensure that they are given not just comprehension questions but tasks which encourage reflection and opinions on what has been read. Hellier and Richards (2005) make the point that it is also useful to remind pupils what they are *not* reading for, as discarding information can be most difficult for pupils regardless of ability.

3   *Use active or 'guided' reading strategies.* Reading can make an important contribution to your lessons if you have chosen and planned strategies appropriate to your lesson objectives. There are a wide range of activities for your choice, several well-documented in DfES (2004), *Literacy in History* and Hellier and Richards (2005). These include asking your pupils to:

  a   Highlight, underline, label, or annotate the text to meet a specific search; at times you could set the challenge to find information against a specified time.

  b   Transfer information from the text to a list, grid, chart, Venn diagram, etc., for example for categorising the causes of an event.

  c   Summarise the content in a sentence or present, say, the essence of a piece of source material as a speech bubble.

  d   Work in pairs on completion activities such as cloze exercises or putting paragraphs into their correct sequence.

  e   Work in groups on a collection of sources, in which individuals describe and summarise for each other.

  f   Read one section of the material at a time as you seek to scaffold their reading.

In addition you might consider the merits of reading aloud. This could involve yourself modelling your approach to reading having notes the issues and questions that can arise in your preparation. Lewis and Wray (2000) advocate the value of inviting pupils to read aloud as a means of helping understanding as some pupils would welcome this use of an auditory approach to reading, including bi-lingual pupils.

4   *Ensure the pupils have the necessary reference skills.* Some pupils can become frustrated and disillusioned if they spend their time unprofitably, simply because they lack the appropriate reference skills – the ability to use the indexing system, dictionaries, encyclopaedias and contents pages. To this we can add CD-ROM and internet materials, which again will require reading ability.

5   *Differentiation* is an ever-present issue. *Ensure the reading material is appropriate for the ability of the pupils.* There will be times when sources are too complex for some pupils and need to be 'doctored' or even rewritten, although some might argue that if such is the case, then the source was inappropriate in the first place. Wilson (1985) has suggested that too much doctoring can leave the reading material a very arid, boring product. There is a case for leaving some difficult aspects of the reading in

place if the general tone is likely to be more stimulating and the sense of period to be retained. It is a question of balancing one need against another. It is not 'cheating' for teachers to provide a commentary as a way of helping pupils to grasp the essence of documents and sources: Fines (1994), and Chapman (2006) argue that pupils can cope with quite challenging documents *if the teacher helps and guides them through in a skilful manner.*

In your use of reading in the history classroom it is of benefit to your pupils, and your lessons if you emphasise the status of reading in learning history. Seek to create an environment for reading both in the classroom and beyond. The recent archiving of newspapers has provided excellent resources for providing high quality reading resources for pupils to use outside the classroom (see Chapter 9).

The more pupils are familiar with the use of reading at Key Stage 3, the more they will be able to build on this in their later studies. However, always remember that whatever strategies you employ there is always the need to have thought through how you will draw out the learning from that reading.

PUPIL TALK

There are occasions when you ask the pupils to be quiet and talking constitutes a breach of classroom rules. Nevertheless, there are other times when pupils need to be encouraged to talk as a means of advancing their learning. 'Speaking and listening' is an important part of the National Literacy Strategy. The learning of history offers many opportunities for the effective use of speaking and learning. Strategies to use a variety of activities involving pupils talking and listening need not be seen as an imposition. With experience you learn that well-prepared use of pupil talk can considerably advance your pupils' historical knowledge. In their report for 2004/5 HMI noted that history lessons showed too little emphasis given to discussion and group work, aware how much the various uses of pupil talk can advance their learning in history.

HOW CAN THE USE OF PUPIL TALK ADVANCE PUPILS' LEARNING IN HISTORY?

1   It helps to combat the *diffidence* of some pupils, who either through shyness or a fear of being wrong prefer to remain silent. A reluctance to speak may also stem from the idea that learning a subject such as history requires the ability to speak in the formal standard English of the textbook, alien from most pupils' usual form of speaking. Luff (2001) makes the point that speaking and listening does not come naturally to many adolescents so that it is important to devise activities in which they are encouraged to speak. Trying out their ideas in groups or even as a pair can be an enormous confidence booster, which might encourage such pupils to repeat them in a plenary session. Skill in 'drawing out' pupils so that they regularly contribute orally to the lessons can make pupils feel much more positive and involved in the subject.

2   Barnes and Todd (1977) emphasized the need for pupils to be able to rework new information, new ideas and new vocabulary *in their own terms*, if their understanding is to be advanced. Once pupils have assimilated the new material, they are then more likely to be able to use it in a more formal manner to a wider audience.

3   Encouraging pupil talk can be particularly helpful in the development of pupils' *understanding of historical concepts*. The work of Lee *et al.* (1995) suggests that pupils can often develop more powerful ideas for understanding the past talking to each other about problems of change, cause and explanation. Also Clark (2001) demonstrates how 'causal explanation' is about competing possibilities and pupils need to be comfortable with using the speculative language of possibility within their arguments'. Hence the encouragement to use 'might have', 'could have', 'if' and 'probably'. Similarly, use can be made of 'oral frames' to help pupils' speaking and listening. This can involve helping to structure pupils' discussion by involving useful phrases such as, for example, for explaining cause and effect, 'the result is', 'triggering', 'the effect of this was' or even 'precipitating'.

4   In contrast to writing, talk has the advantage of *speed*. *Literacy in History* (2004) notes how 'talk is quick, fluid and shared and can do some things better that writing, for example, exploratory work'. And Luff (2001) reminds us, speed appeals to young people. Pupil talk encourages the quick absorption of ideas and of opposing views. He sees value in speaking, which demands the ability to absorb and marshal ideas quickly, something, which will be needed when writing under the pressure of time.

WHAT KIND OF ACTIVITIES CAN BE USED TO MAKE CONSTRUCTIVE USE OF PUPIL TALK?

- asking and answering questions;
- creating or identifying definitions of subject specific words;
- drawing out similarities and differences;
- defending and justifying a point of view;
- explaining a process;
- explaining or summarizing the content of a source;
- creating mind or concept maps;
- participating in pair or group discussion;
- presentations – by individuals or groups, often illustrated;
- involvement in debates, controversies, sometimes with a competitive element;
- use of varieties of roleplay.

In planning to use activities involving pupil talk, it is important for you to consider how your choice maximises pupil involvement, not allowing certain pupils to dominate the talking but do their share of listening to others. It is also important to keep emphasising that activities involving pupil talk are not a 'light option'. Because they may also be enjoyable it does not make them any less valid as a serious learning activity. The point is often worth repeating in the plenary session, where pupils can often realise just what they have learnt from the activity.

It is also important to keep in mind that there is a progression issue with the use of pupil talk. It can be helpful to move pupils on from being over reliant on reading from a prepared script, or from extensive written notes, and on towards 'thinking on their feet' as they move through the secondary school.

USE OF GROUP WORK

The value of the use of group work has over the years been a source of debate among teachers but it has now established an important place in the history teacher's repertoire of teaching methods. As with all methods, if group work is poorly or inappropriately organised, it provides little advancement in the pupils' learning. Much depends on your understanding of the potential problems and your ability to anticipate these. Such problems can include the following:

- the need to ensure pupils keep 'on task';
- the concern that some pupils in each group are not contributing;
- the likelihood that pupils are given too much control of the pace of the lesson;
- concentration on the obvious, eschewing the more thought-provoking issues;
- reluctance of any group member to give feedback in a plenary;
- can slow down the coverage of the content;
- At times, the classroom layout of desks or tables is not helpful to any whole class teaching which may precede or follow the group work.

Nevertheless, there are many situations when you find pupils can be more motivated in group activities than being a passive recipient of class teaching. Used well group work is an excellent vehicle for all the positive values of pupil talk described above. The key, as so often, is in the planning.

SUCCESSFUL USE OF GROUP ACTIVITIES IN HISTORY MAY BE POSITIVELY INFLUENCED BY THE FOLLOWING STRATEGIES

1   Ensure that the pupils have sufficient background knowledge to be able to complete the tasks they have been given. They are aware of this and it influences the enthusiasm with which they set about the activity. Furthermore the tasks should be sufficiently challenging to motivate and require collaboration. For example, try to turn the topic into a problem in a way that interests the pupils. A discussion on whether Queen Elizabeth I should order the execution of Mary, Queen of Scots, would not work well if the pupils are not bothered whether she dies or not.

2   Think about the way the groups are organised, by ability, friendship groups, mixed gender, choice of this depends on the tasks involved. The use of grouping by ability is not as frequently used as it might be in history lessons. You should explore the possibilities of this and the opportunities it can give you as a teacher to change your role from asking questions

appropriate to the group, taking interim feedback or being a temporary group member. Goodwin (2006) recommends putting pupils in groups before entering the room or having place cards on the desks.

3   Think about how each group may have to allocate tasks or roles, e.g. recording discussion, completing pro formas, chairing, to ensure all participate or presenter of group decisions.

4   Be precise in your thinking about the materials the groups need.

5   Give clear instructions. It is fundamental that the pupils have a clear idea of what they are to do and understand the value of what they are doing and how this contributes to their historical understanding. In particular, think carefully about the starting point of any group activity.

6   Employ strategies to maintain the pace of work. At times there are several stages to the activity so time-checks and interim targets can be employed. Many 'card sort' activities have successive stages. Perhaps most important is the need for group activities to have an end product, for example a decision or set of conclusions, a presentation or a display.

7   Finally, in your follow-up, there is value at times in discussing how the group work went, what has been learnt so the pupils realise that pupil talk is real work with tangible results.

Although there are advantages in using the same group formation whenever you decide to use group work, such as the speed of the transition to the activity, there are times when it may be preferable to make use of different ways of organising group work. The methods cited below have the advantage of seeking to maximise pupil involvement by changing the audience, increasing listening skills and minimising the often tedious and repetitive reporting back stage. The *Literacy Across the Curriculum* material included the following strategies, which are all very adaptable for the teaching of history (DfEE, 2001).

DIFFERENT WAYS OF ORGANISING GROUP WORK

Strategy	Example
Envoys Following group discussion, conclusions/decisions, one group member moves to join another group to explain and summarise these results and to find out what the new group thought.	This can be a useful format for encouraging discussion and decision making when dealing with contentious issues and ones, which require some understanding of attitudes at the time. Questions such as 'Did Louis XVI deserve to die?' and 'Was the Poor law Amendment Act of 1834 a good way to deal with poverty?'
Snowball This involves changing the group size. After the initial discussion and familiarisation with the content in pairs, the two become four and later an eight as they retell and develop ideas.	*Literacy in History* (2004) describes a snowball activity in which pairs are given a causation enquiry. The pupils are asked to divide a set of events/ influences into two columns, share their answers with an enlarged group and add anything new. The feedback asks for two answers from each column.
Rainbow Another way of changing the audience is to give each pupil in a group a different colour and then	Given the need for the group to discuss from an informed position, some approaches may be best placed towards the end of a topic. For example

later all those of the same colour join and retell the original's findings.

Jigsaw
This has the advantage of covering a range of material. The topic is divided and each group becomes an 'expert'. A spokesperson reports back in the plenary, when all the 'pieces of the topic are put together.

when discussing the importance of a topic, 'Whose was the most important contribution to the Industrial Revolution?' Or significance: given a list of reasons why a topic is significant, which is most significant and why?

This approach can be useful when an enquiry involves the use of a range of sources some of which need time for reading. Groups can summarise their findings. The plenary must ensure pupils do not remain 'experts' in their own part of the jigsaw. Useful for the study of historical interpretations.

ROLEPLAY

As you gain in confidence and seek to extend the range of methods you can employ, you will find that there are many topics, which are suitable for the use of roleplay. This is another learning activity which can involve a wide range of pupils of different abilities and in some formats can be really beneficial to kinaesthetic learners, who can learn best when they are physically involved. Role play is often at its most useful when pupils have to deal with topics which are conceptually quite difficult such as the impact on a community of religious changes at the time of the Reformation. There has been a fear that roleplay can take up too much time as teachers struggle to cover the curriculum, but Dawson and Banham (2002) effectively show that this approach can save time because it helps pupils to understand more clearly through the visual representation and sheer physicality of the activity, the concepts involved and with that a substantial improvement in their writing. In another example of roleplay helping understanding, Duff (1998) presented some useful exemplar materials on helping a year 10 class to understand the circumstances surrounding appeasement and the Munich Conference of 1938. It is important to be open minded about trying out such activities to explore their potential for developing pupils' historical understanding.

Remember that roleplay does not have to be an 'all singing, all dancing' festival of active drama, with all pupils having to write and act their parts. It can sometimes involve a small number of pupils, who have been selected to perform for the rest of the class; it can be done without pupils having to move around the room; and it can be done by simply asking pupils to take part in decision-making exercises based on information sheets or film slides. Some student teachers are reluctant to use roleplay because they envisage it will entail a full-scale dramatic production. Some of the most effective role-plays are quite modest in ambition. Ian Luff (2000, 2003) has proved several ideas for eminently practicable and useful roleplay activities, which do not require inordinate amounts of time and preparation.

For more detail on the use of roleplay, including some of Ian Luff's examples of roleplay and practical demonstration, and suggestions for further reading, go to:
www.uea.ac.uk/~m242/historypgce/roleplay.htm.

WRITING

Of the range of activities, which take place in the learning of history, writing is one of the most important and, at the same time, the least popular among pupils (Adey and Biddulph, 2001; QCA, 2005). Yet, it is principally through pupils' writing that their knowledge and understanding is usually assessed. Writing has been an issue for concern and always presents a challenge to some pupils, but there is evidence of a positive response in recent years to the problems writing in history poses (OFSTED, 2002).

WHAT ARE THE PROBLEMS WHICH PUPILS FACE WHEN GIVEN WRITTEN TASKS?

1   *Lack of audience and purpose.* Pupils are unlikely to produce the quality of written work of which they are capable if they are unclear about the purpose of the exercise and unsure about the intended audience. A vague, general invitation to write something about a topic is not likely to motivate the pupils, who may see it as a means of filling the remaining time left in the lesson and may well invite the usual delaying tactics. Instead the pupils need to have a clear idea of the purpose of the task and there is much to be gained by varying the audience and not just assuming this is always the teacher. Cottingham and Daborn (1999) found that teachers were able to note how writing improved when there was clarity of purpose and audience.

2   *Information.* A problem experienced by some beginning teachers is that they ask pupils to produce written work based on insufficient information. If they are asked to base their piece on a few sentences from a textbook then the pupils are unlikely to be motivated and will be disappointed with the result. Basically insufficient time and thought has been given to the preparation for the task. By contrast, having too much information can also cause problems. Pupils seem overwhelmed by the detail, having to handle too much at the same time.

3   *Relevance.* Pupils have difficulties working out what information is relevant to the task. At worst some settle for selecting and copying those sentences, which they hope might meet the task. In this way weaker GCSE candidates will merely write out or paraphrase a sentence or two from a source in a hit or miss fashion. Counsell (1997) has noted pupils' difficulties distinguishing between the general and the particular; they have problems seeing the difference between the larger point and an example. Similarly, Cottingham and Daborn (1999) found that pupils have difficulty distinguishing significant conclusions and supporting evidence from the irrelevant and the superficial with the resulting tendency to write an unselective narrative. This is a problem that extends to A level students, who often need to be taught how to make notes from an academic text with awareness of what they are looking for, otherwise their notes (revealingly) may be a random selection of facts.

4   *Language.* In addition to the considerable challenges which written work in any subject presents to pupils, the specific tasks set in history have their

own problems with language. Counsell (1997) has effectively identified the difficulties pupils have when they are asked to produce analytical and discursive writing. Pupils lack the skills and conventions required for such writing, for example, appropriate ways of beginning sentences and paragraphs and the use of modal verbs.

STRATEGIES FOR IMPROVING THE QUALITY OF YOUR STUDENTS' WRITTEN WORK

1   *Preparation*. The problems which pupils can encounter with written work show the importance of preparation and clearly written work should not be perceived as the 'end-on' part of the learning process. Writing should not merely be an outcome but a valuable pedagogical tool for developing higher order thinking in history (Counsell, 1997). You will benefit from thinking about the ways different types of writing activities can be incorporated into your lesson planning. For doing this, it is useful to apply to history teaching the advice from *Literacy Across the Curriculum*.

   • Establish both the purpose and the audience of the writing.
   • Ensure the pupils have something to say and enough information for the task.
   • Give the pupils opportunities to develop, shape and revise ideas.
   • Encourage collaboration during planning and drafting.
   • Make sure the pupils have access to reference material such as word banks, glossaries as well as historical resources.
   • Build in opportunities for feedback both during and after writing.

   (DfEE, 2001)

2   *Presentation*. You will find your pupils will benefit from being made aware of your expectations of the final product of their writing. Be explicit about 'success criteria'. Cottingham and Daborn (1999) found that pupils responded positively to the exposure to and analysis of examples of extended writing as models for their own writing. At times there is a case for writing standard English, at others rough jottings will suffice. It could be that pupils use different ends of their exercise book for these different writing requirements. You need to *consider how the pupils' exercise book is to be used*. There may be a case, particularly with GCSE classes, for having two exercise books, each serving a different writing function and each intended for a different audience. Rough notes, jottings, draft versions, recording of ideas, summaries of group decisions in one book; more formal writing and recording of information in another. Do not always be concerned with tidiness as pupils work out their ideas. On some occasions work is set out on whiteboards or on separate paper especially if there is to be a display of pupil work.

3   *Clarity of instructions* A very common feature of student teachers is the limited quality of their instructions. To avoid having to stop the class when they have settled to their work to clarify directions and give further guidance, it is important that you have thought through exactly what

instructions you need to give. You need to anticipate the pupils' requirements about lay out, length of work, use of proper sentences, whether they write out the question, ensure they write in their own words and understand the basis upon which you will be marking the work.

4   *Process*. Behind these considerations of the mechanics of how written work is presented, lies a much more fundamental point about *how you encourage pupils to do themselves justice with their work*. It can be argued that in the past insufficient attention was given to the process by which pupils achieve the quality of work expected, especially extended writing. However, the last decade has experienced a considerable improvement in the way teachers have anticipated the problems outlined above and have adopted strategies by which they may be overcome. For this Counsell (1997) has provided valuable guidance. Her Historical Association booklet, *Analytical and Discursive Writing in National Curriculum History at Key Stage 3: A Practical Guide* is very much a positive document, which encourages you to discount the siren voices which deny pupils' capability. Her message is clearly that pupils can achieve a great deal in their writing if the problems are properly addressed. These are in many ways organisational. Hence the recommendation to employ a whole range of sorting and classifying activities to help pupils deal with the information, encourage their historical thinking by various forms of classification, identify what is relevant, and structure their writing. The degree to which the 'scaffolding' of support for writing is provided can vary according to the extent to which the pupils are proficient in extended writing. With a year 7 class, which is being introduced to the idea of essay work this might entail writing a first sentence for each paragraph; where proficiency is variable within the same teaching group it might be achieved by providing suggestions for introductory and linking sentences on the classroom walls.

> 'Some sources suggest that . . .'
> 'However, others suggest . . .'
> 'Sources which have something in common are . . .'
> 'We cannot be sure about *x* because . . .'
> 'A source which sheds some light on this is . . .'
> 'Another important factor was . . .' (Counsell, 1997: 31)

Counsell also uses the idea of 'the zone of relevance', to help pupils to grasp that not all sources of information are relevant (and therefore 'evidence') for a particular question or enquiry. As an example, she suggests that the following statements are given to pupils whose task is to find out why the Great Fire of London got out of control and spread so quickly:

- town officials did not believe that it was going to spread and took no action at the start;
- houses in London were built very close together;
- most buildings were made of wood;
- someone started a fire in Pudding Lane;
- water supplies were unusually low in 1666;

- fire fighting equipment was not good enough to cope with a large fire;
- throughout London, heating and lighting were provided by fire.

They are asked to place in the 'zone of relevance' the statements containing information which helps to answer the question posed (Counsell, 1997: 42). The idea can also be used to develop the idea of 'topic relevance' and 'question' relevance', by incorporating statements which have neither topic nor question relevance.

Writing frames can be helpful but they should be flexible enough to allow pupils to amend them, and they should be encouraged to construct their own frames at times. Bakalis (2003) gives a detailed account of how teaching pupils to structure a paragraph at the same time advances their historical understanding by considering the opening statement, its explanation, substantiation and conclusion. In this way pupils were encouraged to make their thought processes both logical and explicit and helped them towards greater understanding of key concepts.

Counsell (1997) again seeks to meet the language problems with a range of strategies such as 'clever starters', a selection of starting phrases or words, sentence stems or paragraph openers, which can be on permanent display in the classroom. There can also be 'starters' for different types of historical questions such as causation. Other ways of helping pupils to start and to structure their writing include the use of mind maps and concept maps. Such activities bring together several of the language skills encouraged by the National Strategy. Goodwin (2006) shows how through discussion the creation of a mind map of the First World War trenches became an effective plan for a piece of written work on that subject. Similarly, Van Drie and Van Boxtel (2003) showed the value of pairs working with concept cards. This was used not only to help pupils' understanding of the concepts but also to create a structure for the outline of an essay. Counsell (1997, 2004) makes the important point that as pupils progress, 'scaffolding' such as writing frames needs to be removed. The long term aim is to bring pupils to a point where they can write autonomously, without support.

The range of written work

You will find it helpful to keep in mind the range of written work that is possible in the learning of history. Curtis (1994) suggests an audit of how writing is used in history involving not only the types of written task undertaken by pupils but also how they are prepared for such tasks. There could be various ways of presenting such an audit. Here, six types of writing are identified and discussed.

Descriptive

You will find such writing is a prominent feature of Key Stage 3.

Types

These can include transferring into writing representations such as pictures, maps, diagrams and time-charts; describing historical sites; writing comparisons of photographs and sources.

Use and differentiation

Many pupils feel comfortable with descriptive writing, but the less able pupils may need something which has already been written (e.g. completing a paragraph begun by the teacher or sequencing activities, which involve rewriting in the correct order statements linked to pictures). Gap-filling exercises are frequently used. These can offer useful support, but you should look for every opportunity to move the pupils on from such tasks and encourage them to use their own words. *Many pupils may also need to be encouraged to go beyond description.* A common experience is for pupils, when asked to compare two sources, to describe each in turn without commenting on the differences.

The nature of this writing particularly is determined by its function and the person for whom it is intended.

Types

Such writing could include rough jottings, notes for discussion, notes for group presentation or notes taken on a site visit. Alternatively the recording may be notes, which the pupil need to use at a later date in preparation for an examination.

Use and differentiation

Note-making is an activity that plays a significant role in history teaching but OFSTED have noted as a weakness that drafting and note-making are often not well-developed. There may be a case for developing skills in note-making, but in such a way that the practice also serves to reinforce and extend the pupil's understanding. The emphasis therefore is not on 'note-taking' but on 'note-making' as the pupils use their own words and not those dictated by the teacher or copied verbatim from the board or the textbook. Your task is to help the pupils, in varying degrees according to their ability, to structure their notes. Following initial information, derived from teacher exposition, the viewing and discussion of a video, or the analysis of sources, the abler pupils in all years of the secondary school are quite capable of making their own notes given some structure in the form of sub-headings on the board, spellings of proper names and any statistics involved. The amount of information will be extended for the average pupils, whilst with the slower pupils note making follows greater reinforcement and requests to write a complete sentences extending what has been written on the board. The weakest may complete sentences the teacher has begun but still with some scope for their own words. If reference is to be made to information in books, *try to structure the work so that copying can be avoided.* Pupils are more likely to understand the content if they are required to express it in their own words.

Expressive

This is the 'personal' aspect of writing, where pupils are allowed to write with a more personal voice, in contrast to situations where the fear of making mistakes stifles opinion. In the words of Levine (1981) 'to suppress the 'self' is to suppress the means of 'understanding.'

Types

Such writing can include the preparation for debate, comments on a video, on group decisions or participation in a roleplay.

Use and differentiation

Differentiation is often achieved by the extent to which evidence is used to support such opinion.

Imaginative

Another writing activity that is released from the more formal, impersonal kind of writing is that which is more creative and inventive.

Types

Such creative efforts can involve writing from the perspective of someone in the past, diaries, reports, eye-witness accounts, letters, plays, provided that the imaginative work is rooted in evidence to create a genuinely historical activity.

Use and differentiation

It is worthy of note that often through this type of writing a pupil can display a greater understanding of the historical context than other writing might suggest. Imaginative work can also cover the consideration of hypotheses, the 'what if' questions. Differentiation is usually by outcome and, again, the extent to which the work is rooted in historical evidence.

Analytical/evaluative

As made explicit in the task, which follows, the quality of this type of writing is greatly influenced by the methodology, which precedes it, as the problems inherent in this type of writing are tackled.

Types

Examples of such writing include pupils being asked to group together and classify ideas and data and employ the relevant vocabulary to describe such grouping; the analysis of changes, causes and consequences or in the evaluation of sources and interpretations.

Use and differentiation

Much of Counsell's work (1997, 2004) is very relevant here with the intention to reduce gradually the support offered. For the able, beware of the restrictive nature of writing frames and also note the possibilities for the able to service their own analysis by creating their own categories, sorting cards and format of response.

Synthesis

This is arguably the most demanding of the written tasks you can set in the teaching of history, where pupils are required to reconstruct an event, create an extended explanation, answer a question at length or present an interpretation – all compositions based on a variety of evidence. Such a synthesis could take the form of a piece of narrative writing. Lang (2003) has described the writing of narrative as an underrated skill, which deserves to be restored as a valid intellectual exercise capable of rigorous assessment. The value of historical narrative is also considered in the Historical Association report, *History 14–19* (2005), with further emphasis on the construction of a narrative as a high order skill in need of rehabilitation.

Use and differentiation

For example, if pupils are to compile a comprehensive answer to questions such as 'What was it like living in (your home town) during the Second World War?' they need to be taken through a series of stages of research, recording, classifying and writing if they are to achieve a satisfactory synthesis. Further consideration is given to the writing which results from 'historical enquiries' in Chapter 6.

Reducing information

When pupils are asked to reduce information, they are required to think. Whether the reduction is in the form of summary, ranking, forming continuums, or sorting, the pupil has to make some conscious decisions. They are forced at some level into engaging with the text.

Use and differentiation: some examples of asking pupils to reduce information

In not more than 100 words . . .
Which event was the turning point . . .?
Which are the main points, and which the supporting points?
Who is the most important person in this event and why?
Underline the five most important words or phrases . . .
On a postcard/post-it note, write a summary of the article . . .
On three PowerPoint slides, tell the story of . . .
Make a spider diagram to sum up . . .
Draw up a list of six bullet points
Think of a headline/soundbite/slogan . . .

Summary and key points

You have been encouraged to consider what assumptions you may be making in how you choose to cover a topic, assumptions about the contribution to pupils' understanding when required to listen, read, talk and write. Such consideration helps you to anticipate potential difficulties in the approaches and the materials you choose to use and to employ strategies to help the pupils succeed. This often means, helping pupils *through* such difficulties rather than helping them to get *round* them: in Counsell's phrase, not teaching *by avoidance* with a negative 'can't do' approach but seeking to help all pupils. The styles of teaching you adopt reflects your understanding of the processes by which the pupils learn.

The key points, which this chapter has emphasised are that you avoid getting into too repetitious a style with a very limited range of approaches and are prepared to take some risks as your confidence grows. Look carefully at any reading material before you use it and try to anticipate any potential difficulties it may create. Remember it is your job to sell the subject, to demonstrate a genuine interest in the past and to ensure the pupils value the contribution of history to their education. Consider the value of using 'higher' order questions and also of creating situations for pupils to ask questions. Reading can be both underused and badly used – think carefully about how you can maximise the use of reading materials but be careful not to use the textbook as an easy option. This chapter has attempted to emphasise that pupils often only understand historical content if they are given the opportunities to express it in their own way – hence the importance of activities which include the structured use of pupil talk and the opportunities to write in their own words. Finally you are encouraged to carry out an audit of the variety of writing activities you set over a period of time as a means of ensuring you employ the range covered by this chapter.

For further resources on the issues covered in this chapter, and suggestions for further reading, go to www.uea.ac.uk/~m242/historypgce/.

REFERENCES

Adey, K. and Biddulph, M. (2001) 'The influence of pupil perceptions on subject choice at 14+ in geography and history', *Educational Studies*, Vol. 27, No. 4: 439–50.

Bakalis, M. (2003) 'Direct teaching of paragraph cohesion', *Teaching History*, No. 110: 18–26.

Banham, D. (1998) 'Getting ready for the grand prix: learning how to build a substantiated argument in Year 7', *Teaching History*, No. 92: 6–15.

Banham D. and Dawson, I. (2002) 'Thinking from the inside: je suis le roi', *Teaching History*, No. 108: 12–18.

Barnes, D. (1976) *From Communication to Curriculum*, London: Penguin.

Barnes, D. and Todd, F. (1977) *Communicating Learning in Small Groups*, London: RKP.

Barnes, D., Britton, J. and Rosen H. (1969) *Language, Learner and the School*, London: Penguin.

Bloom, B.S. (1956) *Taxonomy of Educational Objectives: Cognitive Domain*, London: David McKay.

Bullock, A. (1975) *A Language for Life* (The Bullock Report), London: HMSO.

Burson, W. (1963) *Principles of Teaching History*, London: Methuen.

Capel, S., Leask, M. and Turner, T. (2005) *Learning to Teach in the Secondary School*, Oxon: Routledge.

Clark, V. (2001) 'Illuminating the shadow: making progress happen in causal thinking through speaking and listening', *Teaching History*, No. 105: 26–33.

Chapman, A. (2006) 'Asses, archers and assumptions: strategies for improving thinking skills in history in Years 9 to 13', *Teaching History*, No. 123: 6–13.

Cottingham, M. and Daborn, J. (1999) 'What impacts can the development of literacy teaching have on the teaching and learning of history'. Conclusions at: http://www.tda.gov.uk/upload/resources/pdf/c/cottingham-daborn.pdf, accessed 10 October 2007.

Counsell, C. (1997) *Analytical and Discursive Writing in National Curriculum History at Key Stage 3*, A Practical Guide, London: Historical Association.

Counsell, C. (2004) *History and Literacy in Year 7: Building the Lesson around the Text*, London: Longman.

Cowie, E. (1979) *History and the Slow-learning Child*, London: Historical Association.

Curtis, S. (1994) 'Communication in history', *Teaching History*, No. 77: 25–30.

Dawson, I. and Banham, D. (2002) 'Thinking from inside: je suis le roi', *Teaching History*, No. 108: 12–18.

DfEE (2001) *Literacy Across the Curriculum*, London: DfEE.

DfES (2004) *Literacy in History*, London: DfES. Online at http://www.standards.dfes.gov.uk./secondary/keystage3/downloads/fs_litxc_h1025204.pdf. Last accessed 4 January 2008.

Duff, R. (1998) 'Appeasement role play: the alternative to Munich', *Teaching History*, No. 90: 17–19.

Edwards, A.D. (1978) 'The language of history', in A.K. Dickinson and P.J. Lee, *History Teaching and Historical Understanding*, Oxford: Heinemann: 54–71.

Edwards, A.D. and Furlong, V.J. (1978) *The Language of Teaching*, Oxford: Heinemann.

Edwards A.D. and Westgate, D. (1987) *Investigating Classroom Talk*, Lewes: Falmer.

Fines, J. (1994) Address at Historical Association Conference, Manchester, September.

Garvey, B. and Krug, M. (1977) *Models of History Teaching in the Secondary School*, Oxford: Oxford University Press.

Goodwin, S. (2006) 'Learning strategies and approaches' in M. Hunt (ed.), *A Practical Guide to Teaching History in the Secondary School*, Oxon: RoutledgeFalmer: 27–36.

Gunning, D. (1978) *The Teaching of History*, London: Croom Helm.

Hellier, D. and Richards, H. (2005) 'Do we have to read all this? Encouraging students to read for understanding', *Teaching History*, No. 118: 44–8.

Historical Association (2005) *History 14–19. Report and Recommendations to the Secretary of State*, London: Historical Association.

Husbands, C. (1996) *What is History Teaching?* Buckingham: Open University Press.

Husbands, C., Kitson, A. and Pendry, A. (2003) *Understanding History Teaching*, Buckingham: Open University Press.

Lacey, R. (2006) *Great Tales from English History* (3 volumes), London: Little Brown.

Lang, S. (2003) 'Narrative – the underrated skill', *Teaching History*, No. 110: 8–13.

Lee, P., Ashby, R. and Dickinson, A. (1995) 'Progression in children's ideas about history', in M. Hughes (ed.), *Progression in Learning*, BERA Dialogues II, Clevedon: Multilingual Matters: 50–81.

Levine, N. (1981) *Language, Teaching and Learning: No. 5 History*, London: Ward Lock Educational.

Lewis, M. and Wray, D. (2000) *Literacy in the Secondary School*, London: David Fulton.

Luff, I. (2000) 'I've been in the Reichstag: rethinking role play', *Teaching History*, No. 100: 8–17.

Luff, I. (2001) 'Beyond I speak, you listen, boy! Exploring diversity of attitudes and experiences through speaking and listening', *Teaching History*, No. 105: 10–18.

Luff, I. (2003) 'Stretching the straightjacket of assessment: use of role play and practical demonstration to enrich pupils' experience of history at GCSE and beyond', *Teaching History*, No. 113: 26–35.

Lunzer, E. and Gardner, K. (1979) *The Effective Use of Reading, for the Schools Council*, Oxford: Heinemann.

McCully, A. (1997) 'Key questions, planning and extended writing', *Teaching History*.

OFSTED, (2002) *History in Secondary Schools*, subject reports series 2001–2, HMI 813, London: OFSTED.

OFSTED (2005) *History in Secondary Schools*, Annual report for 2004/5, London: OFSTED.

QCA (2005) Pupil perceptions of history at Key Stage 3. Online at http://www.qca.org.uk/qca_6391.aspx. Accessed 10 October 2007.

Rudham, R. (2001) 'A noisy classroom is a thinking classroom, speaking and listening in Year 7 history', *Teaching History*, No. 105: 35–41.

Schools Council (1978) *Writing across the Curriculum Project, Writing in Geography, History and Social Studies*, London: Ward Lock.

Scott, A. (2006) 'Essay writing for everyone: an investigation into different methods used to teach Year 9 to write an essay', *Teaching History*, No. 123: 26–36.

Torbé, M. (1981) *The Climate for Learning*, London: Ward Lock Educational.

Van Drie, J. and Van Boxtel, C. (2003) 'Developing conceptual understanding through talk and mapping', *Teaching History*, No. 110: 27–31.

Wilkinson, A. (2006) 'Little Jack Horner and polite revolutionaries: putting the story back into history', *Teaching History*, No. 123: 16–20.

Wilson, M.D. (1985) *History for Pupils with Learning Difficulties*, London: Hodder and Stoughton.

5 Developing historical understanding (1): time, cause, change, diversity and significance

INTRODUCTION

One consequence of recent developments in the teaching and learning of history is an emphasis on the importance of key concepts in history (see Chapter 2). This chapter considers how you might set about teaching some of these concepts. It is now generally accepted that the more sophisticated your pupils' understanding of these concepts, when related to historical content, the greater is the depth of their historical understanding.

OBJECTIVES

By the end of this chapter you should be able to:

- understand of the contribution of the concepts of time, cause, change, diversity and significance to pupils' historical understanding;
- recognise some common misconceptions which pupils may have when confronted with these concepts;
- identify some problems pupils may experience in understanding the characteristic features and diversity of particular periods and societies;
- devise a range of teaching strategies with which to develop your pupils' understanding of these concepts.

THE IMPORTANCE OF KEY CONCEPTS IN THE TEACHING AND LEARNING OF HISTORY

An awareness of the importance of chronology and overview helps to ensure that history is not reduced to dismembered and isolated gobbets of the past, which are not reconciled into a coherent framework or useable 'mental map' of the past by pupils. One of your responsibilities as a history teacher is to provide *an overview of the past* so that pupils emerge from school history with some sense of the stages which humans have gone through to get to where we are today. When covering particular events or topics, some attempt must be made to put them in their overall historical context if the pupils are to develop a meaningful sense of the past.

Concentration on such concepts helps the move away from an image of learning history as one represented by 'stories from the past' or of factual content which has, in the eyes of pupils, very little connection with the business of living at the beginning of the twenty first century. The understanding and use of key concepts in history helps to underline the significance of historical events and processes. Sansom (1987) argued that the application of these concepts, or 'tools of thought', helps to turn information into historical knowledge. It is also possible to assert that, even when a pupil's recall of specific detail diminishes, the understanding that comes from conclusions about the significance of an event or events is the enduring educational outcome.

Your pupils today live in a world of constant and rapid change and the historical perspective helps them to place such changes into a wider context and to begin to understand the complex and interrelated nature of the causes of change. At the same time there are aspects of life that do not change. Pupils today share a common humanity with people in the past and there is much to learn from the study of the response of different peoples, groups and individuals to situations that confront them. An emphasis on these concepts also presents a useful guide to the choice of topics within a syllabus, when the amount of time available means there has to be a discerning selection of the content you choose to teach. Finally, as we hope to demonstrate in the chapter, your pupils are more likely to succeed in developing this aspect of their historical understanding if they are actively engaged in their use of knowledge.

TEACHING PUPILS ABOUT TIME

It would seem to be a reasonable proposition to suggest that part of the function of school history should be to give pupils some understanding of time and chronology. If pupils are to make sense of history, they need to have some idea about how we 'measure' and reference events in history in terms of when they occurred, and to build up a mental framework of the past. Although secondary pupils have studied history for at least six years, there may still be 'black holes' in their grasp of fundamental aspects of the concept of time.

It should be remembered that under the original NC for history, it was possible to get to Level 10 in all of the attainment targets for the subject, without knowing what century you were living in, or what AD and BC meant. Time was, at least to some extent, a neglected and forgotten element of the subject, and this was reflected in the text books which were published at the inception of the National Curriculum. A survey of over 1,000 year 7 pupils found that many did not know which century they were living in, what AD meant, or what words such as 'reign', or 'chronology' meant (Haydn and Levy, 1995). When asked about the reasons for these deficiencies, some heads of history suggested that there was an assumption that 'all that had been covered at primary school', or that they had just taken such understanding for granted, or that as it was not part of the '45 boxes' of the original Attainment Targets, it had not been a focus for teaching and assessment. Whatever the reasons, it is important that you do not assume that all your pupils possess a clear grasp of the rudiments of time and chronology. Whereas time was a comparatively peripheral concern of the original NC for history, its status has been restored in the revised versions, and chronology is one of the 'key concepts' of the most recent version of the NC for history at Key Stage 3, to be introduced in September 2008.

One advantage of the NC has been that all pupils have had some instruction in history at Key Stages 1 and 2, but as pupils are of differing abilities, and have come from different feeder schools, it would be surprising if they all arrived at secondary school with a similar understanding about time. One of the tasks of the history teacher is to investigate and develop some insight into what knowledge and understandings pupils bring with them *before* you start to teach the topic or concept in question. Time may well have been approached in a very different manner in various primary schools; some have learnt through family trees and timelines, others have started with ancient history and worked forward. Some already have a sound grasp of dating systems and some idea of a general 'framework' of the past, others may have passed through Key Stages 1 and 2 without having mastered even the lowest levels of attainment in this domain of history.

Task 5.1 A diagnostic exercise on children's understanding of time

The following weblink provides an example of a diagnostic test of children's understanding of some aspects of time, which might be given to year 7 pupils in order to elicit their grasp of some elements of the concept of time: www.uea.ac.uk/~m242/historypgce/time/t1/time1.htm.

With the permission of your tutor and if the pupils have not already been subjected to such a test, give the test to a group of pupils and analyse their responses. The test should take pupils between five and 15 minutes to complete. The test attempts to address pupils' understanding of dating systems, their ability to understand and manipulate 'centuries', and their familiarity with some time-related vocabulary. If the pupils have already done a similar form of test, ask your tutor how the pupils performed, and what 'gaps' there were in their grasp of basic time concepts. When the pupils have completed the test, analyse their responses to examine where there are gaps in their understanding of time. What activities might you devise in order to rectify any deficiencies in their understanding of time?

APPROACHES TO TIME AND CHRONOLOGY

The test in Task 5.1 addresses a particular strand of children's understanding of time; that of the 'mechanics' of time – dating systems and conventions, basic time vocabulary, how time 'works'. Although this is important, there are other aspects of time which children need to address. One of these is an understanding of chronology, and a developing sense of the order of events in history. Children should develop a mental framework of the past through the study of history. As the History Working Group's Final Report pointed out:

> A grasp of the sequence of events is fundamental to an understanding of the relationship between events, and such concepts as cause and change. Chronology, therefore, provides a mental framwork or map which gives significance and coherence to the study of history.
>
> (DES, 1990)

The tendency in recent years to study 'patches' or 'themes' in history, rather than a measured and even (but superficial?) progression from 'The Romans towards the present day', has meant that not all pupils have a clear grasp of the overall unfolding of events in history. The nature of the GCSE exam, with its emphasis on the critical examination of sources, means that it might be possible to gain full marks on a source-based question on the Second World War, without necessarily knowing who was on what side, and who won. There are also some areas of history where is it essential to have a clear grasp of the precise *order* of events as a necessary, if not sufficient basis for providing a coherent explanation or analysis of a historical event, such as the outbreak of the First World War, or the campaigns of 1066. Understanding of 'deep time' – the distant past stretching back to pre-history, the Stone Age and the formation of the earth might also be a facet of time which might be addressed in the course of school history. An understanding of what is meant by the term 'prehistory' can help to give pupils some insight into the nature of the discipline of history itself.

It might be helpful to classify the teaching and learning of time into categories so that you have a clear sense of the various facets of time which need to be addressed in the development of pupils' understanding of the past. For convenience, we have labelled these T1 to T4.

T1 = The mechanics of time – dating systems and conventions, time vocabulary, how time works. In the same way that pupils need to understand the 24 hour clock. If they are studying history, they need to know 'the clock of history'.

T2 = The framework of the past; building up a map of the past in terms of a developing sense of what bits of history fit in where. The chronology and sequence of strands of history, for example, the changing nature of monarchy in Britain over the centuries, the evolution of methods of transport, warfare, energy.

T3 = Building up an increasing range of historical topics or episodes where pupils have a sound grasp of the order in which events unfolded. This might include areas such as the changes in religious policy in England in the sixteenth and seventeenth centuries, the key events and turning points in the Second World War, or an understanding of the chronology of the French Revolution. If pupils have a confident grasp of the order of events *and* can explain why each event occurred, they are some way towards being able to construct an explanation of elements of the past.

T4 = Developing pupils' understanding of 'deep time'. Giving pupils an understanding of the scale of the past, from the formation of the Earth, through prehistory to the development of writing and on to AD Part of this is helping pupils through misconceptions about when humans appeared on Earth, and when 'history' started.

TEACHING STRATEGIES

Your skills of exposition in providing narrative frameworks of the past is an important part of developing pupils' grasp of time and chronology, including an awareness that pupils do not possess the map of the past that some teachers take for granted. The use of timelines in the classroom, as well as in exercise books, can be helpful. The development of sequencing exercises, whether on cards, for group work, in exercise books, on the blackboard, or on a word processor can provide activities which require pupils to think through the precise order of events, using inference as well as knowledge, but there is a danger of sequencing for its own sake; that is, constructing arbitrary lists of historical events which have no necessary connection with each other. Dawson (2004) offers a range of well thought out 'overview' activities, and his website, 'Thinking History', provides a number of eminently practicable 'active learning' approaches to the development of pupils' understanding of chronology (www.thinkinghistory.com).

The following are examples of exercises which might be given to pupils to develop their understanding of some of these facets of time and chronology.

T1 exercises

a   The following words are all used to note an amount or length of time. Organise them into the correct order, putting the shortest at the top, and the longest at the bottom.

shortest	year
	hour
	decade
	second
	millennium
	century
	minute
	week
	month
longest	day

b   The following are all terms, which are used to describe periods of time in history. Place them in the table below, where you think they belong, and then put them in order, with the earliest at the top of each column, and the most recent at the bottom.

Renaissance   Stone Age   Tudor   Pre-Raphaelite   Bronze Age   Hanoverian
Ancient   Pre-Industrial   Plantagenet   Medieval   Modern   Reformation
Victorian   Gothic   Norman   Postmodern   Early Modern   Georgian
Dark Ages
Impressionist   Cubist   Space Age   Prehistory   Regency   Restoration
Windsor

This is an example which might be appropriate for very able, or older pupils, but it would be fairly easy to draft simpler versions. The most able pupils might be asked to identify their own categories.

Royal Family	General terms	Architecture	Named after historical events	Painting

For examples of T2/3/4 exercises, go to www.uea.ac.uk/~m242/historypgce/time/framework.htm

---

Task 5.2 Devising an exercise on time

1   With the permission of your tutor, try out an exercise on time, and evaluate its results.
2   Try to devise an exercise of your own, which might be used by pupils at Key Stage 3 or 4, which is focused on one of these aspects of pupils' understanding of time.
3   Try to devise a pupil activity which attempts to develop pupils' understanding of T4 ('deep time'), or ask pupils about their ideas about the distant past.

A recent survey found that only 4 per cent of people knew that the Battle of Waterloo was fought in 1815. Is this a dreadful indictment of history teachers, or have history teachers better things to do than stuff children's heads with dates? How important is it that pupils should learn 'key' dates in British history? For the views of some pupils, history teachers and historians, see: www.uea.ac.uk/~m242/historypgce/time/dates/dateswelcome.htm.

Further information about children's understanding of time, research findings, and suggested activities can be found at: http://www.uea.ac.uk/~m242/historypgce/time/.

CULTURAL, ETHNIC AND RELIGIOUS DIVERSITY

Under the most recent Key Stage 3 specifications, 'cultural, ethnic and religious diversity' becomes one of the six 'Key Concepts' in the NC for history. The previous requirement that pupils should be taught to describe and analyse the 'characteristic features' of periods and societies studied (DfEE/QCA, 1999) is no longer explicit, but this does not mean that helping pupils to understand characteristic features of periods and societies studied ceases to be a concern of history teachers. A real challenge for the history teacher is to prevent pupils lapsing into stereotypes and lazy generalisations about the past, and to get pupils to understand that periods and societies can have characteristic features, whilst still possessing diversity within those patterns and features (for example, urbanisation and the factory system were a feature of the Industrial Revolution, but this does not mean that everyone worked in factories and lived in cities after the invention of the Spinning Jenny and Compton's Mule).

What are the perceived educational outcomes of studying 'the range of ideas, beliefs and attitudes of people' of particular periods and societies? Why is it considered important that pupils analyse the 'social, cultural, religious and ethnic diversity' of particular societies? Is it possible that one of the objectives is the expectation that the analysis of societies, diverse in time and place, will produce in Britain a society which is more tolerant and understanding of people who hold beliefs and attitudes which are different from their own? Is it that through this study pupils are encouraged to re-examine their own system of values and beliefs? This is where the study of history makes a contribution to the pupil's growing personal awareness by having 'the richest storehouse of human experience and an unrivalled opportunity to reflect on other people's feelings and actions' (Wilson, 1986). The idea here is that school history should be more than just the pupil's cognitive development; it should also address the 'affective' domain of values and attitudes. Illingworth is firmly positioned among those teachers who emphasise history's contribution to the pupils' personal development (2000: 20). He wants pupils 'to feel outraged, inspired and moved by events in the past and to develop their own ideas of right and wrong from this experience.' So, for example, he has no difficulty extending the study of persecution in the past to present day examples such as bullying in schools. History's role is seen as one of drawing out the moral issues that arise from the topics that are studied.

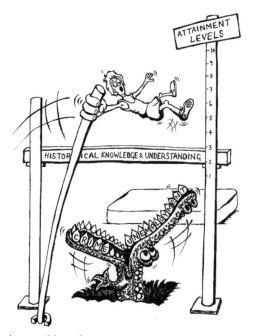

Figure 5.1 History for better citizens?

Some history teachers may prefer to stress that this concept should be seen more as an aspect of historical understanding. Thus, a second objective behind this concept is the necessity for the historian to try to explain why people thought and acted in the way they did in a particular situation. Such an emphasis sees the examination of past beliefs and attitudes as an aspect of historical causation and motivation. Hamilton and McConnell feel that to avoid empathy is 'to reduce history to a science': 'At its core history is about what people have done and why they have done it and to ignore the importance of their mindset and the pressures of the influences upon them is to misunderstand the past' (Hamilton and McConnell, 2003: 19). This emphasis would also contribute to the value of teaching about the social, cultural, religious and ethnic diversity in an explanation of events in the past.

Task 5.3 School history and the affective domain

1 Discuss with the history teachers and student history teachers, with whom you work, their views on the idea of school history as a vehicle for developing particular values and attitudes in pupils, such as respect for cultural diversity and tolerance. What other values and attitudes (if any) should school history attempt to cultivate? How much should this be left to Personal, Social and Health Education (PHSE)?

2 Cunningham (2003) found in her research that teachers usually had difficulties with their approach because they were trying to negotiate complicated or irreconcilable goals. Discuss with your tutor and other history teachers how they seek to resolve these four dilemmas identified by Cunningham and discussed in this chapter:

   a How to harness imagination while keeping it tied to evidence.
   b Whether to frame empathy in personal or historical terms.
   c Whether to encourage identification and emotional connection with historical figures.
   d Balancing empathy and moral judgement.

3 Discuss with colleagues and peers (and perhaps A Level pupils) what the characteristic features of 'Britishness' were in the early years of the twentieth century, as against the middle of the nineteenth century. This should give you an indication of the complexity and salience of such issues. What might be the pros and cons of discussing 'Britishness' with younger pupils?

PROBLEMS PUPILS MIGHT EXPERIENCE

The challenge you have of encouraging pupils to be able to understand past societies with a set of ideas, beliefs and attitudes very different from those commonly held today is one that has been a concern of history teachers for over 20 years. The experience of the GCSE has shown just how difficult that challenge has been with 15 and 16 year olds and so this is even more challenging when dealing with pupils at Key Stage 3. Many would agree with Lee and Ashby (1987) that entertaining the beliefs, goals and values of other people is a difficult intellectual achievement. They argue that it is difficult because it requires high level thinking to be able to hold such features in the mind as inert knowledge, but to be able to work with them in such a way that the pupil can understand and explain what people did in the past. Let us try to analyse the problems and difficulties adolescents are likely to experience in trying to understand the characteristic features of societies remote in time and place from their own.

An important part of learning history is the ability to understand the ideas, beliefs and attitudes of different periods and societies. By understanding we mean not just the ability to recall and describe but to acknowledge that for those times and places, such ideas made good sense and did present a rational explanation of their actions. Yet this can create real problems for pupils in the secondary school. For them it is a major conceptual leap when the values and norms of behaviour might be so different from the world in which they live. For them, in the words of L.P. Hartley, 'the past is a foreign country, people did things differently there'. It requires significant adjustments to be made if they are to get to grips with the very unfamiliar ways of people living in the past. To achieve this the pupils need to discard a collection of notions that can detract from the quality of their understanding.

One such notion is the idea, common to many pupils in the secondary school, that people in the past were intellectually inferior to people today and that the further one goes back in time, the more inferior they get. This is not surprising as the evidence of material advances surround the modern pupils and their understanding of the evolution of man would also encourage such thinking. Ashby and Lee (1987) have noted that the inability of the pupils to recognise that people in the past could not have known what the pupil of today knows and takes for granted and this can lead them to be contemptuous of past actions. Yet this dismissive attitude has to be surmounted if the pupil is to develop his or her historical understanding. You need to encourage your pupils to appreciate that what is 'strange' and 'different' is not necessarily 'stupid' or inferior.

Conversely, another notion that can often limit understanding of past societies and cultures, is one where the pupil makes too great an assumption that people in the past were the same as people today, a view that makes little concession to the changes that have occurred over time. Of course, we do have a common humanity with people of different times and places and the assumptions that pupils make are understandable for that reason. The danger is that such thinking is likely to encourage anachronistic representations of the past by the pupil attributing to people in the past, ideas and reactions, which could not have prevailed at the time. Even then the short length of time that adolescents have lived and the limited situations they have encountered make it more difficult for them to project their experiences into past situations. Your task is to encourage pupils to understand why such ideas and attitudes were held and how these would influence peoples' actions.

To do this your pupils need to possess considerable background knowledge of the cultures and religions involved. Much of this knowledge involves abstract ideas, which are themselves difficult for most pupils to understand. The challenge to the teacher is first not to make assumptions about the pupils' prior knowledge but also to become skilled in expressing the generalisations in terms concrete enough for pupils to understand. For example, teaching the Reformation to year 8 pupils can be a difficult task if pupils are to achieve a good understanding of the range of ideas and beliefs of the sixteenth and seventeenth centuries. Additionally, your pupils may find it difficult to communicate such ideas in a way that show that they clearly understand and are not merely repeating what they have heard or learnt by rote. All these problems have profound implications for the strategies you choose when you come to teach this particular aspect of historical understanding.

Task 5.4 Developing an understanding of pupils' ideas about past societies

1   In your placement schools find out how the history department seeks to meet the requirements relating to 'diversity'. Which topics are considered appropriate for the development of this Key Concept?

2   With the permission of your tutor, discuss with a group of pupils the following questions.

    a   Do you think people in the past were less intelligent then people today?

    b   What different ideas would people in (the fourteenth century) have in comparison with people today?

    c   Why do you think ideas and attitudes were different?

    d   Do you think all people living in (the fourteenth century) held the same ideas?

TEACHING APPROACHES

As noted in Chapter 4 you are likely to be successful in developing your pupils' historical understanding if the pupils are more actively involved in their own learning. Whatever the unfamiliar ideas and attitudes are, they need to be able to apply them and rework them in terms which are meaningful to them. This often means placing the use of such ideas in a specific context, which is not too vague for the pupil to handle. Pupils are more likely to understand ideas and beliefs which are new and strange to them if they are asked to employ them as if they were their own. They need to be presented with experiences and tasks which require them to express such ideas in their own words. Many pupils find this difficult and many make mistakes. Yet this is an important point for you to consider. By setting up situations and exercises that could lead to anachronistic statements you can assess more effectively the limitations of the pupils' understanding.

Many exercises designed to develop pupils' understanding of particular periods and societies have limited success because the pupils have been given insufficient background information with which to work. *Too little background information* encourages the far-fetched, fanciful and non-historical. Thus it is important that plenty of attention is given to setting a framework of background knowledge before any exercise is set. This can often involve the comprehension and analysis of evidence, for, as ever, many of these elements of knowledge, skills and understanding overlap. This could be achieved by whole-class teaching and question and answer, or by pupils analysing sources in groups with the task of listing the ideas and attitudes that they think emerge from the sources. Having ensured the pupils have an adequate background knowledge, what else might you consider to achieve success?

The best efforts are often those which are set *in a very precise time and place*. Pupils find it easier to achieve some synthesis of the information available to them if it has such limitations placed upon it. Lack of precision and vague instructions often characterise the 'Imagine you were . . .' type of exercise. Such tasks tend to be overused and have at times opened this whole approach to ridicule. Bad examples of this method require pupils to place themselves in a situation, frequently gruesome, and describe their feelings. 'Imagine you are a soldier at the Battle of X' is one such example – some pupils have fought in several battles from Hastings to D–Day – and the descriptive writing which tends to emanate from such tasks is often more appropriate to the development of skills in English rather than the advancement of the pupils' historical knowledge and under-standing. Such tasks only encouraged work of very limited value and, what is more, most pupils were aware of this.

Where such approaches were used, and overused, lack of detailed knowledge usually meant that pupils' responses were limited to statements which reflected common feel-ings, a transmission of everyday experiences and emotions into the past but lacking any real historical substance. As such the result was more creative writing than a vehicle to explore understanding of unfamiliar ideas, beliefs and attitudes. The task set needs to be well-structured and thoughtful. An example of such precision was an assignment, which sought to analyse the ideas and attitudes prevalent in a Lancashire textile town in 1866. Based on a real event, the pupils had studied the destruction by fire of two local mills, the consequences for the town in those days before the welfare state and also the con-temporary attitudes of teachers and the clergy. For this they had used newspaper accounts, personal accounts and extracts from school log books. The exercise was a child's view of destruction incorporating the comments which were made by significant adults about the disaster.

Task 5.5 The role of historical empathy

The word 'empathy has been used sparingly in writing this section. It does not appear in any of the GCSE or NC documentation. Its use has given rise to a great deal of controversy during the last decades.

1   To gain something of the flavour of that debate, read and make notes on three articles from *Teaching History*. They are 'Empathy and history' by Anne Low-Beer and 'Some reflections on empathy in history' by John Cairns. Both of these are in the April 1989 issue. The third, 'Historical empathy – R.I.P.?' by Peter Clements appeared in October 1996. A helpful 'thumbnail' summary of the empathy debate can be found in 'Empathy: in a nutshell', *Teaching History*, No. 100, August: 25. There is also a useful summary of the debate in Rob Phillips (1998) *History Teaching, Nationhood and the State*, Cassell: 20–1.
2   Using your notes discuss with your tutor the advantages and disadvantages of using historical empathy in the classroom.

Further consideration of 'empathy' in school history can be found at http://www.uea.ac.uk/~m242/historypgce/empathy/.

It is usually helpful to consider the 'audience' of the task. This often works best if that 'audience' is also of the period, *a contemporary audience*, the recipient of a report or petition. Cunningham found that one difficulty teachers face is to decide whether to frame a task in personal or historical terms (Cunningham, 2004). She cites as an example the use of 'you' in setting a task. She decides that it is best used in a historical context such as 'You are (named contemporary person)', followed by details, rather than just 'you', meaning you, the pupil, placed in a historical situation, which can lead to much confusion.

Resolving dilemmas or decision-making can produce useful assignments

In such exercises pupils are required to describe a difficult choice of action which a person or group of people in the past may have had to make. The pupils have to examine those factors which might influence their choice and in so doing take account that such a decision involves the application of ideas and attitudes which were different from those prevalent today. For example, the pupil might be asked, as a novice in a monastery or nunnery, to decide whether to take the vows and stay or to leave. What would be the pros and cons of such a decision for a person in medieval times. Such an exercise is arguably better than the more familiar 'The day in the life of a monk'. Other examples of decision-making designed to develop understanding of diverse and unfamiliar attitudes could be whether, as a Member of Parliament, to vote against a Bill to abolish the Slave Trade in 1789. It is important to emphasise that such exercises need to be 'rooted in evidence' and as such, while there is scope for the use of imagination, it must conform to what can be substantiated by the evidence available and not given a free rein. Lee has correctly emphasised that historical imagination 'must be tied to evidence in some way and so historical imagination cannot be creative in the same way as in literature, painting or music' (Lee, 1984: 86).

Historical imagination can be encouraged in many formats such as pages from a diary, which can cover successive days or significant days reflecting change and development. A well-used task is to invite pupils to write a letter in which past ideas and attitudes are revealed. At times, two letters, where the recipient responds with different views although still consistent with those held at the time. Pupils can be asked to write news-paper accounts, eye-witness reports or petitions for or against some proposal, for example, a new canal or votes for women. In all cases whatever is written involves the use of the imagination but it must be grounded in historical knowledge, which can be substantiated by evidence. By using a medium such as a letter the pupils are being asked to transfer sometimes difficult abstract ideas into their own words and into more con-crete situations that is meaningful to them.

More ambitious activities can include an attempt to utilise roleplay as a means of developing understanding, following a methodology suggested in Chapter 4. This again can use a variety of formats and can also involve decision-making. Roleplay can be used successfully to encourage the understanding of differing attitudes towards enclosures, of a parish's reactions to religious changes in the sixteenth century, to the ideas of a local board of health to the news of the arrival of cholera in the town in 1831. At a more advanced level, Hamilton and McConnell described their successful use of roleplay in helping year 13 pupils to understand the concept of empire from the point of view of the colonial power by showing the pressures placed upon Bismarck concluding with an activity where the pupils were Bismarck and had to make decisions bearing in mind the various problems and pressures he faced (Hamil-ton and McConnell, 2003).

Where appropriate, other evidence that can be successfully incorporated into imaginative work could be a historical site and the exercise makes use of a familiar landscape for example a castle, monastery, street or canal. There may be times, perhaps with older pupils, although it has been done successfully by year 7 pupils, where your pupils can be encouraged to reference the sources behind some of the statements. How-ever, they also need to ensure their work does not follow the sources too closely and come close to paraphrasing.

Finally, although some teachers may still be reluctant to use historical fiction within the history classroom, Martin and Brooke have shown how this genre can be used effectively to encourage pupils themselves to create fictional pieces themselves in which they can develop their understanding of past attitudes and beliefs. They do emphasise as always that such activities must be solidly rooted in evidence studied beforehand. Then, again provided the piece is not too ambitious, has not too many characters and is limited in time and space, then success can follow (Martin and Brooke, 2002).

Much of the success of such tasks depends on the preparation you have done to enable you to set the work. You need to be very clear in your mind exactly what *is the purpose of the task you are setting*, to be able to articulate the precise objectives you have in mind. Careful thought here helps the way in which you formulate the task. When you have decided what you want the pupils to do, go back to the objectives and assess whether such a task enables the pupils meet the targets you are setting. There are times when a poorly set exercise gives pupils little chance of indicating their understanding of past ideas, beliefs and attitudes. Having precise objectives means you also have to be clear about the assessment criteria you are going to employ when you come to mark the pupils' work. There is a good case here for letting the pupils know what these criteria are, so they can take account of them as they plan and complete their work.

CAUSE AND CONSEQUENCE

Cause and consequence are arguably the most complex of the Key Concepts under consideration. They are difficult to teach because it is easy to make assumptions about the extent of your pupils' understanding of cause and consequence.

Traditionally causes were dealt with as a list of information. Any analysis that had been done was achieved by the teacher or the author of the textbook, rarely by the pupils. Pupils were presented with a list of causes and consequences of an event and committed these to memory to reproduce for assessment. There was very little attempt here to encourage pupils' thought about the nature of the concept involved and thus developing their historical understanding. The National Curriculum Council (NCC) noted that there have been critics of this traditional approach since the early days of this century. Some enlightened history teachers saw the important methodological implications of not relying on the teacher to do all the intellectual work but 'pupils themselves should be generalising, analysing, judging and explaining' (NCC, 1993). The challenge is in trying to get the balance right between providing structure and selected materials and allowing the pupils to have some ownership of an enquiry. This is not easy and usually involves adjustments and improvements as a topic is repeated. Many teachers would now accept that the teaching of this concept needs to be the focus of a series of lessons rather than just one objective as part of a lesson. Such a scheme would most likely cover different aspects of understanding causation. So, as ever, you need to be precise about what it is you want the pupils to understand about historical causation. Chambers includes the following:

- To know that there are reasons why an event happened.
- To highlight causes from a narrative account.
- To make links between causes.
- To organise causes into categories.
- To distinguish between the long-term (trends) and the short-term (triggers) causes of events.
- To order causes in a hierarchy of importance.

(Chambers, 2006)

COMMON MISCONCEPTIONS ABOUT CAUSE AND CONSEQUENCE

First, pupils can look upon causes as being facts in themselves. Shemilt (1980) noted in his evaluation of the 13–16 Schools Council project that many highly intelligent adolescents treated the word 'cause' as though it refers not to the connection between events but to the properties of one of the events. He also noted the prevalence of the opinion that causes are everything that happened before. For such pupils a cause is something of an agent, which has the ability to make something happen. Thompson (1984) suggested that *bad* 'traditional' teaching helped to reinforce this kind of misunderstanding by treating causes in exactly the same way as events in history.

Second, monocausal explanations. Shemilt also noted that many pupils are happy to settle for one cause for a particular event; they like the clear-cut conclusion without any complexities. To them any other causes are superfluous. Such simplicity of understanding is attractive but represents a very limited understanding of the concept. For example, if one asked pupils to account for the building of the turnpike road between Manchester and Rochdale in 1755 some pupils would feel that the fact that the existing roads were bad and in great need of repair to be sufficient for the answer; no additional explanation was necessary. Such a limited response fails to tackle the complexity of the question, where it would be necessary to know who were the people pressing for the setting up of a trust and for what reasons; whether they had they the services of a well-known surveyor available at that time; where precisely would the road be built and whether this brought advantages to some of the promoters; what trades or goods would be most likely to benefit and how had it been possible to defeat any local opposition. The challenge for teachers would be how to encourage pupils not to settle for the most obvious monocausal explanation. This is not always that easy. Indeed, Lee (1998) has indicated that adolescent pupils may have difficulty with causal thinking because it is 'counter intuitive' to many of them who naturally think the last event is necessarily the most important.

Third, another possible disadvantage of listing causes in a traditional manner was that it took away any analysis which took account of the order in which the causes might have had their effect and the inter-play between events and causes. The Balkan Wars of 1912–13 were not as such a cause of the First World War but they contributed to the demands for self-determination and the heightened resistance of the multinational empires towards this development. At times a distinction was drawn between long and short-term causes and similarly long- and short-term consequences but this was often a means of categorising information rather than a basis for discussion about the nature of the concept or indeed how distant a long-term cause had to be to qualify for this category.

Fourth, we also have the problem of *causal determinism*. Scott (1990) indicates that this can occur when pupils liken the concept of causation in history to a scientific interpretation. This is encouraged when words such as 'catalyst' are used (it may be better to use words like 'triggers'). Confusion with *scientific causation* can lead to an almost mechanistic interpretation of causation. It is possible to see here the beginning of the attraction of adolescents towards the conclusion that some historical events were 'inevitable'. It is almost as if, given a certain combination of causes, an event was 'bound to happen'. The outcome is not only predictable, it is inevitable. This 'scientific' view of causation at least has the merit of logic and not least the importance of the interrelationship of causes. However, only the more sophisticated pupil is likely to be able to distinguish between the scientific and the historical mode of causal explanation and is able to understand the 'uniqueness' of a historical event, the sheer unpredictability of events involving both individuals and groups of people. Howells (1998) recommends the value of looking at an episode in some depth to consider chance factors and of relating conclusions of that episode to the wider question of inevitability. *One of your tasks is to encourage pupils to be sceptical about claims that an event was inevitable.*

Fifth, this 'uniqueness', which is such an important feature of historical content, stems from the central fact that history is the study of human beings in the past and human beings are themselves unique and unpredictable. Consequently historians have to concern themselves with motivation, which is in itself an important aspect of the concept of causation. Pupils should be able to discriminate between understanding motive and cause and not see the two as synonymous.

Finally, nevertheless, there may be something of a paradox here, which could be confusing to pupils. While emphasising the 'uniqueness' of events and their causes, the nature of the learning process often means there is need to categorise and assimilate language, which describes categories and concepts. Consequently an important function of learning the concept of cause and consequence is to enable pupils to understand and use words such as 'social', 'political', 'economic', technological' and other adjectives we may wish to use to describe categories of causes, mindful of the fact such terms can be employed in the explanation of widely different events.

Task 5.6 Identifying pupils' assumptions about cause and consequence

When you have covered an appropriate topic, present the class with a list made up of causes and events. Ask the class, in pairs, to identify which are the causes and which are the events and give reasons for their choice. Then consider:

1   The teaching points to make at the conclusion of this exercise.
2   With a class, or a group of pupils, discuss the following questions.
    a   Do you think the (selected event just covered) was inevitable, i.e. was bound to have happened?
    b   How might you decide which cause was the most important?
    c   What do you understand by the terms, short- and long-term causes?
    d   Why might it be difficult to work out the consequences of an event?
3   In the light of this discussion, what points do you need to emphasise when teaching these concepts?

To remove many of the misunderstandings noted above, you should be prepared to invest time in the careful study of causal connections and give pupils the opportunity to work out their own ideas and thinking. To this end activities need to be meaningful and not just a question of labelling, processing and listing to meet assessment statements.

WHAT TO CONSIDER WHEN PLANNING A SET OF LESSONS FOCUSING ON HISTORICAL CAUSATION?

- What experience the pupils have already had. Ask the teacher what has been covered and on which aspects of this Key Concept there has been focus.

- When to introduce the concept? Various choices can be made, the choice often determined by the topic.

  1. *At the end.* A retrospective review of factors causing an event after the pupils have been informed of the preceding events. This has the advantage of a series of stories leaving the final outcome to reveal itself. A story with an interesting ending before any analysis begins.

  2. *At the beginning.* It has become increasingly attractive to begin with the final major event and then pose the question, 'Why did it happen?'. Howells (1998) felt pupils find this approach attractive as 'big questions excite children'. Again, Clark (2001) believed causal skills need to be demonstrated within a 'problem-solving framework' Coverage of the content then uses the overarching question as a constant reference-point and as a means of adjusting hypotheses. Chambers (2006) used the execution of Charles I to begin a set of lessons on the causes of the English Civil War and describes the different activities to developing an understanding of why the king met his death.

- How prepared are the pupils?

  1. As ever, you need to ensure that the pupils have *sufficient knowledge of the content* of the topic in order to make sense of any causation exercises to set them. Categorisation exercises have little meaning if pupils cannot relate the activity to the content detail and may merely look for 'clues' in the words presented to them without having any real understanding. Without knowledge causation exercises can seem meaningless.

  2. Have they the *appropriate vocabulary* for their analysis? What are the range of words they need for different ways of categorising and explaining causes? Chapman provides a useful way for you to consider this vocabulary. There would be words related to (a) 'content', for example, political, economic, religious, etc.; (b) 'time', for example, short-term, long-term, etc.; (c) 'role', which could include words like 'trigger', 'catalyst' and 'pre-conditions'; and (d) 'weight', which encourages words that help describe the relative importance of causes. Chapman devised exercises, some unhistorical, to encourage his pupils to become familiar with the vocabulary of historical causation (Chapman, 2003).

STRATEGIES FOR TEACHING THE CONCEPTS OF CAUSE AND CONSEQUENCE

Matching exercises

There are various ways such exercises can be approached. Often pupils are presented with two columns – one of events another of causes and the task is to match items from one column with another and then explain the reasons for the choice.

Group work using causation cards

Example (with a year 9 class). After a detailed study of a topic on the coming of the railways, the pupils were placed in groups and each group received a set of cards on each of which was written a possible cause of the building of a specified (local) railway line. Each card was numbered to facilitate discussion.

1	Dissatisfaction with canal companies' freight charges.
2	Availability of a labour force prepared to move around the country.
3	Civic pride/rivalry.
4	Demands for the faster transport by many trades and industries.
5	Successful trials of steam locomotives.
6	Appointment of skilled engineer.
7	Leadership of local business people.
8	Use of wrought iron rails.
9	Defeat of opponents (canals, turnpikes, rival railway companies, land owners, coach firms) in Parliament.
10	Courage, foresight of bankers.
11	Spirit of the age (progress, eagerness to improve, enterprising climate).
12	Earlier experience of railway traction using horses.
13	Discovery of steam power.
14	Existence of iron industry capable of meeting requests of engineers.
15	Availability of hard-working skilled engineers.
16	Dissatisfaction with the speed of land transport.
17	Knowledge and skill in capital accumulation, share-holding, joint-stock capital.

Having received these cards the groups then were asked to perform a series of tasks, each followed by a class discussion. These tasks included the categorisation of the cause on the cards. With most groups it would be necessary to identify the categories and to explain these beforehand, but with some able groups it is a useful challenge to ask them to create their own categories. In the following feedback discussion the results of the groups are compared and from this activity it is possible to create a spray-diagram in which the categories of causes are grouped together. Later, this spray-diagram could assist the writing of a piece of extended writing on the reasons for the building of the specified railway.

A further activity was to ask the groups to identify from the cards those, which they considered to be short-term and long-term causes. An extension of this, in an attempt to deal with the issue of the ordering of the effect of the causes, could be to ask the pupils to try to place the causes along some imaginary or real timeline. Finally the pupils were asked to consider which causes were the most important and which the least important.

With able pupils, who have some familiarity with the use of causation cards, once a topic has been covered it may be possible for them to devise their own cards and for groups to compare the results. It is possible to use this approach with older pupils when the selection of particular causes as being the most important is seen to indicate something about the attitude towards causation of the historian. Questions such as which cards might a Marxist historian be likely to choose as the most important can be considered. In this there is a link with Chapter 6 on historical interpretations.

'WHY THEN?' ACTIVITIES

It is important to keep asking this question particularly in those circumstances when the long-term causes have been in place for so long. If the condition of the French peasants was worse in 1722 than it was in 1789, why did the revolution take place at the later date? Also, why not in 1722? This is useful to dissuade pupils from the attraction of the inevitability of events.

Research by Lee *et al.* provides not only interesting information on the development of pupils' ideas about causation and explanation, but excellent examples of 'pupil-friendly' tasks, which address some of the complexities outlined above, particularly with regard to the interrelationship of causes, and pupils' ability to discriminate between fact, reason and cause (Lee *et al.*, 1996).

LINKING CONSEQUENCE AND CAUSE

In the development of such key concepts as cause and consequence over the past three decades, it is probably fair to say that consequence has been the poor relation and received far less attention. However, there have been recent attempts to take a more holistic approach by seeking to link consequence to cause as a means of achieving a better understanding of causation. Clark believes that 'the consequence of a chain of events generally needs to be shown first' (Clark, 2001: 27). Chapman goes further and feels that work on causation should focus as much on consequence as it does on categorisation. He suggests this approach is particularly valuable when students are attempting to evaluate the relative importance of causes. By asking students to work out the effects of each cause he found that this not only encouraged useful debate but helped to sharpen historical understanding (Chapman, 2003).

CHANGE AND CONTINUITY

For many decades history teachers have been aware of the underlying importance of the concept of change and continuity but only in the last three decades have the reasons for its importance been articulated in pedagogic terms with attention to the way change in particular may be misunderstood by pupils and students. Again much of the research, which underpins this emphasis, comes from the Schools History Project (SHP). Attractive text-books associated with this module were produced by Scott and organised in such a way that the concepts of change and continuity are given a clear and comprehensive emphasis (Scott, 1987). Textbooks, such as those covering the history of medicine, offer plenty of ideas about utilising these concepts, which can be adapted to other content areas.

COMMON MISCONCEPTIONS ABOUT CHANGE AND CONTINUITY

As in the case of the concepts of cause and consequence, you may find that it is possible that your expectations of your pupils' understanding of these concepts may be too high. You need to be aware of the possible misconceptions, which pupils may have if you are to succeed in developing their historical understanding.

Thompson (1984) concluded that 'change' is a historical concept that adolescents initially find difficult to entertain in any but everyday use. Pupils can understand change in relation to different times but their appreciation of the nature and scope of change varies very much from pupil to pupil. A feature of Shemilt's research (1980) was to note how many pupils saw change as an episodic not as a continuous process. One change (event) was not seen as in any way connected with changes (events) preceding it in time. This limited understanding tends to be reinforced by a syllabus, which is itself episodic, which moves from one topic to another with little apparent relationship to that which precedes or follows. There is a case to be made for a syllabus which has a chronological base so that the process of change can be better addressed.

Shemilt also noted the difficulty children may have with the idea of historical change seems to stem from their inability to imagine the daily life which give the events their meaning. History lessons can so often present pupils with a succession of events with little reference to the context in which they occur and as a result the pupils are not sure of what precisely it is that changes – hence, the value of making such changes personal by the use of roleplay or writing from an individual perspective.

You may also find it rewarding to find out how pupils interpret the idea of 'progress' over time. It is quite common for young people to assume that the changes that occur over time may all be seen to be for the better. Consequently there is value in stopping to consider whether this was always the case. What were the consequences of the discovery of gunpowder? Did this represent progress? Such questions prompt a consideration of some of the wider issues that the study of history can generate, showing the subject is well placed in the humanities.

A further misconception that often needs to be corrected is that through the pupils' tendency to compartmentalise their history, the episodic approach, they may assume that changes occur at once. Suddenly one changes from the domestic system to the factory system. Yet what can make the concept even more confusing for pupils is the fact that while some things change others do not. Change is not clear cut and to that degree requires a level of understanding which is quite sophisticated and not easily achieved by many pupils.

STRATEGIES FOR THE TEACHING OF THE CONCEPTS OF CHANGE AND CONTINUITY

Emphasising overviews

Arguably the most important of all the strategies used to teach change and continuity is the use of overviews. It is important to make sure the pupils are able to see how the content covered or to be covered presents an overview or framework from which a discussion of change and continuity may develop. Overviews help to give pupils a broader understanding of the past. The requirement to use a combination of 'overview, thematic and depth studies' can be made into a valuable integrated part of a scheme (QCA, 2007: 115).

Too often there has been a tendency to move from one block of content to another without sufficient emphasis on the overview, which helps to show the significance of the study. An episodic approach misses many opportunities to develop important features of historical understanding. As in the past overviews were simply used to link the chosen topics, in what was called the 'patch' method. However giving overviews a central role in a scheme emphasises the overall importance of the topics studied.

Overviews can be used at different times during the teaching of a scheme. It may be useful to present an outline framework at the beginning of a topic or scheme to assist understanding and then return to the framework when the detail has been covered to ask questions related to the concept. Such a framework can also be used for reference while teaching a topic to aid the understanding of particularly complex content. For Banham (2000) the key is not to think of overview in isolation but to combine, blend and integrate it with topics dealt with in depth. He shows how the study of the King John is enhanced by relating the content to a range of wider issues such as the nature of medieval kingship. Looking for the wider issues not only helps understanding but also contributes to covering the curriculum.

With some topics it may be preferable to study an overview at the completion of a topic. Here you can make good use of the knowledge the pupils have gained to encourage the consideration of a whole range of issues arising that help to develop their historical understanding, drawing out key issues and making connections with content covered earlier in the history curriculum or with their experience of life today.

A study of the Poor Law Amendment Act of 1834 raises the issue of how a country deals with poverty and pupils may be asked to recall how the poor were treated in the sixteenth century and then think about how they are treated today. The term 'zero-ing' has been used to describe the rush to start a new topic just when the point has been reached when that content covered can be usefully developed to address some of the key concepts and offer further challenges to the pupils. It is often important that you give thought to these 'matters arising' when completing the details of a study.

First, imaginative presentation of changes in the form of illustrated time–charts, time-lines, diagrams or graphs: these may be drawn to highlight periods of slow or rapid change and again help to place the content under study in an overall context. There are times when it may be necessary to limit the precise accuracy of presentation in order to make general points in some imaginative diagrams.

For example, a topic which benefits from a time-chart is the French Revolution, which may be said to be not one but a series of revolutions. To assist understanding it can be helpful to create a time-chart, which emphasises this succession of changes. Such a chart could also form the basis for a wall display. How much detail is included depends on the ability level of the class, but the idea of an overview is to ensure the changes are not obscured by too much factual 'clutter'. As the topic is covered in more detail, the chart is a useful reference point for pupils.

Second, graphs can also be an effective way of demonstrating change, or indeed, lack of change. Barnes (2002) showed how effective use was made of a graph to plot progress above time. Using information brought from three enquiries about progress in social conditions, in economic performance and in democracy and the franchise between 1750 and 1900, three lines were plotted and drawn in different colours. The resulting graph gave rise to them making valuable comparisons, connections and the relationship between different types of change.

Third, comparative exercises: for some time, 'similarity' and 'difference' have been identified as concepts in themselves. However, it is possible to use of these terms more as an effective strategy for teaching the concepts of change and continuity. They are often used most productively at the beginning of a topic and make a relatively straightforward entry into the discussion of more demanding concepts such as causation. The use of 'similarity and difference' approaches nearly always involves pupils in making comparisons, which in turn can encourage varying degrees of analysis. Such comparisons often work well with pictures or other visual materials, but can also involve with effect cartographical and statistical material. You will find that most of the attractively produced textbooks of recent years make good use of comparisons and so material for their use is not too difficult to find. Even so, there is always scope for your individual initiative in the acquisition of appropriate resources. Evidence from the local environment and from local history will usually add to the interest of lessons, as can skilfully chosen analogies from aspects of contemporary life closer to pupils' own interests and experiences. While most emphasis may be placed on the differences, it is also important to look for similarities.

There are a variety of ways in which comparative exercise can be used to further the pupils' understanding of the concepts of change and continuity (see Figures 5.2 and 5.3). One is the *then–now technique*. This is most likely when pupils have some familiarity with the present-day example, especially involving the use of physical evidence. Contrasting a modern day street with a photograph of the same street in Edwardian times encourages plenty of discussion about what has changed and what has remained the same. Booth *et al.* show how comparison of a Victorian and present-day kitchen can also bring out many facets of continuity and change (Booth *et al.*, 1987).

As part of a lesson on towns in the sixteenth century, the following two lists were written on the board.

Sixteenth century		Recent times (1977)	
1	London (200,000)	1	London (7,030,000)
2	Norwich (15,000)	2	Birmingham (1,050,100)
3	Bristol (12,000)	3	Leeds (734,000)
4	York (11,500)	4	Sheffield (547,000)
5	Exeter (9,000)	5	Liverpool (535,000)
6	Newcastle (9,000)	6	Manchester (491,000)
7	Chester (5,400)	7	Bradford (464,200)
8	Hull (5,000)	8	Bristol (409,000)
9	Coventry (4,000)	9	Coventry (340,000)
10	Manchester (3,500)	10	Nottingham (282,000)

After first identifying the changes featured in these lists, the pupils were asked to consider why such changes had occurred. How did we account for the disappearance of some towns and the appearance of others?

Figure 5.2 An example of a then–now exercise: town populations – comparison of the sixteenth century with recent times

---

This time pupils were given two maps, one showing the open fields, common lands and meadow and the nucleated village of pre-enclosure times and the other showing the effects on the landscape of the introduction of enclosures. The pupils were first invited to identify the similarities and differences between the two maps as a basis for a study of the changes, which had taken place and the reasons for those changes.

Figure 5.3 An example of a before–after exercise: the effects of enclosure

Fourth, comparison of the implication of change for identified people living at the time or at contrasting times. There is plenty of potential here for simulation exercises, role play and the use of 'radio' plays, for example, in approaching topics such as enclosures, the change from the domestic system to the factory system; religious changes of the sixteenth and seventeenth centuries.

Fifth, encouraging speculation: teachers may gain useful insights into how pupils are assimilating the concept by asking them to consider what changes might be experienced by people living at a certain time, when they were 30 years older or by the time of their grandchildren.

> *Example*: year 7 pupils have spent two or three lessons extracting information from the local census returns for 1861. From this information they have been able to construct bar charts showing the different occupations of the people living in 1861, the age and gender distribution and details of the inhabitants' place of birth. As an additional task the pupils were set the following tasks:
>
> - Make a list of those jobs or occupations, which you think would *grow* in number in the next 30 years, that is, by 1891.
> - Make a list of those jobs or occupations, which you think would *decline* in number, that means, there would be less of them, by 1891.
>
> Give reasons for your judgements.
> The answers given would be quite informative of the pupils' understanding and also could be checked by a comparison with the 1891 census returns.

Sixth, use of hypothetical questions. Although there has in the past some reluctance by history teachers to ask questions which invited speculation on what did not happen, it can be a useful way to emphasise the significance of a change or indeed lack of change. For example, consider what might have happened if Henry Tudor had been defeated at the Battle of Bosworth or what might have been the result had the Spanish Armada been successful in 1588?

Seventh, sequencing activities (such as those suggested earlier in this chapter on chronology, in which pupils have to reorganise events in the order in which they occurred). The best of these are where the selection of detail allows pupils to think through decisions using inference and their general understandings, rather than exercises which are purely reliant on memorisation. Such activities are a further example of how the concepts covered by this chapter interrelate as the concepts of change and continuity owe much to an understanding of chronology.

Eighth, following the completion of a topic, inviting discussion on what the pupils consider to be significant *turning-points* in the events which have developed.

Finally, spot the anachronisms activity. This can be both an amusing and yet revealing activity. Pupils are presented with a picture or a passage of writing which contains several errors of an anachronistic nature and are challenged to identify the deliberate mistakes. Alternatively they could be asked to identify which of two accounts is genuine and give reasons for their choice.

SIGNIFICANCE

Although for decades many good history teachers have almost instinctively emphasised the significance of the topics they have taught, it can be argued that this particular element has not received the same attention as, for example, causation or historical interpretations. Lomas (1990) was able to indicate the possibilities of a greater emphasis on significance in his Historical Association pamphlet and those six pages remain a good starting point for your consideration of the concept. The NC for history requires pupils to consider 'the significance of events, people and developments in their historical context and in the present day' (QCA, 2007: 113). The draft revision of the curriculum to be introduced in September 2008, gives significance the status of one of six 'Key Concepts' and will require pupils to 'assess the significance of events, people and developments in their historical context and in the present day'. These statements raise several important questions for history teachers.

How does the study of historical significance help pupils to value the importance and relevance of history?

The relatively recent emphasis on the use of overviews to counter the traditional episodic sequence of topics has helped pupils to understand how the topic they are studying fits into a bigger picture. Often this is achieved by placing content within a wider, overarching enquiry question. Emphasising historical significance is not the same as using overviews but it is not too great a leap for this to be done. Hammond (2001) was able to show how by placing the Holocaust within the bigger picture of persecution over time and the suffering of many groups of people in the Second World War, her pupils were able to identify the particular significance of the Nazi treatment of the Jews. Again, Phillips (2002) made the connection with overviews with the enquiry question, 'How important is the Industrial Revolution to our lives today?' He made the point that emphasising a topic's place within a wider perspective can often be a way of increasing pupils' interest in topics, which might have been deemed uninteresting by some teachers. He thought this was particularly the case with economic and social history topics. Similarly, Hunt showed that similar positive responses could be achieved in the study of the Agricultural Revolution by emphasising its significance within a wider context (Hunt, 2006). Often the value of local history can be underlined by drawing out its contribution to the understanding of national and indeed international developments.

Many topics require attempts to explain human conduct and motivation and the pupils' historical understanding is enhanced if an explanation can relate to the way people thought at the time. It is then a small step to make explicit the connections with other knowledge the pupils possess to be able to deepen their general understanding of what can motivate people in certain situations.

Consideration of themes such as how the country was governed, changes in trade and industry, public welfare and many others seem more coherent when pulled together. Adolescents are particularly attracted by content which invites comment on the social and moral questions involved, as may be seen in the popularity of the unit on 'The Black Peoples of America'. There are many topics which you cover where you can draw out how the significance of specific events to a wider consideration of human conduct and motivation and thus raise fundamental questions, which are important for young people to consider. Harris and Rea (2006) have stressed the need to help pupils to understand how history is meaningful. They want history teachers to show how the past touches the pupils' own lives and how people in the past often had to deal with the same issues as people today. Such considerations in turn necessitate the use of generalisations and with them the need to understand and use a range of abstract concepts such as freedom, equality, inflation, slavery, taxation, class, depression and many more. Studying real people in real situations helps your pupils gain a better understanding of these terms. Part of the answer to this first question may lead to an accusation of 'presentism', the notion that for an event to be significant it must be related to the present, when that is by no means always the case. However, thinking through how the topics you teach do still touch the lives of today's citizens can only enhance your understanding and teaching of this concept.

What makes an event, person or issue significant?

The question, which is perhaps the most central to the teaching and learning of historical significance is: what makes an event historically significant? This may seem the most straightforward approach to the concept but, like so much about significance, it is quite complex. There are been various attempts to answer this question including an early one by Partington (1980) and, more recently, by Counsell (2004). They both offer five criteria.

Partington		Counsell's five 'R's	
An event is historically significant if it has:		An event is historically significant if it is:	
1	Importance – to people living in the past.	1	Remarkable – was remarked on by people living at the time.
2	Profundity – because of the depth with which people's lives have been affected.	2	Remembered – was important at some stage in history with the collective memory of a group.
3	Quantity – because of the number of people who have been affected.	3	Resonant – is possible to connect with experience, beliefs, situations across time and space.
4	Durability – because of the length of time people's lives have been affected.	4	Resulting in change – had consequences for the future.
5	Relevance – because it makes a contribution to an increased understanding of present life.	5	Revealing of some other aspect of the past.

Task 5.7 Evaluating historical significance

It is a characteristic of this concept and debates about it that opinions differ about the validity and weight of these criteria, but they do help to stimulate your thinking.

1   To encourage thinking about how you might use these criteria in the classroom, take each of the ten criteria in turn and try to define then in words which you think most Key Stage 3 pupils would be able to understand.

2   Is it possible to rank these criteria in order of importance? Do all the criteria make a valid contribution? Can any be used on their own or do all the criteria of one or the other need to be fulfilled for an event to have historical significance? Would you add any others?

3   Study your department schemes for Key Stage 3 for the next term. Take each topic in turn and, using the criteria, consider how you would explain to your pupils the historical significance of the topic.

4   With a group of pupils, and the permission of your tutor, ask them to rank the following in order of their significance and to explain their decisions.

an atomic bomb dropped on Hiroshima in 1945;
a fire burns down a local factory in your town in 1893;
a fire burns down much of London in 1666;
Anne Boleyn executed in the reign of Henry VIII;
the opening of the Manchester to Liverpool Railway 1830;
the execution of Charles I in 1649;
the sinking of the Titanic in 1912.

5   Select one major event from three of the Studies for Key Stage 3. Try to create a spray-diagram (some call them spider-charts) which shows the significance of the event, e.g. the Black Death, the Battle of Bosworth, the defeat of the Spanish Armada.

6   When observing a history lesson in your placement school, try to identify what you think is the significance of the topic being taught. How much is this being communicated to the pupils?

Osowiecki (2004, 2005) using Counsell's criteria and particularly that of remarkability, showed how effectively this could be applied to a study of the significance of Renaissance figures and through that of the Renaissance itself. On occasions you may be in a position to explain to your pupils why you chose to teach the topic they are studying in preference to other topics you might have taught. What gave your choice historical significance? Both Wrenn (2002), Counsell (2004) and Bradshaw (2006) stress the importance of encouraging pupils to offer their own ideas about why an event or person they have been studying is significant and so worthy of its place in the syllabus. It is likely that your able pupils will soon consider how the criteria might change depending on why you are studying a certain event or purpose. They may well feel the decision of a town to establish a local sanitary authority in 1870 is more significant for the local historian of that town than the Franco–Prussian war of the same year. So, can a local event meet the criteria listed in the table? Does, therefore, as Lee (1998) would affirm, the significance of an event only make sense within a particular account. Does significance for purpose make its contribution to what makes an event significant? What has been well established is that pupils should come to realise that the significance of an event or a person is not fixed in time, is not a 'given' as it might sometimes appear, is relative and is indeed a matter of debate.

Is there value in categorising types of historical significance?

In dealing with this concept it is useful to consider how the categorisation of various types of significance can help understanding. Both Partington and Counsell include in their criteria a reference to judgements about the significance of an event by contemporaries, events which may not be afforded the same significance today but which were at an earlier time. Such significance would come under the category of short-term. By contrast, some events, which did not seem significant at the time, may be so regarded with the passage of time. Similarly, applying categories often used with causation, an event could be assessed from a choice of its political, economic, social, religious or military significance. And just as causation has 'triggers' and 'catalysts' so historical significance needs to use words such as 'symbolic' and 'cultural'. More recently Cercadillo has made another attempt at categorising types of significance. She identified six types: contemporary, causal, pattern – 'significance as part of a pattern of change or as a turning point', symbolic, revelatory – 'appealing to events or processes which reveal something about individuals or society' and present. She also showed how some of these types could be the basis for a progression model for the assessment of pupils' understanding of the concept (Cercadillo, 2006).

How can historical significance be used as a 'meta-concept'?

The complexity of the concept of historical significance may be partially explained by the notion that it is different from the other key concepts in that it is an over-arching 'meta-concept' that can use the other second order concepts (see Chapter 2) and deepen knowledge of historical understanding. Counsell (2004) noted that, 'when pupils work on significance, they are really standing outside all the usual concepts and could be drawing on any of them.' Bradshaw (2006) suggests that 'in fact most of the second-order concepts are brought into play during a historical significance enquiry. Consider then its application to other second order concepts. In many cases such application invites familiar decision-making activities, group work, 'elimination debates', and card-sorts. In the case of chronology and change, there is plenty of mileage for debate in selecting 'significant turning-points'. For example, which of the series of acts to extend the franchise was the key turning-point? Similarly, which of the Education Acts from 1833 to 1944 held the greatest historical significance and for what? When historical evidence is applied to the question of significance, it is territory that has been familiar to history teachers for decades. So many will have automatically stressed the significance of the Domesday Book, Sutton Hoo, the Rosetta Stone, the remains of First World War trenches and many more. And yet, there is also the issue of the selection of evidence that may be described as significant. When a historian reads a documentary source and sees certain parts as historically significant, what determines that choice?

Furthermore, the study of historical significance can enhance understanding of another key concept – interpretations. Hunt (2003) suggested that the application of significance can be a useful tool to challenge the promotion of particular perspectives when the question is asked, 'What is the significance of such an interpretation?' Wrenn picks up this point when he used Equiano's diary to help pupils to understand why others have judged a certain story significant and why this may not always be so. He concludes that work on 'interpretations' of history can both support work on significance and take it further' (Wrenn, 2002).

In considering the significance of causes of events, once more the concept of significance demonstrates its potential for taking an explanation beyond its immediate context and making connections, that vital activity in studying significance, with other periods. What gives a cause a greater significance? Often the answer is in the way patterns and repetitions of such causes occur in different contexts, some disheartening such as religious and ethnic divisions and poverty, others more positive such as co-operation between individuals or nations.

Consequence is considered last because again, while, as with causes, one might consider the most significant consequence, it needs a more rigorous examination because there is real value in exploring the differences between consequences and significance. Hunt (2003) would claim that greater understanding of historical significance is more likely to be achieved if there is a clear distinction between the two. Thus, while the consequences of an event contributes towards its significance, it is the wider issues, often value-laden, that give it its significance, what Counsell (2004) describes as 'getting beyond consequences'. Also Bradshaw (2006) finds that 'for historical significance teaching to be meaningful it needs to be more than just about consequences, it needs to deal with the ethereal nature of judgements about historical significance and make them real.' For example, consider the Labour election victory of 1945. Listed among its consequences would be the establishment of the National Health Service, the nationalisation of steel, coal, transport and the railways and the continuation of rationing. However, it may be argued that the significance of installing a Labour government with a large majority was its contribution to the wider, enduring debate about the relative merits of nationalisation as opposed to privatisation, the role of the state and, with rationing, state-imposed equality restricting the free market. In this example, significance is seen to be concerned with enduring issues that arose from events and they are often more abstract than statements of consequences. In the year 9 or 10 classroom, it is not impractical for you to try to draw out historical significance in this way.

Task 5.8 Matters for discussion

Historical significance is a complex yet immensely rewarding concept. It does require much hard-thinking on how it is to be used and presents plenty of issues for discussion, many ongoing, continually revised and none resolved. Using the content of this section and your own knowledge and experience, consider the following:

1   When, how often, and with which topics would it be appropriate to employ consideration of historical significance with your pupils?
2   Must the historical significance of an individual, event or issue always be related to the present day for it to be meaningful and relevant to the pupils?
3   Can an event, which was a failure, have historical significance?
4   How can the study of historical significance contribute towards citizenship education?
5   How would you assess a pupil's ability to understand historical significance? What might serve as a progression model for the assessment of pupils' understanding of historical significance?

THE PRINCIPAL OBJECTIVES FOR LEARNING THE CONCEPT OF 'SIGNIFICANCE'

As noted above, it is increasingly important that you should try to be proactive in asserting the relevance and significance of the topic you are teaching in the widest terms. Howells (1998) made a valid point when suggesting that 'this notion of significance must inform the learning objectives at some period in the lesson sequence'. To this end you may find it helpful to consider the value of this set of objectives, developed and augmented from those of Lomas (1990), when you seek to meet the requirements of this concept.

The importance of significance in the teaching of history is that it enables the pupils to:

1   understand that history operates on the basis that some events and changes are more important than others;

2   establish criteria for assessing the significance of events, people or changes in the past;

3   understand that some events, which may have seemed significant at the time, were not, while the significance of other events is only recognised later, sometimes many years later;

4   understand that different people have different ideas about which events, issues or changes are significant;

5   be able to understand *why* people may hold different ideas about what has been significant;

6   understand that the significance of an event or change is determined by the nature of the historical enquiry;

7   understand that relatively minor events can be highly significant, for example, they have 'symbolic' significance;

8   be able to distinguish between the consequences of an event and its significance;

9   understand that an event or change usually becomes significant because of its connection with other events.

STRATEGIES FOR THE TEACHING OF HISTORICAL SIGNIFICANCE

Strategies for emphasising significance can involve a range of approaches. Most frequently this occurs within your usual teaching routines, looking for opportunities to ask questions relating to the significance of events, people and changes either at the beginning or end of a lesson or topic. For example at the end of a topic or unit pupils could be asked to justify their selection of the six most important events covered.

Many successful strategies for teaching historical significance involve decision-making exercises. Hunt (2000) includes several examples of such activities. These included giving pupils a set of explanations why an event was significant and asking them to choose the best three, giving also the reasons for their choice. Alternatively, pupils could be given a set of cards explaining *why* the study of a topic is important and are then asked to decide which is the most important. There are opportunities for roleplay in which rival inventors, political leaders, physicians, generals, reformers, etc. assert the significance of their contribution. As a history teacher you should always try to keep abreast of current events and issues, and where appropriate, link these to the topics you are covering or have covered in your teaching. Try to look for opportunities to point out links, which will not always be obvious to your pupils, especially when they involve the wider issues such as attitudes and responses to poverty, crime, technological change, oppression and disease.

SUMMARY AND KEY POINTS

The teaching of the key concepts covered in this chapter provides you with the potential for some stimulating and successful lessons. That success is aided if you have a good understanding of the likely problems many pupils may experience in handling these key concepts. The challenge for you is to keep reinforcing the significance of the events you cover and the wider relevance of the concepts involved. In that way you help your pupils to realise that history is not just about the acquisition of knowledge but how you apply that knowledge.

 For suggestions for further reading and more resources and information about the concepts discussed in this chapter, go to: www.uea.ac.uk/~m242/historypgce/welcome.htm.

REFERENCES

Ashby, R. and Lee, P.J. (1987) 'Children's concepts of empathy and understanding in history', in C. Portal (ed.) *The History Curriculum for Teachers*, Lewes: Falmer Press: 62–88.

Banham, D. (2000) 'The return of King John: using depth to strengthen the overview in the teaching of political change', *Teaching History*, No. 99: 22–31.

Barnes, S. (2002) 'Revealing the big picture: patterns, shapes and images at key stage 3', *Teaching History*, No. 107: 6–13.

Booth, M., Culpin, C. and Macintosh, H. (1987) *Teaching GCSE History*, London: Hodder and Stoughton.

Bradshaw, M. (2006) 'Creating controversy in the classroom: making progress with historical significance', *Teaching History*, No. 125: 18–25.

Byrom, J. and Riley, M. (2003) 'Professional wrestling in the history department: a case study in the planning and teaching of the British Empire at KS3', *Teaching History*, No. 112: 6–13.

Cairnes, J. (1989) 'Some reflections on empathy in history', *Teaching History*, No. 55: 13–18.

Cercadillo, L. (2006) 'Maybe they haven't decided yet what is right. English and Spanish perspectives on teaching historical significance', *Teaching History*, No. 125: 6–9.

Chambers, C. (2006) Teaching causal reasoning', Chapter 6 in M. Hunt (ed.), *A Practical Guide to Teaching History in the Secondary School*, Oxon: Routledge: 49–58.

Chapman, A. (2003) 'Camels, diamonds and counterfactuals: a model for teaching causal reasoning', *Teaching History*. No. 112: 46–53.

Clark, V. (2001) 'Illuminating the shadow: making progress happen in causal thinking through speaking and listening', *Teaching History*, No. 105: 26–33.

Clements, P. (1996) 'Historical empathy – RIP?', *Teaching History*, No. 55: 11–16.

Counsell, C. (2004) 'Looking through a Josephine Butler-shaped window: focusing pupils' thinking on historical significance', *Teaching History*, No. 114: 30–3.

Cunningham, D.L. (2004) 'Empathy without illusions', *Teaching History*, No. 114: 24–9.

Dawson, I. (2004) 'Time for chronology? Ideas for developing chronological understanding, *Teaching History*, No. 117: 14–24.

DES (1985) *GCSE: The National Criteria*, London: HMSO.

DES (1990) *History in the National Curriculum, Final Report*, London: HMSO, para 3.18.

DfEE/QCA (1999) *History: The National Curriculum for History*, London: DfEE/QCA

Hamilton, A. and McConnell, T. (2003) 'Using this map and all your knowledge, become Bismarck', *Teaching History*, No. 112: 15–19.

Hammond, K. (2001) 'From horror to history: teaching pupils to reflect on significance', *Teaching History*, No. 104: 15–23.

Harris, R. and Rea, A. (2006) 'Making history meaningful: helping pupils to see why history matters', *Teaching History*, No. 125: 28–36.

Haydn, T. (1995) 'Teaching children about time', *Teaching History*, No. 81: 11–12.

Haydn, T. and Levy, R. (1995) *Partnership and School Improvement: Teaching Children about Time*, London: Institute of Education.

Howells, G. (1998) 'Being ambitious with the causes of World War 1: interrogating inevitability', *Teaching History*, No. 92: 16–19.

Howells, G. (2002) 'Ranking and classify: teaching political concepts to post-16 students', *Teaching History*, No. 106: 33–6.

Hunt, M. (2000) 'Teaching historical significance', in J. Arthur and R. Phillips (eds), *Issues in History Teaching*, London: Routledge: 39–53.

Hunt, M. (2003) 'Historical significance', in *Past Forward: A Vision for School History 2002–2012'*, London: Historical Association: 33–6.

Hunt, M. (2006) 'Why teach history?', Chapter 2 in M. Hunt (ed.), *A Practical Guide to Teaching History in the Secondary School*, Oxon: Routledge: 3–14.

Husbands C. and Pendry, A. (2000) 'Thinking and feeling: pupils' preconceptions about the past and historical understanding', in J. Arthur, and R. Phillips (eds), *Issues in History Teaching*, London: Routledge: 125–34.

Illingworth, S. (2000) 'Hearts, minds and souls: exploring values through history', *Teaching History*, No. 100: 20–4.

Kitson, A. (2001) 'Challenging stereotypes and avoiding the superficial, a suggested approach to teaching the holocaust', *Teaching History*, No. 104: 41–8.

Lee, P.J. (1984) 'Historical imagination', in A.R. Dickinson, P.J. Lee and P.J. Rogers, *Learning History*, London: Heinemann: 85–116.

Lee, P.J. (1998) 'A lot of guesswork goes on. Children's understanding of historical accounts', *Teaching History*, No. 92: 29–32.

Lee, P. and Ashby, R. (1987) Children's concepts of empathy and understanding in history', in C. Portal (ed.) *The History Curriculum for Teachers*, London: Falmer: 62–88.

Lee, P. and Ashby, R. (2001) 'Empathy, perspective and rational understanding in social studies', in O.L. Davis, S. Foster, and E. Yaeger (eds), *Historical Empathy and Perspective Taking in the Social Studies*, New York: Rowman and Littlefield.

Lee P.J., Dickinson, A.R. and Ashby, R. (1996) 'Children making sense of history', *Education 3–13:* 13–19.

Levine, N. (1981) *Language, Teaching and Learning: 5. History*, London: Ward Lock Educational.

Lomas, T. (1990) *Teaching and Assessing Historical Understanding*, London: Historical Association.

Low-Beer, A. (1989) 'Empathy and history', *Teaching History*, No. 55: 8–12.

NCC (1993) *Teaching History at Key Stage 3*, York: NCC.

Martin D. and Brooke, Beth (2002) 'Getting personal: making effective use of historical fiction in the history classroom', *Teaching History*, No. 108: 30–5.

Osowiecki, M. (2004) 'Seeing, learning and doing the Renaissance, part 1', *Teaching History*, No. 117: 34–9.

Osowiecki, M. (2005) 'Seeing, learning and doing the Renaissance, part 2' *Teaching History*, No. 118: 17–25.

Partington, G. (1980) *The Idea of an Historical Education*, Windsor: NFER.

Phillips, R. (2002) 'Historical significance – the forgotten "Key Element"?', *Teaching History*, No. 106: 14–19.

QCA (2007) History, programme of study: key stage 3, London: QCA. Online at http://curriculum.qca.org.uk/subjects/history/. Accessed 11 October 2007.

Riley, M. (1997) 'Big stories and big pictures: making outlines and overviews interesting', *Teaching History*, No. 88: 20–3.

Sansom, C. (1987) 'Concepts, skills and content: a development approach to the history syllabus', in C. Portal (ed.) *The History Curriculum for Teachers*, Lewes: Falmer Press.

Scott, J. (1987) *Medicine Through Time: A Study in Development*, Edinburgh: Holmes McDougall.

Scott, J. (1990) *Understanding Cause and Effect* (Teaching History Research Group), London: Longman.

Shemilt, D. (1980) *History 13–16: Evaluation*, Edinburgh: Holmes McDougall.

Thompson, D. (1984) 'Understanding the past: procedures and content', in A.R. Dickinson, P.J. Lee and P.J. Rogers, *Learning History*, London: Heinemann: 168–86.

Wilson, M.D. (1986) *History for Pupils with Learning Difficulties*, London: Hodder and Stoughton.

Wrenn, A. (2002) 'Equiano – voice of silent slaves', *Teaching History*, No. 107: 13–19.

6 Developing historical understanding (2): interpretation and enquiry

INTRODUCTION

In this chapter we shall consider the teaching of two more facets or domains of historical understanding: interpretations of history and historical enquiry. In the revised version of Key Stage 3 introduced in September 2008, interpretation is described as a 'Key Concept', and enquiry, a 'Key Process' (see QCA, 2007a: 111–13 for an explanation of the differences between these two designations). The idea of historical enquiry has been established within the curriculum for quite some time, although the more recent emphasis on enquiries rather than on source skills is a welcome advance. Historical interpretations, while giving rise to some stimulating and enjoyable lessons, has also proved to be one of the most difficult elements of the history curriculum to implement. Successive OFSTED reports have identified interpretations as the weakest area and found schools reluctant to include the element as much as they should. An OFSTED Conference in 2004 focusing on the teaching of interpretations in history reported that 'there is little evidence that schools are giving sufficient time to understanding interpretations of history' (quoted in QCA 2007b). While teachers often discuss contemporary viewpoints of past events, it is much less common for them to show pupils how different people today interpret the past: this is the area seen by QCA as appearing to be the most problematic. There are also concerns about the difficulties of assessing pupils' understanding of interpretations. Student teachers often find this concept to be one of the most challenging aspects of their history teaching. For these reasons, we are giving most emphasis in this chapter to the teaching of historical interpretations.

OBJECTIVES

By the end of this chapter you should be able to:

- explain what is meant by both historical interpretations and enquiry in the context of the secondary school curriculum;

- understand the challenges, issues and problems facing both teachers and pupils when studying historical interpretations;
- identify the wide range of interpretations and reconstructions which can provide material for the study of this element;
- deploy some of the strategies and approaches that can be used for the teaching of interpretations of history;
- set up enquiry-based projects and schemes of work.

THE CHALLENGE OF TEACHING HISTORICAL INTERPRETATIONS

The challenges with which you are faced may be briefly summarised. It is important that you make a clear distinction in your planning between 'sources' and 'interpretations'. Particularly in the early days of the NC there was much confusion of the two with the result that interpretations were approached with the already established 'source skills' approach such as reliability and bias. A clear understanding of the distinction helps you in your choice of appropriate learning objectives and selection of material. Other challenges stem from a variety of pupil misconceptions and stumbling blocks, which inhibit their understanding. You may well discover that some pupils find the idea of differing views of a topic or an individual to be a waste of time and they just want to know what is right, so this presents you with the challenge of explaining why they are studying historical interpretations. It is not always easy to convince pupils that there is not just one common answer. While many pupils can identify *how* interpretations may differ, they struggle to explain *why* this should be the case. They particularly might struggle to explain why different people thought differently even when having the same information available. Other misconceptions you may need to challenge are pupils' conviction of the supremacy of 'eye-witness' accounts in contrast to those of people who were not living at the time; the pupils' preference for written interpretations and a distrust of other representations and indeed a general inclination to dismiss what may be termed 'opinion' with a preference for 'facts'. Finally, there is the thorny issue mentioned by OFSTED, that of assessing pupils' progress in understanding historical interpretations. This itself presents several problems. First, there is considerable scepticism about both the validity and the appropriateness of the levels statements for interpretations, a concern that the progression implied does not relate to how pupils' understanding actually develops and thus making its application difficult for teachers; second, there is the problem that when the statements are linked to mark schemes they encourage formulaic responses, which mask the assessment of real understanding.

It can be argued that for many years teachers have encouraged their pupils to be aware that the way the subject-matter of history is presented is replete with interpretations. The very terms, in which some people and events are described, encourage some discussion of the reasons why such words are used. Why was 'the Glorious Revolution of 1688' so called? Who called the period between 1629 and 1640 'the eleven years tyranny'? Why was the extension of the franchise to just over another 200,000 men called 'the Great Reform Act'? Who decided that Alfred was Great, Elizabeth I was Good, and her sister Bloody? It is also reasonable to ask how much the use of words such as 'revolution', 'progress' and 'civilisation' involve interpretations. Consider the use of the word 'reform'. Today pupils might well consider how the word 'reform' can be used uncritically in news bulletins implying 'a change for the better', even though it is a matter of opinion whether that is the case.

However, since 1990 much progress has been made and Davies and Williams (1998) present an excellent starting point for you to study the earlier developments in the teaching of this element. Most history teachers working in England believe that learning about historical interpretations is an important aspect of studying history. It is a further example of the emphasis of how *the processes by which history is communicated* may be used as a basis for developing your pupils' historical understanding. Encouraging pupils to be aware of the way historical events, people and situations may be differently interpreted, reduces the opportunities for the imposition of 'one version' history with all its potential dangers. An understanding of why such different interpretations occur might make a valuable contribution to the further development of a democratic society. At the same time the range of historical interpretations can give you the basis for producing some interesting lessons, using materials which might not have been considered appropriate a few decades ago.

Task 6.1 Identifying the use of historical interpretations

1   During your school experience discuss with your subject tutor how the depart-ment seeks to meet the requirements of this Key Concept within the study units. Note which topics have been chosen as being suitable for the development of the pupils' understanding of interpretations. Find out what range of approaches are planned and discuss how these may differ according to the ability of the pupils.

2   Collect a variety of textbooks, which have been written for the Key Stage 3 study units and investigate the materials and task designed for the study of historical inter-pretations. Note any particularly useful examples for future reference.

INTERPRETATIONS OF HISTORY: ISSUES AND CONCERNS

How can we define historical interpretations?

It is helpful to be clear in your own mind about what is meant by historical inter-pretations when used in the context of the secondary school. You need to be clear about how this aspect of the teaching and learning of history is distinguished from that range of skills associated with the use of sources. Sometimes the distinction has been made that interpretations are only linked to secondary sources. Yet the distinction between primary and secondary sources can sometimes be blurred and often depends on the purpose for which the source is used, rather than when the source was produced. It is perhaps better to think of an interpretation, as Sue Bennett has suggested, as 'a conscious interpretation of the past, which *normally draws together different sources of information*' (Bennett, 1995). In other words, as with the other second order concepts, interpretations is a *second-stage* activity that usually follows the study of the content and the completion of activities to develop an understanding of that content. Further clarification on this question was provided by the School Curriculum and Assessment Authority (SCAA) (1996):

Questions on representations and interpretations are likely to concentrate on the process by which the interpretation was created, its purpose, audience and validity. On the other hand, questions relating to source evaluation are likely to concentrate on comprehension, inference, utility and reliability.

More recently Scott Harrison made the point that 'the use of the word interpretations' in this Key Concept 'is distinctive from the generic term "to interpret", as in "interpreting sources of evidence" ' (Harrison, 2004). Furthermore, 'conscious interpretations' will be found in *a greater variety of representations* than those normally covered by the 'use of sources' (for example, historical stories and novels, museum displays as well as pupils' own interpretations). Such variety increases the potential for adding interest to history lessons.

Potential confusion also lies between 'interpretations' and the use of the 'characteristic features of past societies' covered in the previous chapter. The concern of 'interpretations' is *not* the knowledge of ideas and attitudes in the past, which may be very different from those prevalent today. It may, however, be necessary to explore how the ideas and attitudes of the past are related to different interpretations. Indeed, Tony McAleavy (1993: 15) made the point when he wrote, 'an interpretation of history is a conscious reflection on the past and *not* the ideas and attitudes of participants in past events'.

So, to summarise our definition, interpretations of history can be presented in many forms; they represent a deliberate and thoughtful attempt to reconstruct and explain events in the past; to be of any worth they must be rooted in genuine evidence and normally that means they are drawn from several different sources of information.

Debates on what constitutes a historical interpretation

As the study of historical interpretations has evolved since 1990 and teachers have sought ways of making the concepts involved accessible to secondary school pupils, several debates have emerged over what constitutes a historical interpretation. In one debate there is some tension between the conviction that pupils need to study 'real secondary sources', representations of historians' views and pupils being asked to create their own interpretations. Mastin and Wallace (2006: 6) hold the view that 'the work of assessing interpretations must involve real interpretations', in other words, 'real' secondary sources. A pupil simply constructing their own opinion of say, the empire, is not what is understood by this Key Concept. Similarly, a discussion paper for the OFSTED Conference (2004) noted that it had been argued that one of the common errors made by teachers in their planning of work on interpretations was that it is about pupils doing some interpreting on their own. Several found the activity 'Cromwell – hero or villain?', where pupils used sources rather than interpretations to form their answers, was not a study of interpretations. Mastin and Wallace do accept that pupils creating their own interpretations could be used as a way into understanding the concept and this highlights one of the challenges for you. What strategies can be employed to introduce pupils to this Key Concept? Encouraging pupils to create their own interpretations is one strategy that is widely used. In doing this teachers are trying to get the pupils to understand the *process* by which interpretations are made by going through something akin to that process themselves. Such an approach could involve giving half the class one set of sources and the other half an alternative and contrasting set with a resultant variety of activities to explore and ask questions about the process. QCA (2007b) have stated 'that it is important that teachers help pupils to understand how individuals construct an interpretation and the constraints which influence their decision making' and so they advocate the use of pupils making their own interpretations of the past. It is a means to an end and Pam Harper's (1993) conclusion from some time ago is still valid today when she wrote:

> activities where a class is divided into two and in role play of the story of the Boudiccan revolt from the point of view of the Iceni or the Romans will not in themselves enable pupils to work towards an understanding of interpretations of history. Only if the pupils spend time analysing their interpretations of events and compare them with the available evidence will such work be related to historical interpretations.

Another debate concerns what would be acceptable as interpretations. Within this there is a discussion about the validity of photographs in contrast to paintings – is the former 'a conscious interpretation of the past?' Then there is the question of the time-scale. Does an interpretation have to be some time after an event for it to meet definitions of historical interpretations? Can an eye-witness account be an interpretation? Task 6.2 Invites you to consider and discuss what you think constitutes a historical interpretation.

Task 6.2 What constitutes a historical interpretation?

Give a copy of the following list to your tutor or head of department and ask them to tick those items, which are thought to be historical interpretations and note the reasons for not ticking any items. Do the same yourself and compare notes.

Domesday Book	Film *Culloden*
War memorials	Museum display re 'Trafalgar'
Pepys' description of the Great Fire	Frith's 'Railway Station' painting

Photograph of Wellington's statue	A newspaper cartoon
A castle	Opinion of two fictional characters with
TV programme *Blackadder*.	opposing views, e.g. Royalist /Puritan upon
History textbook	past events.
Dickens' *Oliver Twist*	

Issues of teaching historical interpretations

Apart from the challenges noted in the introduction to the chapter, the emergence of historical interpretations as an aspect of learning history in all years of the secondary school raises a series of issues for the teacher. You find that your lessons are more successful if you are able to anticipate the difficulties your pupils might encounter. Consider the following:

Knowledge

If the study of historical interpretations is to be a valuable learning experience, pupils and students must have a reasonably detailed knowledge of the topic which is the subject matter of the interpretations. They need a factual basis to enable them to understand the interpretation in the context of events and a basis for making worthwhile comparisons. As greater demands are made of the students, for example, to assess and evaluate inter-pretations, these could be of very limited value if the student is insufficiently informed on the subject matter.

However, how that content is initially presented or 'discovered' by the student could influence later work on interpretations. It may be a case of what information to give and what not to give. So, should you have some exercises involving historical interpretations to follow, then how the groundwork of necessary information is presented needs careful consideration. Basically, the question is, what do the pupils or students need to know and understand in order to complete work on interpretations with success?

Accessibility

Perhaps the most far-reaching and possibly frustrating problem for teachers seeking to teach historical interpretations is that of accessibility. The principal barrier to under-standing is that of language; complex sentence structure and unfamiliar words have for many years presented a problem for teachers and examiners alike, as indicated in Chapter 4. To this may now be added the adult language of historians as they present their interpretations of people and situations in the past. At times such interpretations rest on nuances and shades of opinion too subtle for some pupils. While the variety and range of interpretations can add to the interest and stimulation of the study, the language of poetry or folk songs can also present problems of accessibility. Cartoons and satirical drawings may again be too subtle for some pupils. In all cases the challenge to you as a teacher is to try to make such interpretations and representations accessible to the pupils and without distorting the meaning or in the case of assessment removing too much of the skill or understanding one is trying to assess. The problem of accessibility therefore is linked to that of differentiation. Yet at the same time as being aware of the problems of accessibility, it is quite possible that your abler pupils could be capable of exploring more complex interpretations, especially if studied in a structured manner. Lengthier texts can increase the potential for analysing the process involved with the use of evidence as well as enabling pupils to match an interpretation with their own knowledge. Sinclair (2006) and Woolley (2003) have described such use of challenging interpretations.

Progression

The revised attainment target for the history NC presents a more logical progression in the description of a pupils' developing understanding of historical interpretations. That progression of knowing, describing, explaining and evaluating, which can be extracted from the level descriptions, follows a well-established model. Consistent with this, most pupils find it easier to explain *how* interpretations differ rather than *why*. Whereas many feel comfortable in describing the differences between the interpretations by analysing the data presented to them in a variety of media, they then struggle to explain those differences, particularly when they have to draw upon information not immediately before them. Many might settle for the obvious, for example, 'because they were written by different people living at different times', which while correct is not the depth of insight one might be looking for.

Even so, there are times when you may feel that the progression described does not conform to your experience in setting and assessing your pupils' work. Be prepared to find individual pupils responding differently when using different types of interpretations and different contexts. It is not necessarily regression but shows the complexity of the task. It is likely that any assessment would need to take account of a range of exercises, where assessment is enquiry and context specific. There have been criticisms of the level descriptions because they fail to give sufficient emphasis to the process by which interpretations are compiled and the suggestion is that if due attention is given to process in a succession of activities then determining pupil progress becomes much easier. Lee and Shemilt also identify the progression of pupils' thinking as pupils try to explain why historical accounts differ and seek to encourage pupils to go well beyond the kind of simple answers mentioned above (Lee and Shemilt, 2004). Lee advanced a set of levels often with a range of understanding within the level. They were:

- Stories are the same and only differ in the way they are told.
- Stories differ because of the availability of knowledge yet within this the responses range from 'not being there' to 'interpretation of evidence'.
- Different accounts differ about the past because the past is complex.
- Focus on the role of the author with a range of from biased views to selection of evidence as a legitimate personal move.
- Accounts are not complete so it is in the nature of historical accounts to differ.

(Lee, 1998: 29–32)

Some of these statements are quite insightful and sophisticated and demonstrate a burgeoning development of historical understanding. Lee and Shemilt indicated further developments of their research when setting the goal of pupils understanding that two historical accounts of an event can *legitimately* differ and be consistent with acceptable use of the evidence available. This approach is sophisticated but Lee and Shemilt believe this is possible with the younger pupils and can lead to pupils having positive thoughts about history and appreciate the value of different perspectives. To approach this goal the pupil needs to progress through several 'break through' points such as:

1   Abandoning the idea that only contemporaries could write a true account (a common misconception noted at the beginning of the chapter) and even worse, if contemporary accounts do not exist, all other histories are fabrications.
2   An appreciation that there can never be the *perfect* representation of an event but there can be an infinite number of possible descriptions of it.
3   An acceptance that accounts may differ legitimately without merely being matters of opinion (Lee and Shemilt, 2004).

Task 6.3 Considering pupils' progression in understanding historical interpretations

1   Using the information provided in this chapter about common misconceptions, which pupils may have of historical interpretations and the progressive statements from Lee and Shemilt's research, devise a list of questions, which you could employ at appropriate times when you are teaching a topic which targets this concept.

> 2   Ask your subject tutor or head of department if you could interview two groups of pupils of differing abilities, who have recently studied a topic, which targeted historical interpretations. Using some of your list and using the historical topic they have studied, consider how you will initiate a discussion with the groups. Although aware of the limitations of this activity, see if you can tease out their problems with this concept. Compare how the two different groups responded.

Background of the interpretations

Linked to the difficulties with progression, implying a progression of understanding, is that of knowledge of the background of the interpreters. That background information might be correctly but superficially expressed as 'He was a royalist' or 'She was a French Protestant' or, with older pupils, 'He was a Marxist historian', but such information would need to have a fuller explanation, which requires further layers of knowledge. Should it be necessary to determine that an interpretation of a much earlier event reflected the spirit of the times of the person responsible for the interpretation, then that requires knowledge not only of the event being interpreted but also of the times of the interpreter. Card has called this process 'seeing double' – one historical period's visualisation of another. Using the example of painting, she shows how the artist – even one who has done a great deal of research – usually projects back into the subject, the values, ethics, manners and sometimes the costumes of the artists' own period (Card, 2004). The result is the double vision of studying two periods of history. However, sometimes when the background of the interpreter is reduced to a brief attribution, as for assessment, then there can arise the dangers of stereotyping as if, say, all Victorians held the same views.

Conveying genuine understanding

When presented with such issues as accessibility, progression and author background, one approach chosen, particularly if external examinations are involved, is for teachers to present user-friendly packages of interpretations for the examination candidate to recall and reproduce within the examination room. Then, what is being assessed is an awareness of the differing interpretations and the ability to recall accurately. What is less likely is that the candidates have had the opportunity to work through the processes involved in understanding interpretations. McAleavy (2003) doubts very much whether the use of 'gobbet questions' with minimal background is likely to encourage critical thinking but is more likely to produce a set of stereotypical responses (McAleavy, 2003). In Howells' view 'the one line source description and date encourages simplistic comments on creating an interpretation and this greatly diminishes the historian's art (Howells, 2005). For perhaps what is worse, many candidates will see this for what it is to the detriment of a positive attitude towards the subject. Similarly Davies and Williams asked how pupils can form valid judgements on the basis of 35 minutes' reading of a few highly selective sources (Davies and Williams, 1998). There is a danger here that assessment practices at Key Stage 4 could have a detrimental influence on the teaching of historical interpretations with younger pupils. The challenge for you as a teacher is how to create situations, which can *genuinely assess an understanding of historical inter-pretations*, an *application* of principles and knowledge rather than diligent recall and formulaic responses.

Confusion of certainty and uncertainty

A problem inherent in the study of historical interpretations is that, while for some it encourages valuable insights into the nature of events, people and issues in the past, for others there is a danger that such a study could promote a rather negative attitude towards history as a subject. For the latter they need to be assured that they are learning something that is accurate and 'correct', knowledge that they can now 'possess' to put alongside their knowledge of other subjects. To them, if history is too frequently presented as a mass of uncertainty, represented by different viewpoints, they may become disenchanted with the subject. *You need to constantly emphasise that what is accepted* forms the framework of our historical knowledge and assure your pupils that a great deal of what they learn falls into this category. At the same time as stressing that what really adds interest to the subject are the questions such uncontested knowledge raises. We accept that the Normans won the Battle of Hastings in 1066, what may be open to interpretation is how much that event affected England and Wales in the years that followed. Perhaps for this reason, in your schemes of work for Key Stage 3 you need to limit the concentration on interpretations according to the ability of the class or pupils within a class. Pupils and students need to be able to understand the educational outcomes that arise from such study and be able to recognise their relevance for the world in which they are growing up. For all these risks, the successful use of informed scepticism and the ability to make discerning and considered judgements about alternatives is extremely helpful to pupils in life after school. And even in school Lee and Shemilt were able to show that there was a positive appreciation of historical interpretations when pupils came to understand that historians could hold legitimate differing interpretations of the same evidence (Lee and Shemilt, 2004). Perhaps, the key message here is to be always seeking to emphasise the positive.

Sensitivity

The final issue for your consideration is that of the need to be sensitive to the way differing interpretations could affect your pupils not just in mixed racial schools but in all schools. Many departments teach the Crusades and are very conscious of the need for sensitivity and balance in their selection of material, particularly the need to ensure the inclusion of positive images for all pupils. Be aware of the potential dangers. A recent study, *The British Media and Muslim Representation* (2007) complained that popular films have helped to demonise Muslims as violent, dangerous and threatening, thus reinforcing prejudices. Significantly, the report argued that it was not the fact that they were negative images but that they were the only images. Therein lies your guide – it is not a question of making topics 'no-go' areas for differing interpretations but rather ensuing balance and positive images. The same point may be applied to the treatment of the slave trade and its abolition. Wrenn, in an article about Equiano, noted that 'societies, people, religious cultures and states often create role models or people of iconic value to reinforce their identities. The same is true of black identities' (Wrenn, 2002: 15). He goes on to reassert one of the aims of learning interpretations, relevant to a consideration of sensitive content, by noting that 'interpretations of history is one rigorous, analytical tool, which we can use to help pupils to resist and question racist attitudes'. Grosvenor (1999) has noted how often the black experience has either been excluded or seen in problematic terms and suggests that one aspect of the study of interpretations would be 'to teach pupils how such interpretations and representations have arisen'. Sensitivity is not limited to different races and cultures but can also be a factor with pupils from different social backgrounds. Thus there is a case for the sensitive handling of interpretations of poverty and its causes. Finally, McCully and Pilgrim (2004) have shown how by the use of two fictional characters to present opposing views of major events in Irish history the characters reflected on their own allegiances. In this way the teachers were seeking to explore the relationship between particular contemporary perspectives and the way the past is interpreted and in so doing offered the pupils a way forward in understanding the forces that divide society. Using fictional characters made it less personal.

Task 6.4 Sensitivity and interpretation

A useful long-term pursuit for you to contemplate is to collect old history textbooks. This is not always that easy as many departments have problems of space and old books soon disappear. Even so there are plenty still around and they can provide some useful material for your lessons, especially on historical interpretations.

1   With a series of textbooks written over time (you could be lucky and find some over 100 years old), examine how they approach a set of topics which you think would or should be treated differently today.
2   Examine a set of modern history textbooks to note with what sensitivity and with what images presented, they cover topics and groups such as the Crusades, the slave trade, poverty, the British Empire, China, the portrayal of different nationalities.

APPROACHES TO DEVELOPING PUPILS' UNDERSTANDING OF HISTORICAL INTERPRETATIONS

1 Planning development

The teaching of historical interpretations is more likely to be successful if there has been a sufficient investment of time in the preparatory activities *before* the interpretations can be considered. The following diagram gives some indication of the stages through which the teaching of interpretations can move.

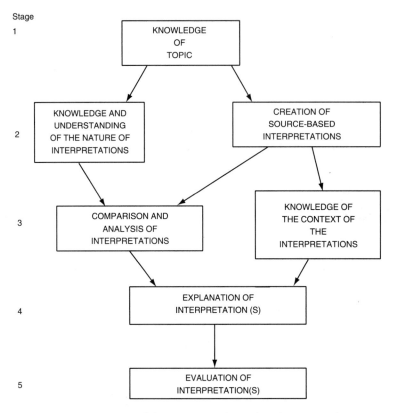

This diagram summarises some of the points made in the chapter to this point. Stages 1 and 2 represent the preparatory stages for the study of interpretations. The knowledge of the topic and the identification of the interpretation are vital preliminaries for the successful completion of the higher levels of analysis, explanation and evaluation. The key question is: do the pupils have sufficient information from which to be able to draw meaningful conclusions and to make valid comments on the interpretations they are studying? Without sufficient knowledge the pupils will become frustrated and lose motivation. It has been suggested that only when the activities described as stage 3 and above are reached is the real study of interpretations underway. Only if pupils spend time analysing their interpretations of the events and compare them with the available evidence can such work be related to the assessment of pupils' understanding of interpretations. Further knowledge about the authors of the interpretations and the context in which they were working would be needed if the pupils are to be able to tackle successfully stage 4 – an explanation of interpretations.

2 Explaining the purpose

There are times when studying the different interpretations might seem to some pupils a rather arcane and dry exercise, irritating in its uncertainties and lacking the interest of the original story. To counter this possible reaction, it is both advisable and educationally useful for pupils to be able to *appreciate the value of such exercises*. Your pupils always need to be encouraged to see the relevance of the aspects of the historical study they pursue to the world in which they are growing up. An important element of this is to *compare the varying interpretations of past events to current ones* and be able to show how sometimes what may be presented as an unequivocal truth is really an interpretation. Some current issues may be too complex for Key Stage 3 pupils. Even so they can probably understand why and how people who once wrote of Nelson Mandela as a terrorist are now prepared to accept him as a great leader.

3 The range and diversity of historical interpretations

An important feature of this element is the need for pupils to appreciate the breadth and variety of interpretations. Because they may regard history as a school subject with content that has to be learnt, it is easy for them to fail to appreciate just how widely used history can be and that much of its use involves somebody's interpretation. They will soon appreciate the point when you refer to well-known cinematic interpretations such as 'Robin Hood' or 'Ben Hur'. References to interpretations, which are familiar to the pupils, form a useful starting-point for the development of their understanding. This can be extended to include historical stories and novels, drama, cartoons, museum displays, guides and displays at historical sites, popular views about the past as well as your pupils' own interpretations. Valuable as it is for pupils to know the range of interpretations, Lee and Shemilt (2004) correctly warn against such knowledge being the height of your ambitions for your pupils. Many teachers have found them capable of much more.

Task 6.5 Encouraging pupils to understand the range and diversity of historical interpretations

The death of Thomas à Becket: see the Becket materials at: www.uea.ac.uk/~m242/historypgce/interp/welcome.htm.

Study the resources and suggested activities on the death of Becket. In most history departments the topic of Becket is covered in year 7. Consequently any suggestions for activities involving interpretations must only consider those appropriate for such young pupils. The example and the activities set out on the website therefore have as their main objective the task of familiarising the pupils with the range and sometimes the unusual nature of interpretations.

4 Asking questions about interpretations

An important part of the teaching of historical interpretations is the development of pupils' skills in asking questions about an interpretation. It is possible to create a sequence of questions, which provides a useful basis for such questioning. The table shows two sets of questions which pupils could be encouraged to employ to a range of interpretations and a range of topics. The first list is taken, with some adaptations, from Pam Harper (1993) and the second a more recent one used by Counsell *et al.* (2004) at an OFSTED Conference. Compare the two and use them to design your own set, possibly for display on the classroom wall.

1993		2004	
•	Who produced it? What was his or her starting-point?	1	What is it?
		2	What is it saying?
•	What do we know about the person who produced it?		• What does it say/show explicitly?
			• What does it say implicitly?
•	Why was it produced?	3	How and why was it constructed?
•	Where was it produced?		• What was the purpose and the audience
•	What sources were used and how valid were they?		i to persuade?
•	Who was the intended audience?		ii to entertain?
•	What was the purpose of the interpretation?		iii to inform?
	○ to amuse or entertain?		iii to communicate?
	○ to sell the past or an image of it?		iii to commemorate?
	○ to inform?	4	What is the relationship between the interpretation and the available evidence?
	○ to create myths?		
	○ to search for truth?	5	Which parts are factual, points of view or imagined?
	○ to justify or explain the present?		
	○ to influence current and future policies and discussions?	6	How has the interpretation been affected by the context in which it was created?
•	Are some interpretations more convincing/ plausible/trustworthy than others and if so why?		i ideology?
			ii values?
			iii nationality?
			iv personalit?
			v expectations?

In spite of the passage of time the lists have much in common. However, with the greater experience now available the more recent list shows a clearer focus on purpose, process and perspective. However, take care in your use of questioning, selecting those which are appropriate for the materials you are using and the ability of your pupils. You need to ensure they have access to the information needed to answer the questions.

5 Identifying and explaining differences

You find that there is a logical sequence as you take your pupils to a point where they are in a position to begin to explain differences in interpretations. Your first task is to ensure your pupils understand the content of the interpretation. This might require some editing of the original statement or prompting to note the significant details of, for example, a picture or a poem. Then the pupils can be set the task of comparing the differences and the similarities. Once these have been identified can begin the real task of explanation. At this point your pupils can begin to apply the questions set out above. What is important is that your planning takes into account what the pupils will need, while *allowing pupils some scope for initiative and insight*.

Task 6.6 Setting an exercise to identify and explain differences of interpretation

Presented below are two extracts, which show two very different interpretations of Thomas Becket. On the left-hand side of each extract are the actual words of the author, on the right is an attempt to make the content more accessible.

Using these extracts, work out a sequence of activities for your pupils to enable them to begin to offer explanations of these differing interpretations and to make some attempt at evaluating them. You may find these further extracts from John Harvey of use:

'Again and again kings with a truly regal achievement to their credit are found to have . . . their memory besmirched by historians.'

'Becket got what he asked for, but Henry, as generous and as just as he was free from petty spite, was left burdened with murder and sacrilege for the remaining twenty years of his life.'

Interpretation 1 From John Harvey, *The Plantagenets*, 1959: 45.

Nothing could be more misleading than the notion of a saintly man of God ill-treated by a tyrannical potentate. It was said that Henry was never known to choose an unworthy friend, but Becket's worthiness is a matter of opinion. Extraordinary mixture of well-to-do-man-about-town, witty and extravagant, and self-willed, self-torturing, and it must be said, self-advertising churchman, Thomas Becket won for himself an outstanding place in history by his genius for manoeuvring other parties into the wrong.

The idea that Becket was a saintly man of God, who was harshly treated by a cruel King is far from the truth. People said Henry always chose good friends, but whether Becket was a good friend is a matter of opinion. Becket was an unusual mixture of well-off man-about-town. He was witty but wasteful. He was a stubborn, self-torturing and, it must be said, a churchman who was keen to show off. Thomas Becket won for himself an outstanding place in history because he was a genius at making other people appear to be in the wrong.

Interpretation 2 John Morris, SJ, *The Life and Martyrdom of Saint Thomas Becket, Archbishop of Canterbury*, 1859: 91. Morris was a Jesuit, that is a member of the Catholic Society of Jesus, founded by Ignatius Loyola.

The personal hostility which King Henry was now beginning to entertain against St. Thomas, soon found rent in an attack upon the liberties of the clergy. This was a part of the King's policy of self-aggrandisement in which he had been restrained by the Saint, whilst he exercised influence over him.

The personal hostility, which King Henry was now beginning to show against Saint Thomas, was soon seen in an attack upon the rights of the clergy. This was a part of the King's policy of increasing his own importance. Before that, in the days when the Saint was able to influence the King, Thomas had been a restraining influence.

6 Explaining why historical interpretations might change

In order to meet the requirements of this area of knowledge, skills and understanding, pupils need to be able to explain 'how and why some historical events, people, situations and changes have been interpreted differently'. Part of that explanation involves an understanding of how circumstances might change which can influence an interpretation. To summarise these changing circumstances it is possible to create a spray-diagram. Here is an example showing some factors; no doubt there are others. Able pupils could be asked to try to design a diagram before being given a final version. Having drawn the diagram, most abilities might be asked to write a sentence or two explaining each point. Most would find it useful to have some examples of each point also.

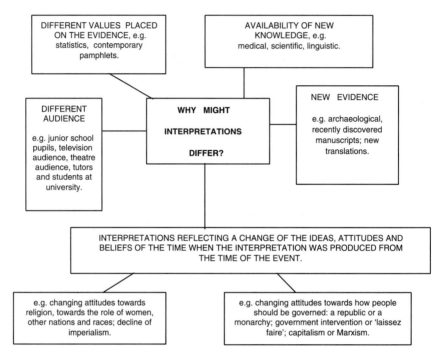

Evaluating historical interpretations

Some teachers are sceptical about whether the evaluation of historical interpretations is an appropriate activity for most secondary school pupils, believing it would be expecting too much of them to be asked to sit in judgement of what could be the result of long-term academic study by a reputable historian. Pupils are aware of their limitations and would see such an activity as contrived and artificial. However, there are situations when the evaluation of interpretations can offer rewarding insights for pupils studying this Key Concept. Such activity usually involves asking your pupils to apply their knowledge of a topic to certain types of interpretations and representations to see if they are consistent with their knowledge and understanding. Many rise to the challenge of offering their opinion as individuals or as a group. A further advance would be, after studying a range of sources, to evaluate an interpretation for its consistency with the understanding they have gained from their study of the evidence. To this end the following list of objectives deriving from the 2004 OFSTED Conference on interpretations should be helpful. Pupils should:

- know how to identify the internal evidence from the interpretation they are considering;
- be able to make inferences from the comparison of different interpretations;
- understand how the interpretation is affected by the context in which it was created;

- make judgements on the effectiveness of a history written as propaganda;
- understand the role of history where the context is unhistorical;
- make an informed judgement about the interpretation, which, depending on the type of question, might include objectivity, completeness, accuracy or the extent of these things.

(OFSTED, 2004)

Examples of strategies

Although there are many challenges, debates and unresolved issues associated with the teaching of historical interpretations, the teaching of this concept can provide you with some of your most imaginative and stimulating lessons. In planning to teach this Key Concept, you may find that it is more likely to succeed if placed within a wider overarching enquiry. This means that your pupils will be better informed both to understand the interpretations presented to them and make informed comments about them. One-off interpretation lessons are more likely to have the same deadening effect as context-free source skill exercises. Furthermore, placing interpretations within an enquiry will also make it easier for pupils to understand the process by which an interpretation has been constructed and as noted already understanding the process is a great step to a more sophisticated understanding of the concept. Also, studying interpretations makes it easier for pupils to answer those questions listed above.

The use of a variety of children's books, old-fashioned history textbooks and popular historical story books

For pupils who have had little experience in considering historical interpretations, the use of history books intended for a younger audience than themselves, can provide a useful introduction. The NCC (1993) described the use by year 7 pupils of a view of William the Conqueror based on a Ladybird book by L. Du Garde Peach, published in 1956. Pupils were asked to compare that interpretation with their own knowledge and try to explain the limitations of the Ladybird view. Similarly, a year 8 class could be presented with the following extract from *The Story of Queen Elizabeth*, Ladybird, 1958, by the same author:

> Queen Elizabeth reigned over England for forty-five years. When she came to the throne England was poor. When she died, England was rich, prosperous, united and happy. Her reign saw the beginnings of what came to be the British Empire. The fighting sailors of her reign and the great victory over the Spanish Armada made England one of the greatest countries of Europe. Much of this was due to the character of Elizabeth herself. She never despaired and she never gave in.

Again, pupils could consider whether all these statements are confirmed by their knowledge and discuss why the author has chosen to present such an interpretation. This encourages a useful discussion of the relationship of an interpretation to its intended audience. With able pupils it could also be the starting point for an enquiry into 'How accurate is "the Elizabethan legend"?'

The study of historical interpretations can also generate a *revived use for some old textbooks*. Quotations from some such books, written in the late nineteenth century or early twentieth century can tell as much about the times in which they were written as the topic they were writing about. This particularly applies to comments about the British colonies and other countries, where the books often had an imperialist and condescending tone. Others sought to use the study of the past as a vehicle for moral lessons for the pupils; as such they encourage the consideration of the author's purpose in writing a historical textbook.

Drawings, paintings

Another relatively straightforward approach to the study of historical interpretations is through drawings and artistic reconstructions. Returning to the Ladybird books, these are attractively illustrated and yet it may be useful for pupils to think about such pictures as interpretations. How much do the pictures showing the social background of the times present a sanitised, attractive representation of what was often dirty and unhygienic. How much is the artist influenced by the nature of the audience? Similarly, artistic reconstructions in textbooks can be the subject of such questions.

An alternative approach to interpretations through drawing is *to encourage the pupils to draw their ideas about a topic*. This can offer useful clues about the pupils' understanding of that topic. Wilson (1985) has shown how successful this can be with pupils of generally low ability. Apart from using drawings as a welcome alternative to the symbolic meaning of language, encouraging pupils' drawing helps them to realise that what they produce is the product of their own imagination – 'history not necessarily as it was, but as they think it is'. The comparison of each other's interpretative drawings and the ensuing explanation of the differences enables the pupils to be operating at stage 3 of the diagram. Furthermore, as Wilson also points out, this subtle distinction between fact and inter-pretation is less clear when children are presented with visual material, which is the product of the imagination of others, including the illustrations of modern textbooks.

Much can be gained from the pupils' own interpretation of pictures. For example, a photograph of a painting by A.F. Tait of the Stockport Viaduct (1842), soon after its completion, was passed round a year 9 class studying the nineteenth-century industrial town. Individually, they were asked to write down one or more adjectives that came to mind when they analysed the photograph. In the following feedback, a variety of con-trasting interpretations emerged. Most saw a smoky, grimy factory town beneath this massive viaduct, while others produced words such as 'romantic', and 'magnificent'. These differences generated a useful discussion about the painter's purpose, about how people in 1842 might have felt about the new viaduct and its railway, and why so many pupils had emphasised the dirty aspect of the town. The discussion then moved on to consider further comparisons reflecting different viewpoints.

Use of historical fiction

In more recent years teachers have overcome some reluctance to make use of historical fiction in their history lessons. It has become generally accepted that such literature can be a useful aid to pupil interest and understanding. By following the experience of individual characters placed in past situations, it is easier for many pupils to begin to comprehend situations very different from their own experience. Any concern about the lack of authenticity of such a medium has been dispelled to a degree by the good fortune of having had in the past half century some excellent writers of historical fiction for young people. Such writers spent many hours of solid research on the background of their novel. The very nature of such fiction means that it represents an author's interpretation of an event or past environment. So, while extracts from such literature with the wealth of detail that is often included, are an excellent aid to understanding in themselves, they can also be used to develop further pupils' understanding of historical interpretations. Consider the following description of exploited child labour in the factories of the early industrialisation. The passage is taken from a novel, excellent for this purpose, *The Devil's Mill* by Walter Unsworth:

> If Jeremy was overawed by the machinery and the noise, he did not fail to notice his fellow apprentices. What he saw was not encouraging: thin, ragged children with pinched faces, some only seven or eight years old and so tiny that they had to stand on stools to reach their machines. The boys wore only shirt and trousers, though the mill was damp and cold, the girls plain, pinafore dresses. All were barefoot, with unkempt hair, and incredibly dirty.
>
> Though these things in themselves were bad enough it was the faces of the children which alarmed Jeremy. Pale, sickly, their faces had set into a look of utter hopelessness. He felt a cold chill of apprehension to think that these were his companions of the future and he wondered whether he too would become like them.

Such a passage could precipitate the use of some of the questions about interpretations listed above. It would be particularly useful for pupils to consider not only the purpose of the author and the intended audience but also the extent to which they think it represents an accurate picture of such factories. Furthermore, such a passage could be used either to introduce the topic of child labour in factories to be followed by the use of contemporary sources to examine whether the passage was supported by such evidence. Alternatively, the use of the extract could, as in the procedure indicated by the diagram near the beginning of this section, follow the study of child labour and so enable the pupils to move from analysis through to evaluation. An alternative and effective way of using historical fiction is to encourage pupils to write their own. Martin and Brooke (2002) have shown that given structured guidance and using their own search for supportive evidence, pupils can find such an activity both stimulating and effective in developing their historical understanding.

 The EACH Project at: http://www.historicalfiction.org.uk/ is an invaluable resource for the use of historical fiction in history teaching.

Use of groups

Successful lessons may be based on giving different sets of evidence to different groups within the classroom. In their discussions the groups are asked to produce a set of conclusions based upon the information available to them. When their responses are fielded and recorded, one of the points that emerges from the ensuing discussion is the conclusion that interpretations will differ because they draw upon different evidence. A lesson using such an approach was given to a year 8 class studying the Moghul Empire. The groups were asked to answer the question, 'Who won the battle of Panipat?' Two different duplicated and contrasting sheets were in use, some pupils had Sheet A, others Sheet B. Sheet A was fictitious. The different views were later recorded in a chart on the board. The teacher then analysed the results and asked the pupils a series of questions about the conflicting interpretations. Destroying the fictitious sheet before them, the teacher then asked the pupils to consider the significance for historians of having only one side of evidence on which to base their interpretation of events. Again it is worth re-emphasising the importance of the follow-up work in re-informing the significance of issues that had emerged from the discussion. Sometimes student teachers do not allow sufficient time for this important follow-up to the activity, assuming that the group activity itself will be sufficient for the objectives of the lesson to have been met.

In one of many card sort possibilities for teaching historical interpretations, Howells (2005) showed how, following lessons on the English Civil War, different distribution of cards describing long term causes/blockers (actions which would stop the war/short term causes), would reveal different interpretations of the war and lead on to a valuable debate about determinist/Marxist or chance/accidental factors. QCA (2007b) also advocate several card-sorting exercises to explore the question of the relationship between underpinning evidence and different interpretations of the past. One method begins with an explanation of the topic by the teacher. The pupils are then given a number of evidence cards and asked to sort them in a way that shows particular pieces of evidence can be used to support particular interpretations, for example different views of the fairness of the Treaty of Versailles.

Group work may also be one way of studying how different periods have interpreted an event or a historical figure, for example, in compiling obituaries supposedly written at different times, thereby helping to develop Card's 'double vision' of interpretations. More elaborately, as part of a larger enquiry, groups might be used for understanding changing attitudes towards the British Empire. Mastin and Wallace (2006) described how different sources from (i) around 1897, (ii) 1960–70 and (iii) contemporary times can be used to show how different periods of history produced differing interpretations of the empire.

This last example raises a further debate about the extent to which your pupils study of historical interpretations should concentrate on the process or whether some aspects of historiography present a legitimate approach to the study of the concept. McAleavy (2000) found teachers to be reluctant to use historiography but feels that it presents scope for introducing real historical debate at Key Stage 3, believing that academic histories are neglected and can be accessible to pupils of this age.

Use of video, film, internet

Amongst the most stimulating aids to the understanding of historical interpretations is the use that can be made of videos and films. These vary greatly in their nature.

The use of film material does raise legitimate questions about the use or neglect of historical evidence, the purpose of the interpretation and, again, how the nature of the intended audience can affect the interpretation. A familiar anecdote on this theme may be retold of how the film director, Eisenstein, in his reconstruction of the Bolshevik Revolution of 1917, did more damage to the Winter Palace when shooting the film than was ever achieved during the actual revolution. Clips from that film have been used in documentaries and news programmes for many years, since the film was made in 1922, to the extent that Eisenstein's reconstruction is often assumed to be the actual event.

Pupils will be familiar with various historical 'epics', such as *Gladiator* and costume dramas frequently repeated on television. Such reconstructions could be useful starting-points for the study of a topic. Useful discussion can focus on the degree of artistic licence involved to add drama to the reconstruction.

The rapid development of the internet has brought a range of opportunities and challenges to the teacher of historical interpretations. ICT has a chapter of its own and the wider issues and strategies are explored there. Even so, as a student you will already be familiar with some of its uses but it is well worth exploring it again through the eyes of the student teacher.

Task 6.7 Using the internet for teaching historical interpretations

1   Discuss with your department how they make use of the internet in their planning and teaching. Have they any rules or guidelines about how and how not to make use of this resource?

2   *Either* select a topic you are likely to be teaching in a few weeks' time. Surf the web to find out what materials are available related to that topic. These might include: useful short summaries of content which extends the content of the textbook; various and differing visual images; controversial views/propaganda; academic debates; material on teacher-orientated websites.

Or collect material for studying historical interpretations of Richard I (Richard the Lionheart). How could you make accessible the interpretations of: John Gillingham, Amin Maalouf, Réné Grousset, Bishop William Stubbs, Nigel Saul, Richard of Devizes and pictorial representations from the sixteenth to the nineteenth century?

Use of drama

The use of a variety of forms of drama can provide a valuable approach to the study of historical interpretations. Any printed play is itself an interpretation and there are times, when material on a historical topic, could be used appropriately in the classroom. Another approach could involve 'playlets' (usually read out as radio plays rather than acted), about three or four pages only in length, written by the teacher. It is surprising how quickly such materials can be produced and how often such an effort is rewarded with a successful lesson. This is an increasingly popular way of dealing with some of the conceptually difficult topics, which occur in the medieval period. To retain consistency with the definition of an interpretation established earlier in the chapter, such a playlet should also include some indication of the sources on which it is based.

Once pupils have become familiar with the format of a play, with some classes, they can be given an opportunity to write their own playlets. This should not be too onerous a task. The *real* work on interpretations will occur when the pupils are given an opportunity to compare the results and to try and account for the differences.

Use of roleplay

Another increasingly popular but valuable approach used in history teaching is that of roleplay. Its main purpose is usually to help the pupils to comprehend complex issues in format that they can understand by making situations more personal and immediate. Such an approach can also be used to help the understanding of historical interpretations.

The use of familiar media formats can also be used to good effect. A year 9 class was asked, in groups, to prepare a radio programme on the Peterloo Massacre. Different pupils within the groups were to be interviewed presenting different interpretations of the event. Each interpretation was based on a collection of primary sources made available to the pupils. The discussion which followed the group work then sought in sequence to (1) identify, (2) explain and finally (3) evaluate the differences that emerged.

HISTORICAL ENQUIRY

In the version of the NC for history at Key Stage 3 to be introduced in September 2008, historical enquiry is described as a 'Key Process', and this will hopefully help you to encourage pupils to use sources not as discrete and often arid exercises, removed from their context, but as a means of mounting a set of enquiries. In other words, 'sources' may be seen as an aspect of 'resources' available to aid the development of historical understanding.

The emphasis on pupil enquiries and investigations is a helpful way of developing pupils' interest in history and their historical understanding. The limitations of some of the coursework produced for the Certificate of Secondary Education before the advent of GCSE probably helped create a deprecatory attitude towards the history 'project' if it involved a 'scrap-book' of copied extracts and cuttings. This created an understandable dislike of 'projects' if they were so lacking in rigour and challenge. However, pupil enquiries, if they are well organised, can offer plenty of challenge and scope for individual initiative. SCAA (1996) emphasises the point in noting that 'independence in carrying out research and in making historical judgements is an important characteristic of work at higher levels'. Local history can offer many opportunities for pupils to pursue their own historical enquiries, and if used appropriately some of the more thoughtfully designed ICT materials can provide a useful resource for pupil investigations. The British Library's structured investigations based around their CD-ROM, *Medieval Realms, Making of the UK* and *Britain, 1750–1900*, are a good example of this (British Library, 1994, 1998, 2000).

Task 6.8 Encouraging the use of enquiries in local history

Local history sources can provide the basis for many stimulating enquiries for pupils of all ages and abilities in the secondary school. They are particularly useful if your locality can provide examples, which help your pupils to understand national history. Fieldwork, site investigations and the use of local history libraries can give an extra dimension to the learning of history.

The following activity for year 7 classes can help to develop their understanding of the use of sources for a series of enquiries. As with all valuable lessons involving enquiries, appropriate materials need to be accumulated. For this activity you need to acquire a set of census returns for, say, 1861 for the area in which you are teaching, then:

1   Divide the data into approximately equal amounts of data for six groups (a population of 800 people would result in two A4 pages of data per group).
2   Explain to the class that they are going to find out what occupations the people living in their area had in 1861.
3   Using the entry for a particular household, explain each of the columns and give the class some details of how the census returns were acquired.

4   Appoint two pupils whose task is to move round the groups collecting and collating the data.
5   Appoint another pupil who will then use to data to create a bar chart on the board.
6   The groups will then complete the following sheet and the collators complete their totals (suitably amended for your area and data).

GROUP . . .

We have found that in . . . in 1861 there were:

1_____	servants or house servants	_____
2_____	labourers; farm labourers	_____
3_____	laundresses; washerwomen	_____
4_____	housewives; housekeepers	_____
5_____	gardeners	_____
6_____	cotton factory workers (winders, weavers, spinners, calico printers, dyers, agents)	_____
7_____	farmers	_____
8_____	craftsmen (blacksmiths, stone masons, wheelwrights, joiners, shoemakers, carpenters)	_____
9_____	warehousemen	_____
10_____	salespeople (beerhouse keepers, butchers, grocers, saleswomen, provision dealer, hosier)	_____
11_____	jobs related to travel (railway porter, carter, grooms, coachmen, carriers, footmen, paviours)	_____
12_____	craftswomen	_____
13_____	professional jobs (teachers, police, nurses, clerks, cashiers)	_____
14_____	merchants, manufacturers	_____

An important part of the investigation will be a discussion of the final bar chart and the questions that can emerge. Further enquiries using the same data could include an analysis of the age range of the population and an investigation into their places of birth.

Linking the census data to the maps of the time can add interest to the enquiry, especially when the pupils can make a connection with past and present place names. The first edition of the 6 inch series of Ordnance Survey maps are now accessible through the website of the Landmark Information Group http://www.old-maps.co.uk/.

The use of historical enquiries would help towards meeting OFSTED (1995) comments about the need to give pupils more responsibility for their own learning. Their review also notes that in addition to the underuse of libraries that 'too often pupils appear to be given access to only a limited range of texts and the teaching of research and retrieval skills is not developed sufficiently'. You find that there are great opportunities for differentiated work if you can encourage pupils to use their initiative to complete enquiry-based projects. The website includes details of such an enquiry-based project on the Peasants' Revolt.

The word 'enquiry' has several resonances and has been used to describe other types of enquiry other than the 'project' type just described. The word enquiry with its implication of searching, activity and problem-solving has been usefully adapted to describe overarching questions which form the basis of a series of lessons. As noted in

Chapter 5 in the discussion of the use of overviews, these are very helpful in enabling your pupils to see the 'big picture'. They usually include the use of evidence. Riley defined such a historical enquiry as:

> A planning device for knitting together a sequence of lessons, so that all the learning activities – teacher exposition, narrative, source-work, role-play, plenary – all move toward the resolution of an interesting historical problem by means of substantial motivating activity at the end.

He suggests ten questions, which can be asked to inform the planning:

1   Is this area of content significant?
2   How can we turn this area of content into a rigorous and motivating enquiry question?
3   Can we focus the enquiry on individual people?
4   How will pupils communicate their understanding through an engaging end product?
5   How will we hook them in at the start of the enquiry?
6   How will we sequence the learning for maximum motivation?
7   How can we help pupils to choose and use information?
8   How can we create learning activities which appeal to different intelligences?
9   How will we create 'mini-hooks' to engage learners with particular tasks?
10   How will we create rich resources rather than grubby gobbets?

(Riley, 2006a: 2)

Task 6.9 Deconstructing enquiry question schemes

Ask you subject tutor or head of department for some examples of work based on the idea of historical enquiry. Analyse the lessons to identify the role of the pupils and the skills and knowledge they need to employ. Consider how the lessons can contribute towards the pupils being able to reach their own conclusions to the enquiry question.

Chambers shows the kind of enquiry questions, which might be used to focus an enquiry on the concept of causal reasoning. He includes questions such as:

'"There would have been no civil war if Charles I had avoided war with Scotland." How far do you agree with this viewpoint?'
'Is it possible to explain why Britain became the First Industrial Nation?'
'How important a factor was rebellion in persuading the British to end slavery in the Caribbean in 1833?'
'Why did it take so much longer for British women to get the vote?'
'"Hitler came to power largely because he was able to convince enough people that he had impressive individual qualities as a leader." How far do you agree with this explanation of Hitler's rise to power in Germany?'

(Chambers, 2006)

You might analyse the different formats that have been used to create these enquiry questions and consider how they could be applied to content areas with which you are particularly familiar

SUMMARY AND KEY POINTS

The teaching of interpretations of history gives you the opportunity to plan and deliver lessons, which can be imaginative, interesting and of great educational value. We have seen that it is important that the pupils have a clear understanding of how the study of historical interpretations differs from source skills and also to know why we consider them to be important. This can be quite a challenge to the new teacher, who needs to be aware of the possible learning difficulties pupils might experience. The chapter has stressed that problems can arise through insufficiency of content, the pupils' limited comprehension, their need to have the confidence to move from describing to explanation and, where appropriate on to evaluation, and at the same time your pupils do not feel there is nothing in history about which we can be certain. Your pupils need to understand why it is important for them to study historical interpretations. Success is more likely if you try to utilise a range of types of interpretations, some of which the pupils might be surprised to find that they can form part of their history lessons. This in turn encourages you to employ a range of media and of teaching styles.

The chapter concludes by emphasising the point that the development of source skills is likely to be more successful if they are seen by the pupils to have a purpose. Such skills are to be seen as the means by which they can carry out historical enquiries rather than as exercises in source skills, divorced from their context and without any evident utility.

For further resources and suggestions for further reading in these areas, go to: www.uea.ac.uk/~m242/historypgce/interp/welcome.htm.

REFERENCES

Bennett, S. (1995) *The Teaching and Assessment of Interpretations and Representations in History: A Discussion Paper*, London: SCAA.

Bowen, P. (1995) 'Secondary history teaching and the OFSTED inspections', *Teaching History*, No. 80: 12–16.

British Library (1994) *Medieval Realms*, CD-ROM, London: British Library.

British Library (1998) *The Making of the UK*, CD-ROM, London: British Library.

British Library (2000) *Britain 1750–1900*, CD-ROM, London: British Library.

Card, J. (2004) 'Seeing double. How one period visualises another', *Teaching History*, No. 117: 6–11.

Chambers, C. (2006) 'Teaching causal reasoning', Chapter 6 in M. Hunt (ed.), *A Practical Guide to Teaching History in the Secondary School*, Oxon: RoutledgeFalmer: 49–59.

Counsell, C., Riley, M. and Byrom J. (2004) Presentation to OFSTED Conference on Historical Interpretations.

Davis, I. and Williams, R. (1998) 'Interpretations of history: issues for teachers in the development of pupils' understanding', *Teaching History*, No. 91: 36–41.

Dearing, R. (1994) *The National Curriculum and its Assessment*, London: SCAA.

DES (1990) *History in the National Curriculum*, London: HMSO.

DfE (1995) *History in the National Curriculum*, London: HMSO.

Grosvenor, I. (1999) 'History and the perils of multiculturalism', *Teaching History*, No. 97: 37–40.

Harper, P. (1993) 'Using the attainment targets in key stage 2: AT2, interpretations of history', *Teaching History*, No. 72: 11–13.

Harrison, S. (2004) Address to OFSTED Conference on historical interpretations, June–July 2004.

Howells, G. (2005) 'Interpretations and history teaching. Why Ronald Hutton's "Debates in Stuart History" matters', *Teaching History*, No. 121: 29–35.

Lee, P. (1998) 'A lot of guesswork goes on: children's understanding of historical accounts', *Teaching History*, No. 92: 29–32.

Lee, P. and Shemilt, D. (2004) 'I just wish we could go back in the past and find out what really happened: progression in understanding about historical accounts', *Teaching History*, No. 117: 25–31.

McAleavy, T. (1993) 'Using the attainment targets at KS3: AT2, interpretations of history', *Teaching History*, No. 72: 14–17.

McAleavy, T. (2000) 'Teaching about interpretations', Chapter 6 in J. Arthur and R. Phillips (eds), *Issues in History Teaching*, London: Routledge: 72–82.

McAleavy, T. (2003) 'Interpretations of history', in M. Riley and R. Harris (eds), *Past Forward*, London: Historical Association: 42–4.

McCully, A. and Pilgrim, N. (2004) 'They took Ireland away from us and we've got to fight to get it back', *Teaching History*, No. 114: 17–21.

Martin, D. and Brooke, B. (2002) 'Getting personal and making effective use of historical fiction in the history classroom', *Teaching History*, No. 108: 30–5.

Mastin, S. and Wallace, P. (2006) 'Why don't the Chinese play cricket? Rethinking progression in historical interpretations through the British Empire', *Teaching History*, No. 122: 6–14.

NCC (1993) *Teaching History at Key Stage 3*, York: NCC, 50–8.

OFSTED (1993) *History: Key Stages 1, 2 and 3: The Implementation of the Curricular Requirements of the Education Reform Act*, London: HMSO.

OFSTED (1995) *History: A Review of Inspection Findings, 1993–94*, London: HMSO.

OFSTED (2004) *Report of Conference on Historical Interpretations*, June–July 2004.

Pendry, A., Atha, J., Carden, S., Courtenay, L., Keegh, C. and Ruston, K. (1997) 'Pupil preconceptions in history', *Teaching History*, No. 86: 18–20.

QCA (2007a) 'History, programme of study: key stage 3', London: QCA. Online at http://curriculum.qca.org.uk/subjects/history/. Accessed 11 October 2007.

QCA (2007b) 'Innovating with history websites', how to teach about interpretations at key stages 1 to 3'. Online at www.qca.org.uk/history/innovating.

Riley, M. (2006a) Quoted in 'Final report: Historical Association's key stage 2–3 History Transition Project, London: Historical Association. Online at: www.historytransition.org.uk. Accessed 11 October 2007.

Riley, M. (2006b) Historical enquiries and interpretations, conference presentation. Online at http://czv.e2bn.net/e2bn/leas/c99/schools/czv/web/riley.htm. Accessed 11 October 2007.

SCAA (1996) *Exemplification of Standards in History, Key Stage 3*, London: SCAA.

SCAA (1997) *The Assessment of Interpretations and Representations and Use of Sources in GCSE History Examinations*, London: SCAA.

Scott, B. (1994) 'A post-Dearing look at history: interpretations of history', *Teaching History*, No. 75: 20–6.

Sinclair, Y. (2006) 'Teaching historical interpretations', Chapter 7 in M. Hunt, *A Practical Guide to Teaching History in the Secondary School*, Oxon: Routledge.

Teaching History (2000) No.99, contains several articles, which are invaluable in giving guidance on the structuring of worthwhile and stimulating enquiry activities.

Towill, E. (1997) 'The constructive use of role play at key stage 3', *Teaching History*, No. 86: 8–13.

Wilson, M.D. (1985) *History for Pupils with Learning Difficulties*, London: Hodder and Stoughton.

Woolley, M. (2003) 'Really weird and freaky: using a Thomas Hardy short story as a source of evidence in the year 8 classroom', *Teaching History*, No. 111: 6–11.

Wrenn, A. (1999) 'Substantial sculptures or sad little plaques? Making "interpretations matter to Year 9', *Teaching History*, No. 97: 21–8.

Wrenn, A. (2002) 'Equiano-voice of silent slaves', *Teaching History*, No. 107: 13–19.

7 Ensuring inclusion in the history classroom

INTRODUCTION

When you qualify to teach, you enter a school system where there are massive differences in the extent to which pupils from different backgrounds fulfil their educational potential (see, for example, Gilborn, 2000; Ajegbo, 2007). Some teachers, departments and schools make a big difference to the attainment of pupils from groups who often underachieve 'nationally'. Issues of equality of opportunity and educational inclusion are therefore very high-profile and important in current policy debates on education. Ensuring inclusion means responding to the diverse needs of each individual pupil. This means respecting cultural diversity, as well as making the curriculum accessible to all learners. It is the teacher's role to enable each pupil to feel part of the learning process, and to make sure that they achieve their 'personal best'.

The NC Inclusion Statement (DfEE/QCA, 1999) states that:

> When planning, teachers should set high expectations and provide opportunities for all pupils to achieve, including boys and girls, pupils with special educational needs, pupils with disabilities, pupils from all social and cultural backgrounds, pupils of different ethnic groups including travellers, refugees and asylum seekers, and those from diverse linguistic backgrounds.

It emphasises the need for teachers to 'plan their approaches to teaching and learning so that all pupils can take part in lessons fully and effectively'. The NC states three main principles which are essential to develop this more inclusive curriculum:

a   setting suitable learning challenges;
b   responding to pupils' diverse learning needs;
c   Overcoming potential barriers to learning and assessment for individuals and groups of pupils.

(DfEE/QCA, 1999)

The importance of being able to address issues of equality of opportunity and cultural, ethnic and religious diversity are also strongly emphasised in the standards for QTS (see Standards Q1, Q10, Q14, Q19, Q20, Q21, TDA, 2007), and the NC for history introduced in September 2008 includes the 'Key Concept' of 'cultural, ethnic and religious diversity' (see QCA, 2007: 112, or online at http://curriculum.qca.org.uk/subjects/history/). It is also helpful for you to read the section on inclusion in history in the new NC for history at Key Stage 3 (QCA, 2007) which can also be accessed at http://curriculum.qca.org.uk/subjects/history/.

OBJECTIVES

At the end of this chapter you should be able to:

- understand the range of learning needs you are likely to encounter in school, including Special Educational Needs (SEN), and the needs of pupils who are learning English as an Additional Language, of the very able, and of pupils who are disabled;
- identify factors which are preventing pupils from performing to the best of their ability in the subject;
- understand how your teaching can be culturally relevant to your pupils;
- understand the educational context in which teaching and learning take place with regard to pupils with learning needs;
- know about a variety of teaching strategies to help pupils with different learning needs.

VALUING EVERY PUPIL

Teachers need to respect all pupils as individuals and as learners. The government's 'Every Child Matters' initiative (DfES, 2004, see also www.everychildmatters.gov.uk/aims) distinguishes five strands in a child's wellbeing. These are to be healtly, to stay safe, to enjoy and achieve, to make a positive contribution, and to achieve economic wellbeing. Effective teachers try to encourage a positive contribution from their pupils by creating a collaborative classroom ethos. An attempt to 'meet and greet' individuals as they enter your classroom, together with a positive word or an exhortation to improve as they leave shows that you are aware of their presence, and value their contributions. Grosvenor (2000) also gives further guidance on creating a positive ethos in the history classroom. Effective classroom management is integral to this positive ethos. Some helpful strategies for this are outlined in the NC Inclusion Statement (DfES/QCA, 1999, online at www.nc.uk.net/inclusion.html).

Providing incentives for each individual to engage with learning is also part of creating an inclusive classroom. The ideas in Chapter 10 on gathering instant feedback from pupils may also be helpful to involve all pupils in class activities as an alternative to the standard question and answer sessions. This chapter also suggests various approaches, including self and peer assessment, to encourage pupils to move on in their learning. Other needs which you encounter as a student teacher are the needs of pupils in year 7, who may struggle with the transition from primary school. For pupils with a disability or other additional needs, it is often harder to reorientate themselves, and to respond to the more formal relationships required with subject teachers, and the loss of close relationships with the class teacher (see www.historytransition.org.uk for history specific guidance on this issue). Certain Special Educational Needs such as dyslexia often lead to difficulties in personal organisation. This should be considered as you plan their homework in particular. It is worth exploring what support is available to help with homework within the school. You may also encounter certain religious or cultural sensitivities, so you need to exercise tact and sensitivity.

Task 7.1 Valuing the individual

Discuss with your tutor how teachers can encourage a sense of belonging from individual pupils. Observe a lesson, and list all the ways in which you see this happen. Can you identify any pupils with additional needs – either from the pupils' or the teacher's behaviour?

As you observe try to note down how many individual pupils interact with the teacher, and whether the interactions appear positive or negative. Can you learn anything about how a positive classroom environment is created and maintained?

A HISTORY CURRICULUM FOR ALL

It is important that pupils perceive our teaching to be relevant to their own lives. The revised NC for history (QCA, 2007) makes explicit reference to history's role in fostering personal identity, and specifically mentions history's contribution to promoting mutual understanding in a multicultural society. The QCA document *Respect for All* (QCA, 2001) stresses 'the need for all pupils, regardless of their cultural heritage, to value cultural diversity and be equipped to challenge racist assumptions'. As Grosvenor (2000: 149) stated, 'History is always about selection'. The way that you approach topics, and the selections and choices you make, can make a big difference to the extent to which history is relevant to the lives and situations of your pupils.

It is possible to exercise some flexibility in planning the curriculum, even as a student teacher, if this is done through discussions with your subject tutor. Positive curriculum choices at Key Stage 3 may involve learning about varied cultures, for example settlers and invaders, Islamic civilisations and the Crusades, the British Empire and the Transatlantic slave trade, the Holocaust, the role of the British Empire in the two world wars. Often pupils enjoy this kind of study provided the teacher has the skills to bring it alive for them. There are certain opportunities to teach non-European histories at GCSE and GCE A level. The NC for history introduced in September 2008 continues to offer choice in selection of subject content to teachers, with a more thematic approach and emphasis on overviews of the past (QCA, 2007). This should give more scope for schools to tailor the curriculum around the interests of their pupils. Where the choice of topics is beyond your control, try to adopt an inclusive approach. A few general principles concerning selection of resources follow:

Principle	Examples
Use resources that include people from all backgrounds (culture, gender, class).	Posters, pictures, books. See teaching materials available from *Hidden History Express* (2006) for example.
Look into 'hidden histories'.	<ul><li>Count references to women and to men, in the index of a textbook.</li><li>Discuss number of pages given to a topic such as the Transatlantic slave trade.</li><li>Consider why certain groups do not feature in history textbooks, which could lead to research into their histories.</li></ul>
Show that Britain has been a diverse society for many centuries.	<ul><li>*QCA's Respect for All* web pages (QCA, 2001b) give details of how one school broadened a study of the Norman Conquest into an investigation of the bigger question 'Who are the British?' Lyndon's article (2006) explains how black history can be woven into the curriculum rather than just visited at particular points.</li><li>Grovesnor (2000) gave examples of black people, whose role could be investigated as part of a traditional study of the English Reformation, radicals in the nineteenth century or the suffragettes.</li></ul>
Avoid presenting a picture of a particular cultural group solely as victims. Present positive role models and successes of different cultures.	<ul><li>The successful slave revolution on the island of Saint-Domingue in the 1790s could be a case study.</li><li>Case studies of resistance to the Holocaust could be Rabbi Leo Baeck, who resisted Nazi authority by peaceful methods in Therersienstadt, or the armed uprising in the Warsaw ghetto in April 1943. The story of Abba Kovner, who advocated armed uprising in the Vilna Ghetto, is recounted in the Holocaust Memorial Day Education Pack (DfEE, 2000).</li><li>The struggle of African slaves can be compared with the struggle of British workers in the nineteenth century, then with the struggle of British women for their rights, and the struggle of peoples in British Empire to achieve independence in the twentieth century.</li></ul>
Show that victims of atrocities did not always belong to the same race.	<ul><li>Some French prisoners of war were transported to America through the Transatlantic slave trade.</li><li>Sinti and Roma, and the Slavs, as well as Jews, were murdered by the Nazis.</li></ul>
Show positive achievements within larger conflicts.	<ul><li>Case studies of Christians who helped Jews during the Holocaust, for example Swedish diplomat Raoul Wallenburg or Albert Bedane in the Channel Islands, or Danish fishermen who ferried almost all of Denmark's Jewish population to safety in Sweden in 1943.</li></ul>

INCLUDING PUPILS WITH SPECIAL EDUCATIONAL NEEDS: WHAT THE LEGISLATION SAYS

It is estimated that approximately 1 in 5 children will have some form of SEN which will require additional provision in school (Warnock, 1978; OFSTED, 2004). Approximately 1 in 30 children have a statement of SEN, which describes the pupil's needs and requires an action plan for the provision being made. This provision is legally binding. The most important legislation is the Code of Practice for Special Educational Needs. This was published in 1994, and revised in 2001 (DfES, 2001a). The code confirmed the key principle, present in policy since the Warnock Report of 1978, that, in nearly every case, pupils with special educational needs would be educated in the main-stream classroom. It states that children have special educational needs if they 'have a significantly greater difficulty in learning than the majority of children of the same age' or if they 'have a disability which prevents or hinders them from making use of educational facilities of a kind generally provided for children of the same age in schools'.

The Code of Practice requires all subject teachers to identify pupils with SEN in their classes. It stipulates a five stage process, as follow:

1   recognition of the pupil's SEN;
2   provision of greater differentiation for the SEN pupil;
3   use of outside specialists by the school;
4   consideration of the need for a statutory assessment;
5   assessment of a pupil for a possible SEN statement.

The Revised Code of Practice further specifies three stages of provision, once a pupil is identified as not learning effectively through the usual methods of differentiation. These are:

- School Action, whereby the pupil needs additional support, which can be pro-vided within the school. This may involve extra tuition or in-class support, different learning materials or special equipment.
- School Action Plus, whereby some additional support is provided by specialist agencies external to the school.
- A statement.

(DfES, 2001a)

Strategies employed to enable a pupil with SEN to progress should be recorded within an Individual Education Plan (IEP). It is the responsibility of the Special Educational Needs co-ordinator (SENCO) to write and review the IEP in collaboration with colleagues.

Many teachers have found that the range of needs encountered in a mainstream classroom has become greater in recent years, partly because of the closure of a number of special schools across the country. This is most likely to be considered a problem where the needs are social and behavioural as well as educational. For more detailed discussion of inclusion and SEN, see Peacey, 2005.

THE NATIONAL CURRICULUM AND SPECIAL EDUCATIONAL NEEDS

The statutory inclusion statement of the NC requires staff to modify the programmes of study to give all pupils relevant and appropriately challenging work at each key stage. The NC guidance allows teachers the discretion to teach pupils material designed for earlier key stages, where appropriate.

 See www.uea.ac.uk/~m242/historypgce/welcome.htm for further details about issues of inclusion and diversity.

RECOGNISING BARRIERS TO LEARNING

First it is important to consider which pupils are struggling with tasks you set and why. History contains many abstract terms and concepts which, if not introduced at the right level, will cause ambiguity and confusion in the minds of all pupils. The linguistic demands of the subject are high and you need to be constantly aware of both the language you use in communicating with pupils, and of the demand placed on pupils' literacy skills and experience (see Chapter 4). Lomas (2005) identified some of the common difficulties experienced by learners of history. Teachers who are concerned about inclusion will attempt to address these difficulties as far as possible.

Pupils with SEN may experience particular barriers. The history department and the SENCO at your placement school can be consulted about which of your pupils are identified as having SEN and what are their specific learning needs. Data such as reading ages, Cognitive Abilities Tests (CATs) and Standard Assessment Tasks (SATs) scores will be helpful (see www.uea.ac.uk/~m242/historypgce/assess/welcome.htm for more detail on these means of assessment).

There is a highly informative chapter on different types of SEN in Luff and Harris (2004), which gives details of the main characteristics for each type of need, and how the subject teacher can help to meet it (see also Peacey, 2005).

Task 7.2 Recognising SEN

During your school experience find out what the school and department policy is concerning the identification of pupils with SEN, including exceptionally able pupils. Does the school have a whole-school approach to SEN with a written statement of policy? How does the history department interpret the school's SEN policy in terms of individual education plans and departmental strategies for pupils with special educational needs?

From the list of learning difficulties recognised by the Code of Practice, observe one history class and try and identify any learning difficulties that the pupils have. In particular look at:

- ability;
- motivation and interests;
- maturity;
- preferred learning styles;
- behaviour;

- reading and writing skills;
- listening skills;
- communication skills;
- memory.

DISABILITY

Many pupils who have disabilities learn alongside their peers, with little need for additional support beyond physical aids such as a wheelchair, a hearing aid, or equipment to aid vision. The SEN and Disability Act of 2001 obliged schools to take reasonable steps to ensure that pupils who are disabled are not placed at a substantial disadvantage in their education, and to plan to increase the extent to which they can participate in the curriculum, make the physical environment more accessible and ensure the written material is accessible (DfES, 2001b). Any specific difficulties must be recognised and planned for. This might mean printing your resources in larger type, or reducing the amount of homework required and so on. It is particularly important that pupils who are disabled feel a sense of belonging, especially during the teenage years. This can come through interaction with peers, and sometimes with others who are also disabled.

A sensitive and aware teacher can make a big difference to the climate within which disabled pupils work in a class, and to the extent to which they are socially and logistically integrated into the class. Part of this is forethought: a wheelchair can make it difficult for a pupil to get into the classroom, but minor readjustments to chairs and desks can make it easier to enter the room without embarrassment.

In some ways, pupils with learning disabilities want to be treated the same as other pupils. Student teachers should try to talk to disabled pupils and pupils with learning disabilities in the same tone, manner and intonation as they would to other pupils, and should be careful not to adopt a mannered 'caring' inflection or 'poor little mite' manner.

SOME APPROACHES TO TEACHING HISTORY TO PUPILS WITH SPECIAL EDUCATIONAL NEEDS

A flexible, but carefully structured, approach to teaching and learning helps ensure that all of your pupils make progress. It should not be assumed pupils with SEN cannot enjoy history. All pupils can respond to history which is captivating. It is important not to teach to the lowest common denominator, simplifying everything. It is critical to consider when and what kind of differentiation is necessary. It is not a productive use of your time to provide different learning experiences and differentiated materials *all of the time*. A useful start is to consider ways of stimulating your pupils and capturing their attention, by use of a variety of approaches which will appeal pupils of all abilities and with different preferred learning styles.

Planning and teacher input

The teacher concerned about inclusion holds high expectations of pupils with SEN, as of any other pupils, seeks to recognise the difficulties faced by individuals in learning history, and helps them improve their conceptual understanding and literacy skills in order to access the learning more easily. These pupils are considered in lesson plans which incorporate a range of strategies to bring alive the subject matter, as well as differentation. Approaches may include story-telling, the media, drawings, discussion, field trips, model making, roleplay, drama, information technology and visual displays in an attempt to make history more concrete for pupils with SEN. Group work is often a useful tool to encourage maximum participation and learning for pupils with SEN. Exploratory talk is crucial for pupils in development of their understanding and confidence. There are lots of ideas about organising group work and roleplay in Chapter 4. It is important to remember that challenge in learning, as well as access to learning, is as important to pupils with SEN as to able pupils.

Consider how to build in opportunities for success for everyone early in the lesson sequence. A lesson which appeals to all pupils could focus on some kind of initial stimulus to 'hook' pupils into the lesson, and secure the motivation needed to pursue some difficult thinking, reading or writing. Use of historical narrative is often popular (see Chapter 4). The Foundation Subjects Strand of the Key Stage 3 National Strategy (2002) refers to the importance of starters. Starters can serve a key purpose for settling the class, but their power to engage the class in learning should also be valued. Use of pictures, artefacts, card sorts, puzzles to solve, DVD clips, etc., can engage pupils of all abilities and backgrounds. Phillips' article (2001) contained helpful ideas on use of initial stimulus material. Harris (2005) argued that a suitable stimulus can help pupils to care about what happened in the past, and therefore engage them in the lesson from the start. He showed the pitfalls of over-simplification of complex topics for less able pupils, whereby they can be deprived of the knowledge necessary to make sense of the issues. If the work is made engaging and accessible, with obstacles such as reading and writing carefully placed, it can make a real difference to the extent to which pupils with learning difficulties *commit themselves* to learning in history.

As a student teacher, you may be surprised at how often many pupils require repeated reinforcement of what you have said. Teacher talk in class must be pitched at the appropriate level for the pupils to understand. Use open questions to permit some response from the pupils which you can build upon. Do not assume that closed questions are always easier, as they may require factual recall, which is difficult for some pupils.

Reading

It is often the case that pupils with SEN have a lower level of language development than that of their peers, and as suggested in Chapter 4, difficulties in reading can be one of the biggest obstacles in learning history. Many practical suggestions for strategies to aid reading are given in Chapter 4. Remember that your supporting explanation of written materials, and individual help given to pupils can help to make more difficult written materials accessible, as can shared reading of the text. If you are able to skilfully 'guide' pupils through pieces of reading, it can open up a broader and more potentially interesting range of resources for pupils.

Writing

The communication of ideas in writing is obviously critical in the learning of history. At times, we can reduce the amount of writing required, or simplify or scaffold (Burton, 205: 250–1) the process for pupils with SEN. However, we should not try to avoid it completely. The list below gives ideas to help pupils with SEN. Further ideas on improving pupils' writing in general can be found in Chapter 4.

- Repeat explanation of the task both orally and in writing.
- Question individuals to check that they have understood what is required.
- Think carefully about exactly what it is you are asking pupils to do. The use of imaginative writing, for example, requires first that the pupils be able to describe and record.
- Model the type of writing required, e.g. provide a first sentence or introductory paragraph.
- Beware of the difficulty in an apparently easy task such as copying from a board. Copying from a sheet on the desk is easier.
- If pupils are slow in starting the written task, check that the obstacle does not lie in reading text or instructions. If it does, try to give individual support, or to pair them with a classmate who can help.
- Reassure pupils as they work that they are doing the right thing.

Worksheets

Some suggestions follow about the mechanics of adapting worksheets for pupils with SEN.

- Use a high ratio of picture to print.
- Make instructions short and simple, possibly in the form of bullet points.
- Sources can be put into text boxes to make them more easy to find for reference.
- The language of any text may have to be adapted, or difficult words explained in brackets. Text can be broken up with diagrams and illustrations.
- Avoid fonts sizes below 14.
- Some specific learning difficulties or disabilities mean that pupils need text at font size 20 plus with double spacing between lines. Printing worksheets on pale coloured paper may also be helpful.

- Questions should refer to text on the same page, avoiding the need to turn pages to find an answer. It is better to print a 2 page worksheet on one sheet of A3 than on two pages of A4.
- Give hints as to where to find answers.

Tasks can be broken up by:

- producing gap fills, with or without the missing words provided, or with first letters provided;
- deciding if a given statement is true or false;
- sequencing events;
- choosing the correct ending to a sentence from several;
- matching heads and tails of sentences;
- cutting and pasting instead of writing out long answers;
- providing some space for pupils to write down their own ideas, however briefly.

For ideas about checking the readability of a text, see the section of the website relating to inclusion and diversity issues. www.uea.ac.uk/~m242/historypgce/welcome.htm.

Published materials

Several publishers provide specialised textbooks for less able pupils (see, for instance, Robson, 1993; Kennedy, 1994; Buxton, 1991). Many of these books provide suggestions for work which is accessible to pupils of limited ability, but which address historical understanding. The Schools History Project (SHP) has put together resource packs particularly designed to support pupils with special educational needs, and which make imaginative and thoughtful use of picture packs (see, for instance, Shephard and Brown, 1994).

Task 7.4 Learning from published SEN resources for history

Either from your placement school or from the resources centre at your IHE, look through at least one of the textbooks or resource packs designed for pupils with SEN and examine how they attempt to retain genuinely historical activities whilst ensuring that materials are rendered accessible to pupils. Examples include Heinemann's 'Foundation History' series, (e.g. Kennedy, 1994), Oxford's 'Access to History' series, (e.g. Robson, 1993), and the SHP materials published by Murray mentioned above.

Having looked through the materials, try to devise an exercise for pupils with SEN for one of your teaching groups which attempts to adapt some of the principles and strategies used in the published materials.

Differentiation

Differentiation means matching tasks to pupils' ability. All classrooms contain pupils of different abilities, even when they are theoretically setted or banded. When you are placed in a new school, you need to find out the policy on setting. If groups are setted, how many sets are there, and on what basis has their composition been decided? If sets apply across two or more subjects, for reasons of timetabling, problems may arise in placing individuals. Some schools prefer solely mixed ability teaching on the grounds of numbers or behaviour or positive social reasons such as fear of stereotyping pupils in lower sets.

There are a number of ways of achieving differentiation. Some of these are explained in Chapter 10. Stephen (2006) gives an overview of the strengths and weaknesses of various methods. The starting point is an awareness of what and when to differentiate. Careful use of visual resources, and active learning activities, such as those outlined below, should reduce the need for differentiation of resources and tasks. Cunnah (2000) outlines the challenge to teachers to examine their learning environment and the actual process of learning as a whole, affirming that successful differentiation includes a full range of approaches. Less obvious methods, such as the level of support offered to each pupil, or the use of different groupings to allow pupils to support each other can be highly effective.

When written tasks are important to the learning objectives, some differentiation of the task is usually required. An alternative to the production and distribution of differentiated worksheets could be to give pupils the choice of a 'help sheet' if they are struggling with a task in a textbook or on a worksheet. This may include glossaries, memory prompts, multi-choice answers, tick boxes, etc. Pupils with very low levels of English or severe special needs may be given some part of the answers as a 'given' (see overleaf) to get them started and into the task. The advantages of using supplementary materials, rather than different materials, are that they can be given out with the minimum of fuss. Pupils with SEN can work from the same materials as their classmates, and may see progress at the point where they no longer need the help sheet. Help sheets are also useful for homework.

Another popular method is stepped worksheets, where all pupils given the same materials but the tasks show an incline of difficulty with the simplest first. This can be clarified on the sheet, with tasks labelled as foundation, middle, higher, or levels 3, 4, 5 and so on. The advantage of this approach is that it is simple to manage, and it helps avoid any stigma attached to a separate resource given to less able pupils. However they may become disheartened that they never finish the sheet, and may be tempted to attempt tasks that are too difficult.

Further guidance on differentiation can be found on the website (www.uea.ac.uk/~m242/historypgce) and in Lowe, 2005.

This was used as a help sheet where the standard task was to write a diary extract for a slave.

My capture, 28 June 1777

Read the sentences and decide on a sensible order. Number the sentences in the boxes. The first one has been done for you.

We saw the white slave traders give cloth to the African chief who brought the slaves.	
They made us walk to the coast with our legs chained to each other's.	
They came at night and took me from my home.	1
They whipped us if we walked too slowly.	
They captured lots of people from my village.	
They crammed us into a rowing boat to take us to the slave ship.	

Now complete this sentence.

I felt . . . . because . . . .
. . . .

Now consider the following:

1   What skills are being tested?
2   What input might be needed to give this pupil the knowledge to complete this task?
3   Where has challenge been left in the differentiated task?
4   Where might this pupil still experience difficulty with this task, and what kind of support would you offer?
5   If this task proved too easy, how could you add extra challenge?

Figure 7.1 An example of a task designed for pupils with SEN

Task 7.5 Thinking about differentiation

As preparation for this activity you should read A. Lewis (1992) on the practical listing of the types of differentiation in Vol. 19, No. 1 of the *British Journal of Special Education*. You should then observe a particular pupil throughout a lesson or shadow him or her through a whole day of lessons. Make notes and comment on their performance in a range of activities in each of the classes.

From your notes try to identify:

- the extent to which pupils were on or off task;
- how interested they were in each lesson;
- how many contributions they made in the lesson;
- the quality of their written work;
- the extent to which they appeared to understand the purpose of the tasks they were engaged in;
- how they responded when they encountered difficulties with tasks assigned to them;
- to what extent pupils were able to work things out for themselves.

What do your notes tell you about differentiation? Try and meet with the school's SENCO to discuss the SEN policy in the school.

Task 7.6 Building up a
repertoire of approaches to
teaching pupils with SEN

During your school experience, if possible, observe a number of lessons of mixed-ability classes and observe the strategies the classroom teacher uses in working with pupils who have the following learning difficulties:

poor organisational skills;
lack of confidence;
poor presentation;
poor language skills;
isolation from other pupils;
poor writing skills;
lack of interest;
short concentration span;
physical impairments;
weak general knowledge, reluctance to contribute orally.

Discuss with your tutor the approaches which can be used to help pupils through their learning difficulties. You may find the booklet by the Association of Teachers and Lecturers recommended in the further reading section of this chapter useful.

Read John Hull's article in *Teaching History* entitled 'Practical points on teaching history to less able secondary pupils' (October 1980). You will see that he lists a number of examples of how to exercise historical skills which include:

- analysis;
- vocabulary acquisition;
- synthesis;
- inference;
- comprehension;
- memorisation;
- sequencing.

Choose one of these skills and design a lesson plan and worksheet for a year 8 which incorporates one of these skills as its aim.

The use of visual resouces

Many pupils learn well when they can visualise the concepts they are learning about, or when they are enabled to present their ideas in a visual format. Lesson planning designed to include pupils with SEN, as well as English as an Additional Language may be focused on pictorial resources. See Stephen (2006) for ideas on how to use a picture as a starter. Luff and Harris (2004: 61) also included some practical ideas for use with visual learners. Unwin (1981) explained how great depth of understanding can be teased out of a visual source. Similarly, maps can be used as pictorial sources. Pupils could be given a number of maps of the local area at different dates, and could be asked to highlight the differences, before finding out how and why the area changed. Haward's (2005) *Seeing History: Visual Learning Strategies and Resources* is another valuable resource.

Getting pupils to devise board games can be a very popular activity. Some examples could be a snakes and ladders game depicting the ups and downs of medieval town life, or those facing a factory worker during the industrial revolution. The board could include pictures or symbols from the time in question, to encourage use of knowledge and creative skills. The level of difficulty in devising a board game can be reduced by giving pupils ideas to incorporate.

Many learners benefit from the use of living graphs, charts, timelines, diagrams, mind or concept maps to display information rather than lengthy, written notes (see Ian Dawson's 'Thinking History' website for a wide range of examples of these approaches: www.thinkinghistory.org.uk). A graph could be used, for example, to show changing attitudes in the First World War where date is plotted against morale (from positive to negative). Pupils add labels to show why attitudes changed, instead of writing in paragraphs. Getting pupils to transfer information from written form to a visual format can be modelled by the teacher as a form of support and guidance for pupils. Farmer and Knight (1995) suggest a variety of activities for working on diagrams, including completions of a diagram such as a pyramid showing the feudal system, whereby the task can be made easier by giving some of the answers or giving a list of points from which to choose, or correcting mistakes. They also suggest the drawing of strip cartoons to emphasise the key features of a story. To save time, these could be sequenced rather then drawn out. Cartoon strips can also be used to represent a specific point of view within a story.

The process and benefits of concept mapping are explained in an article by Jamet van Drie and Carla van Boxtel (2003). A mind map is a complex tool to summarise information and categorise into big points and little points. Mind maps lend themselves well to differentiation by outcome, since they can display any amount of information and understanding of links between ideas. Some explanation of the process of classification is beneficial to pupils before the technique is learnt. They could recall familiar examples of classification, such as different aisles in a supermarket, then discuss why it is useful to classify information about history.

Use of active techniques that appeal to the kinaesthetic learner

Many pupils with SEN prefer to learn by more practical methods. These could include activities such as card sorts and roleplays. Bear in mind that when a card sort is complete, the findings may not have to be written up. Cutting and pasting could be a time-saving alternative. A variation of card sorts is a pairs game, which involves pairing cards from a selection, explaining why they go together. Other approaches could be placing labels on a diagram or picture, putting together the pieces of a jigsaw, or human timelines, where individual pupils have large cards showing events and have to physically put themselves into the correct order. Luff and Harris (1994) refer to 'human continuums', which might involve 'best to worst' in the case of monarchs, or arranging ideas on a political spectrum. They further suggest that pupils organise themselves in a line of social order. This can similarly be done with sentences showing diverse views about a topic, whereby pupils have to group themselves according to the type of view. Another possible starter activity is 'Find the source', whereby pupils have to find sources which have been placed around the classroom in order to complete a chart containing a clue about each source. This encourages close study of sources, as well as immediate participation in the lesson. It can be a hook into complex analysis to be developed later in the lesson. Further information about roleplays can be found at the website (www.uea.ac.uk/~m242/historypgce), on the 'Thinking History' website (www.thinkinghistory.com), and in Ian Luff's articles on roleplay in *Teaching History* (Luff, 1999, 2001).

Activities for auditory learners

Some pupils with SEN will respond better to auditory stimuli than to written or visual ones. To maximise their learning, consider the use of oral sources other than your own voice, including music or recordings of the spoken word, commonly found on CD-ROMs.

Alternatively, pupils can present their ideas orally, either through making casette or video recordings. Group work can be presented orally, and teacher assessment made. Where a teaching assistant is present, part of his or her role may be to assist in recoding the pupils' ideas. A further idea is the talking essay, a class effort whereby different groups take on different paragraphs of the essay, using 'talking frames' to guide them. They could be given prompts such as 'Our change was significant because . . .'. Such group talk can also be fostered by giving groups a different extract from a story, or alternatively a picture, and asking them to sequence them as a class. This involves high levels of communication, especially when done to a strict time limit.

Working with a teaching assistant

The role of the teaching assistant can be to assist in planning and differentiating materials as well as to encourage concentration and to reinforce aspects of learning for individual pupils, praising achievement. They can help with assessment of a pupil's understanding, possibly by use of a tape recorder. The teaching assistant should be aware of the learning objectives, whilst the class teacher should be aware of the needs of the pupils requiring support and of the IEP. You need to discuss who is going to be supported and how. Adversely, too much one on one support could have a detrimental effect, either on the pupil's ability to work independently or on their self image. It is often most effective for a teaching assistant to work with a group of pupils, or to circulate and work with different individuals. This also encourages other pupils to respond well to both adults in the room. If the pupils supported have difficulties, do not assume that it is solely the job of the learning assistant to deal with them. It is important for both adults to be involved. Nor should you assume that because a teaching assistant is present, the targeted pupils will automatically be able to follow the usual curriculum.

MEETING THE NEEDS OF PUPILS WHO SPEAK ENGLISH AS AN ADDITIONAL LANGUAGE

Teaching pupils who speak English as an additional language (EAL) is a growing challenge in secondary schools across the country. EAL is not the same as SEN, although the barriers to learning for pupils with EAL may not derive solely from language issues. As Hart (1996) explains, the development of language support for children with EAL has followed a pattern broadly similar to that for children with SEN, with many pupils being withdrawn from mainstream classes for specialist language help until the later 1980s following the Swann Report (DES, 1985). There was a move towards 'immersion' and integration in the 1990s.

SOME APPROACHES TO TEACHING PUPILS WITH EAL

Identifying need

The school should hold data on pupils' national and linguistic background. It may be harder to find out about the pupil's family circumstances, previous schooling and level of ability. Where possible, talk to the pupils themselves.

The situation that you encounter in different schools varies. Each LEA has an Ethnic Minority Achievement Service (EMA). EMA will allocate staff to schools where there is the greatest perceived need. These specialist staff usually run some withdrawal groups for beginners in English, as well as supporting lessons. Where provision is streched, history lessons may not be targeted for support and you may find pupils with very little English arriving in your lessons part way through a term. EMA staff will be able to offer advice, and may assist in preparing resources. In addition, you may teach pupils at various stages of English language acquisition. Bilingual learners who have always lived in Britain, or have been through a British primary school, should be competent in the use of oral English, and often in written English. However, many who have a strong command of 'playground English' may struggle with the language of learning. The role of the history teacher in an inclusive classroom is to promote learning of history with a focus on the language necessary to understand the content and complete the tasks. Hounslow Language Support services offer an excellent history specific booklet on supporting EAL pupils in history (http://www.hvec.org.uk/HvecMain/index.asp).

Some pupils, including asylum seekers, may be affected by traumatic experiences. Your priority here may be to make them feel welcome, and not excluded from the proceedings. A special effort to greet them, learn their name or find a task for them to do, may enhance their motivation, as their language skills improve. Even things like remembering to make 'friendly' eye contact at intervals can help pupils to feel accepted and welcome in your classroom.

The learning environment

Your overall approach, which must plan for inclusion, is critical. Drawing pupils into your lesson can be achieved by the ideas outlined above under visual literacy, and careful thought about the use of classroom display and supplementary materials for EAL learners (see Stephen, 2006 and Parr, 1996 for further development of these points).

Pupils who are in the very early stages of English language acquistion find it hard to follow much of a history lesson. It is especially difficult in classes where there are only one or two learners with EAL, and it may be some time before they have the confidence to speak in class. Where pupils find themselves in a class with others who share their first language, it is easier to integrate, but arguably harder to make the shift to use of English for communication. The challenge for the teacher is to ease the process by giving as many cues as possible. These could involve gestures to reinforce what is being said, and use of pictures to help illustrate key points in a talk. For pupils whose first language employs a different script, there is a greater need than usual for clear writing on the board. Try to watch these pupils to see how much they appear to understand. Give regular words of encouragement.

For beginners in English, it is worthwhile to develop separate work, such as labelling pictures, colouring certain parts of a diagram in a specified colour, matching words and meanings, writing out dates in order, completing sentences based on a short text or even copying in order to engage pupils in some way in your topic.

Interpreters and support teachers

Various types of support may be available in the classroom, including

- support from an EMA-funded specialist teacher;
- support from an EMA-funded classroom assistant in the lesson;
- support from someone who speaks the pupil's home language in the lesson;
- support from teacher/adviser with planning and resources outside the lesson.

The OFSTED report 'Managing support for the attainment of pupils from ethnic minority groups' (OFSTED, 2001) stresses the need when planning jointly with EMA staff, to ensure that the focus is on the content of the lesson, with appropriate cognitive challenge, but with a parallel focus on the language necessary to complete the task. Useful guidance on the role of a support teacher can also be found in an article by Malaya (1996).

Use of first language in the classroom

Encouraging use of the first language values the individual and his or her culture. Furthermore, pupils who can transfer their understanding from the spoken to the written word, or from one language to another, show understanding rather than rote learning. Some teachers are wary that use of first language may lead to exclusion of others or to disputes about what is being said. It also limits the teacher's control. Such concerns can only be allayed by setting specific boundaries. Many teachers prefer the use of English unless there is an express suggestion otherwise and for a clearly defined purpose.

Exploratory dialogue in the pupils' first language can take place within a group, and should then be fed back to the class through a pupil interpreter. It is most effective given the presence of another adult in the room. According to the paper 'Access and Engagement in History' (DfES, 2002), pupils should be encouraged to use their first language in lessons when:

- the cognitive challenge is likely to be high;
- they are still developing proficiency in English;
- oral rehearsal helps reflection, for example, before responding to a text, artefact or historical source.

It may not, however, be appropriate for pupils to use their first language when:

- they need to practise the target language to improve fluency;
- they need oral rehearsal in the target language so that they are prepared for writing tasks;
- they need to take risks in their spoken English in order to build confidence.

Bilingual dictionaries can help with transfer of language, although difficulties arise where there is more than one meaning or context for a given word. Dictionaries are best used with guidance. Various online translation services are now available, sometimes free of charge. These may be quite useful for translating particular words, but less so for translating longer passages. If there are interpreters working at the school, it is helpful to ask them to write out key words in both languages. Older pupils could also help with this. The lists could then be stuck on classroom walls or pasted into books. Pupils with EAL could be given lists of key words, with their meanings, for each topic, and then asked to write out the word in their first language. The learning of words could be set as homework.

Supporting oral work

Oral work is central to an inclusive classroom. Some suggestions as to its successful practice follow:

- In a question and answer session, inform your pupils with EAL in advance of the question to be posed to them, to allow them to rehearse an answer.
- Wait more than 15 seconds for a pupil with EAL to answer your question.
- Clarify the purpose of listening tasks and talk and use listening or talking frames, as you would a writing frame (see Counsell, 1997).
- Organise groups so that pupils with EAL hear a positive English language model.
- Use written prompt cards such as 'The evidence tells us that . . .' or 'The most likely explanation is . . .' to start sentences.
- Provide key words and meanings in advance.
- Consider the place of oral presentations as a form of assessment.

Supporting reading and writing

Many of the same techniques which apply to pupils with SEN can be applied here, such as the use of Directed Activities Related to Texts (DARTs) – see Capel *et al.*, 2005: 265–9 for further explanation of this term – modelling reading and writing, paragraph headings for text or writing, structured questions and writing frames. Depending on your lesson objectives, it will be possible at times to reduce the amount of written work required using methods outlined earlier in the chapter.

The DfES publication, 'Access and Engagement in History' (2002) points out specific confusions for pupils with EAL over the following:

- cultural references – for example, references to common aspects of life in Britain;
- the use of written sources from periods in the past where the use of English is different from the way the language is used today;
- reference in text, where meaning is carried across sentences and paragraphs through reference (to previously stated nouns) using pronouns ('it', 'they', 'he', 'she');
- imagery – metaphors, similes, idiomatic phrases;
- use of the passive voice;
- contextual definitions of words that can have different meanings from those encountered elsewhere, such as *depression*;
- subject-specific vocabulary.

The report also states that 'Pupils learning EAL may show patterns of error when writing in English in their history lessons which are related to their experience of the structures of their first language.' It suggests diagnostic marking to ascertain the most commonly made errors. These can indicate writing targets for individuals or groups of pupils.

Task 7.7 Planning a lesson for pupils with EAL

Plan a lesson using a 10 minute video extract available in the department where you are working. Watch the extract and note down any words that will need to be explained in advance. Devise a listening frame to encourage active listening. Then devise a group task exploring the new learning. This may involve picking out and weighing up different causes or interpretations of events, or explaining the achievements of an individual. Then write down some questions to be used as a plenary. Which questions would you direct to pupils with EAL?

MEETING THE NEEDS OF ABLE PUPILS IN THE HISTORY CLASSROOM

QCA guidance identifies talented learners as those who have abilities in practical subjects, and gifted learners as those with abilities in academic subjects, including history (QCA, 2001–2). All schools are required to keep lists, by subject, of pupils who are gifted and/or talented. The QCA suggestion is that the list contain pupils working at the top 5–10 per cent of the school's cohort, regardless of the school's overall ability levels. Whilst the school should adopt an overall approach to working with these pupils, it is the responsibility of the classroom teacher to ensure that suitable learning challenges are set and learning needs are met. This is not always easy for student teachers, for whom factors such as classroom management can seem a more pressing priority. However, if their needs are not met, able pupils can quickly lose motivation and become distracted or disruptive.

Your first task, as a student teacher, is to identify your very able pupils. The conclusions of the NAGTY History Think Tank (2005) identifed 21 characteristics of high achievement in history. These included an appreciation of the intrinsic value of historical learning and an enjoyment of the process, an unwillingness to be easily satisfied, a hunger for knowledge of the past, an ability to read historical materials actively and critically, as well as more sophisticated analytical powers.

As you begin teaching your own classes the class teacher should be able to offer information on gifted pupils. Some rapidly identify themselves in discussion, whilst others prefer to keep their abilities well hidden. Early assessment of written work is helpful, but you may be surprised to find that some articulate pupils with excellent powers of reasoning do not express themselves so fluently in writing. Some schools may still identify such pupils as gifted. Barriers to writing, which may be connected with cultural background, can be alleviated by some techniques described elsewhere in this chapter.

Task 7.8 Identifying able pupils in the history classroom

With the permission of your tutor, when you have become reasonably familiar with one of your teaching groups, make a conscious attempt to identify any pupils who you feel may be particularly able in history, by examining their work and talking to them. What is it about their work and their oral responses which indicates exceptional ability? Look out for pupils who may appear very able because of motivation and workrate, but may fall behind their gifted peers when it comes to work requiring critical thinking. Consider the following characteristics, and see if your observations reveal any others:

- powers of concentration;
- critical judgement and evaluation of evidence;
- ability to argue logically;
- attention to detail;
- easy concept formation;
- originality and imagination;
- fluency and sophistication of extended writing.

There are a number of strategies which can be employed to assist the history teacher with more able pupils. Extension or enrichment work can be beneficial, particularly in a mixed ability context. Worksheets could include extension tasks involving higher order thinking, and possibly extra research. A selection of tasks could also be ready for pupils who finish work early or do not need to spend time on some of the less demanding activities you have set for the class. Many history teachers keep an 'archive' of newspaper and journal articles on historical topics which can be given as extension work or home-work (see Chapter 8). Access to library and web resources is essential. Any reading of historical matter can help to extend vocabulary, and sense of period or place as well as enhancing direct subject knowledge. In the same way that publishers have attempted to provide materials for less able pupils, the 'Fast track' series attempts to provide extension tasks for able pupils (Aylett, 1993).

Some able pupils, however, may resent being asked to do separate work. Your planning for their needs should not be simply bolted onto your main lesson plan. Class activities which involve challenging thinking, often through oral work, group work, research and independent enquiry can prove very successful for all pupils, including the most able. Some suggestions follow. The NAGTY report (2005) is worth consulting for detail on extending pupils' thinking about sources and interpretations of history.

Activity	Examples	Skills employed	Organisation
Puzzles.	Quiz questions Identifying the author or the source of certain words, e.g. 'We're here because we're here because . . .' (sung by soldiers in the First World War). Identify the lesson's learning objectives retrospectively. Two pupils hold a conversation in role before their classmates, whose task is to work out who they are.	Lateral thinking, deduction and inference or research. Revising prior learning.	Set on notice board each week. Prizes for strong answers. See Fisher (2002) for details about using mysteries as full lessons. Plenary targeting very able pupils.
Word games.	Devising mnemonics Finding shorter words within longer ones. Odd one out games. Classify words from a long list, which might straddle several historical topics.	Exploring vocabulary and historical ideas. Discussing and weighing up alternative answers, justifying choices.	Useful lesson starters.
Chronology exercises.	Deduce order of key events without being given dates.	Powers of reasoning. Collaborative talk.	Can be done in groups or as a whole class exercise where each pupil receives a card with one event written onto it.
Consider events from different perspectives.	Write a script for persuasive speeches by two rivals. Produce an information leaflet about First World War trench life, first from a soldier's point of view, second from the government's point of view. Show film footage of an event, with sound turned off, and ask pupils to write their own commentary, from two different viewpoints. Footage from the Blitz could be used as German propaganda or as a British government information film.	Understanding of diverse views and creative thinking.	These tasks could be powerful learning tools for all pupils, although the less able may need more scaffolding of their responses. Examine speeches from a different time period as a model. Give examples of ironic writing as a model.
Write an obituary for a chosen individual (see Senior and Whybra, 2005).		Summary based on selection of significant points.	Specify number of words and a particular style, e.g. serious, humorous or provocative, based on a model piece from a newspaper.

Think up pithy headings for pieces of film, or for extracts from a book.		Extended reading and summary.	
Directed empathy exercises.	Decisions facing Charles I or his opponents in the 1630s. Setting up a factory in the 1700s. Discussions preceeding the Treaty of Versailles. Responses to Hitler's foreign policy in the 1930s.	Understanding of contemporary knowledge and constraints. Weighing up alternative solutions. Justifying choices.	Many commercial decision making exercises have been produced. Clear roles should be ascribed and a clear context outlined, possibly to be explained by your gifted pupils. Pupils can either choose from a range of possible decisions, or devise their own. Reasons for their choices must be clearly explained. Debriefing is crucial. Very able pupils should be asked to analyse factors that made their task difficult, and to explain the methods of thought that helped them. This will help them to transfer learning across topics and curriculum areas.
Historical debate, either in role or set in the present.	Courtroom drama, for example Mary Queen of Scots or Charles I. Responsibility for the outbreak of war. Government censorship during wartime or Truman's decision to drop the atomic bomb. Relative significance of different factors in the Industrial Revolution.	Reasoning, listening and persuasion. Questioning different moral positions.	A whole lesson could be set aside with a limited time given to prepare arguments based on prior learning. Provide strict guidelines on who speaks, preferably thought up by the pupils themselves.
Open-ended and research based questions.	This might lend itself well to the Twentieth Century Programme of Study, as pupils tend to have their own areas of interest and some background knowledge about this. A project could also be linked to work on their own heritage or family histories.	Research. Time management. Justifying choices.	Works well with a top set. Pupils could pick their own topics, and set their own questions within certain parameters. They could select their own sources of information and to justify their choice. Pupils could be given a specific task to do each week or fortnight, and monitor each other's progress.

Activity	Examples	Skills employed	Organisation
Additional opportunities such as historical visits, guest speakers, or web debates (see *Teaching History* 124, 2006 for ideas).	Older members of the community or local academics could be invited.	Enriching learning experiences. Considering the importance of history in the world around us.	
Redesigning public architecture (see Nagty report 2005) or revising street names.	Many public buildings in Liverpool show connections with the Transatlantic slave trade.	Local knowledge. Links with tourism industry.	Provide or visit examples. Consult maps for street names and consider their derivation.

Some questions permit all pupils to offer suggestions, but ones which operate at very differing intellectual levels of response. Some of these questions may be appropriate for the whole class, others might be better suited to extension activities for the able.

- In 1851, Britain was arguably the greatest power in the world. Many people feel that this is no longer the case. How do we measure the 'greatness' of nations, and why do you think that Britain is less 'great' than she was in 1851? (For those who feel that the subject of British decline is not an appropriate topic for school history, the question might allow for a discussion of whether Great Britain has declined or not. One interesting statistic is that in 1904, Britain won over 50 gold medals in the Olympic Games, in 1996 she won only one. What reasons might pupils suggest for this change?)
- How was it that William the Conqueror's army of no more than 20,000 men managed to conquer a country with a population of over 1 million?
- In what ways and to what extent was life in England different in 1485 from 1065?
- William the Conqueror, Richard II and Henry VIII all had to put down revolts against their government. Which of them faced greater difficulties in crushing the revolts and why? Would it be easier or harder to put down revolts today? Give reasons for your answer.
- Why did William the Conqueror succeed where Philip II (1588), Napoleon (1805) and Hitler (1940) failed?
- Why did people stop building castles?
- Was King John a good or a bad king? What are the criteria for good government today? What does the ordinary person want from the government? How much do the answers to the above questions apply to the medieval period?
- What happened to poor and/or old people in (a) Elizabethan Times, (b) in the years before and after 1834, (c) in 1908–14, (d) after 1945? What was the attitude and/or policy of the government with regard to poor and/or old people at these times?

Figure 7.2 Questions for able pupils

SUMMARY AND KEY POINTS

We have seen that ultimately, the success of the inclusive classroom rests upon the teacher's efforts to make the curriculum accessible to all pupils. History is taught in such a way that all pupils, including those with SEN, want to learn. This is achieved partly by the provision of appropriate materials, partly by the careful planning of teaching methods and delivery of your lessons. It is an ongoing professional process, which needs to be adapted to individual learners. Support is available in schools from fellow history teachers, the SENCO, and possibly EMA staff. It is important not to adopt a defeatist attitude. History lessons can be made enjoyable, yet challenging. Where pupils are engaged in the work, the experience is more rewarding for the teacher. It is worth adding that inclusion is not *just* a technical issue; the personality, warmth, skills of interaction, and care and concern of the teacher also contribute to pupils' sense of being valued in the classroom.

For further information and resources about aspect of inclusion in the history classroom, including a section on 'Taking equal opportunities seriously', go to the inclusion section of the website: www.uea.ac.uk/~m242/historypgce/welcome.htm.

REFERENCES

Ajegbo, K. (2007) *Diversity and Citizenship (The Ajegbo Report)*, London: DfES.

Association for Teachers and Lecturers (1994) *Practical Information and Ideas on Teaching Pupils with Special Educational Needs in Mainstream Schools and Colleges*, London: ATL.

Aylett, J. (1993) *History Fast Track, 1750–1900*, Fast Track Series, London: Hodder and Stoughton.

Bradshaw, M. (2006) 'Creating controversy in the classroom: making progress with historical significance', *Teaching History*, No. 125: 18–25.

Burton, D. (2005) 'Ways pupils learn', in S. Capel, M. Leask and T. Turner, *Learning to Teach in Secondary School: A Companion to School Experience*, 4th edition, Oxon: RoutledgeFalmer: 244–57.

Byers, R. and Rose, R. (1996) *Planning the Curriculum for Pupils with SEN: A Practical Guide*, London: David Fulton.

Buxton, S. (1991) *The Action History* series of textbooks, London: Hodder & Stoughton, (e.g. *Medieval Times*, 1991).

Capel, S., Leask, M. and Turner, T. (eds) (2005) *Learning to Teach in the Secondary School: A Companion to School Experience*, Oxon: Routledge.

Counsell, C. (1997) *Analytical and Discursive Writing at Key Stage 3*, London: Historical Association.

Cunnah, W. (2000) 'History teaching, literacy and special educational needs', in J. Arthur and R. Phillips (eds), *Issues in History Teaching*, London: Routledge: 113–24.

DES (1985) *Education for All (The Swann Report)*, London: DES.

DfE (1994) *The Code of Practice and the Identification and Assessment of Special Educational Needs*, London: HMSO.

DfEE/QCA (1999) *History: The National Curriculum for England*, London: DfEE/QCA.

DfEE (2000) *Holocaust Memorial Day Education Pack*, P47/42392/1100/54 ref. HMEP, London: DfEE.

DfES (2001a) 'Special educational needs: code of practice', London: DfES. Online at www.teachernet.gov.uk/_doc/3724/SENCodeOfPractice.pdf. Accessed 13 October 2007.

DfES (2001b) *Special Educational Needs and Disability Act*, London: DfES.

DfES (2002) *Access and Engagement in History*, London: DfES.

DfES (2004) *The Children Act*, London: DfES.

DfES (2007) *Standards for Qualified Teacher Status*, London: DfES.

Diversity and Inclusion Team (2006) *Hidden History Express*, Manchester: Manchester LEA.

Farmer, A. and Knight, P. (1995) *Active History in Key Stages 3 and 4*, London: David Fulton.

Fisher, P. with Wilkinson, I. and Leat, D. (2002) *Thinking through History*, Cambridge: Chris Kington.

Frederickson, N. and Cline, T. (2002) *Special Educational Needs, Inclusion and Diversity*, Buckingham: Open University Press.

Frow, M. (1997) *Roots of the Future: Ethnic Diversity in the Making of Britain*, London: Commission for Racial Equality.

Fullan, M. (1999) *Change Forces: The Sequel*, Lewes: Falmer Press.

Gilborn, G. (2000) *Educational Inequality: Mapping Race, Class and Gender. A Synthesis of Research*, London: OFSTED.

Grosvenor, I. (2000) 'History for the nation: multiculturalism and the teaching of history', in J. Arthur and R. Phillips (eds), *Issues in History Teaching*, London: Routledge: 148–58.

Harris, R. 'Does differentation have to mean different?' *Teaching History*, No. 118: 5–13.

Hart, S. (ed.) (1996) *Differentiation and the Secondary Curriulum: Debates and Dilemmas*, London: Routledge.

Haward, T. (2005) *Seeing History: Visual Learning Strategies and Resources for Key Stage 3*, Stafford: Network Educational Press.

Husbands, C., Kitson, A. and Pendry, A (2003) *Understanding History Teaching*, Maidenhead: Open University Press.

Imperial War Museum packs – 'The empire needs men', 'Together', London: Imperial War Museum.

Kennedy, P. (1994) *The Making of the United Kingdom*, Foundation History Series, Oxford: Heinemann.

Lomas, T. (2005) 'New ideas in develping pupils' learning in key stage 3 and 4 history', address to SHP Conference, Leeds.

Lowe, W. (2005) 'Meeting individual differences: pupil grouping, progression and differentiation', in S. Capel, M. Leask and T. Turner (eds), *Learning to Teach in Secondary School: A Companion to School Experience*, 4th edition, Oxon: RoutledgeFalmer: 153–67.

Luff, I. (1999) 'I've been to the Reichstage: rethinking roleplay', *Teaching History*, No. 100: 8–17.

Luff. I. (2001) 'Beyond I speak, you listen boy! Exploring diversity of attitudes and experiences through speaking and listening', *Teaching History*, No. 105: 10–18.

Luff, I. and Harris, R. (2004) *Meeting SEN in the Curriculum: History*, London: David Fulton.

Lyndon, D. 'Integrating black British history into the curriculum', *Teaching History* No. 122: 37–42. (See also Lyndon's website: www.blackhistory4schools.com.)

Malaya, J. (1996) 'The case of blilingual learners', in S. Hart (ed.), *Differentiation and the Secondary Curriulum: Debates and Dilemmas*, London: Routledge.

NAGTY History Think Tank (2005) 'Supporting high achievement in history: conclusions of the NAGTY history think tank'. Online at: http://www.historyyearbookonline.co.uk/articles/nagty.shtml. Accessed 13 October 2007.

OFSTED (2001) *Managing Support for the Attainment of Pupils from Ethnic Minority Groups*, London, OFSTED.

OFSTED (2004) *Special Educational Needs and Disability: Towards Inclusive Schools*, 2004, ref HMI 2206, London: OFSTED.

Parr, N. (1996) 'I belong here – they speak my kind of language', in S. Hart (ed.), *Differentiation and the Secondary Curriculum: Debates and Dilemmas*, London: Routledge.

Peacey, N. (2005) 'Introduction to inclusion, special educational needs and disability', in S. Capel, M. Leask and T. Turner (eds), *Learning to Teach in Secondary School: A Companion to School Experience*, 4th edition, Oxon: RoutledgeFalmer: 227–42.

Phillips, R. (2001) 'Making history curious: using initial stimulus material to promote enquiry, thinking and literacy', *Teaching History*, No. 105: 19–25.

QCA (2001–2) 'Guidance on Teaching the Gifted and Talented'. Online at www.nc.uk.net/gt/general/index.htm. Accessed 13 October 2007.

QCA (2001a) 'Planning, teaching and assessing the curricuum for pupils with learning difficulties: history'. Online at www.nc.uk.net/ld/Hi_content.html. Accessed 13 October 2007.

QCA (2001b) 'Respect for all'. Online at: http://www.qca.org.uk/qca_6753.aspx. Accessed 13 October 2007.

QCA (2007) 'History: programme of study, key stage 3', London: QCA, available online at: http://curriculum.qca.org.uk/subjects/history/, accessed 13 October 2007.

Robson, W. (1993) *Britain 1750–1900*, Access to History Series, Oxford: Oxford University Press.

Senior, J. and Whybra, J. (2005) *Enrichment Activities for Gifted Children*, Salisbury: Optimus.

Shephard, C. and Brown, B (1994) *Britain 1750–1900*, Special Needs Support Materials, London: John Murray.

Stephen, A. (2006) 'Ensuring inclusion in the classroom', in M. Hunt (ed.), *A Practical Guide to Teaching History in the Secondary School*, Oxon: RoutledgeFalmer: 70–80.

Sweerts, E. and Grice, J. (2002) 'Hitting the right note: how useful is the music of African–Americans to historians?', *Teaching History*, No. 108: 36–41.

Teaching History (2006) *Teaching the Most Able*, No. 124.

Teare, B. (2006) *Problem-Solving and Thinking Skills: Resources for Able and Talented Children*, London: Network Continuum Education.

Unwin, R (1981) *The Visual Dimension in the Study and Teaching of History*, Historical Association pamphlet no. 49, London: Historical Association.

Van Drie, J. and van Boxtel, C. (2003) 'Developing conceptual understanding through talk and mapping', *Teaching History*, No. 110: 27–31.

Warnock, M. (1978) *The Warnock Report: Special Educational Needs*, London: HMSO.

8 The use of new technology in the history classroom

A key question: to what extent are you able to make full use of the potential of new technology for improving teaching and learning in history?

Figure 8.1 Wired up?

INTRODUCTION

What do the Standards for Qualified Teacher Status (TDA, 2007) have to say about the use of ICT in subject teaching? It is important to be aware of the implications of the standards relating to ICT from the start of the course. By the end of the course you have got to be proficient in all of them, whether you are passionately enthusiastic or uncertain, sceptical and daunted by the prospect of using ICT in your teaching. Being able to use new technology to improve teaching and learning in your subject is not an optional extra. Whereas a decade ago, there were many history teachers who were profoundly sceptical about the use of ICT in the history classroom, and some who argued that it was possible to be a perfectly effective history teacher without using ICT (see, for instance, Dickinson, 1998; Easdown, 2000), there are now few history teachers who believe that you can eschew the use of new technology without in some ways limiting the learning opportunities of your pupils (Haydn, 2004). Given that history is now seen by some as being about 'learning to manage complex subjects and manipulate data' (Rollason, 1998), it would be surprising if ICT was not capable of contributing to teaching and learning in history.

Being proficient and imaginative in terms of integrating the use of ICT into your teaching is also helpful in terms of securing employment at the end of your course of education. One survey (Haydn, 2004), found that well over half of the applicants for history posts were asked about their proficiency in ICT, and in some cases, those inter-viewing expressed the hope that the NQT appointed would be able to play a prominent part or even take the lead in developing the use of ICT in the history department. But becoming proficient in ICT is about more than just helping you to secure a teaching job; if you are accomplished in this area it can make it much easier to teach history in a way that is varied, powerful and interesting for pupils. If you are a history teacher, new technology is your friend and ally.

All history teachers are somewhere on the continuum below. Very few of them are at either extreme of the continuum. Your overarching objective in this area of competence should be to be as far as possible towards the right hand end of the continuum as possible by the start of your NQT year.

Teacher is unaware of, or unable to use ICT to improve the quality of teaching and learning in history.

Teacher is able to fully exploit the potential of ICT for improving the quality of teaching and learning in history.

Figure 8.2 Developing competence in ICT: a continuum

OBJECTIVES

By the end of this chapter you should be able to:

- appreciate the importance of ICT competence for your professional development;
- state what is required in terms of the standards for QTS in the area of ICT;
- identify the range and breadth of new technology applications which might be relevant to the history classroom;
- understand the various aspects of developing competence in ICT, particularly the difference between personal proficiency and classroom experience;
- understand that with many aspects of new technology, there is a continuum in terms of the degree of relaxed assurance and effectiveness with which you are able to use new technology to enhance the quality of teaching and learning in the classroom;
- list some ideas about how ICT can be used in the history classroom.

SOME THINGS TO KEEP IN MIND

The use of ICT in history teaching poses difficult questions for history teachers and student teachers. Although politicians of all parties have waxed lyrical about the transformative potential of ICT, and have tended to see it as an unproblematic educational miracle, official reports and surveys present an ambivalent picture about the use of ICT in the history classroom. A major OFSTED survey of the use of ICT in secondary schools described progress as very uneven, with 'slow growth, a few green shoots'. The survey revealed that history lessons which incorporated the use of ICT were on average *less satisfactory* than lessons where ICT was not used (Harrison, 2003). A DfEE survey of the use of ICT found that in spite of massive spending on computers, approximately 60 per cent of teachers made little or no use of computers in their classroom teaching (ImpaCT 2, 2002). So – sometimes the technology can get in the way of the learning or be ineffective – it doesn't necessarily make your lessons better. Also, there are difficult choices to make in terms of what facets of ICT to explore in your teaching. There are now dozens of avenues to explore in terms of finding out about, and using new technology in your teaching, which ones should you prioritise? You have to think what to do with all this stuff, how to make intelligent use of it. You will have read about (and perhaps already been involved in) a world of Web 2.0, blogs, wikis, podcasts and so on. But how are you going to adapt them to improve your lessons? There are a lot of very boring podcasts out there whose best use might be as punishments for pupils who misbehave, and the number of 'dead' blogs, rotting and abandoned in cyberspace was recently estimated at 200 million ('Why are so many people blogging off?', *Guardian*, 27 March 2007). Presentation software like PowerPoint does not have the same effect on learners as it did when it was first used. Is there anyone reading this who has not at one point or another been severely bored by a PowerPoint presentation (or heard the phrase 'death by PowerPoint')? There is no necessary correlation between the sophistication of the technology, and the degree to which it improves teaching and learning. Often very simple 'lo-tec' applications can be very effective and powerful. The bottom line is the extent to which you are able to *apply* new technology to improve pupils' learning. It is not primarily a question of the extent to which you are technologically 'gifted' when you start the course, it is about how good a learner you are. It is an area where some student teachers make much more progress than others, and you need to be proactive, display initiative, and put aside some dedicated time to this agenda rather than just 'waiting for the answer lady to come round'.

THE STANDARDS FOR QTS RELATING TO ICT

Some of the Standards for QTS (TDA, 2007) relate directly to ICT, others less directly. In terms of the standards relating directly to ICT, you must:

- Have passed the professional skills test in ICT (Q16).
- Know how to use skills in ICT to support your teaching and wider professional activity (Q17).
- Design opportunities for learners to develop their ICT skills (Q23).
- Use a range of teaching strategies and resources, including e-learning (Q25a).

Other standards have a less direct bearing on your progress in exploring the use of new technology to improve your teaching: it is part of reflecting on and improving your practice and taking responsibility for identifying and meeting your developing professional needs (Q7) and identifying priorities for your early professional development in the context of induction (Q8). ICT can also play an important role in providing access and challenge for pupils of all abilities and 'personalising' elements of the work they have to do (Q10), and planning worthwhile and engaging homework tasks (Q24). Although less explicit than in earlier versions of the Standards for QTS, ICT can also make it much easier to make progress in the important area of motivating and engaging pupils in learning by providing access to vivid, intriguing and attractive teaching resources.

THE 'C' IN ICT

One of the most far reaching consequences of the information revolution is the exponential increase in the speed and breadth of information dissemination. If there are good ideas about history teaching, it is now much easier to tell history teachers about them. In the UK, at least in education, 'IT' has been replaced by 'ICT' to reflect the importance of communications technology. Communications technology includes the telephone and the fax machine, as well as the internet, with the world wide web and email, electronic conferencing and 'bulletin boards', through intranet systems, and video conferencing. There are now several important 'hubs' (sometimes called 'gateway' sites, or 'portals'), which are essential sources of information for student history teachers. You need to be familiar with these, if you are to keep abreast of recent developments in both history, and ICT. A list of some internet sites which history student teachers have found helpful is provided in Figure 9.1 in Chapter 9. In addition to the major internet sites for teaching history, there are also a number of online forums for history teachers to share their questions, interests and resources. Some student teachers use such forms to develop their capability in ICT; some sites focus on technological issues, others on providing ideas and content for lessons. One further thing you should keep in mind is that web resources and sites are often transient. Sometimes URLs change; content is pruned or sites become defunct. Sometimes you find that they have moved elsewhere. Other times, the resource has disappeared from cyber space altogether. It is worth refining your searching techniques (see, for example, the 'advanced search' facility in Google), but if you find 'gems' on the internet, it is helpful to make your own 'capture' of them before they disappear.

A list of some of the most commonly used sites for history teachers is given in Figure 9.1 in Chapter 9. Here are some other sites which are in one way or another 'forums' for history teachers, and sites which focus on more technical aspects of using ICT in school history:

E-help (www.e-help.eu) A major European project bringing together many of the history teachers who are doing interesting things with ICT in school history. Probably the most helpful link is to the seminars which describe the work that these teachers have been doing: (http://educationforum.ipbhost.com/index.php?showforum=246 or follow the link from the front page of the 'Spartacus' site).

School history forum: www.schoolhistory.co.uk/forum

The Education Forum:
http://educationforum.ipbhost.com/index.php? act=idx

Mr Belshaw: http://teaching.mrbelshaw.co.uk

Ed Podesta's blog: www.podesta.org.uk

Innovative History: www.innovativehistory.net

TES: www.tes.co.uk/section/staffroom

Although you should be alert to the potential of communications technology for augmenting your resources, you should also keep in mind that access to information is the first step in learning, not the final one. You need to think through what you are going to do with the information, how you use it to improve your teaching, and pupils' learning in history. It is very easy to accumulate a bigger and bigger list of websites, CD-ROMs, etc., which you don't actually deploy in your teaching. Some time must be devoted to thinking what to do with all the information, and finding a balance between acquiring it, and deploying it.

WHAT DOES IT MEAN 'TO BE GOOD AT ICT' IN HISTORY TEACHING?

Initial teacher education courses attempt to lay solid foundations to build on. They do not generally produce experts. It is important to be realistic about what can be achieved in initial teacher education, where you have many other areas of competence to develop. (If you are really struggling with class management issues, should you really be trying to learn 'Flash' software?) It is also important to stress that objectives should not be limited to the development of *personal* proficiency in ICT. Research has shown that there is only a limited correlation between personal expertise in ICT and subsequent classroom use (Downes, 1993). Objectives might helpfully be divided into four discrete areas. You have to consider all four areas if you are to be in a position to use ICT effectively in your NQT year.

Personal competence

You should try to develop a reasonable 'base' of personal proficiency in the use of ICT. It may not be possible to develop assured and expert levels of competence in a comprehensive range of applications, but to think about what might constitute a foundation which would give you access to a wide range of eminently usable and realistic opportunities for using ICT in the history classroom in your NQT year.

Awareness of what there is to think about in terms of history and ICT

You should be aware of the breadth of ICT applications and ideas which can be used in the history classroom, even if you do not have time to fully explore the potential of all applications. It is important to keep abreast of new developments and ideas by reading the regular sections on ICT in *Teaching History*, the *TES*, and other relevant journals and websites.

Levels of competence

You must bear in mind that in all facets of competence in ICT, there is a continuum between ignorance and inadequacy on the one hand, and expert levels of proficiency and knowledge on the other. Ideas for progression in competence in some of the domains of ICT are suggested later in the chapter. The important thing is not to see competence as a line at which your development stops once you have achieved basic levels. A clear grasp of levels of expertise to aspire to, and a commitment to getting there are important attributes, even if you do not attain expert levels in the course of your initial teacher education. Often progression is in terms of being able to get to a degree of confidence with the ICT application where the teacher can get *the pupils* using ICT applications constructively and creatively to 'do history', rather than just using ICT themselves.

Classroom use of ICT

Perhaps the most important – and challenging element – is to develop a depth of classroom experience in the use of ICT. No matter how sophisticated your personal levels of expertise in ICT, it is only when you can successfully incorporate that expertise into your classroom teaching that ICT can enhance the learning experiences of pupils. It is only by trying things out in a classroom with real, live pupils that you (eventually) develop a relaxed assurance in the classroom use of ICT. This is in some ways the most problematic of the four areas. History departments vary in the extent to which they have access to state of the art ICT facilities and departmental expertise in ICT, so you need to adopt a flexible and proactive approach, *and use your own initiative* to make progress in the use of ICT in the history classroom. It is partly (and perhaps largely) a question of application and attitude over the course of your education rather than your level of expertise in ICT when you start the course.

Easdown notes the negative preconceptions of some student history teachers in the early stages of their course, including one student who remarked that 'Computers are becoming increasingly important in education, and I'm afraid it's going to get worse' (Easdown, 1997). The process of developing classroom assurance in the use of ICT is in some ways akin to learning to ride a bike or learning to change gear in a car – effortless and enjoyable once proficiency has been acquired, but nerve-racking and requiring a degree of will and determination to persevere in the first stages. What is important here is that a climate of learning is created in which you are not afraid to experiment, to take chances, and even to 'fail' in some lessons, as long as this is not done with cavalier disregard of the needs of the pupils in your care (although reckless 'overdosing' on ICT by student teachers is a comparatively rare phenomenon). Short term agendas of 'That was a reasonable lesson', need to be balanced against longer term consideration of developing a complete range of pedagogical skills and methods, so that you do not arrive at your NQT post having employed cautious and 'survival-oriented' teaching techniques, before going on to inflict a staple diet of worksheets and word searches for the rest of your teaching career. Because of this, it is better to attempt the incorporation of computers into lessons, and risk the possibility of everything not working out perfectly on the first occasion, than not to use computers at all. Given the variables in facilities, expertise, and attitudes to ICT in different schools, departments and university tutors, the extent to which you progress towards expert levels of competence in the use of new technology in the classroom depends to at least some extent on the extent to which you are prepared to try things out and experiment, and use your initiative and make time for developing ICT skills over the course of the year.

> **Task 8.1 Investigating attitudes to ICT**
>
> Talk to the teachers you are working with in school, and to your peers on the course. What are their experiences and views on the potential of ICT for improving teaching and learning in history, and what avenues for exploration and development do they recommend?

DEVELOPMENT OF PRACTICAL EFFECTIVENESS IN THE USE OF ICT

If you are to arrive at your NQT post as a technologically enabled history teacher, you have to get to grips with a wide range of new technology applications. Part (but only part) of this agenda is your own range and depth of expertise in being able to use new technology. The following exercises were designed to get student teachers to think about what there is to think about in terms of the ontology of new technology - exactly what do you have to think about in terms of becoming technologically 'enabled' in ICT in the history classroom?

> **Task 8.2 Which applications are most important to a history teacher? Prioritising your exploration of ICT agendas**
>
> New technology applications offer different advantages and opportunities according to the nature of the subject discipline. For instance, history teachers tend to make more use of the television and DVD recordings than maths teachers. Data logging is invaluable to science teachers, but of no interest or relevance to history teachers.

Look at the following list of new technology applications, and think about whether they are (1) essential, (2) fairly important, (3) of peripheral interest, or (4) irrelevant to the secondary history teacher. Also, what are the time implications of exploring the potential of these applications? Are some going to be easier and quicker to get to grips with than others, what should your priorities be in exploring and developing your proficiency in ICT?

wikis   video camera   mind mapping software   desktop publishing
history websites   image manipulation   use of virtual learning environments
overhead projector   photocopier   word processing exercises   Flash
databases   spreadsheets   presentation software (e.g. PowerPoint)
History CD-ROMs   history teacher forums   podcasts   blogs
web authoring   digital camera   digital video   webquests   scanner

Task 8.3 What is your ICT quotient? Thinking about what it means 'to be good' at ICT in history teaching

Work through the questions and try to give an honest answer as to your current state of competence, according to these criteria. The idea is that when you add up the scores, you get some idea about what there is to think about in terms of history and ICT, and where you are on the continuum between novice and expert levels of competence in various aspects of ICT. It is important to bear in mind that it's not about 'coverage' (acquiring basic proficiency in all applications); the 'bottom line' in terms of new technology is not that you become personally proficient, but that you are able to use new technology to enhance the quality of teaching and learning in your teaching.

1   Computers – range of hardware platforms

I don't know how to use any computer hardware system. **0**
I can only confidently use one computer hardware system. **4**
I am confident using PC and Mac systems. **10**

2   Computers – level of technical capability

None. **0**
Very basic – can just about get round the system but sometimes get stuck. **3**
Quite confident: I know how to do most things (file management, multi-tasking, integrating and transferring bits and pieces from different applications). **7**
All this plus can usually reconfigure and fix the system without having to send for the support person when something won't work. **10**

3   Digital camera

I am aware of what they are. **1**
I can use one. **3**
I can use a digital camera to transfer pictures into other applications. **7**
I use them in my teaching and preparation of lessons, on field trips, etc. **10**

4   Image editing packages

I know what they do. **1**
I can make some sort of picture using them. **3**
I am confident in using most features of art packages. **6**
I can use them and am aware of how they can be used in teaching. **8**
I regularly make use of them in my preparation of resources and teaching. **10**

5   Voice recognition software

I know what it is. **1**
I can just about use it. **3**
I can use it proficiently. **6**
I have used it successfully in my teaching. **10**

6   Word processing

I can't word process. **0**
I can do basic word processing. (moving and adjusting text, saving and printing, etc.). **3**
I am confident and accomplished in word processing and can do most things. **5**
I can use some of the advanced features of word processors. **7**
I can 'find my way' around most word processing packages. **9**
I am aware of the ways in which the word processor can be used by history teachers to help to develop pupils' historical understanding. **12**

7   Data-handling

I don't know what data-handling is. **0**
I know what it is but I don't know how to do it. **2**
I know how to use a data handling package or commercially produced datafile. **5**
I know how to construct my own datafile using a data-handling package. **7**
I know what sort of questions to ask of history datafiles. **9**
I feel confident that I could teach/demonstrate how to construct a datafile to a group of students. **10**
I could do all this using a variety of data-handling packages. **12**
I can do all this and am confident that I could teach pupils how to use a datahandling package. **15**

8   Spreadsheets

I'm not sure what they are and what you can do with them. **0**
I know what they are but don't know how to use a spreadsheet application. **2**
I know the difference between a database and a spreadsheet. **4**
I know how to use a spreadsheet application. **6**
I know how to use spreadsheets for a variety of purposes. **8**
I know how to use a range of spreadsheet applications. **10**
I can use them and know ways in which history teachers can make use of them. **12**

9   Desktop publishing

I'm not sure what this is. **0**
I know what it is but can't use a DTP application. **1**
I have a basic grasp of a DTP application. **5**
I have a fluent grasp of a DTP application. **7**
I know how to use several DTP packages. **10**
I know how to use DTP applications and have used them successfully in a classroom context. **12**

10   CD-ROM

I'm not sure what they are. **0**
I know what CD-ROM means/stands for. **2**
I can use a CD-ROM. **5**
I am confident in the use of a range of CD-ROMs. **8**
I know how to use them and I am aware of a range of activities using CD-ROMs which can be used to enhance learning outcomes in my subject. **12**

11   Authoring and presentation packages (PowerPoint/Inspirations/Photostory, etc.)

I'm not sure what they do. **0**
I know how to find my way around a presentation which has been made. **4**
I can use one of these packages to construct my own multimedia presentation. **7**
I am confident in the use of several of these applications. **10**
I know how to use them and how they could be used effectively to enhance teaching and learning in my subject. **12**

12   The internet

I'm not sure what it is. **0**
I know what it is but have not used it. **2**
I have surfed cyberspace on the world wide web. **4**
I have some idea about where I'm going and how to find my way around cyberspace. **6**
I know how to transfer files to my personal webspace. **8**
I know how to put my own stuff up on the web. **10**
I can use the internet and have several ideas for using it to enhance teaching and learning in history. **15**
I know how to set up a personal or departmental website. **18**
I already have a well designed and educationally useful website. **20**

13   e-mail

I know what it is. **1**
I know how to send and receive simple e-mail messages. **3**
I know how to send and download attachments. **5**
I know how to do nicknames and pass messages on. **7**
I know how to take part in electronic conferencing. **10**
I can use it and know how to set up conferencing activities for pupils. **14**

14   Scanner

I know what it does. **1**
I know how to use one. **3**
I know how to use both flat-bed and hand held versions. **5**
I know how to use scanners and have used them to improve resources for pupils. **8**
I regularly use scanners to improve my lesson resources. **10**

15   Video/DVD recorder

I don't know how to use a video/DVD recorder. **0**
I can use video/DVD recorder to tape and replay TV programmes. **2**
I can use the advance timer on VCR/DVD to tape a TV programme. **4**
I can use the advance timer to tape several TV programmes at a time. **6**
I can do tape to tape editing of video/DVD programmes. **8**
I can use an editing suite to edit and add my own sound track to video/DVD extracts. **10**
I can do all this and have a developing range of video/DVD extracts which I can use to enhance teaching and learning in my subject. **14**

16   Video camera

I don't know how to use a video camera. **0**
I think I know how to use a video camera, might need a quick revision session. **4**
I am confident in the use of the video camera. **7**
I can transfer video camera footage to a computer and save it. **9**
I know ways of using the video camera with pupils to improve the quality of their learning and their enthusiasm for the subject. **12**

17   Film strip/slide/carousel projector

I don't know how to use any of them. **0**
I'm OK on ones that I'm familiar with, but not all models. **3**
I feel confident in using any of this equipment. **5**
I even know which way the slides go without having to do it by trial and error. **7**
I know how to use them and how found ways of using slides to improve some of my lessons. **10**

18   Overhead projector

I don't know how to use an OHP. **0**
I can use one but I'm not sure about how to do all the adjustments, (focusing, etc.). **3**
I am completely confident about all aspects of OHP use. **5**
I even know how to change the bulb if one blows. **7**
I know how to use them and have frequently used them to improve the quality of my presentation of lessons to pupils. **10**

19   Making transparencies for OHP

I don't know how to do this. **0**
I can make them using OHP pens, handwritten. **2**
I can make them using a computer graphics package and photocopier. **4**
I can use computer slide presentation packages (PowerPoint, etc.) to do them using the computer, OHP and LCD machine. **8**
I have a collection of transparencies which have helped me to improve the quality of my presentation of lessons to pupils. **10**

20   Photocopier

I don't know how to use one. **0**
I can make simple single or multiple copies. **2**
I can also do enlarge/reduce. **3**
I also know how to do back to back copies. **5**
I have made imaginative and effective use of the photocopier to improve the quality of some of my lessons. **10**

21   Digital video editing

Don't know what it is. **0**
Know what it does but can't use it. **2**
Can use digital video editing software. **4**
Feel confident using digital video editing applications with real live children. **10**
Can get pupils to use digital video editing activities in history. **14**

22   Using electronic whiteboards

I'm vaguely aware of what they are and what they do. **1**
I know how to link them up and make basic use of them. **4**
I can use them successfully as part of my teaching. **7**
I know a wide range of ways that they can be used to enhance teaching and learning in history. **12**

23   Data projectors

What? **0**
I know how to set up and use a data projector. **3**
I sometimes use the data projector as part of my teaching to improve the quality of the lessons. **6**
The use of the data projector has had a big impact on improving my teaching. **10**

24 **Wikis**

I don't know what they are. **0**
Know what they are but haven't accessed one. **1**
Have accessed one or more wikis. **3**
Know how to incorporate wikis in my teaching. **5**
Can get my pupils involved in work constructing and editing wikis. **8**

25 **Blogs**

Know what they are. **1**
Have accessed some. **3**
Am familiar with some history blogs. **5**
Have my own blog. **7**
Have my pupils working with blogs and constructing their own history blogs. **10**

26 **Podcasts**

Know what they are. **1**
Have accessed some. **3**
Can make a podcast. **5**
Use them for homeworks. **8**
Can get my pupils making podcasts of their own. **12**

27 **Web authoring tools**

Know what they are. **1**
Can use Flash, Captivate, Audacity, Hot Potatoes, etc. **5**
Work with pupils using these applications. **10**

28 **Accessing E-resources**

Can't use any of them. **0**
Vaguely know what they are but don't use them. **1**
Can use some of them (Metalib, History Resource, TTRB, Pathé News, etc.). **5**
Use most of them and use RSS feeds to update resources. **10**

Max = 321

Remember that your personal proficiency in ICT is only part of the learning agenda. You also need to think about which of these applications is useful to you as a history teacher. In what ways you can make use of the applications, and what are the classroom management implications of their use? Discuss with your tutor and with other student teachers which ICT applications you should prioritise in terms of developing your ICT competence for the history classroom. (Are there any respects in which the 'weighting' of the scores is 'wrong'?) It can be interesting to do the quotient at the start of your course of education, half way through, and towards the end of the course.

If you are at the start of your course, you may well have a limited grasp of the ways in which some of these applications can be used in the history classroom. A particularly important facet of your development in ICT competence is to investigate how these applications can be used in the context of the history classroom.

THE USE AND ABUSE OF NEW TECHNOLOGY: TELEVISION, VIDEO AND DVD RECORDINGS

'That passed the time.' 'It would have passed anyway.'

(Samuel Beckett, *Waiting for Godot*)

The development of new technology offers a wide range of opportunities to history teachers and has had a profound effect on the way in which history is taught. It is also important to bear in mind that with nearly all applications, there is a continuum between 'I don't even know what it is and what it does', and 'I feel confident that I can fully exploit the potential of this technology in my teaching.' Nearly all student teachers know how to use a photocopier, but not all of them know how to do back to back copies, reductions and enlargements, etc. (It is also important to find out departmental norms and conventions on photocopying and be aware of its costs to the department.) Similarly, nearly all student teachers use the television and video recorder in the course of their teaching, but not everyone starts their NQT year with an accomplished and relaxed assurance in the use of the video camera in the classroom. A more developed version of this continuum is given in Figure 8.3.

ICT can be interpreted in a broader sense than merely applying to the use of computers. It is important to note that with most areas of new technology, continuums of competence exist. You may be able to use an overhead projector, but could you change the bulb if necessary? You might be able to use e-mail, but do you know how to send attachments?

Progression in competence

Acquisition: dimly aware that video/DVD extracts can be used in history lessons.

Novice: able to operate the machine and play departmental video/DVD resources as part of a lesson.

Advanced beginner: able to use departmental video and DVD resources selectively and discerningly, intelligently selecting appropriate excerpts, and incorporating them adroitly into the lesson as a whole to enhance the quality of teaching and learning.

Competence: contributes to departmental resources by using initiative and forethought to tape suitable material, able to plan the lesson to make maximum use of extracts, always watches and selects before use in class and uses to a clear purpose: doesn't use as an 'anaesthetic' or to pass the time.

Proficient: builds up coherent collections on topics/themes and is able to *edit* materials to maximise their efficiency, enhancing departmental resources, can use video camera in the classroom as part of lesson activity to enhance quality of teaching and learning. Handles classroom management implications of such exercises skilfully and without chaos and disruption.

Expert: makes maximum use of material available to build up collections of skilfully edited and effective extracts, and deploys them to maximum effect in the classroom. Accomplished and appropriate use of video camera and able to use editing software to make polished final versions of material. Can teach pupils how to edit film extracts using programmes such as Windows Movie Maker.

Figure 8.3 Use of television, video and DVD recordings

In addition to developing in terms of depth of technical proficiency in the use of television and video, you will also become aware of the *breadth and range* of ways of incorporating video and DVD extracts into your lessons. There are more imaginative ways of using video as a resource than simply sticking on a schools broadcast and playing through the whole series, over consecutive lessons. There is also the question of whether and when to use the pause button, to ask questions, and when ICT might be appropriate to give the pupils things to do that will reduce the 'passive' nature of watching television.

Figure 8.4 gives a summary of some of the reasons for the use of video and DVD extracts in the history classroom.

1	To get the pupils' attention.
2	To cover broad stretches of content quickly.
3	To provide an engaging 'starter' activity.
4	To make a point more vividly or forcefully.
5	To 'break the lesson up'.
6	To provide directed questions for pupils to note and then discuss.
7	To engage pupils' emotions.
8	To get pupils to guess what followed on from the extract shown.
9	To get pupils to supply their own 'script' for an extract.
10	To illustrate a concept.
11	To compare two different versions of events.
12	To help make history interesting and accessible.
13	To enable pupils to watch a video roleplay they have made.
14	To help to get you through a lesson with a difficult class.
15	To get out of actually having to teach the pupils yourself.

Figure 8.4 Ways of using the television and video recorder in history

For student teachers in the first stages of their practical teaching, the video and DVD extracts can seem like a godsend, particularly with difficult classes. For understandable reasons, for some, the perfect 40 minute lesson with 9Z on a Friday afternoon would be to show an episode of *Blackadder*, set a worksheet or homework on it, and for the bell to go. Although part of the agenda of learning to teach is about becoming relaxed and comfortable in the classroom, learning to talk to pupils in an appropriate manner, and learning about 'survival' and coping strategies, even in the early stages of practical teaching, thought needs to be given to the question of using resources so that they maximise effective learning for pupils. Video and DVD extracts can be used as an 'anaesthetic', or to pass the time, but this is clearly bad practice. You need to think about how you use the video extract to promote effective learning by pupils. There may be some excepts and programmes which 'stand on their own', and do not require follow up and interpretation. One example of this is the practice of showing the *World at War* programme on the Holocaust, from start to finish, with no introductory or follow up remarks from the teacher. Some history teachers feel that this is the most powerful and effective way of getting pupils to think about the Holocaust. Usually, however, the extent to which the video excerpt promotes historical understanding in pupils depends on what is said and done afterwards – on the quality of the follow up work by you, the teacher, whether this is in the form of teacher exposition and questioning, or pupil activities. It is important to remember that in spite of the claims made for the use of new technology in the classroom, whether involving the use of computers or other forms of new technology, there is no *automatic* learning dividend in using ICT; the use of new technology can have negative as well as positive effects on learning; it depends how adroitly and thoughtfully ICT is used. A computer is like most other things in teaching, the quality and the inspiration comes from you, it is not in the machine.

Task 8.4 Use of video extracts

One commonly used extract is the 'What have the Romans ever done for us?' extract, from the film, *The Life of Brian*. Although the pupils may well find the extract amusing, and ICT has hopefully served the purpose of engaging their attention in the past, what might the history teacher do to derive the maximum benefit from the extract after showing it?

Select a video extract which you might use as part of a lesson, and explain what you and/or the pupils would do after you had shown the extract, and what you hope the learning outcomes would be. Discuss the use of video resources with your tutor.

FORMULATING AN AGENDA FOR THE DEVELOPMENT OF ICT COMPETENCE

The development of personal and classroom proficiency in ICT has time management implications. You cannot have ICT instantly transferred, or injected into you; there is no substitute for spending time becoming familiar with applications and software. As you have to balance developing competence in ICT with other demands, you will probably have to prioritise your agenda for ICT. You cannot reach expert levels in all the above areas. Are there any guidelines or principles on which to construct an agenda for development in ICT?

As you are at different stages in terms of personal expertise in ICT, and work in a variety of school contexts, it is not sensible to lay down a template or formula for developing competence in ICT. Much depends on how the department you are working in is using ICT, which strands of ICT you work with in taught sessions on your course, which aspects of ICT have attracted your interest or that of your tutors. Personal competence in ICT constitutes a necessary but not sufficient part of the requirements for QTS; classroom application and understanding the attributes of ICT applications in relation to teaching and learning history are other important elements. There are, however, some applications which might be given priority because nearly all schools possess the necessary software. 'Generic' applications (which are not subject specific) such as word processing, PowerPoint, data handling software, and the internet are particularly helpful in that they can be used in a wide variety of contexts. You can devise your own, cost-free activities, and there are an increasing number of examples of activities which can be accessed on the main history and ICT websites (see Figure 9.1, Chapter 9).

If you are starting your course with absolutely no knowledge of ICT, the following might be stages of competence to consider over the course of the year in some of these applications; phases which you might move through if you were determined to become accomplished in ICT by the end of the year. (The idea of progression in competence from novice to advanced levels is based on the model of progression in competence developed by the Science department at the Institute of Education, University of London.)

Novice	To find out about databases and spreadsheets, even if it is just the level of knowing what they are and what sort of things you can do with them in history lessons.
Advanced beginner	To look at the data handling applications which are available in the school you are working in, and if possible, observe someone at school or at university using a data handling package in order to get a basic idea of how to use it.
Competent	To be able to use a database or data handling package which you are familiar with as part of a lesson.
Proficient	To develop and use in class, a data handling exercise which you have devised and put on disk yourself.
Advanced	To be sufficiently assured and confident in the use of data handling packages that you can use your lessons to teach the pupils how to compile a history data-file and interrogate it.

Figure 8.5 Degrees of ICT competence – data handling

Task 8.5 Progression in ICT competence – the internet

What would a similar continuum of competence on the internet and teaching and learning in history look like, from novice to advanced levels of competence? In what ways can the internet be used to enhance the quality of teaching and learning in history, in relation to the five areas of historical knowledge, skills and understanding? If possible, discuss this with fellow student teachers and the colleagues you work with. (It might also help to look at the section of the ICT quotient relating to the internet and discuss the extent to which you agree with the weighting of the scores.)

For more information on the use of the internet in history teaching, see: http://www.uea.ac.uk/~m242/historypgce/ict/.

DEVELOPING CLASSROOM CONFIDENCE IN THE USE OF ICT

Some of your use of ICT is within an 'ordinary' classroom, using a data projector, and (possibly) an interactive whiteboard, but there are also occasions when you want to use an ICT suite because you want the pupils to be working on the computers. However accomplished you are in terms of personal ICT capability, it is not as useful as also having developed your classroom experience, using ICT with real, live pupils. This can only be done in school. One of the most important aspects of competence is being relaxed and confident about using ICT in your teaching. There are some general considerations which make this easier.

1   When they first use ICT in the classroom, most student teachers (and some teachers) do so with a degree of trepidation about how it will go,

whether everything will work, whether the pupils will do everything they are supposed to, whether you will get through everything in the time available, etc.

One way to minimise these concerns is to use computers in such a way that they are merely an incidental part of the lesson, rather than the delivery and success of the lesson being entirely dependent on ICT. It is generally more stressful if you have booked the ICT suite for an 'all singing, all dancing' computer extravaganza, rather than simply letting them have a quick look at the timeline on Encarta, or getting them to print off a couple of documents to work on back at their desks.

2   Try to find out about, and use, quick, simple and reliable programs/ exercises. Some applications are useful not primarily because they are brilliant at developing children's historical skills and understanding, but because they are easy to use, and therefore build up your confidence and faith in the use of ICT. You can get onto the ambitious stuff when you've (hopefully) got a few successful ICT lessons 'under your belt'.

3   It's not cheating to ask for help and support, even if it's just asking where an ICT literate person will be that lesson in case you need a hand with some technical hiccup. Find out if there are any members of staff or fellow student teachers with an interest in ICT. If there is no one in the department who is seriously into ICT, see if the ICT coordinator is able to help in any way, and talk about your ICT interests with the School Tutor, who may know the right channels and contacts for developing your ICT capability. It may also be possible to observe other members of staff using computers, even if it's not in history.

4   Use ICT with a teaching group that you feel reasonably comfortable with. Not 9Z on a Friday afternoon, and not a class where your control of proceedings might be a bit shaky at the best of times.

5   Have a 'Plan B', so that if there is a problem you can simply say, 'Never mind we'll do something else and get on to that next week', or 'Here's one I printed out earlier'.

6   Try to have mastered the software in rehearsal if possible so that you can concentrate on the classroom management implications of the lesson (throughput of pupils for example).

7   Think carefully about the planning of the non-computer aspects of the lesson. Devise work that is accessible and that lasts a reasonable length of time so that you are making life as easy for yourself as possible.

8   School ICT suites are usually free at some point in the week; try to make use of them, and your fellow students, by 'sub-contracting' the task of finding out about different areas of ICT and sharing the expertise you develop over the course of the year.

9   Make the most of your school placement to develop your ICT experience. This is often a propitious time for working with small groups of pupils, or developing support materials for the software which the school possesses, or simply developing your familiarity with various items of software. In some cases it is an opportunity for the student teacher to repay help and support rendered, by helping the department with its ICT needs and resources.

10 'Throughput' considerations: some ICT applications are excellent but very time consuming. One of the challenges facing history teachers in deploying the use of ICT is to think of activities where the use of the computer can be integrated into the lesson so as to provide quick, effective and eminently practicable activities which do not take up massive amounts of curriculum time.

11 Problems of access: not all schools possess the facilities to provide everyday access to computers. Part of the challenge of learning to be a teacher is how to make the best of what is available and the art of the possible. Developing proficiency in the classroom use of ICT is partly about your resourcefulness, initiative, patience, diplomacy and tenacity. Even if you have to do things at lunch time, after school, or with small groups of pupils rather than whole classes, try to fit in work with pupils if at all possible. Doing it in the staff room, with fellow student teachers, or at your ITE institution is not quite the same as doing ICT with pupils.

12 Work out a basic checklist before the lesson such as the one suggested below.

---

1 Are you familiar with the ICT application you will be using?
2 How will you put the ICT exercise into the context of the history topic you're doing (before, during or after the pupils are on the computers)?
3 How long will it take the pupils to do the ICT task?
4 Are you clear, and will they be clear about exactly what they have to do? (Will you need support materials?)
5 What will you do if the network is down and the computers aren't working?
6 How will you arrange the groupings?
7 What work will they do/what points will you make after they've been on the computer?
8 Do the pupils have the historical knowledge to undertake the task?

Figure 8.6 Using ICT in a computer suite: classroom management considerations, a checklist

It is important to remember that different applications of ICT are helpful and valuable in different ways. With some applications, the principal benefit might be the enthusiasm it elicits in pupils and the extent to which it draws them into an enthusiasm for learning about the past, even if the extent to which it develops intrinsically historical understanding is marginal. With others, it might be the development of knowledge, skills and understandings which are part of the attainment targets for ICT, with others, the main benefit may be an enhanced understanding of historical processes, concepts, knowledge or skills. Sometimes applications are helpful because they are easy to use, and to incorporate into classroom use, and thus help to develop the teacher's confidence in the use of ICT – in the short term they might benefit the teacher more than the pupils but this may result in a longer term 'pay-off' for pupils who are working with teachers who are comfortable with a broad range of ICT applications. It is unusual to come across an application which possesses all of these attributes; the important thing is to have a clear awareness of what (if any) benefits are being bestowed by the use of ICT.

Differences between individual schools and departments means that ICT will be easier for some student teachers than others to develop ICT competence. Some of you will work in schools where use of computers in the classroom is highly developed, with easy access to computers. Others may work in schools where, for various reasons, this is not the case. Some may well have a subject supervisor who is heavily committed to ICT, and to some extent acts as a 'personal trainer'. Others have to be very much more reliant on their own initiative and the hardware and software resources of the ICTE institution in order to make progress. If your department, or your tutor isn't heavily 'into' ICT, you have to use your initiative more in order to make progress.

Task 8.6 Tracking the QTS Standards related to ICT

Before the end of your final block of teaching experience, examine your teaching file, and look for evidence to support the claim that you are someone who is able to use ICT to enhance and improve the quality of learning in your history lessons, and that you have evidence to support the claim that you are competent in all strands of the QTS Standards relating to ICT (see earlier in this chapter for details). If there is little or no evidence to support this claim, try to plan, teach and evaluate some lessons which focus on this area of competence.

IN WHAT WAYS CAN YOU USE ICT IN YOUR HISTORY TEACHING?

Building collections

Ben Walsh argues that history teachers need to build up what he calls 'learning packages'; collections of resources plucked from the internet, but perhaps also including some resources from other sources, which mean that when you have to teach a topic, you have a wealth of ideas and resources, way beyond what is available in the textbook and the departmental filing cabinets. If this seems an anodyne or dull use of new technology, you should keep in mind that it might be the development which has had the greatest impact on history teachers' practice over the past decade. At its most basic, the learning package can be little more than a collection of images on particular topics, events or individuals, gleaned from Google images, to complement teacher exposition. At a more advanced level, it can be a combination of 'impact' moving image extracts, powerful written testimony and sources and web interactivities for pupils to explore further. For further development of the idea of the learning package, with some examples, see Walsh (2003). The facility of the internet to showcase specialist collections on particular historical themes means that much of the time and effort that used to go into scavenging for resources has been done for the history teacher. The following are just a few examples of sites that can act as valuable first ports of call when you are thinking how to put together lessons on the topics listed below.

As well as 'meta-sites' for history teachers (see Figure 9.1, Chapter 9), the internet is also valuable for 'niche' sites, where a range of obsessives (usually but not always harmless) have put together rich collections of resources and links to particular historical topics and themes.

First World War: www.worldwar1.com
The Holocaust: www.remember.org
The Cold War: www.learningcurve.gov.uk/coldwar/default.htm
Schools History Project: www.leedstrinity.ac.uk/shp (for those teaching SHP courses)
Transition issues: www.historytransition.org.uk

Google's 'page ranking' system means that a simple Google search throws up the sites that most people find useful. John Simkin's 'Spartacus' site (www.spartacus.schoolnet.co.uk) is another common starting point for teachers starting their search for powerful and appropriate materials for their lessons.

Figure 8.7 Useful websites on particular topics

Task 8.7 Selecting from and using internet resources

Look at the list of websites for history teachers given in Figure 9.1 (Chapter 9). They have been chosen partly because they are substantial sites. Select one of the sites, and choose some materials which could then be used as part of a lesson. Think through in detail how you would actually *use* the resources in the lesson. This might be as part of a worksheet or group activity for pupils. It might involve using the web pages 'live', using a data projector in your classroom, or with small groups taking it in turns to use a computer. You should be clear about how the material will develop pupils' historical knowledge, skills and understanding, and how the material offers 'value added' in terms of pupils' learning, compared to using textbooks or other resources.

Extending learning time in history

One of the main problems that history teachers face is that the subject does not get much time on the school timetable and there are a lot to things to get through (not just in terms of subject content) if pupils are to receive a first rate historical education. Making good use of ICT can be a way of getting pupils to (often willingly) do as much work outside the history classroom as inside it. Given the increase in access to computers over the past decade, there are very few pupils who cannot get access to the internet either at school, at the library or at home over a period of several days. Use of the internet can make it much easier to set worthwhile and meaningful tasks for homework. Giving pupils *preparatory* homeworks, where they find out about topics *before* the lesson, can also make for better discussion and debate in class, and more confident pupil performance in general.

Task 8.8 Exploring the feasibility of internet based homeworks

Discuss with the teachers you are working with the possibilities of using the internet as part of homework activities. Schools vary considerably in terms of pupil access to the internet; if access is limited, it can help to give pupils several days to complete the homework, and to have pupils working in groups, where they are able to 'sub-contract' the work involved.

Keeping in touch with peers and colleagues (and sometimes pupils as well)

Many ITE institutions and schools now have Virtual Learning Environments (VLEs) and content management systems such as *Blackboard, WEbCT, Moodle, Uniservity,* which make possible 'virtual' communication between groups. This can be a helpful way of sub-contracting tasks and sharing resources, as well as just keeping in touch with your peers when you are on teaching placement.

Using the internet to develop pupils' information literacy

Teaching pupils how to make mature use of the internet should be an essential element of a historical education for the twenty-first century. This means not jut being able to search for and locate information efficiently, but to evaluate the status of information, and to make intelligent judgements from analysing a range of information from different sources. In the words of Reuben Moore (2000: 35):

> We [history teachers] must use the internet . . . it is not a passing trend . . . young people will use it in their daily lives, no matter what they choose to do with them. And on the internet, they will continue to confront interpretations and representations of history. All adults, no matter what they do with their lives, need to be able to see how and why the historical interpretations that bombard them are constructed. Otherwise they are prey to propaganda and manipulation, not to mention cynicism or a lack of regard for the truth.

The internet is a fantastic resource for teaching the key concept of interpretations and presenting multiple perspectives on events and individuals, and presenting history as 'contested, problematic, and above all else, an argument' (Arnold, 2000: 13). (For some examples of the use of the internet for teaching interpretations, see www.uea.ac.uk/~m242/historypgce/interp/welcome.htm.)

There is some evidence to suggest that many pupils do not have a sound grasp of the weaknesses of the internet as a source of information (Haydn, 2003). As Walsh (2005) points out, 'dodgy' internet sources can be invaluable for getting across the point that the internet is not a straightforward or inherently reliable source of information. The vast, confusing and contradictory nature of internet sources can be a major asset in getting across to pupils that history is a construct; that someone has selected, omitted, edited and combined information, not taken a factual 'snapshot' of the past. This means that pupils need to learn about the principles of procedure which a historian would use to try and 'get at the truth' in the face of these difficulties. Walsh (2005: 98–103), November (www.anovember.com/articles/zack.html) and Teachers TV (http://www.teachers.tv/video/5425) offer useful resources and teaching approaches in this area. Teaching pupils about the meaning of URL syntax can be another way of developing pupils' internet literacy (see the ICT section of the website for further detail on this).

Word processing exercises

Walsh has pointed out that the word processor is not just a typewriter,

> It can search, annotate, organise, classify, draft, reorganise, redraft and save that fundamental of the historian, the written word. When we consider these processes and the difficulties which they represent for so many of our students, the true power and value of the word processor becomes clear. It is not a typewriter, it is an awesome tool for handling information in written form.
>
> (Walsh, 1998: 6)

The use of tables, Venn diagrams and writing frames can give pupils tools to sort out the 'vastness' of history and get it under control. Limiting the text length of pupil responses and making them think about reducing the amount of information available (see Chapter 4) can avoid what Walsh (2005) terms 'Encarta syndrome', where pupils simply copy and paste large chunks of text without reading or understanding it.

 For some examples of word processing exercises for developing pupils' understanding of time and chronology, see: http://www.uea.ac.uk/~m242/historypgce/time/.

Desk top publishing exercises

Desk top publishing exercises also lend themselves to work in the history classroom, particularly with regard to the Key Concept of 'Interpretations'. Pupils can be asked to report on historical events form different perspectives, for instance, a Norman and Saxon report on the Battle of Hastings, German and British front page coverage of the Battle of Britain, pro- and anti-suffragette reports on the death of Emily Wilding Davison and so on. It is important however to make sure that you build in 'real' history into the process, to ensure that this does not become simply an exercise in English or presentation. This can be done by referencing details to source materials used by pupils, and explaining to pupils the nuanced techniques of propaganda, with examples and discussion of real newspaper front pages.

Data handling in history

Computers enable us to manipulate, interrogate and test hypotheses on information much more quickly than would be the case of having to read through and take notes on information provided. Once the collection of information has been put on a data handling package, pupils can create bar charts and pie charts which enable them to see significant patterns in the data, and to explore a range of hypotheses deriving from the data. There are some datasets on the internet; one example is the Commonwealth War Graves Commission site (http://www.cwgc.org/). This can be used to get pupils to explore local or family connections with the First World War, and the site contains an education section explaining how it might be used. Many history departments purchased copies of the BECTa/Historical Association package (1998) on datahandling, *History using IT: Searching for Patterns in the Past using Databases and Spreadsheets*, and this remains a sound introduction to data handling activities on the history classroom. Walsh (2005: 57–75) also provides a range of suggestions for using census data and other electronically available datasets, and Martin (2003) also provides a range of data handling activities which are practicable and which genuinely develop pupils' historical understanding. It is possible to buy commercially produced history datafiles; once you know how to use a data handling package, you can put your own datafiles on to a computer, some pupils can construct a datafile and then interrogate it to test hypotheses. As in many other areas of ICT, it is helpful to be able to get to a stage where the pupils can work autonomously and construct meaning for themselves from the sources and applications they are working with.

Web quests

A web quest is an inquiry-oriented lesson format in which most or all the information that learners work with comes from the web. The model was developed at San Diego State University in 1995 and the site is a useful resource for templates and examples of web quests (http://webquest.org/index.php). Typing 'History Webquest' into a Google search is another way of finding examples of History web quests. There is a lot of research which suggests that just letting pupils loose on the internet in an unstructured way is not a time effective way of using ICT, and yet in the longer term, we do want to bring pupils to a point where they can make autonomous use of the internet in a mature and intelligent way. Good web quests therefore ask questions relating to internet literacy and the reliability of internet sources, as well as the enquiry questions about the topic or person being studied. The basic idea of the web quest is a simple one; that the teacher explores the web first and prepares a path or possible paths for the pupils, which problematise the enquiry question and require the pupils to evaluate the information they are guided through, rather than simply collecting it. Topics of historical controversy (dropping the atom bomb, whether General Haig was 'a butcher', Munich 1938, the wars with Iraq) are therefore fertile territory for web quests. Good web quests require a lot of patient teacher research on the topic in question and intelligent choice of enquiry questions. Some examples of web quests are given in the ICT section of the website (www.uea.ac.uk/~m242/historypgce/ict/welcome.htm).

Using the digital archives of newspapers

Perhaps principally for use with older and more able pupils, but even the tabloid press has potentially interesting and usable headlines and lead stories. Although they can seem dull, long and devoid of images, newspapers often contain high quality pieces from some of the world's greatest writers. Introducing pupils to quality writing from the broadsheet newspapers, and getting pupils to read some of these articles can be an important step in moving from the 'bite-size' and 'picture' mentality which prevails in many textbooks, to being able to sustain concentration and persevere with longer and more challenging sections of extended writing. If they are going to go on to university, which some of them will, they need to get into the idea of reading extended text which has no pictures in it. They can also develop pupils' understanding of the important concept of 'polem-ics', and that not all writing aspires to be 'fair and balanced (see, for instance, Glancey's writing on Britain's role in Iraq in the first British war with Iraq in the 1920s at: http://arts.guardian.co.uk/critic/feature/0,,941850,00.html (for a hyperlinked list of history relevant newspaper articles, go to www.uea.ac.uk/~m242/historypgce/ict/paperboy.htm.

Wikipedia and wikis

A wiki is a website that allows visitors to add, remove and edit content. The most famous and by far the biggest wiki is wikipedia (www.wikipedia.org). Many history departments now use the school's virtual learning environment or content management systems to set up wikis that are 'internal' to the school, so that pupils can engage in what might be termed a form of 'knowledge construction', which can also involve argument, debate and the reconciling of different opinions and perspectives. Wikipedia has a history specific section, and just using wikipedia on its own, without setting up internal wikis, can be an interesting exercise, as the extracts in Figure 8.8 show. However, in terms of active learning and pupil involvement, wikis where pupils collectively try to construct an encyclopaedia entry for a person, event or concept are a good example of genuinely interactive learning.

Views on famous people and events from the past are often disputed, as well as the precise meaning of concepts such as fascism, liberalism or neo-conservatism.
 The following extracts from the wikipedia entry on 'appeasement' gives an example of this:

a the 'official' wikipedia definition of appeasement:
 A policy of accepting the imposed conditions of an aggressor in lieu of armed resistance, usually at the sacrifice of principles. Usually it means giving into demands of an aggressor in order to avoid war. Since <u>World War II</u>, the term has gained a negative connotation in the British government, in politics and in general, of weakness, cowardice and self-deception.
b (From the section on 'different views of appeasement')
 The meaning of the term 'appeasement' has changed throughout the years. According to <u>Paul Kennedy</u> in his <u>*Strategy and Diplomacy*</u>, <u>1983</u>, appeasement is
 'the policy of settling international quarrels by admitting and satisfying grievances through rational negotiation and compromise, thereby avoiding the resort to an armed conflict which would be, expensive, bloody and possibly dangerous.' It gained its negative reputation for its use in the build up to World War II. It had previously been employed by the British government successfully, see the <u>Treaty with Ireland 1921</u>.

(This is followed by quotes on appeasement from Gilbert, Dilks and Churchill.)

Figure 8.8 Using wikipedia

Blogs

Blogs are online diaries, and given that large numbers of pupils now have some form of online presence through social networking sites such as Myspace, Facebook, MSN Messenger, etc., you will be tapping into media that pupils are generally familiar with. Ed Podesta has a good example of what can be done with a teacher-led blog (www.podesta.org.uk), but blogs can again be 'internal' to the school environment, and can be good for showcasing pupils' work, generating discussion between pupils and giving feedback on pupils' work. To look at a range of examples of history department blogs, just type in a Google search for 'history department blogs'.

Podcasts

Podcasts are audiofiles which can be downloaded onto pupils' MP3 players, ipods, or computers. There are hundreds of history podcasts available (just type in 'history pod-cast' on a Google search), but not all of them are a thrilling and engaging listening experience, and there are issues of age and ability appropriateness. They can be helpful for revision for some pupils who like 'audio' based learning, and the BBCs 'Bitsize' revision site has a large range of audio files for downloading (www.bbc.co.uk/schools/gcsebitesize/audio/history/index.shtml). Historians have also started to use the medium of podcasts. At the time of writing, the Downing Street website has a podcast of a talk between Tony Blair and Simon Schama, which can be listened to or printed off (www.pm.gov.uk/output/Page11325.asp), and the National Archives has a podcast by Professor Barry Coward, 'Was the Cromwellian Protectorate a dictatorship?' (www.nationalarchives.gov.uk/podcast/barry-coward-cromwell.mp3?pod=rss%20).
Some internet podcasts may well have a short 'shelf-life', but they can be saved and downloaded, and a Google search should unearth current ones. Again, a step forward in terms of active learning and pupil engagement can be for pupils to produce their own podcasts. The development of downloadable software such as 'Audacity' (http://audacity.sourceforge.net/) which makes it easy to make and save audiofiles, has made this a rela-tively straightforward exercise.

Web interactivities and toolkits

Given that some schools now have wireless technology, it is now possible to get pupils using a wide range of the interactive features of history websites. Sometimes these are fairly 'light' starter activities or end of lesson games and quizzes, but they are not all limited to 'just a bit of fun' type activities. They can range from PowerPoint presenta-tions to 'virtual interviews' with historical figures, and simulations and decision making exercises. Russel Tarr's 'Active History' site (www.activehistory.co.uk) has a large range of such activities. Although it is a subscription site, it usually has a 'free' section as well. Further examples are given in the ICT section of the website (www.uea.ac.uk/~m242/historypgce/ict/welcome.htm). Tarr also hosts 'Classtools', which provides templates for history teachers to design their own ICT based activities for pupils (www.classtools.net). 'Hot Potatoes' is another site which provides such activities (http://hotpot.uvic.ca/). See the discussion at the 'School History' site for further detail about online simulation activities in history: www.schoolhistory.co.uk/forum/index.php?showtopic=1876. (You might also want to explore the potential of Googlefight (www.googlefight.com) as a 'starter' for discussions about historical significance.)

Departmental websites

Richard Jones (2007) makes the point that a departmental web site can help you to keep your resources organised, and engage both pupils and parents in making progress in history, and his site is a powerful example of what departmental websites can aspire to (see reference below). They can be particularly helpful for revision activities. Further details of history department websites are given on the ICT section of the website, and Chris Higgins' e-help seminar talks about how to create and maintain a departmental website: (http://educationforum.ipbhost.com/index.php?showforum=246).

Interactive whiteboards

Opinion appears to be divided as to whether these are invaluable assets for the history teacher or expensive toys that just do 'eye candy' stuff. There is evidence to suggest that skilful use of interactive whiteboards motivates and engages pupils in learning (BECTa, 2004) but they are expensive, not universally available, and some history teachers swear by the 'cheap and cheerful' option of a mobile mouse and keyboard. You should try to ensure that you at least explore the world of whiteboards so that you can make your own mind up on this. An e-help seminar by Roy Huggins on the use of interactive whiteboards can be accessed at: http://educationforum.ipbhost.com/index.php?showforum=246.

PowerPoint presentations

These can be riveting or dire. There is an art to using PowerPoint in a way that engages pupils and makes pupils think about history in a way that develops their historical understanding. This is not just a question of how technically sophisticated your presentations are. It is about imagination, creativity and a good understanding of the pedagogy of school history. How good will your PowerPoint presentations be by the end of your education? With the increased access to whole class projection facilities, it is a question that is relevant to most history departments and student teachers. As there is not room to fully explore this issue here, there is a section on the ICT section of the website about 'how to make PowerPoint less boring'.

Voting technology

Not all history departments have access to voting sets but they are becoming increasingly common in schools, even if the history department does not have their own set. If you are working in a school where there is access to such technology, try to talk to some of the teachers who use it. Walsh (2006) warns of the danger of just using them for banks of multiple choice tests, and suggests a range of ways of using voting technology to promote discussion and debate in the history classroom. Although the technology is not cheap, it does have the potential to make learning genuinely interactive, and to make pupils think. As with many other aspects of ICT in history, there is an e-help seminar on this (see URL above) as well as a section on the Historical Association's website.

Digital video

This is perhaps one of the most exciting recent developments relating to school history and ICT. The incorporation of easy to use moving image editing software (such as, for example, Windows Movie Maker) into the standard 'package' for personal computers, and the accessibility of moving image files on the internet and video cameras within history departments has made it easy for pupils to make and edit films, and to put their own subtitles and commentary on them. There are also three e-help seminars on digital video (by Ben Walsh, Richard Jones and Peter Tollmar), and a section on the use of digital video (pages 133–56) in Ben Walsh's book, *Exciting ICT in History* (2005). There is not space within this chapter to do full justice to this, but there is a section on the ICT section of the website which provides more depth on this.

Two important resources

Two resources which are invaluable for giving an indication of the *breadth* of ways in which ICT can make it easier for history teachers to teach their subject more effectively are Ben Walsh's book (2005) *Exciting History*, and Richard Jones' departmental website, which at the time of writing is between online 'homes' and has no current URL. When it finds a new home, the URL will be provided in the ICT section of the website (www.uea.ac.uk/~m242/historypgce/ict/welcome.htm).

BE CAREFUL NOT TO...

Don't just carry on collecting more and more web addresses without thinking about how you might use them in your teaching. It is important to achieve a balance between acquiring more resources, and deploying them effectively in your teaching. It is possible to browse the web for hours, and encounter fascinating material, but end up with nothing that you will use in a lesson.

SUMMARY AND KEY POINTS

Developing competence in ICT in a way that fulfils the requirements for QTS means that you not only need to develop personal proficiency in ICT, you must also have a clear grasp of the ways in which ICT can contribute to effective learning in history. You must make every effort, whatever the circumstances of your school placements, to get as much experience in the use of ICT applications as possible; *classroom* experience is particularly helpful. You also need to consider the classroom management factors which influence the successful use of ICT, and to be able to evaluate the impact of the use of computers in the classroom. It is not a question of how much you use computers, or the breadth of applications used; what matters most is how effectively you are able to use new technology to improve the quality of your lessons. With many applications, it is not a question of competence, but of *levels* of expertise, in terms of your understanding of both the technology, and the pedagogy of the subject you are teaching. Investing time and thought into how you can harness the use of ICT and take full advantage of the rich resources of the internet can have massive benefits in terms of making it much easier to motive and engage pupils in learning.

For further reading and resources on the use of ICT in history teaching, and examples of some of the uses of ICT mentioned in this chapter see: www.uea.ac.uk/~m242/historypgce/ict.

REFERENCES

Arnold, J. (2000) *History: A Very Short Introduction*, Oxford: Oxford University Press.

BECTa (2004) *Getting the Most From Your Interactive Whiteboard: A Guide for Secondary Schools*, Coventry: BECTa.

Dickinson, A. (1998) 'History using IT: past, present and future', *Teaching History*, No. 93: 16–20.

Downes, T. (1993) 'Student teachers' experiences in using computers during teaching practice', *Journal of Computer Assisted Learning*, Vol. 9, No. 1: 17–33.

Easdown, G. (1997) 'IT in initial teacher education: a survey of feelings and preconceptions', in A. Pendry and C. O'Neill (eds), *Principles and Practice: Analytical Perspectives on Curriculum Reform and Changing Pedagogy for History Teacher Educators*, Lancaster: Standing Conference of History Teacher Educators (SCHTE): 102–12.

Easdown, E. (2000) 'History teachers and ICT', in G. Easdown (ed.), *Innovation and Methodology: Opportunities and Constraints in History Teacher Education*, Lancaster: HTEN: 19–35.

Harrison, S. (2003) 'The use of ICT for history teaching: slow growth, a few green shoots. Findings of HMI inspection 1999–2001', in T. Haydn and C. Counsell (eds), *History, ICT and Learning in the Secondary School*, London: RoutledgeFalmer: 38–51.

Haydn, T. (2003) 'What do they do with the information? Working towards genuine interactivity with history and ICT', in T. Haydn and C. Counsell (eds), *History, ICT and Learning*, London: RoutledgeFalmer: 192–224.

Haydn, T. (2004) 'The use of ICT in history teaching in secondary schools in England and Wales, 1970–2003', Unpublished PhD thesis, University of London.

ImpaCT 2 (2002) *The Impact of ICT on Pupil Learning and Attainment*, Coventry: BECTa.

Jones, R. (2007) Unpublished seminar, 'The creative use of ICT in history teaching', University of East Anglia, Norwich, 30 May.

Martin, D. (2003) 'Relating the general to the particular: data handling and historical learning', in T. Haydn and C. Counsell (eds), *History, ICT and Learning*, London: RoutledgeFalmer: 134–51.

Moore, R. (2000) 'Using the internet to teach about interpretations in years 9 and 12', *Teaching History*, No. 101: 35–9.

Rollason, D. (1998) Quoted in *Daily Telegraph*, 29 October.

TDA (2007) *Professional Standards for Teachers: QTS*, London: TDA.

Walsh, B. (1998) 'Why Gerry likes history now: the power of the word processor', *Teaching History*, No. 93: 6–15.

Walsh, B. (2003) 'Building learning packages: integrating virtual resources with the real world of teaching and learning', in T. Haydn and C. Counsell (eds), *History, ICT and Learning*, London: RoutledgeFalmer: 109–33.

Walsh, B. (2005) *Exciting ICT in Secondary History*, Stafford, Network Educational Press.

Walsh, B. (2006) 'Beyond multiple choice: voting technology in the history classroom', seminar presentation at e-help conference, Stockholm, October. Online at: http://educationforum. ipbhost.com/index.php?showforum=246. Accessed 13 October 2007.

9 The use of resources in the teaching of history

INTRODUCTION

The NC for history and OFSTED inspection reports stress that to teach history effectively, teachers need to use a range of sources of information, including documents and printed sources, artefacts, pictures, photographs and films, music and oral sources, buildings and sites. This is not just desirable, but necessary if pupils are to derive full benefit from the study of the past.

Effective history teaching is at least in part about having teachers who are adept at acquiring stimulating and appropriate resources, skilfully adapting and combining them, and using them adroitly in the classroom to support a clear plan for learning in history (see Chapter 3). Once you have decided what is to be taught (the content) and how it is to be taught (the teaching strategy) you need to secure the tools necessary (the resources) to ensure and maintain pupil interest and learning, although as noted in Chapter 3, there may be occasions when the discovery of an exciting or unusual resource might be the starting point for the planning of a lesson. You need to develop a knowledge and understanding of the full range of resources available to history teachers. You also need to know how to deploy those resources skilfully and effectively; it's not just a matter of 'chucking lots of stuff at them'.

OFSTED (2006) has been critical of much of the quality and range of the resources used by many teachers in history classrooms and in particular, teachers who confine themselves predominantly to the use of textbooks and worksheets. Recent research commissioned by QCA found that three of the biggest 'turn-offs' for pupils in school history, were too much teacher talk, overuse of textbooks, and too many worksheet exercises (QCA, 2005). This chapter therefore examines the range of resources available to the history teacher, and how they might best be used.

OBJECTIVES

At the end of this chapter you should be able to:

- identify a range of resources available to the history teacher;
- evaluate the suitability of resources for the teaching of history by recognising relevance and appropriateness;
- have confidence in accessing and using resources;
- recognise the tensions and challenges involved in building up an 'archive' of resources for teaching;
- suggest practical ways to use and manage your resources.

PROBLEMS AND POSSIBILITIES WITH RESOURCES

Before detailing some of the major avenues teachers can explore to build up an 'archive' of appropriate and high-quality resources, it might be helpful to highlight some of the issues and tensions teachers have to deal with in the area of resources.

The term 'resource' should be understood as anything that can serve as an object or stimulus for pupils and which a history teacher can effectively use to enhance or extend the teaching or learning of history. Whereas 40 years ago there was a paucity of resources for history teachers to work with (blackboard, chalk, text book, exercise books, some old maps perhaps), nowadays teachers are overwhelmed with materials that can be used in history lessons. As early as 1994, Danks identified 15 different uses of resources for the history teacher and divided them into three categories: 'teaching resources', 'teaching aids' and 'teaching methods'. Teaching aids relate to the use of equipment or mechanical devices such as OHPs, interactive whiteboards, flip charts and television/DVD. Whilst teaching methods and teaching aids are certainly resources in our definition, this chapter focuses on what Danks terms the 'teaching resources' which include: historical sources, field trips, worksheets, websites, text books, computer programs, etc., in other words, items which are used to enrich or enhance the understanding of pupils and the development of historical skills. Teaching with these types of resources often involves an active and investigatory mode of learning. Although some resources are useful for developing your subject knowledge (for instance, history magazines such as *History Today* or *BBC History Magazine*), more often they offer a way of engaging pupils in active participation in learning, in helping pupils to 'do history' rather than simply receive it. With most resources, you have to give considerable thought to how you are going to deploy them in the lesson, it is unusual to find resources that do not require some adaptation, editing or supplementing with other inputs.

THE IMPORTANCE OF INITIATIVE WITH RESOURCES

Initiative and imagination are essential attributes of any history teacher wishing to play a full part in the development of the department's resources. All good history teachers are good 'scavengers', always on the lookout for things that they can use in a lesson, and proactive about exploring a wide range of opportunities for getting hold of high-impact resources that might turn an 'OK' lesson into a memorable one. Some student teachers tend to be overreliant on the resources which the history department possesses. Although this is understandable in the first few weeks of school experience, as the course progresses, you should increasingly be finding and developing your own resources and materials, and feeding them into the departmental stockpile. One of the factors which may well be influential in the department's assessment of your level of competence is the extent to which you have made a positive contribution to the department's resources in the course of your school experience. This can also include contributions to display work and site and museum visits. Remember that by the end of the course, you should be 'autonomous', in the sense of being able to plan for progression in learning for all your classes, over a sustained period. When you qualify, you may have to teach classes for several years. This means that you need to build up a formidable archive of teaching materials, so the sooner you adopt an proactive and energetic approach to developing your archive of teaching ideas and resources, the better.

BUILDING 'LEARNING PACKAGES'

As noted in Chapter 3, if you are a history teacher, week on week you have to put on around 15–20 'shows'. Part of the show derives from your subject knowledge and your knowledge of the NC, GCSE or GCE A level specifications, and the quality of your exposition, questioning and interaction with pupils. But part of the show is based on the quality of the learning materials you bring to bear on the lesson. It is a lot easier to get through a one hour lesson if you have got several high quality resources, perhaps a good starter activity, some good images to go with your initial 'script', a well thought out PowerPoint presentation with appropriate music, a really powerful video or DVD extract, a well thought out card sort or pupil task, a good idea for a 'fun' quiz or plenary and so on. It is easier to relax if you have got a powerful and appropriate collection of resources to support the lesson, and much more nerve racking if you are going in there mainly reliant on your exposition and questioning and a battered old text book. Walsh uses the phrase 'building up learning packages' to sum up the importance of initiative with resources, meaning a conscious attempt to assemble a collection of resources of different kinds (and ideas), so that you can go into lessons with confidence. The phrase 'learning package' simply indicates that usually, teachers go into a series of lessons with a *combination* of resources and ideas from different sources, which when put together thoughtfully and with skill, interspersed with teacher exposition and questioning, provides a stimulating, varied and coherent experience for pupils. In Walsh's words:

> What does this package consist of? It is a combination of intricately stuctured history activities, of multiple software applications, of more 'normal' resources (such as textbooks, fieldwork, TV programmes, paper and pen), of detailed planning for pupils' learning around substantial, motivating historical enquiries and . . . classroom teaching skills, preferably discussed, practised and shared.
> (Walsh, 2003: 110)

It needs to be stressed that this is not just a matter of 'chucking lots of things in'. Coherence is an issue, and it is not a matter of 'how much stuff' there is in a lesson, but rather, how well is it used, how much thought has gone into thinking exactly what the pupils will do with the resource. Experienced teachers are sometimes more accom plished at 'getting a lot out of' an activity or resource. They don't rush through it, and have the composure to let the pupils into the activity and respond to it. If you do get hold of a Second World War gas mask, or a First World War helmet, or a Roman coin, what are you going to do with it, other than just show it to the pupils?

Task 9.1 Initiative with resources

Pick out a topic that you are teaching and make a conscious attempt over several weeks to look out for resources on that topic – try and build up your own 'learning package' on the topic. This can include looking through past articles from *Teaching History, BBC History Magazine, History Today, Radio Times*, the main history internet sites (see Chapter 8), the library, text books, Google images, the newspapers and so on.

In conjunction with the department's scheme of work and relevant text books, consider how and where you would insert some of your collection into your lessons in this topic. What should you keep for the future from your collection, and are there some things that you have collected that you probably will not use and which need to be discarded?

If you work with other student history teachers, compare notes with what they have collected on their topic. Are there any aspects of your collections that you can easily share, and is it possible to 'sub-contract' the development of learning packages across common topics?

Task 9.2 The balance between collecting things and using them

Towards the end of your school placement, look through the resources you have acculated, and make a rough estimate of what percentage of the things you have cut out, photocopied, saved to your hard drive, bought, bookmarked, etc., you have actually used in your teaching. Although it is helpful to 'scavenge' for resources, you need to keep a watchful eye out for the habit of your collecting more and more 'stuff' that you don't ever process into your teaching. It generally takes some time to hone and refine resources into a usable form, and you need to make sure that you are not eschewing the hard 'thinking' work that this involves, in favour of just getting more and more stuff that you don't use.

THE ROLE OF THE INTERNET IN DEVELOPING YOUR 'ARCHIVE' OF RESOURCES

As Harrison pointed out, new technology provides 'an extraordinary supplement to the resources normally available to the history teacher' (Harrison, 2003: 39). It is now next to unthinkable for history teachers not to make use of the internet, but this is not to say that all of them have been able to exploit fully the internet to enhance teaching and learning in their lessons. The internet is a fantastic resource, but it is not unproblematic. For teachers as well as pupils, the problem is partly that there is 'too much stuff'. It is vast and it has not been catalogued in the way that a library is catalogued (at the time of writing, a Google search on the Battle of Stalingrad threw up 792,000 hits). Moreover, there can be a tendency for teachers and student teachers to simply 'browse' or to collect skips full of webpages and references that they do not 'process' into something they actually use in their lessons. The internet can be a fabulous waste of time and energy, and a way of putting off lesson construction, leading to diversion and clutter, rather than the formulation of a high quality learning experience for pupils. Like other materials and resources (see next section) the internet needs to be handled intelligently if it is to be of use to the history teacher. Some teachers are much more accomplished than others in making effective use of the net to improve the quality of teaching and learning with their classes. There is no excuse these days for having boring lessons because the textbook is rather dull and the department's resources aren't great on some topics. There are few topics where there is 'nothing out there'. If you are a history teacher, the internet is your friend. You don't have to come up with all the brilliant, creative and imaginative ideas for your lessons yourself, there are thousands of ideas, activities and resources out there, waiting to be downloaded and used.

MANAGING AND ORGANISING YOUR RESOURCES

Most student teachers start with very little in terms of an archive of resources for use with their teaching groups, and are to a large extent reliant on the history department they are working in for access to resources in the early stages of their teaching. However, you soon accumulate a surprisingly large number of resources of different types, and these need to be sorted and organised efficiently if they are to be used in future and 'kept under control'. Whether you are by nature a highly organised person or not, if you are going to be a teacher, you have got to 'get your act together' and be efficient and well organised in your marshalling of resources, At the most basic level, you must make sure that your teaching file is kept in good order and up to date – most tutors believe that the quality of your teaching file is an important indicator of how good you are as a student teacher. It is unusual to encounter a student teacher who is excellent in the classroom whose teaching file is a mess. Try to keep up to date with your lesson plans and evaluations, don't leave yourself with a big backlog. It is usually best to do evaluations when the lesson is fresh in your mind. It usually saves time in the longer term if you write your lesson plans and evaluations electronically rather than by hand, and try to ensure that you have a sound filing system for e-resources of different kinds. Jones argues that having your own website for your teaching is a very practical way of organising your teaching resources and making sure that things don't get lost or jumbled (Jones, 2007). This is no longer just a question of storing 'favourites', but using flash drives, DVDs and CD-ROMs and portable hard drives to store digital media files that are quite large. With 'paper' resources, make sure you have a sensible filing and storage system that you understand so that you can find things when you need them. Not being able to find things when you need them, and doing things at the last minute are two major causes of stress on teaching placement, and tutors do not like it when you are continually having to interrupt lessons to find scissors, sugar paper, or lesson resources. Allen (2001) has a range of simple and practical suggestions for organising yourself so that you capture all the things that need to be done: you know where things are when you need them, and that you have systems so that all the clutter of teaching is accessible but not in your head and causing stress.

It is also important that you are careful to look after departmental resources. Text and topic books are precious and costly resources; if you give them out, make sure that you count the books in, and don't lend departmental resources to pupils without clearing it with the department, and taking all appropriate administrative measures.

KEEPING IN MIND THE BALANCE BETWEEN STORIES AND SOURCES, DEPTH AND OVERVIEW

Whilst acknowledging that our responsibility as history teachers is to present historical knowledge, as 'tentative, constructed and problematic', and to select sources which enable us to explore these attributes, Hake and Haydn (1995) suggested that we need to keep in mind the balance between narrative and sources in history teaching. They point to the fact that early NC textbooks consisted almost exclusively of a series of double page features on a particular historical topic, dominated by four to six sources and questions focused on these sources. Student teachers of history sometimes model their own materials on those used in professionally produced textbooks. This can lead to excessive use of 'the dreaded two page spread' type of lesson. Inserting pictures and diagrams and breaking-up blocks of text has been at the expense of extended pieces of writing which might provide a clearer grasp of how events unfolded, and the theories surrounding those events.

There is a need to ensure that more detailed accounts and explanations of periods of history are not left out in the move to a more source based approach to history teaching. You need to bear in mind that there needs to be a balance between 'traditional' teaching strategies (sometimes dismissively referred to as 'chalk and talk') and the use of sources in the classroom. As well as understanding what 'history' is, and how it is constructed, it is helpful if pupils have a coherent view of how events, wars and crises have evolved. HMI make the point that pupils who appear to know little do not make a good case for the teaching of history (HMI, 1985:11). Pupils should develop a clear grasp of how we have moved from the past to the present day, in terms of political ideas, methods of warfare, economic and social organisation and so on, in addition to acquiring the skills to analyse and interpret it. Your selection and use of resources should help pupils to build up an overview or 'framework' of the past as well as providing opportunities to analyse sources in detail. Some schools broadcasts, (and BBC, Channel 4 or History Channel series such as, *The Troubled Century*, *A History of Britain*, *The Wars of the Roses*, *The World at War*) are good examples of resources which can provide an overview or general summary of developments in a particular topic over time. The other crucially important resource which can achieve this is your own knowledge and understanding of the past, in the form of the expositions and explanations which you provide for your pupils to provide a link between source based activities. Try to ensure that as you are developing your collections of resources on particular topics, you strike a balance between resources that are good for 'depth' enquiries, and resources which help to provide a broader overview of the topic or theme.

SHARING RESOURCES WITH COLLEAGUES AND OTHER STUDENT HISTORY TEACHERS

How 'smart' are you at sharing resources efficiently with colleagues and peers, and through history teacher forums? This is of course, a two way process. There are lots of ways for history teachers and student teachers to sub-contract the development of resources and share their materials, but again, some teachers are more proactive (and generous) than others. One piece of 'etiquette' is that if you are using someone else's ideas, you acknowledge this with other relevant adults ('This is an idea I got from X at an

SHP workshop', or whatever). If it is something that you observe in someone else's lesson, it is also polite to ask if it is OK to use the idea with your own classes. Most history teachers and student teachers come across 'gems' from time to time. It's fine to keep your eyes open and use other people's ideas, from *Teaching History*, the SHP Conference or whatever, but try and make sure that you are 'a giver', and not someone who ruthlessly grabs other people's stuff and then is reluctant to pass it on to others. 'Generosity of spirit' is another characteristic of good teachers.

WHAT RESOURCES ARE AVAILABLE TO HISTORY TEACHERS?

Textbooks and worksheets

Over the past decade, OFSTED have been consistently critical of the ways in which some history departments use textbooks (see, for example, OFSTED, 1995, 2005). This does not mean that they are against the use of textbooks *per se*. Textbooks are still widely used in secondary history departments, and they can be a helpful support, particularly in the first few weeks of your teaching – most pupils are used to using them, and so there is an element of security and familiarity in making use of this resource. Moreover, there have been dramatic improvements in the design of more recent history textbooks: 'the dreaded two page spread' format of earlier NC text books has been replaced with more varied and imaginative approaches. But if textbooks are to contribute to stimulating and worthwhile learning for pupils, teachers need to use them selectively and critically. You need to be aware of the strengths and limitations of the textbooks you use, and understand that no textbook is perfect. As you think about the lessons you are teaching, you should look at the text book and consider whether there are some aspects of the lesson which the textbook might deliver perfectly well, and where there are areas which require other resources and approaches – not least your own 'supplements' to the information contained in the textbook, and the ability to 'toggle' between the textbook, your exposition and questioning, and other inputs, such as images and activities on the whiteboard, or in a PowerPoint presentation.

 For some examples of newer approach NC history textbooks which have moved away from the '2 page spread' approach, go to: www.uea.ac.uk/~m242/historypgce/welcome.htm.

As well as using textbooks as a resource, you can also create your own worksheets which can complement the use of textbooks, although you must take care not to spend hours putting together a worksheet when a judicious selection of tasks from the textbook might have served just as well as your own creation. One of the advantages of textbooks (and history web resources) is that someone has often done all the time consuming work of putting together a useful group of sources which go well together as a collection for assisting a particular enquiry question. One of the decisions you have to make is whether the tasks and questions that accompany the sources and narrative work perfectly well for your learning objectives for the lesson, or whether they need pruning or adapting.

Most history departments make some use of worksheets to support effective learning. They are not necessarily drab and dull; like most other teaching strategies for history, they are something that can be done well or badly. Common problems with the production of worksheets can be overcome if you consider the pitfalls beforehand. First, your worksheets must cater for the full range of ability in the classroom. This means that you need to use appropriate language (see Chapter 4). It can be helpful to 'scaffold' (support) the use of the worksheet with some explanation and to use the whiteboard or OHP in conjunction with a worksheet. Support materials and extension options might be appropriate to provide access and challenge for the whole class.

Much of the skill in devising good worksheets lies in the quality of task design; creating activities that require pupils to think rather than just remember or comprehend. Requiring pupils to 'reduce' information in some way can be a helpful strategy to remenber here (see Chapter 4). The creation of tables, charts and graphs can also help pupils to select and organise information before processing it further. You should generally try to avoid 'fill in the missing word' exercises that merely test pupils' ability to read. The worksheet should contain tasks that in some way develop or test pupils' historical understanding. There is nothing to stop you incorporating discussion and pairwork tasks in the worksheet – activities do not always have to be written ones. Copying and colouring are almost always bad history practice and you should avoid them in your use of worksheets. Lloyd-Jones provides a sound introduction on how to produce better worksheets and he asks nine questions (summarised below) which are worth considering:

Are your worksheets:

- part of a planned, balanced and coherent course?
- written in language that is easily understood?

Do they:

- provide opportunities for group work and class discussion?
- require pupils to use a variety of sources and resources?
- ask for a variety of responses, including both oral and written?
- cater for the needs of all levels of ability in the class?
- provide for progression and continuity in learning?
- avoid mindless blank filling-in or colouring?
- give clear information and unambiguous instructions? (Lloyd-Jones, 1995)

Task 9.3 Devising a worksheet

Design a worksheet for a year 9 class which complements the use of the textbook you are working with. When you have used the worksheet with the pupils, go through their responses and consider which sections of the worksheet seemed to work best, keeping in mind the checklist above. Did it just pass the time, or did it promote pupils' understanding of what you were trying to teach? Did it provide any useful insight into what pupils do and do not understand which might inform subsequent teaching? Did the pupils work in an assiduous or desultory fashion on the task? In what ways would you amend the worksheet for future use? Would you use it again? Is it possible to have a good, stimulating and worthwhile lesson using just textbook, worksheet and exposition and questioning?

History fieldtrips

It can be argued that by giving pupils something they can actually see and touch, they gain a better understanding of the use of the item, the context in which it is placed and the historical significance of both the artefact and the period of time to which it relates. Teachers have used this argument to theorise that there is a much greater sense of learning and impact on pupils with a single site visit than with the use of a large number of textbooks in class. Teachers need to be realistic about the strengths and limitations of site visits. Nevertheless, if one of the aims of school history is to give pupils an understanding of what history *is*, and how it is constructed, they need to experience history outside the classroom and teachers therefore must look beyond the classroom in their planning. This allows pupils to experience resources in a stimulating environment whether it be historical sites or museums. Participation in history fieldtrips can increase awareness of the nature of history through exposure to a rich variety of sources.

24 Hour museum www.24hourmuseum.org.uk
'Gateway' site to find out about museums in the UK. Some museums have much more advanced internet resources than others. This is a good way of finding out about both the 'real' and 'virtual' assets of a wide range of museums.

Planning a fieldtrip often involves you in extensive enquiries and preparation. You need background information before the visit and an understanding of the disruption and cost to the school. History fieldtrips need to be planned well in advance. They are not spur of the moment ideas. A preliminary visit to the site by the teacher organising the proposed visit is usually vital to check any arrangements and to plan the focus of the visit. You need to contact museum staff or any educational officer at the site before you visit. These officers can provide invaluable information and often they cater for groups of pupils from schools. Coach parking, toilet and eating facilities need to be checked in advance. You will need to do a risk assessment audit of the visit, and you should be familiar with LEA guidelines for trips outside school. You also need to be accompanied by a qualified teacher if you take pupils on a museum visit or fieldtrip.

You may wish to design a worksheet for pupils in order to focus the visit for them. However, it is important that the visit does not become a paperchase with pupils moving from one display to another looking for the right answer on their worksheets. The worksheets should be designed to encourage enquiry and self-discovery on the part of the pupils. You also need to consider how the visit will be followed-up for the maximum learning potential of the visit to be achieved. Pupils could gather evidence together to be used in a number of subsequent lessons. Culpin (1999) provides excellent advice on planning and preparing for fieldtrips.

Task 9.4 What do pupils gain by going outside the classroom?

Rightly or wrongly, 'trips' out are something of a luxury for most secondary schools. They are not something that you can do every week because of the disruption to other lessons. Think of a specific field trip or museum visit which would be feasible for a group of pupils, (this might be a major national museum you are familiar with, or a museum or site which is within easy visiting range of your school placement), and draft an outline plan of what your object-ives would be for the visit, and what activities you would devise to make the experience worthwhile. How would you justify it to the assistant head in charge of cover arrangements and out of school activities?

Task 9.5 Planning visits

In addition to the question of the 'historical' validity of a site or museum visit, there are important logistical considerations which need to be borne in mind. You need to be aware of the possible effects of the visit on the school as a whole, on parents of pupils involved, and on other members of staff.

You have been requested by your tutor to investigate and plan a possible field trip for a year 7 class to the local cathedral as part of their medieval realms study unit. You need to complete a short report on the feasibility of such a visit particularly addressing the following questions:

a   How would your plan affect the school timetable?
b   How many staff would be involved on the day?
c   How much would the visit cost pupils?
d   Could all the pupils pay? If not, where would the money come from?
e   How many pupils would attend and would permission from parents be necessary?
f   Have you considered the school policy on outside visits? Is insurance necessary?
g   Does the site have adequate toilets, parking and eating facilities?
h   What is the justification for the visit? Does it have a clear focus?
i   Would the focus correspond to the aims of the study unit?
j   Is there an educational officer based at the site? Do you need to contact them?
k   Does the site produce its own materials for school visits? Will you use them?
l   Do you need to plan a worksheet? What would it contain?
m   Do you intend to follow the visit up with subsequent lessons on the topic?
n   What other questions would you ask yourself? Are there any other steps you could take to ensure that the visit does not cause problems?

NEWSPAPERS

Newspapers tend to be an underused resource. They have become more accessible and usable since the introduction of internet archiving of newspapers. You can get to most British newspapers by just typing their name into an ordinary internet search. Although they can seem dull, long and devoid of images, newspapers articles can be high quality pieces from some of the world's greatest writers. Introducing pupils to quality writing from the broadsheet newpapers, and getting pupils to read some of these articles can be an important step in moving from the 'bite-size' and 'picture' mentality which prevails in many textbooks, to being able to sustain concentration and persevere with longer and more challenging sections of extended writing. If they are going to go on to university, which some of them will, they need to get into the idea of reading extended text which has no pictures in it. Newspaper headlines and articles can also often be a way of linking the past to the present, so that the relevance of history becomes apparent to pupils. Whenever anything historically controversial happens (introduction of Holocaust Commemoration Day, slavery, debates about Britishness, citizenship), it makes it easy to get a range of newspaper opinion about the issue. Many sites now have a quite sophisti-cated archiving system so that you can get articles published over the past few years.

Some also provide animations, special reports, cartoons, etc. Newspapers are also excellent resources for providing pupils with examples of 'polemics'; an important element of using school history to develop pupils' information and media literacy. The ability to 'hyperlink' to archived newspaper articles makes them very easy to access. Giving pupils a historically oriented newspaper article to read for homework can also be a convenient way of setting high quality homeworks. As well as the broadsheets, the tabloid press also have sites, some better than others, and these can be particularly good for headlines and sensational stories – 'London bus found on the moon', etc.

Theme / concept	Date	Title	Author
Cold War	19/02/2002	'The Soviet threat was a myth'	Andrew Alexander

URL: http://www.guardian.co.uk/comment/story/0,,686910,00.html
Quote: 'Stalin had no intention of attacking the West; we were to blame for the Cold War'

The details above give a link to an article on the Cold War which might be appropriate for GCSE or GCE A Level pupils.
　　Another example, URL: http://www.guardian.co.uk/g2/story/0,,898341,00.html – the views of a dozen historians on the Iraq war.
　　A longer list of such articles with linking URLs can be accessed at: www.uea.ac.uk/~m242/historypgce/ict/paperboy.htm.

Task 9.6 Initiative with resources: newspapers and television

Over a period of several days (a week would be ideal), look through the newspapers and cut out any articles which you might be able to use in your teaching. Look through the listings for television programmes for the week and make a note of programmes which might be of use or relevance to the history teacher other than school broadcasts for history (and, if possible, record them).
　　Compare your collection with someone else's. Are there any 'gems' which are definitely worth keeping? How do you decide which of these resources to 'process' into using in a lesson, which to keep, in case you might use them in the future, and which to throw away because they are not really that useful? How do you set up an efficient way of cataloguing and storing your resources, by topic, by type of resource?

TELEVISION

Arguably, the new technology application which has probably had most impact in the history classroom until recently is television (combined with video recorder or DVD). Most history departments have an archive of moving image recordings, largely taped from television programmes, and that some of these recordings are 'tried and tested', often edited, high impact resources which are very precious to the department. There are some bits of history that are incredibly powerful and moving when deliverd via the moving image, and television has captured many of these moments. However good you are at exposition, it is difficult for you to demonstrate vividly, what an atom bomb going off looks like, whereas television programmes can do this very powerfully. Given that lessons might be an hour or longer, a well chosen, vivid and powerful video/DVD extract can really help to provide a point of focus for a lesson, which is stimulating and accessible for pupils, and which makes it psychologically easier to get through the hour without worrying whether you can hold the attention of the pupils with your exposition and a textbook.

There are some bits of history which have been recorded on television and which are so powerful that having watched the extract, pupils may well remember it for the rest of their lives. As well as providing a variety of focus, use of the moving image can also give you a bit of time to think what you will do next – it can take the pressure off you for a few moments. There is of course the danger that history teachers can use television extracts indiscriminately, as an 'anaesthetic', or mainly to pass the time. (Extracts from *Blackadder* can be fine, but do they need to watch the whole episode?)

Schools broadcasts have improved significantly over the past few years, but they often do not hold pupils' attention for 20 minutes, and usually, video extracts need editing so that short extracts are used, to make a particular point vividly and powerfully. Sometimes schools broadcasts, or more general history programmes can be used to cover broad stretches of content, but you need to be careful about showing longer extracts – you need to watch the pupils not the programme from time to time, to see whether they have switched off and are 'truanting in mind', or turning their minds to messing about because they are bored. Both Channel 4 and the BBC offer a range of history prog-ammes relevant to the history which is taught in schools, and often the whole series of a progamme is broadcast 'back to back' so it can be helpful to look out for such collections in the TV guides (the BBC collections are usually broadcast as past of 'The Learning Zone', from 2.00 a.m., so you need to learn how to use the timer on your video or DVD if you do not know already). This is also when the popular GCSE 'Bitesize' revision progammes for history are broadcast. Teachers TV also has a number of history pro-grammes relevant to history teachers, which are easy to download from the site to watch and use at your convenience, once you have registered (www.teachers.tv).

The *Radio Times* or *TV Times* are invaluable resources for checking to see what history programmes are going to be on television, so that you can be prepared to record them, but beware of recording hundreds of programmes which you never get round to watching, editing and doing something with. Most programmes need careful editing to slect the most powerful and appropriate extracts, and this takes time.

THE HISTORICAL ASSOCIATION

We would advise you in the strongest possible terms to join the Historical Association. Although perhaps the biggest single benefit is access to *Teaching History*, the main profes-sional journal for history teachers (with electronic access to issues of the journal dating back to 1998), there are many other benefits, and the HA website has become increasingly useful to history teachers and student teachers over the past two years. In addition to resources and information about recent developments such as the use of voting technology and a report on the teaching of emotional and controversial issues, there is a regular newsletter to inform teachers and student teachers about regional and national conferences and Continuing Professional Development (CPD) opportunities, materials to promote the subject in schools and online discussion forums. The Historical Association also provides one of the main links between history teachers and academic historians. The 'In a nutshell' feature in *Teaching History* provides one of the most succinct and time effective ways of keeping up to date in the subject, and the 'Move me on' section (see below) is an essential source of information and advice for anyone wishing to become a history teacher. The website for the Historical Association can be found at www.history.org.uk.

'Move me on'
In addition to accessing the best possible resources for your pupils, you need to keep in mind resources for your own professional development. Every issue of *Teaching History* contains a section called 'Move me on', which addresses common problems and issues which student history teachers encounter on placement, and provides practical suggestions for moving forward in various aspects of your practice. You should become familiar with this section of the journal. It is specifically focused on the needs of student history teachers and their tutors.

HISTORY BOOKS, MAGAZINES AND MAPS

The development of the internet has not rendered obselete the written word, and there are a number of books and magazines which are relevant to the development of history teachers' subject knowledge and teaching skills. Many books and magazines contain powerful passages and quotations, and it can be good practice to make a collection of these as you come across them. The usefulness and impact of reading extracts from books, and quotations within PowerPoint presentations can be underestimated. They are often a useful counterpoint to the use of moving and still images, and provide more ways of varying your lesson format. Some examples and recommendations can be found at: www.uea.ac.uk/~m242/historypgce/sk/welcome.htm

There is a degree of irony in the comparative neglect of maps in the history classroom. The increasing prevalence of data projectors and interactive whiteboards in history classrooms has made it much easier to use maps in the history classroom, and many history websites contain 'interactive' maps and animations which can demonstrate change in a very vivid and clear manner (see Smart, 2003 for more detail on this).

There are also books which focus on particular aspects of school history, or teaching techniquess/pedagogy more generally. Amongst these, the following are amongst those which have been commended by former student teachers (a longer list is provided on the website):

Useful books:

Davies, P., Lynch, D. and Davies, R. (2003) *Enlivening Secondary History: 40 Classroom Activities for Teachers and Pupils*, London, RoutledgeFalmer. Provides both ideas and 'worked' examples.

Fisher, P. (2001) *Thinking through History*, Cambridge, Chris Kington.

An influential text which provides insights into ways of teaching history which develop pupils' ability to think, and learn, for themselves.

Ginnis, P. (2002) *The Teacher's Toolkit*, London, Crown House. Not history specific, but contains a vast number of suggestions for broadening your teaching repertoire and excellent on things like task design. Many teachers swear by it.

Murphy, J. (2006) *100 Ideas for Teaching History*, London, Continuum. You shouldn't expect all 100 to work perfectly, but even if just a few of them do, you are increasing your archive of teaching ideas.

Watkin, N. and Ahrenfelt, J. (2006) *100 Ideas for Essential Teaching Skills*, London, Continuum. A mixture of practical and imaginative ideas.

Smart, D. (2000) *Citizenship in History: A Guide for Teachers*, London, Stanley Thornes. Gives an indication of the breadth and range of citizenship issues which can be linked to history, with practical examples of activities.

PEERS AND COLLEAGUES

The teachers you work with, and your fellow student history teachers are obviously a fantastic resource for developing your professional knowledge, skills and abilities in history teaching. To what degree do you share and sub-contract with them efficiently in order to maximise your archive of resources? As noted earlier in this chapter, there are issues of ethics, tact and diplomacy here, as well as ones of organisation and dissemination. You must make sure than you do not alienate peers and colleagues by adopting a rapaciously selfish policy in this area, taking from others and not contributing and sharing yourself, not asking permission to use or borrow things, not acknowledging the provenance of ideas and resources when it is appropriate. This is an area where drive and initiative have to be balanced with sensitivity and professionalism – keep in mind Standards Q6 and Q32 of the standards for QTS here (TDA, 2007: 4, 7).

Another part of this agenda is whether you are a good learner or not (not necessarily the same thing as being highly intelligent). Some student teachers display high levels of acuity in picking up things from the teachers they work with. Others seem much slower to learn from others. Some student teachers seem to learn even before their tutors have said anything to them. Others have to be told time after time, and even then, don't seem to quite 'get it'.

Even with the availability of flash drives (memory sticks), portable hard drives, photocopiers, CD-ROMs, DVDs and virtual learning environments VLEs), there are few communities of history teachers who have organised themselves optimally to share and sub-contract in a way that helps them all to build up a fantastic archive of resources for teaching (mainly because they are too busy rather than lack of collegiality). Think how long it would take just to comprehensively explore *one* major history website. If you work as a group of history student teachers, it can be helpful to make arrangements to 'mine' different sites or different topics, so that between you, you can cover at least a reasonable proportion of all the resources that are now 'out there' for history teachers.

THE INTERNET

By 'out there', we largely mean the internet; a resource with fantastic potential for history teachers, and yet one which is far from unproblematic. It is not just pupils who can waste large amounts of time browsing the internet (see Chapter 8).

To think about...

A question worth asking:

To what extent do you make effective use of the internet for improving your teaching and your development as a history teacher?

You might also think about what proportion of what you bookmark or print off on the internet you turn into something that you actually use in your teaching.

There are different ways of using the internet as a resource. Here are some of them:

Collecting images on particular themes, people and events

At a very basic level, just building up 'collections' of pictures, cartoons, images, newspaper headlines on particular topics can transform fairly anodyne, text laden PowerPoint presentations into something much more interesting and enticing. Together with the use of the scanner, it is possible to build up folders of pictures on topics such as slavery, the industrial revolution, opposition, the Vietnam War or whatever, which can make the topics easier to talk about. Many images have stories that go with them – the boy standing in front of the tank, the soldier executing the Viet Cong prisoner, the girl with the napalm burns, the vulture waiting for the child to die (see website for further details on these and other pictures). Given that political, media and information literacy is a legitimate part of school history (Crick, 1998; DfES/QCA, 1999), it can also be helpful to collect pictures on contemporary figures. A common activity in year 8 is to look at portraits of Elizabeth I; the internet and cartoon archiving make it easy to collect a range of pictures of Elizabeth II which can develop pupils' understanding changes in public attitudes to monarchy over the past 50 years.

Teaching resources and ideas

This is obviously one of the major assets of the internet; to access resources that others have spent a lot of time and money on, with a view to helping you to teach history with stronger, more varied ideas and materials. The following is a list of sites that student teachers have found helpful in this respect. It is obviously far from comprehensive, and a wider list of sites and resources on ICT, and more detail on these sites can be accessed at: www.uea.ac.uk/~m242/historypgce/ict/welcome.htm.

School History: www.schoolhistory.co.uk
The Learning Curve: www.learningcurve.gov.uk
Spartacus: www.spartacus.schoolnet.co.uk
Schools History: www.schoolshistory.org.uk
Active History: www.activehistory.co.uk
Thinking History: www.thinkinghistory.co.uk
BBC History: www.bbc.co.uk/history
Innovating with history: www.qca.org.uk/history/innovating
Burnt Cakes: www.burntcakes.com
I love history: www.ilovehistory.co.uk
Channel 4 History: www.channel4.com/history
John D. Clare site: www.johndclare.net
Compton History: www.comptonhistory.com

Figure 9.1 Some history sites that student teachers have found helpful for ideas and resources for their lessons

It is easy to be overwhelmed by the sheer quantity of information available; you can spend hours just looking through the sites, browsing through various sections, with an almost 'pinball' approach. It can help to have a clear focus to your exploration of the site, and to be clear what you want to find so that your perusal of the site makes a real contribution to the quality of the lesson or series of lessons which you are preparing. You also need a well organised system of folders and files on your computer in order to keep your collection of resources under control. Remember also that lots of the ideas you come across can be adapted for use with other topics; many of the teaching ideas and resources on these sites are eminently transferable to different contexts.

The development of your professional knowledge and access to research and inspection findings

Intelligently used, the internet can make a major contribution to the development of your professional knowledge and understanding. If you look at the standards relating to professional knowledge and understanding in the QTS standards (TDA, 2007: 5–6), the internet can help with nearly all of them. Given that many student teachers will be embarking on courses which have a masters level element, the internet can help you to access articles and reports which enable you to strengthen the theoretical and literature based elements of your written assignments. Even the best of university liberaries can only have so many copies of key texts, which are often not in the library when the relevant assignment is due. More and more literature relating to teacher education and contemporary education policy and practice is now available electronically, and this can be invaluable if you are aware of some of the 'portals' to look for this information. Most academic journals are now downloadable over the net if your institution has a subscription to them, and it is helpful if you learn how to use the library's search engines to find what you want as early in the course as possible. The following are just some of the sites which may be of use or interest.

'Official' sites, sponsored by QCA and the DfES

i   The DfES 'Standards' site: www.standards.dfes.gov.uk/schemes. Part of this site is devoted to suggested schemes of work for history at Key Stages 1–3.

ii NC in Action: www.ncaction.org.uk/subjects/history/index.htm. Uses pupils' work to exemplify NC standards and expectations, with sections on promoting ICT and creativity through history.

iii NC Online: www.curriculumonline.gov.uk/Subjects/Hi/Subject.htm. Resources for teaching NC history and links to other relevant sites.

'Specialist' sites which focus on a particular facet of teaching history

i   Guidance on teaching history to gifted and talented pupils: www.nc.uk.net/gt/history/index.htm. Includes sections on identifying able pupils, inclusion issues and examples of activities and resources.

ii Respect for all: history: www.qca.org.uk/1581.html. Some exemplification materials on good practice in multicultural and anti-racist education in history.

iii 14–19 learning: www.qca.org.uk/14–19. Aims to cover all aspects of planning, teaching and learning within the 14–19 phase.

iv Citizenship and school history at KS3: www.standards.dfes.gov.uk/schemes2/citizenship/sec_hist/. Information to provide guidance on the possible links betweeen citizenship and school history.

v   History Transition: www.historytransition.org.uk. Site designed to help history teachers working in the transition phase between primary and secondary schools.

Task 9.7 Exploring a specialist support site for history

Access the History Transition site (www.historytransition.org.uk) and spend at least 20 minutes finding out about transition and teaching issues in this age range by looking at some of the schemes of work, the education sessions and the final report.

Academic sites

The move in the UK towards many history student teachers incorporating a Masters Degree element to their course of initial teacher education means that it is essential that student teachers demonstrate an understanding and awareness of recent research in history education, not least when they submit their formal written assignments. Most university libraries have electronic access to a wide range of academic journals which have articles detailing research findings in the field of history education. It is important that as early in the course as possible, you learn how to use the library's search facilities for e-journals, but there are also some sites which have free electronic access to academic papers relevant to student history teachers. Amongst these are:

The International Journal of Historical Learning, Teaching and Research: www.centres.ex.ac.uk/historyresource/journalstart.htm.

The Institute of Historical Research: see the resources section at: www.history.ac.uk/resindex.html.

The 'Open Society' section of the Institute of Education, University of London website (see the section on 'Frameworks' and 'Big pictures' of history in an open society'): http://ioewebserver.ioe.ac.uk/ioe/index.html.

Sites designed specifically for student teachers

Millions of pounds have recently been invested in creating Initial Teacher Education Professional Resource Networks (IPRNs) in order to improve access to resources for student teachers. As these have grown and matured, they provide an increasingly rich source of resources for student history teachers, and they give details of a wide range of programmes, reports and research findings which are available on the internet, freeing student teachers from absolute dependence on the library's of their education institution. Teachers TV provides another valuable source of materials and resources. All these resources have easy search systems, although they do require you to register in order to access the full range of features of the site, such as the ability to download and save programmes.

Teacher Training Resource Bank (general resources): www.ttrb.ac.uk
Behaviour for Learning (resources relating to behaviour issues):
    www.behaviour4learning.ac.uk
Multiverse (resources relating to diversity and equal opportunities issues):
    www.multiverse.ac.uk
Teachers TV: www.teachers.tv

Task 9.8 Using internet sites designed to support student teachers

a   Access and watch the Teachers TV programme, 'Secondary ICT: web literacy', which focuses mainly on helping teachers to develop pupils' understanding of the problematic nature of the internet as a resource (http://www.teachers.tv/video/5425). In what ways could you use this programme to develop your teaching strategies in this area. Use the search facility to seee if you can find out what other programmes are avaiable to support secondary history teachers.

b   Go to the Teacher Training Resource Bank (www.ttrb.ac.uk) website and type in 'history' to the site search engine. Choose a resource that is relevant to work that you are doing, either in the classroom or for an assignment, and download it. (This would be one strand of evidence to support your developing compence in Standard Q25a, but it is only of any real use if you read the article rather than simply downloading it.)

General sites designed for teachers

As well as history specific sites (see Figure 9.1), there are a range of sites for teachers which have sub-sections for history teachers. See for example:

Times Educational Supplement Resource Bank: www.tes.co.uk/resources/
    Home.aspx
Birmingham Grid for Learning: www.bgfl.org
London Grid for Learning: http://cms.lgfl.net/lgfl/web/homepage/
TeacherNet: www.teachernet.gov.uk
The Education Forum: www.educationforum.co.uk

SUMMARY AND KEY POINTS

There is no necessary correlation between the sophistication and expense of the resources used and the quality of the learning experience for pupils. It is important that pupils experience a variety of resources and treaching methods, but a lesson which involves no more than teacher talk and pupil talk may be more successful than one involving an array of technological aids. The most important resource of all is you, and the skilful and effective use of the teaching strategies you decide to employ. Often the main resources used by the teacher are talk, the blackboard, displays and the use of paper and note-books. Books, source materials in books and worksheets are also widely used, but slides, videos, roleplay, games, artefacts, computer technology, TV, museums, and fieldtrips are not always feasible in terms of everyday use- access, finance and school organisation often place limits on what can be attempted. Your task is to do the best job possible in the circumstances. Foresight, initiative and imagination are part of the art of using resources effectively, and a sureness of touch in working out 'fitness for purpose' is something which should accrue from increased experience and reflection.

You need to be aware of the problems pupils have in understanding historical sources and consider how best to use sources at different levels as classroom resources. Resources certainly help pupils to be active in their own learning and can often play a significant part in motivating them to do well in history. A greater understanding of the past should be possible when you use a variety of resources in your teaching. The intelligent use of resources ensures that history teaching does not focus on a narrow range of activities. As a general point of professional integrity or etiquette, if you are using someone else's ideas or resources, you should acknowledge their provenance.

BE CAREFUL NOT TO...

Be careful not to fall into just using whatever comes to hand, or what is in the department. One of the performance indicators for student teachers is the extent to which they show initiative, and are proactive and imaginative in scavenging for resources – from *Teaching History*, the newspapers, the internet, the television, the museum shop – potentially brilliant resources are all over the place if you keep an eye out for them.

REFERENCES

Allen, D. (2001) *Getting Things Done*, London: Piatkus.

Crick, B. (1998) *Education for Citizenship and the Teaching of Democracy in Schools: The Crick Report*, London: DfEE.

Culpin, C. (1999) ' "No puzzle, no learning": how to make your site visits rigorous, fascinating and indispensable', *Teaching History*, No. 97: 29–35.

Danks, E.J. (1994) 'Theory and practice: the use of resources and teaching aids in the teaching of history, with particular reference to year eight', *Teaching History*, October, No. 77.

DfEE/QTS (1999) *The National Curriculum for Citizenship*, London: DfEE/QCA.

Hake, C. and Haydn, T. (1995) 'Stories or sources?', *Teaching History*, No. 78: 20–2.

Harrison, S. (2003) 'The use of ICT for teaching history: slow growth, some green shoots', in T. Haydn and C. Counsell (2003) *History, ICT and Learning*, London: RoutledgeFalmer: 37–51.

HMI (1985) *History in the Primary and Secondary Years*, London: HMSO.

Jones, R. (2007) 'The creative use of ICT in history teaching', unpublished seminar, UEA, Norwich, 29 May.

Lloyd-Jones, R. (1995) *How to Produce better Worksheets*, London: Stanley Thornes.

Smart, L. (2003) ICT and maps: a significant development for teachers of history', in T. Haydn and C. Counsell (2003) *History, ICT and Learning*, London: RoutledgeFalmer: 152–75.

OFSTED (1995) *History: A Review of Inspection Findings 1993–4*, London: OFSTED.

OFSTED (2006) *Annual Report of Her Majesty's Chief Inspector of Schools, 2005–6*, London: OFSTED.

QCA (2005) 'Pupil perceptions of history at Key Stage 3', London: QCA. Online at http://www.qca.org.uk/qca_6391.aspx. Accessed 14 October 2007.

TDA (2007) *Professional Standards for Teachers: QTS*, London: TDA.

Walsh, B. (2003) 'Building learning packages: integrating virtual resources with the real world of teaching and learning', in T. Haydn and C. Counsell (eds), *History, ICT and Learning*, London: RoutledgeFalmer: 109–33.

10 Assessment in the classroom

INTRODUCTION

The organisation of a book about teaching, which considers assessment in a separate chapter, and that towards the end of the book, could in itself send out an incorrect message. For it is fundamental that if assessment is to be used successfully by the classroom teacher, it must be integrated within the whole process of planning. The well-worn maxim that 'effective assessment depends on effective planning' is as true as ever. Consequently, the way in which you provide feedback to your pupils and both record and report on their progress, will be very much related to the clarity of your teaching and learning objectives, together with you choice of learning experiences.

In the second part of this chapter we will review the range of approaches to assessment you could consider using, and relating them, where appropriate, to the principles underpinning 'assessment for learning'.

Objectives

At the end of this chapter you should be able to:

- identify some of the key issues which affect the assessment of history;
- understand and deploy the recent recommendations for the use of both the formative and summative assessment of pupils' progress at Key Stage 3;
- set and mark tasks for pupils and record and report on pupils' progress in an appropriate and effective way.

KEY ISSUES IN THE ASSESSMENT OF HISTORY

This important relationship between planning, methods and assessment means that the vast changes in the teaching of history in the last 30 years have also had a considerable impact on how learning in history is assessed. More than a generation ago the principal concerns were to assess the recall of knowledge, to reward the ability to select information relevant to a question and to deploy that knowledge in Standard English. Differentiation was achieved in the accuracy, quantity and literary quality of the answers.

With the evolution of the 'new' history, teachers and examiners had to consider how to assess pupils' progress in their use of sources, their understanding of key concepts, of past ideas and attitudes and, more recently, of historical interpretations and representations. Such changes made it even more imperative that the concept of progression in historical understanding was researched and applied to the assessment of that understanding. The development of 'levels' marking schemes at 16+, and the later TGAT model with its (original) ten levels for the NC, implied the existence of some acceptable theory of how pupils' historical understanding progresses. It may be argued that the problems experienced of both the GCSE and the NC are in part related to the limited and inconsistent application of any theoretical basis, and the lack of a universally acceptable model, which would explain pupils' progression in historical understanding. The June 2004 issue of *Teaching History*, entitled 'Assessment without levels' included several articles, which highlighted the limitations and frustrations of using the NC level descriptions. Burnham and Brown (2004) felt that the descriptions 'do not define the changing ideas, patterns of reasoning and layers of knowledge that make up progression in historical learning'. The issue describes the tensions apparent in some schools between school managers, keen for data on pupil progress, and heads of history disliking the use of level descriptions for half-termly reports or indeed as the basis for assessing individual pieces of work. It is correctly stated that the level descriptions were never intended to be used in this way. Burnham and Brown found them 'too blunt' for individual pieces of work and OFSTED (2003) agreed that descriptions were unlikely to help in creating helpful learning objectives. Hammond (2001) found that 'planning to meet this or that level of causation became reductive and pointless and did not add up to any long-term progression anyway'. A fuller discussion of this aspect of assessment is included when progression is considered later in the chapter. Not only do you need to be aware of this debate but to consider it within the practice of your own school and in the formulation of your lesson objectives, when you will probably agree that finely-tuned precise objectives, task and context-related offer the best prospects of day-to-day assessment.

The diversity of approaches and resources now available to the history teacher encourages the need for a corresponding variety of assessment procedures. You should take note of how some pupils perform better in some situations than others: some are good orally while not so good with written work; some work well in small groups but not so well in whole class situations; while some produce good work if given time and the opportunities for re-drafting mentioned in Chapter 4. So you need to be aware of that variety of assessment possibilities, which extends beyond written responses, but also includes oral assessment together with other more ephemeral, yet significant, evidence of understanding that will occur. A Historical Association report summarised this point in the context of the wider debate:

> There is a broad consensus among educational researchers that a variety of modes of assessment makes that assessment more accurate and reliable. Assessment in history has become much more restricted and uniform. It needs

to be broadened to include much more scope for teacher assessment. There needs to be much more variety for teacher assessment.

(Historical Association, 2005: 4)

These changes in the form of school history and in ideas about assessment over the past few decades have raised important and difficult questions about what it means 'to get better' at history, and how we make sure that the time that we invest in assessment is of maximum benefit to all parties involved in the process. Issues include (1) the use of knowledge, (2) progression, (3) differentiation and (4) the validity and reliability of your assessment.

THE ROLE OF KNOWLEDGE

The role of historical knowledge in assessment has become the subject of much debate. There has taken place what to many would seem to have been a rather artificial debate which sought to place the advocates of knowledge (traditional history) against those of skills (new history), what Counsell has called 'a distracting dichotomy' (Counsell, 1999). Most history teachers accepted that the learning of history required both skills and knowledge. Assessment which attempted to test skills without reference to the historical context was as arid as the recall of information without understanding and was of limited value.

The challenge for you is to determine how that knowledge is to be used. Some pupils gain great satisfaction and a real sense of achievement when they are able to recall information and there is a place for this in your assessment, particularly with the younger pupils. The danger is, of course, that history is once more seen as a subject whose prime objective is the memorisation of facts.

Two issues may be highlighted:

- What is historical knowledge?
- Are there gradations of historical knowledge?

How you respond to these questions will influence your thinking about how you assess your pupils.

WHAT IS HISTORICAL KNOWLEDGE?

If you are trying to assess historical knowledge, you need to have a clear understanding of what this means (see Lee and Ashby, 2000: 199–201 for a helpful discussion of this issue). To those listening to general knowledge quizzes, the answer may seem obvious – the ability to recall historical facts with accuracy. Others may settle for the ability to describe a historical event in some detail. For either of these short answer objective tests or requests to 'write all you know about' would be suitable forms of assessment and were indeed familiar features in the history classroom a couple of decades ago. There may be still a case for the interim testing of factual knowledge but this is seen as securing the basis for further applications of that knowledge. Counsell (1999) justifiably stressed that what matters is the teacher's awareness of the *role of knowledge in future learning*. So, while accepting the need to be able to deploy accurate information, if this is done without also demonstrating understanding, such assessment has little educational value. The issue thus becomes – how can you assess historical knowledge in a way that enables the pupils to show understanding as well?

It is now generally accepted that historical knowledge is much more than factual knowledge and also includes knowledge of explanations of events, changes and issues; and knowledge of the historical process, for example, what procedures do you adopt for analysing evidence or what questions should you ask when confronted by differing interpretations? The issue then is – how can you assess such aspects of historical know-ledge, while still rewarding factual knowledge?

ARE THERE GRADATIONS IN HISTORICAL KNOWLEDGE?

If assessment were to be based solely upon historical knowledge what would be the basis for discrimination? Traditionally, the answers would have centred upon quantity and accuracy. These characteristics continue to feature in criteria for assessment, but the problems of a narrow focus on factual knowledge were increased when 'levels of response' mark schemes began to appear in the early 1980s and even more so with the NC Attainment Target levels. If history was to have an Attainment Target assessing knowledge, what knowledge would characterise level 1 and what level 10? Such a question seemed only to emphasise the limitations of such assessment and, not surprisingly, specific knowledge is not included in the Attainment Target statements. Lee and Shemilt note the limitations of gradations of knowledge based upon substantive concepts such as 'peasant', 'parliament' in contrast to ideas that shape history such as key concepts such as that of evidence (Lee and Shemilt, 2003). It is salutary to note the importance attached to 'Key Concepts' and 'Key Processes' in the recent revision of the NC for history, introduced in September 2008 (http://curriculum.qca.org.uk/subjects/history/, or search the History area of the QCA website, www.qca.org.uk should this change in time).

But can we be so dismissive about the relative value of historical knowledge? It is possible to argue that knowledge will be rewarded either *for the way in which it is acquired* or *for the way in which it is used*. Your pupils' historical knowledge is likely to be worthy of praise if it has been acquired as a result of the use of initiative and the use of enquiry and reference skills: enquiry is one of the 'Key Concepts' in the revised history curriculum. Higher rewards are also likely to be available for knowledge not immediately available to the pupil or candidates in sources or descriptions of a context. Should that knowledge be used to demonstrate the wider significance of a topic, to make links, connections and perhaps generalisations then again this is likely to be graded more highly. Within a levels marking scheme what often pushes a mark to the top of a level is the extent knowledge is used to support that level of understanding. The real requirement is for pupils to be able to *apply* their knowledge to inform their opinions and judgements.

Even though due attention is paid to the use of knowledge, there often remains the need to maintain a balance between rewarding the use of knowledge and the relationship between knowledge and levels of understanding. For example, supposing you were to set a task, the main purpose of which was to assess the pupils' understanding of historical interpretations. Pupil A *described* in detail the differences between the two interpretations and used plenty of factual information to support the answer. Pupil B was able to make some attempt at *explaining* the differences with some, but not a lot, of factual support. Who gets the higher mark? This question of balance has again been a feature of the debate over the last ten years and remains a key issue. What is important is that you continue to think carefully about the relationship between knowledge and understanding. Lee has pointed out that

> learning history is difficult, and does not take place in a flash at 18 or even at 25. It is a gradual process of developing ideas, in which pupils need a great deal of help. A substantial part of what is learned has to be *knowing-how*, not just *knowing-that*. Some of what children have to learn is not itself historical knowledge at all, but provides crutches and tools for assisting them to acquire that knowledge.
>
> (Lee, 1994: 44)

Task 10.1 The role of historical knowledge

1   Discuss with the subject teachers in your school how they encourage their pupils to recall and use their historical knowledge. On what occasions are the pupils required to recall their historical knowledge (a) orally and (b) in writing? Do they have a different emphasis for the ability to recall and use historical knowledge for KS3 pupils in comparison to GCSE pupils? Consider how the responses might influence the objectives you formulate and the tasks you set.

2   With two different age-groups (e.g. year 7 or 8 and year 10), ask the pupils the following question, 'If a pupil is "good at history", how do we know?' Compare their answers with your own answer to this question. What do the pupils' answers tell you about their understanding of history?

3   Present a group of year 7 or 8 pupils with two pictures, related to a topic they have covered, for comparison, e.g. a motte and bailey castle and a concentric castle. Ask the pupils to draw two columns, one headed 'How they differ?' and the other 'Why they differ?' Ask them to try to complete the columns. When assessing their responses, consider the role of knowledge in your final judgement. Are you rewarding the quantity or the quality of the knowledge used?

For further consideration of the nature and role of historical knowledge, see www.uea.ac.uk/~m242/historypgce/sk/welcome.htm.

PROGRESSION

The issue of progression raises fundamental questions, which will influence your whole approach to teaching and setting tasks for pupils. Competence statements Q22 to Q25 (TDA, 2007: 6) stress the importance of continuity and progression within and between classes as well as ensuring you make appropriate demands of your pupils. Yet without an understanding of progression it will be difficult for you to meet these competence statements. Thus, without an understanding of progression you could be in danger of making assumptions about what your pupils can do and understand, failing to understand what seem to be blocks to their progress or repeating tasks, which do not offer sufficient challenge because you are unsure about how to encourage such pupils towards a deeper understanding of the subject.

So what does the concept of progression mean in the context of learning history? More factual knowledge? Extended vocabulary? Better literary skills? The time has surely passed when what made one piece of work better than another was the number of accurate pieces of information that could be counted. Yet such approaches do have an attraction for those seeking reliable standardisation. Rather, if progression is related to historical understanding, what characterises better understanding of key concepts such as causation, change and the attitudes of differing past societies? How can we identify progression in the development of source skills and in the ability to handle historical interpretations? Much has been written to help you to understand the basis for progression in the learning of history. The work of Hallam (1972), Watts (1973), Shemilt (1976), Booth (1983), Dickinson and Lee (1984), Lomas (1989) and Lee and Ashby (2000) covers some of the debate about how children's historical understanding develops and its implications for teachers. More recently QCA (2007) have stated that progression at Key Stage 3 is characterised by:

- the acquisition of an increasing range and depth of historical knowledge, and the ability to make links and connections within and across historical periods;
- deepening understanding of general and specific historical concepts;
- greater understanding of and proficiency in the use of historical skills;
- an increasing ability to apply skills and conceptual understanding across a variety of historical contexts;
- an increasing ability to communicate knowledge and understanding using language appropriately and accurately;
- becoming independent in learning across a variety of situations.

The challenge has been and continues to be for teachers and examiners to translate these characteristics into detailed, specific mark schemes. For over two decades now progression in history has often taken the form of levels and levels mark schemes with the assumption that a pupil progresses up a 'ladder of progress'. The task then is to identify, which level statement most closely fits the work produced by the pupil. It all sounds so straightforward and this is the model of progression used by the National Attainment Target (NCAT), which presents you with levels of attainment, each of which have a collection of statements covering the range of second order concepts. The theory is that these statements can be applied to indicate the level of attainment an individual pupil has reached (see the link to 'Attainment Target' at http:// curriculum.qca.org.uk/subjects/history/).

But, as indicated in the chapter introduction, many teachers have misgivings about the NCAT model of progression. These are voiced in many places and are effectively expressed by Lee and Shemilt. Their concerns about the NCAT model include:

1   Pupils' understanding does not necessarily follow this linear approach. It does not necessarily move up this step-ladder one rung at a time.
2   The use of phrases such as 'beginning to identify' are *weasel* phrases, which in their use, seem to admit the limitations of levels and to encourage the use of sub-levels. They also challenge the evenness of the levels as you cannot really say the gaps between levels are equal.

3   The use of history specific language within the documentation, for example the failure to distinguish between what constitutes 'evidence' and what is 'information'.

4   It is not possible to state that a particular pupil is at say level 5 because progress in one area of the statement is not necessarily balanced by similar progress in another.

5   Possibly one of the most telling points they make is the assumption within the model that the skill of evaluation is a higher level activity and so limited to a few pupils. Many teachers will see the rigidity here does not equate to their class-room experience, where, depending on the context and how the task is set up, many pupils are capable of making evaluations. (This has a familiar ring about it as for many decades hierarchies of types of questions have listed comprehension as a low order activity whereas in practice it depends on the context, as similarly evaluation questions are not necessarily higher order ones.)

6   The use of 'best fit' practice for matching pupils' work to levels seems highly hit and miss; a compromise to produce data which could obscure the detail needed to help pupils make progress. (Lee and Shemilt, 2003)

Where there does seem to be general agreement is that progression in history should be based upon the development of pupils' understanding of its key concepts. Thus, instead of assembling a collection of disparate statements in an arbitrary manner, as Cottingham (2004) concluded, 'the clear implication is that separate progression models are needed for different concepts'. Much work is still needed in their development, then, given such models, departments could then use them to assess pupil progress for each concept across topics, years and Key Stages. In being able to do this, what is clear is that such models need to be secure enough to be applicable to a range of contexts but most of all they need to be user-friendly, unambiguous and not unduly time-consuming in their application. Lee and Shemilt find that there is much to be gained from teachers having a good understanding of the likely misconceptions which pupils may hold about a concept (of the sort indicated in previous chapters) and also of the nature of the water-sheds or barriers they need to overcome in order to make progress in their understanding of a key concept.

Clearly understanding and using ideas about progression in history represents a chal-lenge for all involved in the teaching of history and it is far easier to criticise existing models than it is to create better ones. For the student teacher it is therefore important that you are aware of the difficulties and the possibilities of progression and use this information when constructing specific objectives for the learning of a concept and in devising your own mark schemes.

Task 10.2 Identifying progression in history

You will find it useful to see how various notions of progression have influenced the NC and GCSE.

1   Ask the history department in which you are placed if they have a copy of the original documentation for the 1991 NC specifications for history. Look carefully at all three Attainment Targets and try to identify any principles that underpin the level statements.

> 2   Compare these statements with those in the current Attainment Target for history (online at http://curriculum.qca.org.uk/subjects/history/, and follow the link to 'Attainment Target'). Extract those sentences which are comparable e.g. causation, interpretations, use of sources. How much do they differ? Note the key words 'describe', explain' etc., in the latest version.
>
> 3   Ask your history department if they possess any of the marking schemes produced by a GCSE awarding body. Again analyse these to identify any principles of progression, which underpin the levels of response. (Alternatively, you should be able to access examples from the awarding body websites: www.ocr.org.uk, www.edexcel.org.uk, www.aqa.org.uk.)

DIFFERENTIATION

get it

A further issue, linked to progression, is that of differentiation. It is possible to argue that setting differentiated tasks is one of the most difficult activities in teaching. OFSTED (1995) comment on the general lack of differentiation. 'At worst this saw classes doing the same work which was unchallenging to some of the pupils and inaccessible to others.' In history teaching, any such differentiation must be based on a clear understanding of those factors, which make a task easier or more difficult, hence again the importance of progression. It is important to be aware that there are many factors influencing the extent to which the learning of all pupils can be maximised (see Lewis, 1992; Biggs and Moore, 1993), but two of the commonest approaches to differentiation in the history classroom are 'by outcome' or 'by task'. 'By outcome' means that the whole range of pupils in a class, year or examination cohort, are given the same assessment exercise or examination paper with questions set in such a way that pupils can respond according to their ability. The revised history GCSE continued to use this approach to differentiation even though there are critics of this method, well articulated by Checketts (1996). The GCSE approach may well have encouraged its overuse in secondary schools leading to OFSTED (1995) criticism. Their inspectors felt that inappropriate use 'can become frustrating to pupils who need a more structured approach to enable then to give of their best'. 'Differentiation by outcome' is more likely to work well for tasks, which require creativity, imagination, investigations and empathetic reconstructions, when the pupils have a clear idea of the assessment criteria. 'By outcome' has been described as the more 'comfortable' option by OFSTED and this is because differentiation 'by task' is generally regarded as being more difficult. Planning work, which addresses different levels of conceptual understanding is a skilful business. You need not only to know the abilities of the individual pupils but also to understand the nature of progression in history. You must also remember that another important part of differentiation is the pupil's attitude to the task. If pupils are to perform to their 'personal best' to borrow a phrase used in athletics, it helps if they want to do well and are enthusiastically engaged in the process of learning. As Hallam notes, 'They must want to learn,: if you lose that, you will lose just about everything' (Hallam, 1996). Hallam also stresses the importance of the following factors:

- valuing and encouraging all pupils – including the clever ones and the quiet ones;
- allowing pupils to make mistakes;

- making learning objectives explicit and explaining the criteria for doing the task well;
- providing accurate and positive feedback;
- taking into account that pupils have differing preferred learning styles when planning teaching and assessment activities.

(Hallam, 1996)

Your methods of assessing pupils' achievement in history should keep in mind all these factors.

In issue 98 of *Teaching History*, the 'Move me on' section, for student history teachers and their tutors, focuses on marking and assessment (*Teaching History*, No.98, February, 41–5). As well as identifying common problems and difficulties, the article provides practical strategies for moving forward in marking and assessment. Stephen (2006) provides a wide range of very practical ideas and approaches to differentiation in a wide-ranging chapter on inclusion.

APPLYING DIFFERENTIATION TO YOUR ASSESSMENT

Chapter 7 has included a section on differentiation, which by the application of the principles of assessment for learning means it is integral to the assessment of the activities described. Further points for your consideration are discussed below.

Setting written assessment topics to take account of different abilities requires the consideration of issues such as:

1   Make sure your pupils write as fully as they can. This can be helped by giving precise indications of your expectations. For example, instead of 'give reasons for' ask 'Give at least *five* reasons for'. With younger pupils you might, where appropriate, suggest they write 'at least ten lines' for their answer.

2   The extent to which *you will provide a structure* for the pupils' answers. This might include the use of several short questions in a helpful sequence leading to main question or giving some indications about the required content, for example, providing some causes of an event for comment and then asking pupils to add to this list before writing a full response. In other words, this means helping the pupil by breaking down the task into manageable parts or providing the first sentence of a response. An issue of differentiation arises if you give too much help to the more able pupils, who would be better assessed with a more general or open-ended task.

3   The *format of the tasks* can involve differentiation. This could involve the extent to which you want to include objective items. Such items often require more limited writing and may be appropriate for some pupils. Consequently, you might find some place for making lists, labelling, the completion of sentences, sequencing exercises and, at times, the use of multiple-choice questions. All of these reduce considerably the amount of writing, but also prompt you to keep asking what you are assessing. While there are exceptions, the use of short objective test items could encourage the assessment of knowledge without understanding and, of course, be inappropriate for the ability of many pupils. Another 'rule of thumb' is that the more you reduce the number of sources and

'variables' involved in a task, the more likely you make it more accessible to pupils of lower abilities.

4   A further issue is the relationship between the use of differentiated assessment and norm-referencing. If pupils are set tasks according to their ability so that they can demonstrate what they can do, you may need to have some sensitivity in making the less able pupils aware of the limitations of their success. Other-wise they may hold unrealistic notions about their level of performance when compared with others and assessed against the levels of the Attainment Target. Similarly, you need to take into account the level of support provided when assessing the quality of your pupils' responses.

Task 10.3 Assessment and differentiation

Choose a topic, which you know you will be teaching on your placement to a class with a wide range of ability. When you have familiarised yourself with the content and the available resources, select as a target, an element of the knowledge, skills and understanding in the NC for history, for which that content and those resources presents an appropriate vehicle.

Plan *three* different task-sheets for the different abilities, taking into account the following:

a   the use of language involved for both the instructions and any sources;
b   the appearance of the sheet (where possible making use of ICT facilities);
c   the use of abstract concepts;
d   the variety and nature of any sources used;
e   the range and progression of skills you wish the pupils to employ;
f   your expectations about the amount of knowledge you wish them to use; and
g   your expectations about the length and format of their responses.

Try to ensure that there is a very noticeable difference in demand between the tasks for the ablest and the least able pupils.

Discuss your task sheets with the teacher and, if convenient to the department, use them.

THE VALIDITY AND RELIABILITY OF YOUR ASSESSMENT

In assessing your pupils you need to be constantly aware of the factors that can affect the validity and reliability of the information you acquire. A task may be said to be valid if it achieves what it is intended to do, if it clearly addresses the assessment targets you have in mind. Several factors can limit validity.

First, a most frequent reason for a test being of limited validity is *because the question has been poorly formulated*, that could mean the pupils are confused about what they have to do. It is ambiguous and your instructions are unclear and you may be asking the pupils to try to read your mind and guess what it is you want. Alternatively the question you have devised is actually testing a different set of objectives from what you thought. Finding the best words and phrases for a question or task is much harder than you might initially believe and usually needs plenty of thought and time. Because of this if you do create or find tasks that work well, store them away for future use.

Second, if the tasks are dependent on sources, as many are, then you need to make sure the sources are not inaccessible, and are appropriate for the parameters of the ability levels of the pupils they are designed for.

Third, you also need to consider whether the pupils have access to the *amount of knowledge* they will require for a good answer. Also a test loses validity if the pupils are being assessed on content, skills or concepts which they have not been taught. In the SCAA (1996) Optional Tests and Tasks, the question is constantly asked 'Are the pupils ready for this assessment?' and invites consideration of the knowledge of the content and the understanding of historical concepts required of the pupils if they are to attempt the task with any degree of success. There are implications here for situations where there are several history teachers teaching different classes who are all given the same test or examination. Should your pupils not be given sufficient time to complete a task, this again affects the validity of any assessment made.

A task is potentially less reliable if there are several teachers involved in the marking. Hence the need for clear mark schemes, which can be consistently interpreted and the identification of clear criteria for the marking. This helps to diminish the subjective aspects of marking such as your opinion about an individual pupil's attitude to history, his or her usual behaviour or the clarity of the writing. However, this is easily offset by the welcome and growing trend for departments to consider the assessment of key pieces of assessment across the year and the key stage as a team. The discussion of the mark schemes, the principles behind them and examples of pupil responses is likely to increase reliability. As a student teacher you will find involvement in such discussions makes a valuable contribution to your understanding of good practice.

APPROACHES TO ASSESSMENT IN HISTORY

Assessment is generally more effectively used when it is integrated within the teaching of a topic; planned for, not bolted on at the end as an afterthought. Keep in your mind the idea that the prime objective of assessment is to support learning not just to test it. Trying to achieve this is quite a sophisticated skill as you try to choose assessment strategies which are appropriate to the learning activities in which the pupils are engaged. Acknowledging that assessment is part of effective planning is central to the *assessment for learning* initiative now becoming well established in schools. Many of the aspects of 'assessment for learning' have been familiar to good teachers for many years, but they do help to reinforce good practice and provide very useful guidelines for student teachers. To summarise, in applying 'assessment for learning' you focus on *how* your pupils learn, ensuring the tasks you require of your pupils are both sensitive and instructive, fostering motivation, ensuring your pupils understand the purpose of the tasks and how success will be identified in such a way that they know how to improve and in developing in your pupils a capacity for self-improvement. This is quite a list and could at first seem overwhelming. Consequently it is perhaps better as a student teacher to adopt the policy of gradualism and not expect to fulfil all aspects at once. This is a complex agenda, and it takes time for you to acquire a solid grounding in all aspects of assessment.

Further resources and information on assessment in history can be accessed at: www.uea.ac.uk/~m242/historypgce/assess/welcome.htm.

Further information about assessment more generally, including the use of 'value added' data, can be found at the website for the Association for Achievement and Improvement through Assessment (AAIA): http://www.aaia.org.uk/index800.htm.

Task 10.4 Applying principles of assessment

The following questions are derived from the principles of assessment defined by the Association for Achievement and Improvement through Assessment (AAIA).

i   How can assessment reflect the academic, social, emotional and moral development of the pupils?

ii How can pupils be fully involved in assessment processes so that they can understand how to improve and become independent learners?

iii How can assessment be organised so that pupils work towards long-term as well as short-term goals?

iv How can assessment be used to encourage motivation and enhance pupils' self-esteem?

v   How can I employ a range of assessment strategies in my day-to-day teaching and base my judgements on a wide range of evidence in order to obtain a holistic view of pupils' achievements?

vi What opportunities exist for my assessments to be moderated and discussed?

vii How can I present my assessments in way that is useful to the pupils, the school's assessment policies and also to parents?

1   Using your department's schemes of work for Key Stage 3 consider where and when these principles are likely to be applied.

2   Decide which principles are relevant to your own planning and how you would incorporate them into your schemes.

3   Discuss with your tutor or head of department how the department seeks to apply these principles to the teaching of history at Key Stage 3.

The range of approaches listed below, in which the principles of Task 10.4 are implicit, show the variety of possibilities for the integration of assessment in both your planning and the delivery of your lessons.

DAY-TO-DAY ASSESSMENT

Giving instant feedback: tutors often find that for student teachers, ongoing assessment seems to be one of the hardest things the beginning teacher needs to master. For example, it is found that often a student teacher cannot see that a lesson was wrongly pitched, sometimes too low, frequently too high. That miscalculation could be based on the fact that some pupils have provided correct answers to oral questions even though the answering may have been limited to a few pupils and many may not have followed the lesson. Some ideas for getting a better idea whether all or most pupils have grasped the points and met your objectives are as follows:

- Use of *mini whiteboards* in class sets in folders with pen and rubber. They can be used to write very brief answers to questions, e.g. factual recall, key words or simple understanding. 'Give me a date in the twelfth century' is a question many year 7 pupils can find difficult. This kind of instant feedback can assess the understanding of a concept where the pupils clearly have or have not grasped it. It cannot show the depth of their understanding.
- Use of true/false cards to show simple understanding after reading a text.
- Plenaries involving active participation by everyone, e.g. giving each pupil a card with a key word on it and a pupil has to stand up up when the teacher calls out the meaning to match their word.
- Dominoes as a starter or plenary, i.e. cards telling a story. The pupil with the first card begins a sentence, the next card completes the sentence and starts the next one. Each pupil has a card. Repeat as a class exercise a couple of times, the second time is much easier. Pupils can help each other to make it easier.
- Walking round the classroom looking at books as the pupils write, especially year 7. The difficulty pupils experience in following instructions for writing is often underestimated.
- Use of factual recall exercises. The important role of knowledge has already been discussed and although sometimes unfashionable there still remains a place for encouraging factual recall as part of your instant feedback. Haydn (2005) in his research for QCA found that pupils continue to see their progress in terms of knowledge and while understanding is the goal, there are times when you can use strategies to ensure the pupils have a strong enough factual base to move on to further activities. Again mini white boards are useful.

Self-assessment: teachers are increasingly finding value in encouraging their pupils in the use of self-assessment. Black and Wiliam (1998) have been advocating the use of this type of formative as well as peer assessment for some time. Very much a feature of 'assessment for learning', self-assessment is seen to carry many benefits for the pupils. It encourages a more positive classroom climate by reducing the fear of failure and emphasising what has been achieved, thereby improving the pupil's self-esteem. Pupils benefit from being involved in using and at times creating the 'success' criteria to be used and have a clear idea of what it is they are expected to learn. When applying the criteria they can work out how well they are doing and what they now need to do in order to improve as they reflect upon their own assessment.

You may find it useful to begin in a modest way, making it as simple as possible. Task 10.5 is designed to help you in your earliest efforts. You will see just how important it is that you have a precise understanding of what it is you want your pupils to learn. Note too the importance of giving *all* pupils a chance to succeed and to be able to reflect on their own assessment. From more simple approaches you may be able to move on to using some forms of progression models, possible including concept and context-specific levels.

Task 10.5 Beginning to use pupil self-assessment

1   In planning a sequence of lessons, think about how you can find out whether all your pupils have achieved the objectives. What forms of assessment will you use? When will they take place? At what point will you inform pupils of the ways in which they will be assessed?

2   Include in your planning a piece of work which concludes a set of lessons. Before the pupils attempt it work with them to create the criteria to be used in the assessment.

3   After completion of the piece of work, ask the pupils to create a grid with the criteria down the left-hand side and 'Have I done it?' across the top. Then ask the pupils to go through their work and tick the criteria, which they think they have met.

4   Field the responses. What criteria have been met and what has proved the most difficult? Ask the pupils to indicate what should be the next thing they could do to improve.

Peer assessment: this is in some ways a more sophisticated advance on self-assessment but, if done successfully, can have additional benefits. When experimenting with the use of peer assessment, it is important to give clear and detailed guidance to pupils including some suggestions for areas of focus, and some modelling of exemplar comments. The advantages of peer assessment include giving the pupils an opportunity to talk about their work in a constructive manner, which would involve trying to accommodate subject-specific language into their exchanges; they can learn from each other and benefit from examining each other's work. Opinions might vary about how you pair up the pupils but teachers often find it helps if you put together pupils of a similar ability. Again the follow-up to the paired discussion is crucial, ensuring all pupils have reflected on the assessment and have a clear ides of how to progress.

Modelling: closely linked to the use of self and peer assessment is the use of modelling. This is where you show examples of completed work to the pupils so that they can identify what makes one piece of work better than another and from that learn what they need to make progress. Modelling can be used at different stages throughout a set of lessons: at the beginning of a unit of work by showing the pupils an example of a piece of work and by comparing this with the written learning objectives. With some pupils you may find they need to be shown exactly how to set out their work or begin their work and presenting model answers is a valuable method. As their work develops the pupils can use the model as a guide in order to improve and modify their work. Finally, as a basis for comparison with their own work to help them identify the success criteria, note if they have done better and where they need to make progress. Another modelling activity involves presenting pupils with four different answers to a question and using these to discuss which is the best and for what reasons, considering to what extent they answer the question and meet the assessment objectives.

For an example of this approach, go to: www.uea.ac.uk/~m242/history pgce/assess/welcome.htm.

Using levels: in spite of all the misgivings about and limitations of the NCAT levels discussed at some length earlier, there is every probability that you could find yourself in a school where the history department is required to produce, even on an interim basis, data which indicates the level which the pupil is said to have reached. Consequently you need to work within the system and an important part of your placement would be to find out how the history department uses the NCAT levels and builds them into its schemes of work. It should be remembered that the levels were intended to be used as 'best-fit' end of key stage descriptors for pupils' progress, but departments are not always 'free agents' in terms of school policy on the use of NCAT levels.

As a student teacher you are more concerned with formulating your own assessment criteria and devising your own mark schemes for formative assessment. For this, most teachers would advise making such schemes specific to your precise learning objectives and also very much related to the topic taught. Harrison (2004) confirmed the value of devising precise contextualised diagnostic tasks with mark schemes on specific skills with indicative content knowledge together with annotated examples of pupil responses. This was found to be particularly valuable when tried and tested tasks were used across schools.

When assessing pupils' work a basic but very important question to keep asking yourself is. 'Am I assessing what I think I am assessing?' This can be particularly pertinent when considering the relationship between the understanding of Key Concepts, the use of knowledge and the presentation and the organisation of a piece of work. You need to consider, for example, whether a list of causes of an event with greater reward for the greater number of causes mentioned really demonstrates understanding of the concept. Also, you need to ensure your marking scheme really does reflect the question or the task set and that you are not asking the pupils to guess what you really had in mind. For example, does a question asking the consequences of an event necessarily imply that the pupil should analyse the different types of consequence to achieve the best reward or the highest level?

Task 10.6 Using levels

1 Ask your tutor or head of department for a set of unmarked pieces of work together with the associated assessment objectives.

2 Read through the pupils' work and try to place the pieces in rank order. Teachers generally find it easier to find agreement over rank order than in the allocating marks or levels.

3 With the work in rank order, try to identify the reasons for your decisions. Reflect on what has informed your decisions.

4 Translate these reasons into a marking grid with statements for marks. All statements should be *positive*. Avoid statements which deny marks because of what you feel has been omitted.

5 Check once more your statements against the assessment objectives and the task description.

6 Work out what feedback you would give to (i) the class and (ii) a sample of individual pupils.

7 Compare your results with the conclusions of the teacher who set and marked the work.

Adding variety: there may seem to be an apparent contradiction between those advocating the use of precise, contextualised diagnostic tasks and those favouring the use of a more holistic approach. This need not be the case for both have a place and what form of assessment you use is determined by your purpose. What is evident is that assessment tasks in history should not be a seemingly unending and demotivating diet of tasks replicating the types of questions to be found on GCSE papers. Rather much is to be gained by adding variety to your use of assessment. There are aspects of historical understanding that do not fit easily into a narrow examination format, for example the key concept requiring understanding of attitudes and beliefs of different times as well as the skills employed in well-constructed enquiries. The squeezing of coursework at GCSE has led to a narrowing of assessment formats and a limitation on the range of what studying history entails. The loss of the Local History Project, worth 50 per cent of the marks in one GCSE syllabus and often involving the gamut of key skills and concepts is but one example. However, as Luff (2003) has argued, this need not affect your teaching and formative assessment. He shows with a range of roleplay activities how they can be used to cover effectively a range of external examination objectives, while Guscott (2006) sets out his own guidelines for using roleplay for assessment in which a range of key concepts are covered. Both emphasise the importance of motivation and enjoyment together with the need to provide learning and assessment opportunities for pupils with differing learning styles.

Further variety in assessment may be found in the use of oral presentations either by individuals or by groups. The use of technology such as PowerPoint has added to the attraction of this approach. Such a method, apart from encouraging research skills and the use of the internet, can be used to involve peer assessment when the class assesses the presentations according to agreed criteria. Cain and Neal (2004) combined both presentations, roleplay and display as part of continual assessment for year 8. All groups, given set questions for enquiry, presented their findings in different ways, yet all were subjected to the class's success criteria for what a high quality enquiry should contain. In this way, many facets of learning history were covered in an enjoyable way, developing key historical skills not always covered by conventional examinations.

MARKING RECORDING AND REPORTING ON PUPILS' PROGRESS

OFSTED (2005) noted in the annual history report that while the quality of marking and assessment in history was improving in schools, there remained significant variations between schools. Features that needed attention included the need to give pupils clear indication of how well they were doing, failure to link marking to clear objectives and difficulties in interpreting the NC levels and turning them into workable criteria. Some reporting of pupil progress was too detailed and overly bureaucratic. From those comments it is clearly evident that the challenge is to achieve a balance in your recording of pupil work that is not excessively complex and time-consuming, yet is sufficiently detailed to enable you to build up a profile of a pupil's progress related to their knowledge, skills and understanding in history in a way that highlights both strengths and weaknesses.

Marking pupils' work takes up a significant amount of your time and you will need to give plenty of thought to how you can make the best use of that time. You might consider the value of marking pieces of work in terms of specific objectives not commenting or correcting on everything every time (making sure all realise what is the basis of your marking). As a student teacher you are usually required to follow your department's marking policy, and it is useful to be involved in any discussion that takes place about marking strategies and moderating and standardisation procedures. Many teachers would advocate the value of making meaningful comments in the pupils' books and using various tactics to ensure the pupils understand the comments, respond to them and, where appropriate, use them in future work. Most marking is a part of assessment for learning and this formative assessment should embody the principles of that initiative.

An aspect of formative assessment could be individual target setting, although with the number of pupils a history teacher meets during the course of a week it is not easy to achieve. History departments use various systems to try to involve pupils in setting targets and moving pupils on once a target has been achieved. Such systems include the use of a target sheet, which the pupils stick in their book. The idea is for the teacher to set initial targets and for the teacher and the pupil to review every so often. Some departments use traffic light signals for specific skills. Another method is to use large printed topic cards, which pupils place in a wallet stuck in the back of the exercise book. Pupils replace them with a new ones when they have been achieved.

The recording of pupil progress not only has its uses for the planning of learning but also to meet school requirements about that progress. Often history departments set pieces of work which over time cover the range of key skills and concepts. Such work is placed in a folder for moderation and comparison with previous work. Figure 10.1 is an example of an assessment record sheet used with year 9, showing the use of set tasks, grades, teacher comments and targets for improvement. The information on such a sheet would be the basis for reporting to senior management, discussion with parents and to facilitate continuity.

Grade awarded at end of year 8:

Assessment title	Attainment grade	Effort grade	Teacher comment / targets for improvement
Slavery sources (source skills)			
Slavery essay (causation, understanding, extended writing)			
Golden Age essay (sources, interpretations, extended writing)			
Dunkirk sources (sources, interpretations)			
Other			

Grade awarded on year 9 report:

Figure 10.1 Example of an assessment record sheet for a year 9 pupil

Continuity: assessment and records of assessment are useful tools to aid a smooth transition from year to year and also from one Key Stage to another. Within the secondary school, it is instructive to find out how history departments seek to prepare pupils for the expectations and demands of Key Stage 4. Given the pressures to recruit for the GSCE, consider how this can be achieved in a positive manner. The more pupils see that much of the preparation for Key Stage 4 has been done within Key Stage 3, the more comfortable they will be in opting for history. This could be reinforced by showing pupils the Grade C description for the GCSE, when they would realise how much it reflects that Key Stage 3 work and connects with their records of that work.

Task 10.7 Marking, recording and reporting on pupils' progress

In your placement schools, find out if there is a policy for marking and recording in:

a   the whole school;
b   the faculty; and
c   the history department.

Discuss with your tutors the main features of any policy – purposes and procedures. Does the school use profiling, individual pupil targets, review and self-assessment? Make notes on the procedures and ask to talk to pupils about their progress records.

History subject marking

How is this achieved? What use is made of pupils' exercise books? How do the teachers organise and use their mark book? Do they reflect the main areas of the NC? Is it possible to identify the strengths and weaknesses of individual pupils in their ability to apply knowledge, use skills and understand concepts?
   What use is made of ephemeral evidence – oral responses, contribution to group work, use of initiative in historical enquiries?

Reporting

How is the recorded information translated into material for reporting?

a   to pupils;
b   for the school records; and
c   to parents.

What are the means by which the parents are informed of their child's progress?

SUMMARY AND KEY POINTS

There is more to getting better at history than simple accumulating factual information about the past. Concentration on range of skills and understanding helps to define some of the ways in which pupils make progress in history. The assessment of pupils' progress in history is a highly sophisticated and extremely challenging aspect of your teaching. Although it is acknowledged that assessment is always an imperfect procedure, it is important that you are familiar with some of the pitfalls and are aware of some of the strategies to improve the validity and reliability of your assessment. You benefit from having a good understanding of the key issues involved in the assessment of history, and of the need to integrate assessment into your planning. Such planning should make sure that all the prescribed aspects of knowledge, skills and understanding are covered by the range and diversity of the tasks you offer to cater for the different abilities and aptitudes of your pupils.

It helps if you make sure you are assessing what you think you are assessing, if you have a clear idea about your expectations and these in turn are clearly communicated to the pupils. By working out in advance the kind of responses you are expecting and checking these against your objectives for the exercise, you are more likely to concentrate on these criteria when you come to mark your pupils' work. This adds to the reliability of your assessment by making it more objective and less dependent on 'impression' marking. Further information and resources on assessment, including suggestions for further reading can be accessed at: www.uea.ac.uk/~m242/historypgce/assess/welcome.htm.

REFERENCES

Association for Achievement and Improvement through Assessment (AAIA) www.aaia.org.uk, accessed 13 October 2007.

Biggs, J. and Moore, P. (1993) *The Process of Learning*, New Jersey: Prentice-Hall: Chapter 16.

Black, P. and Wiliam, D. (1998) *Inside the Black Box: Raising Standards through Classroom Assessment*, London: Kings College School of Education.

Booth M. (1983) 'Skills, concepts and attitudes: the development of adolescent children's historical thinking', *History and Theory*, Vol. 22.

Booth M. and Husbands, C. (1993) 'The history National Curriculum in England and Wales: assessment at key stage 3', *The Curriculum Journal*, Vol. 4, No. 1: 21–36.

Burnham, S. and Brown, G. (2004) 'Assessment without level descriptions', *Teaching History*, No. 115: 5–15.

Cain, K. and Neal, C. (2004) 'Opportunities, challenges and questions; continual assessment in Year 8', *Teaching History*, No. 115: 31–6.

Checketts, J. (1996) 'GCSE history: a case for revolution', *Teaching History*, No. 82: 20–2.

Cottingham, M. (2004) 'Dr Black Box or how I learned to stop worrying and love assessment', *Teaching History*, No. 115: 16–23.

Counsell, C. (1999) 'Historical knowledge and historical skills: a distracting dichotomy', Chapter 5 in J. Arthur and R. Phillips (eds), *Issues in History Teaching*, London: Routledge.

DfE (1992), *The Accreditation of Initial Teacher Training: Circular 9/92*, London: HMSO.

DfE (1995) *History in the National Curriculum*, London: HMSO.

DfEE (1998) 'Teaching; high status, high standards', *Requirements for Courses of Initial Teacher Training*, London: Department for Education and Employment.

DfEE/QCA (1999) *History: The National Curriculum for England*, London: DfEE/QCA.

Dickinson A. and Lee P. (1984) 'Making sense of history', in A. Dickinson, P.J. Lee and P.J. Rogers, *Learning History*, Oxford: Heinemann: 117–53.

Dicksee, I. (2006) 'Peer assessment', Chapter 10 in M. Hunt (ed.), *A Practical Guide to Teaching History in the Secondary School*, Oxon: RoutledgeFalmer.

Frith, D.S. and Macintosh, H.G. (1984) *A Teacher's Guide to Assessment*, London: Stanley Thornes.

Guscott, S. (2006) 'Role play as active history', Chapter 5 in M. Hunt (ed.), *A Practical Guide to Teaching History in the Secondary School*, Oxon: RoutledgeFalmer.

Hallam, R.N. (1972) 'Thinking and learning in history', *Teaching History*, Vol. 2, No. 8: 337–46.

Hallam, S. (1996) 'Pupil learning and differentiation', unpublished lecture, Institute of Education, University of London, 17 January.

Hammond, K. (2001) 'From horror to history: teaching pupils to reflect on significance', *Teaching History*, No. 104: 15–23.

Harrison, S. (2004) 'Rigorous, meaningful and robust: practical ways forward for assessment', *Teaching History*, No. 115: 26–30.

Haydn, T. (1994) 'Use and abuses of the TGAT assessment model: the case of history and the 45 boxes', *The Curriculum Journal*, Vol. 5, No. 2: 216–33.

Historical Association (2005) *History 14–19, Report and Recommendations to the Secretary of State*, London: Historical Association.

Lee, P. (1994) 'Historical knowledge and the national curriculum', in H. Bourdillon (ed.), *Teaching History*, London: Routledge: 41–52.

Lee, P. and Ashby, R. (2000) 'Progression on historical understanding 7–14', in P. Stearns, P. Seixas and S. Wineburg, *Teaching, Knowing and Learning History*, New York: New York University Press: 199–222.

Lee, P. and Shemilt, D. (2003) 'A scaffold, not a cage: progression and progression models in history', *Teaching History*, No. 113: 13–23.

Lewis, A. (1992) 'From planning to practice', *British Journal of Special Education*, Vol. 19, No. 1: 24–7.

Lomas T. (1989) *Teaching and Assessing Historical Understanding*, London: Historical Association.

Luff, I. (2003) 'Stretching the strait jacket of assessment: use of role play and practical demonstration to enrich pupils' experience of history and beyond', *Teaching History*, No. 113: 26–35.

OFSTED (1995) *History, A review of Inspection Findings*, London: OFSTED.

OFSTED (2002) Report on invitation conference, 'Assessment in History', London: OFSTED.

OFSTED (2003) *Good Assessment Practice in History*, HMI 1475, London: OFSTED.

OFSTED (2005) *History in Secondary Schools*, London: OFSTED.

QCA (2005) *History, Annual Report on Curriculum and Assessment*, London: QCA.

QCA (2007) The National Curriculum: History, Key Stage 3. Online at http://curriculum. qca.org.uk/subjects/. Last accessed 3 January 2008.

SCAA (1996) *Exemplification of Standards in History*, London: School Curriculum and Assessment Authority.

Shemilt, D. (1976) 'Formal operational thought in history', *Teaching History*, Vol. 4, No. 15: 237–43.

Stephen, A. (2006) 'Ensuring inclusion in the classroom', Chapter 8 in M. Hunt (ed.), *A Practical Guide to Teaching History in the Secondary School*, Oxon: RoutledgeFalmer.

TDA (2007) *Professional Standards for Teachers: Qualified Teacher Status*, London: TDA.

Vermeulen, E. (2000) 'What is progress in history?' *Teaching History*, No. 98: 35–41.

Watts D.G. (1973) *The Learning of History*, London: RKP.

White, C. (1992) *Strategies for the Assessment and Teaching of History*, London: Longman.

11 Teaching for external examinations

INTRODUCTION

Although the balance of your teaching experience during your course is likely to be with Key Stage 3 classes, even within your course, you will almost certainly have responsibility for teaching some classes with examination groups. If your course of initial teacher education is qualifying you to teach pupils aged 11–18, this will include some teaching of GCE AS and A2 classes, as well as GCSE classes. What's different about teaching examination classes – and what is the same?

Teachers care about the progress of all their classes, and are concerned about handing them over for you to 'practise on', whether they are in year 7 or year 12. But whereas slow content coverage with a Key Stage 3 class can be 'retrieved', lessons with exam classes are particularly precious; pupils generally only get one chance to do well in an external examination, and you have to take the gravity of this responsibility on board in your preparation and planning for lessons with exam groups. Time is precious. There is a specification to be covered (and time left for revision towards the end of the course), and pupils do have to remember things and have strong subject content knowledge to do well in history examinations: 'recall' is an important skill both at GCSE and GCE A Level. There is less scope for eclectic approaches with exam classes, and interesting but not strictly relevant diversions. You have to have a clear grasp of the detail of the exam specification (including the assessment objectives and the nature and format of the questions that pupils will be asked), and stick to these things in your teaching. There is a much stricter 'compliance' agenda than with Key Stage 3 teaching, where the teacher has much more autonomy in terms of what topics are covered, in what way, and at what length.

However, some student teachers make the mistake of thinking that many of the principles of subject pedagogy which apply at Key Stage 3 no longer apply, and that with, for instance, GCE A Level teaching groups, you can just deliver your notes, focus purely on content transmission, and not see a need to vary your teaching approaches and find ways of motivating and engaging pupils so that they work as hard outside the lessons as during them. Revision is a particular challenge; how to go over content that the pupils should already be familiar with, in a way that maintains their interest and extends and consolidates their knowledge and understanding. Imagination, initiative and varying your approaches in thinking what to do with topics is just as important with exam classes as with Key Stage 3 groups.

Another difference is that you may well be teaching exam groups 'alongside' their regular teacher, either team teaching, with you sub-contracting responsibility for planning teaching parts of the lesson, or planning and teaching collaboratively, or working with sub-groups of pupils or even individual pupils, to support the regular class teacher. This requires you to be extremely conscientious, flexible and adaptable in your approach.

For reasons which are hopefully obvious, you are unlikely to be given sole responsibility for teaching groups in the year of their external examination over a long period. If some of this seems rather daunting, you should keep in mind that working with examination classes is one of the most purposeful, enjoyable and exciting aspects of being a teacher. You see much more of the pupils over the two years of the course and consequently get to know them much better. To at least some extent, you are working with pupils who have chosen to do the subject in preference to other subjects. It is easier to get to the stage of feeling that you are all on the same side, working together towards shared objectives, and when it is your own exam class, you care very much about how well they do in the exam.

OBJECTIVES

At the end of this chapter you should be able to:

- locate and be familiar with examination options available at GCSE and GCE A level;
- locate and understand the assessment objectives for GCSE and GCE A level examinations;
- identify approaches you may adopt when given a GCSE class to teach;
- list possible approaches you may use when asked to teach an A Level class;
- obtain and use relevant information and resources to approach your teaching for examination classes.

USING INFORMATION FROM AWARDING BODIES

There has been a revolution in the amount of information and guidance for teachers provided by awarding bodies over the past three decades. The three main awarding bodies now provide a wide range of materials to support teachers in preparing their pupils for external examination. In addition to specifications, past papers, coursework options and examiners' reports for particular exams, there are resources guides, notice boards, media reports, roadshows, support meetings, MP3 downloads on technique and preparation, and (more controversially), courses on how to prepare pupils for the exam led by examiners.

You need to familiarise yourself with the examination specifications for the courses you will be teaching in the course of your school experience by reading the information available in the department you are working in, and discussing the exams with the colleagues you are working with. You must also be proactive in accessing the full range of resources made available by the relevant awarding body.

Task 11.1 Familiarising yourself with the range of support materials available from awarding bodies

Your first priority is to acquire 'a grounding' in the exam courses that you are teaching on placement; you can develop your grasp of the range of exams available at GCSE and A Level at a later stage. Your first priority is to prepare as conscientiously and effectively as possible for the pupils who are in your care.

As soon as you know which exam groups you will be teaching, access the relevant awarding body website, download the materials and resources which are available for the particular exam you will be teaching, and then explore the site to familiarise yourself with the full range of services which the awarding body offers.

The web addresses of the three main awarding bodies are:

Edexcel: www.edexcel.org.uk
OCR: www.ocr.org.uk
AQA: www.aqa.org.uk

TEACHING GCSE HISTORY

Background

GCSE, was introduced in 1986, replacing the earlier GCE O Level examination, intended for the most able 20 per cent, and the CSE, which targeted the next 40 per cent of ability. The hope was expressed that GCSE would not just amalgamate the two existing examinations but would extend examination opportunities for candidates of *all* abilities. The GCSE examination also introduced the idea that not all the assessment of a pupils' progress in the subject would be based on the final written examination. All candidates would produce coursework, which had to meet precise assessment objectives, and which would be carefully moderated by Examination Boards (now 'awarding bodies'). Although coursework continues to be recognised as a form of assessment which can suitably complement the end of course examinations, concerns over internet based plagiarism and parental assistance have led to moves to limit both the proportion of marks to be allocated by coursework, and to bring to an end the practice of pupils being able to complete coursework outside the classroom. From 2009, coursework will be done under supervised conditions in school ('Coursework axed to beat GCSE cheats', *Guardian*, 14 June 2007).

Since the inception of GCSE, there have been a number of changes to the subject criteria. The proportion of the specification to be devoted to British history has been set at 25 per cent, because of concerns in some quarters that pupils could 'escape' doing any British history between the ages of 14–16. The original GCSE exam saw a massive reduction in the amount of marks allocated to essay type questions, but more recently, the importance of pupils being able to express their knowledge and understanding in the form of extended writing has been acknowledged and the examination now has a more even balance between short 'source-based' questions, and questions involving extended writing. Another area of controversy was the inclusion of historical empathy in the original assessment objectives, in the form of 'an ability to look at events and issues from the perspectives of people of the past'. This has disappeared in the light of concern over the way in which empathetic understanding would be assessed.

History is one of a very small number of subjects which has one set of examination papers for the full range of GCSE grades. Tiered examination papers (papers targeted at a narrow range of GCSE grades) have been a feature of examinations in some subjects since GCSE was first introduced. Other subjects, including geography, introduced tiered papers in the context of the 1995 revisions to GCSE. The majority of history teachers have long considered it to be desirable for all candidates to sit the same examination papers and believe that it is possible to produce mark schemes that discriminate across the full ability range. A survey carried out by QCA in 1998 endorsed this view; although the proportion of supporters of untiered papers was far lower than on previous occasions. In their responses many teachers surveyed expressed concerns about the accessibility of the question papers to pupils of lower ability. The issue of tiered papers was raised by the tribunal of subject experts who debated the report of the five yearly review into history at 16+ conducted by QCA. The panel of subject experts recommended that at some point in the future, QCA should explore the implications of using tiered papers in GCSE history examinations, and this remains a contentious area of history exams.

The assessment objectives for GCSE history

Given the 'high stakes' nature of external examinations, it is important that there is clarity about exactly what we are measuring when we make judgements on pupils' achievements in the subject. In the examination specifications, this is indicated in the form of assessment objectives. These are the same for all the awarding bodies and all the specification options (the three main boards all offer GCSE courses in Social and Economic History, Modern World History, and the Schools History Project).

Under current GCSE regulations, candidates have to demonstrate their ability to (Assessment Objective 1): recall, select, organise and deploy knowledge of the specification content to communicate it through description, analysis and explanation of: the events, people, changes and issues studied, the key features and characteristics of the periods, societies or situations studied.

(Assessment Objective 2): use historical sources critically in their context, by comprehending, analysing, evaluating and interpreting them.

(Assessment Objective 3): comprehend, analyse, and evaluate, in relation to the historical context, how and why historical events, people, situations and changes have been interpreted and represented in different ways.

Task 11.2 Thinking about progression from Key Stage 3

How do the three assessment objectives above compare to the Attainment Statements in the NC at Key Stage 3? Look through the attainment statements for Key Stage 3 and compare them with the GCSE assessment objectives. To what extent is there continuity in terms of how we are attempting to measure progression in history? Are there any differences?

Teaching approaches for GCSE

As indicated in the previous chapter, the challenge to both teachers and examiners is how to accommodate knowledge within levels of response marking schemes. The specifications are required to include 'extended writing' as one form of assessment of candidates' achievements. The presence of such questions, carrying a substantial percentage of the marks for the paper, influences the way you prepare your pupils for the examination. They benefit from the occasional class essay on a prescribed topic, in which they are given about 25 minutes to complete an answer without reference to books or notes. As Husbands notes:

> It is not primarily the length of the written work which matters, but 'the provision of written tasks as culminations of historical enquiries which extend pupils' capacity to think historically . . . they should be challenging in the ways they ask pupils to complete the move from the accumulation of material, through the sketching of relationships, to the presentation of a statement about the historical material which they have explored.
>
> (Husbands, 1996: 109–10)

One of the challenges you face is how to ensure that pupils answer questions as fully as possible; you also need to get across to pupils that they need to be able to recall their knowledge in the examination – being able to remember what they have learnt is part of the test, as is being able to deploy their knowledge to answer particular questions.

On at least one of your school placements you should find that you are responsible a series of GCSE lessons. You need to think about how to do 'medium term' planning for the topic or topics you have to teach. Here are some suggestions for the preparations you can make for such teaching.

- Study carefully the specific specifications for which the pupils are to be entered, noticing how the assessment objectives are being met by the terminal examinations and the coursework.
- Once you have been told the content areas you have to cover with a class, find out in which part of the examination – coursework or the examination papers – that content is to be used.
- If it is for the examination, find out what are the chief emphases of that particular examination paper – concepts, interpretations, sources. This influences to some extent the way you approach the teaching of the topics you have been given.
- Examine the resources which the department uses for the teaching of that content; find out which books the pupils may take home.
- If the content area is one you have not recently studied, do some background reading to ensure that you are not only familiar with the detail but also your knowledge is wide enough to consider associated causes, consequences and the significance of events.
- With guidance from the teacher, begin to create a scheme of work for the series of lessons. Make sure that the main emphases of that element of the examination to which the content contributes are well represented in your scheme, that is, if sources form a major feature, include source work within the scheme.

- Whatever the paper, your pupils need to support their answers with relevant knowledge. To this end there will be some lessons, usually the earlier ones in a scheme, when you will need to consider how the pupils are to gather and record that knowledge. How much do you tell them? How much do they find out for themselves? Remember that there are tensions here; it is often quicker in terms of specification coverage to use teacher exposition. On the other hand, one of the aims of school history is to enable pupils to find things out for themselves.

- Remember, there are many ways of recording information and there is no reason why a year 10 class should not experience the variety of approaches used at Key Stage 3.

Task 11.3 Studying past papers

Another useful preparatory task is to study the specimen papers of the specifications you are to teach. Look closely at the questions and the associated marking schemes. Consider what teaching and learning strategies you could employ to enable you to be able to tackle such questions.

- What do the pupils need to know?
- What skills do they need to employ?
- How do your answers to these two questions affect your planning and choice of teaching strategies?
- Devise a question of your own that you feel would be appropriate for a GCSE exam. With the permission of your tutor, set the question for a class and think about its effectiveness and limitations, and how you will assess it.

Common mistakes and misconceptions of GCSE candidates

Technique: as a result of your own experience of examinations, you are already familiar with some of the guidance teachers need to give to candidates for external examinations. Advice about *the need to look carefully at the precise wording* of a question and to note that the number of marks available for question determines how much time should be spent on it. Your pupils should be familiar with the requirements of the paper and its rubric by having sight of an earlier paper. There are some candidates who fail to do themselves justice, because they do not follow the rubric or do not read the question properly. Encourage them to look for and understand the *meaning of the key words in a question* such as 'explain', 'compare', 'useful', 'reliable' and 'give reasons for'. They should clearly understand how such words will guide their answers.

Source skills: a common practice with some weaker candidates is to paraphrase the sources on the paper in the hope that such words will contain the answer. This may result from a limited understanding of the content of the source or from familiarity with rather undemanding worksheets, which allow pupils to copy or paraphrase without showing much thought.

There are times when pupils faced with a requirement to compare sources, will, nevertheless, paraphrase or describe each source in turn but without making any comparison. It may be helpful to encourage such pupils to develop certain routines such as completing a table.

	Similarities	Differences	Reasons for differences
Source A			
Source B			

There are some candidates, who, in the belief that the more they write the greater the mark awarded will be, devote much of an answer that requires the interpretations of sources to their description. Some give the impression that they think that assessing a source's utility means describing it.

Another common difficulty is the inability to differentiate between the 'utility' of a source and its 'reliability'. You might find it helpful if the pupils are encouraged to ask questions such as 'Useful for what?', 'Useful for whom?' and to realise that some sources, which contain some inaccuracies, still have their uses for certain enquiries. Some candidates can be too dismissive of such sources.

Again, with reliability, your pupils benefit from being encouraged to ask 'Reliable for what?', which again may not always be determined by the accuracy of some of the details in the source. Your pupils benefit from having set procedures for tackling both source questions and also different interpretations.

Less common now is the misconception that because a source is a 'primary' source it must be more reliable than a secondary source. It may still be worthwhile to pose a question which might explore this idea. (For example, 'Would it be possible for a secondary school pupil in this school to have better knowledge and understanding of what happened at the Battle of Waterloo than a soldier who fought in that battle? Give reasons for your answer.')

Use of knowledge: as discussed in Chapter 10, the role of knowledge generated considerable debate in the first ten years of the GCSE. One of your tasks is to try to encourage your pupils to think about how they use their historical knowledge. In this they should be aware of not relying too much on the information available on the paper but being able to support their opinions with other relevant, accurate information. Such knowledge is likely to push a mark to the top of the level in a mark scheme. The revised GCSE places more emphasis on knowledge and so those candidates who not only display a certain level of conceptual understanding but can also support the answer with knowledge will be rewarded – the more you can encourage your pupils to make use of knowledge to *back up* their statements and judgements the better and the more this is done at Key Stage 3, before the GCSE course, again the better.

Concepts: while it is important to encourage candidates to use their historical knowledge intelligently, there are times when questions dealing with concepts such as causation and change are seen by some pupils as requests for lists. This illustrates one of your problems in teaching GCSE history, namely, how to achieve a balance between teaching a body of knowledge but not giving sets of prepared answers, which may or may not answer the specific question set. Such a balance is often the case with, for example, causation, where a good candidate not only recalls the causes of an event but is able to use them. A recurrent comment from examiners is that candidates need more practice in evaluating the relative merits of different causes of events and of explaining the links between them. In other words, try to encourage your pupils to assess and evaluate rather than merely list, thus, some of the approaches to the teaching of concepts discussed in Chapter 5, are equally applicable to your teaching for the GCSE. So, in this way your pupils will not, for example, recount lists of results without making any attempt to assess and evaluate explicitly whether the changes they mentioned were important.

Task 11.4 Analysis and commentary on GCSE questions

Go to www.uea.ac.uk/~m242/historypgce/exams/welcome.htm
Read through the analysis and commentary on the two GCSE questions detailed on the website. How would you use this information to devise your own levels of response mark scheme for a GCSE type question for your pupils?

Coursework

Although coursework is (at the time of writing) worth a maximum of 25 per cent of the whole examination, it makes a valuable contribution to the variety of learning your pupils' experience. There continue to be aspects of the teaching and learning of history, for example the development of enquiry skills and the use of initiative to acquire, analyse and evaluate sources, which are more appropriately assessed away from the examination room. Coursework can also encourage different and more personal ways of organising and communicating history, consistent with the requirements of the NC at Key Stage 3. As noted in Chapter 10, assessment should form an integral part of the learning process and this is particularly true of GCSE coursework. In the words of one syllabus (1996) 'The coursework element of the syllabus is seen as a taught component which is designed to foster good practice by facilitating imaginative and innovative styles of teaching and learning, so that courses are enjoyable for all participants.' Indeed, while it is the usual case that coursework is presented in written form, the use of film and video, diagrams, models, tape recordings and photographs, if accompanied by adequate explanatory written material, is also allowed. Under the guidance of an awarding body, and provided the assessment objectives are met, schools and colleges are given the freedom to construct their own coursework tasks.

Should you be required to help in the preparation of pupils for their GCSE coursework, you need to be familiar with the assignments which the history department has set and the assessment targets each assignment seeks to meet. The department will have constructed a mark scheme for each of the assignments. As with the preparation for end of course examinations, you need to consider what knowledge, skills and understanding the pupils need to develop before they can attempt the assignments. For many this involves fieldwork. It is likely that pupils have several opportunities to attempt similar tasks for practice before they attempt the coursework that counts towards their final grade.

Task 11.5 Preparation to teach coursework

During your school placement, study the coursework details of the GCSE specifications for which the history department enters its pupils. Among the features you should note are: the way the assessment objectives are applied to the coursework elements; the choice of content available; the number and length of assignments required; the guidance offered by the awarding body for the creation of mark schemes for the assignments, noting the use of progression for the objectives; the administration involved and how this sets the timetable for completion by the pupils; the moderating procedures and any specimen examples made available by the awarding body.

Then, study the coursework proposals of the school to note how these seek to meet the requirements of the awarding body.

Task 11.6 Resources to support GSCE teaching

You don't have to limit yourself to departmental resources and your own ideas for teaching GCSE. There are many websites which have substantial sections on teaching GCSE. Explore some of the sites listed below and consider how you would use or adapt some of the ideas and resources available for topics which you have to teach with your GCSE classes. There are so many resources available that there is always a danger that you can just 'browse' and not collect, organise and deploy resources effectively. Try to make sure that you put together a powerful 'learning package' (see Chapter 8) on at least one of the topics that you are teaching using internet resources, together with material from other sources. (This is just a small selection of what is available. Do a Google search on 'History GCSE' for further options.):

www.historygcse.org
www.schoolhistory.co.uk/revision
www.schoolhistory.co.uk/gcse.html
www.johndclare.net
www.schoolshistory.org.uk/gcse.htm
www.activehistory.co.uk/Miscellaneous/menus/GCSE/menu.htm
www.redhotscott.co.uk/revision
www.burntcakes.com/resources/keystage_4.html
www.revisioncentre.co.uk/gcse/history/index.html.

Valuable advice on preparing pupils for GCSE examinations can also be found in the following articles in *Teaching History*:

Angela Leonard, 'Exceptional performance at GCSE: what makes a starred A?' (1999) No. 95, May: 20–3.

Diana Laffin, ' "My essays could go on forever": using Key Stage 3 to improve pupil performance at GCSE' (2000) No. 98, February: 14–21.

Chris Culpin 'Breaking the 20 year rule: very modern history at GCSE' (2005) No. 120: 11–14.

Entry Level Certificate history

This qualification course was introduced to meet the needs of pupils for whom the GCSE history courses were too demanding, both in terms of their assessment requirements and in the amount of material to be covered.

There are three pass grades: Entry 1, Entry 2 and Entry 3, which are intended to recognise a level of achievement below that of a grade G at GCSE, but candidates who are entered for the Entry Level Certificate qualification may also be entered for GCSE History full or short courses The courses give teachers considerable flexibility in selecting content to study from within the specifications. There is an emphasis on portfolio work, with 'core tasks'. At present, students have to complete a maximum of six assignments, some of which can be selected from board-set assignments, and all of which are designed to match with GCSE topics so that the course can be completed by some pupils within a GCSE class. AQA is changing the assessment from 2008, so that students complete only four tasks instead of eight, dropping the two board-set tests which were previously compulsory. Some departments like the entry level certificate because it gives some pupils a chance to get a certificate where they might otherwise have ended up with nothing, but take up has thus far been modest.

Task 11.7 Developing insight into tasks for less able pupils post Key Stage 3

The suggested frameworks for the Entry Level Certificate in history provide interesting insights into 'official' versions of differentiation in history. Course specification and examples of the sort of work which Entry Level Certificate pupils are asked to undertake can be accessed at:

Edexcel: www.edexcel.org.uk/quals/elc/8916
OCR: www.ocr.org.uk/qualifications/EntryLevelCertificateHistory.html
AQA: www.aqa.org.uk/qual/pdf/AQA3904WSP.PDF.

Examine a range of the tasks which pupils are asked to undertake. What insights do these tasks provide for ways of providing meaningful, worthwhile and genuinely historical activities for less able pupils? It might be helpful to consider the extent to which the Key Stage 3 areas of knowledge, skills and understanding (or from September 2008, key concepts and processes) are embodied in the tasks specified.

Take up for Entry Level qualifications has not traditionally been high. Talk to the history teachers you work with about the pros and cons of entering pupils for the Entry Level Certificate.

The GCSE history pilot

Recent concerns about the appropriateness of the GCSE history exam for all pupils has also led to the development of a 'pilot' history GCSE, which at the time of writing is being trialled by the OCR awarding body. Described as a 'hybrid' examination, it aims to combine the study of history post 14 with vocational elements of experience. In the words of Ken Boston:

> The aim of the pilot is to allow students to make links between the history they study and its application to the world of work. There is now a wide range of employment related to our national heritage. This exciting and innovative approach to history GCSE would give students a rigorous grounding in both the historical knowledge and practical skills they need to take advantage of those opportunities. The combination of academic knowledge and practical

experience is what many employers in this expanding sector want in their recruits.

(Boston, 2006)

Significant features of the specification include:

- an emphasis on internal and teacher assessment;
- flexibility, by offering centres a wide range of optional units and providing opportunities for them to develop these units in ways that reflect local interests and needs;
- enhancing the potential of the history curriculum to address aspects of vocational education;
- emphasising to candidates the importance of history for understanding and participating in both their own communities and the wider world;
- a focus on representations and interpretations of history, particularly those found in the heritage and tourist sectors.

(OCR, 2006)

The pilot was started in September 2006 with about 70 schools. The 'related' or contingent vocational elements include areas such as heritage, archives, museums, galleries, historical sites, archaeology, tourism and the media. The 'hybrid' element involves allowing pupils a range of 'pathways' through the course, including both history specific and general or vocational units, but as well as linking history to vocational areas, the aim of the pilot is to trial new approaches to content and assessment at GCSE. The 'core content' includes a unit on medieval history, a local history enquiry and an international enquiry focused on significant or controversial issues in history. Optional units include:

- heritage management and marketing;
- multimedia in history: bringing the past to life;
- an archaeological enquiry;
- Whose history? Presenting the past;
- change over time;
- missing pages: the migrant experience;
- a society in depth.

The overall aim is to provide a lively and innovative history course for 14–16 year olds that caters for the needs of pupils, is relevant to pupils growing up in the twenty-first century, and which addresses some of the criticisms of the current format of GCSE examinations (see, for example, Culpin, 2002) and the disaffection towards history displayed by some pupils (see Biddulph and Adey, 2003). At this point it is too early to say how successful the hybrid history GCSE pilot will be, and the extent to which it will be 'taken up' post-pilot, but it is important that you have a sound basic knowledge and understanding of the course: it is a potential question at interview for your first post.

TEACHING ADVANCED LEVEL HISTORY

Background

When GCE A Levels were first introduced sixth form education had been a 'prize' won only by the most able, most of whom who were destined for university but by the mid-1990s more than 60 per cent pupils stayed on at school beyond the statutory leaving age and full-time education post-16 was generally perceived to be desirable and an entitlement for all those who wanted it. However, a result of the move to an open access sixth form led to concern about the large number of students who, after two years in the sixth form left school with no qualification to show for their efforts. Initiatives intended to broaden the sixth form curriculum to make it appropriate to students with a variety of career goals had been less successful than hoped and concerns to improve this situation led to the setting up of an enquiry into qualifications 16–19 which was published as the Dearing Report (Dearing, 1997).

The recommendations of the Dearing Report were reviewed and refined by the New Labour administration in 1997 and by September 2000 far reaching changes to the system of qualifications post 16 were finally implemented. In an attempt to ensure parity of esteem of General National Vocational Qualifications (GNVQ) with GCE A level qualifications all qualifications, including GCSE were accredited within a common qualifications framework, whereby GCSE (Grades A–C) is a Level 2 award and a pass grade at GCE A Level or in an advanced vocational qualification is a Level 3 award. A modular structure was introduced for all post-16 qualifications and a grading scale of A–E was to be used.

Perhaps the most radical of the changes implemented in 2000 was the introduction of what was, in effect, an entirely new qualification which could be taken at 17+ and is called the Advanced Subsidiary (AS). This new qualification is gained at the midway point between GCSE and 'A2' level and recognises achievement at a standard reflecting the progress students have made at that midway point in an advanced level course. A full GCE A Level constitutes an AS in the subject (3 modules of study) plus 3 additional modules usually taken in the second year of the sixth form and assessed at the A level standard. The QCA is currently undertaking a review of GCE A Levels across all subjects. For further detail on this, follow the URL given below.

 For commentary offering some insights into the challenges and opportunities of the AS/A2 model, and further details of proposed revisions to the current system, see www.uea.ac.uk/~m242/historypgce/exams/as.htm.

The new specifications continue to offer schools or colleges a good deal of autonomy in terms of what areas of historical content can be taught. There is scope to teach from medieval to modern and the history of a wide range of countries, although the scope for teaching the history of countries in Africa, Asia and Australasia is somewhat limited. At present, there is still opportunity for centres to offer candidates the chance to carry out a personal study which can be selected to meet an individual candidate's own area of interest, but the 'coursework' or personal study component of GCE A Level is one of the elements currently under review. From 1998, additional requirements were placed on awarding bodies in the development of the new specifications. There is now in place a set of nationally agreed criteria for each of the major GCE AS/A Level subjects, including history. These criteria provide the basis for the approval of new specifications at advanced level by QCA, ACCAC and CCEA, the regulatory bodies for England, Wales and Northern Ireland respectively who have the responsibility for ensuring the maintenance of standards and rigour of public examinations. Many of the criteria are common to all subjects at GCE A Level. For example at GCE A Level, all subjects need to provide opportunities for the development of the six key skills and to indicate what aspects assist candidates in their spiritual, moral, social and cultural development as well as the provision at the end of the full advanced level course for the candidates to sit an examination that tests their understanding of the course of study as a whole, a synoptic assessment.

There are also content criteria that are different for each subject. Two aspects of the history content criteria proved to be controversial with the subject officers at the awarding bodies and within the subject community more widely, as they had significant implications for the structure of the current specifications. The first of these was the requirement for all GCE A Level specifications (but not AS specifications) to include a 'substantial element of British history'. A substantial element was subsequently interpreted as one module of the six leading to the full A Level award. The criteria also required the study of change over time of at least 100 years. The requirement to study change over time had been included in the original draft criteria and was a response to a perception from the history community, particularly historians in university departments, that A Level courses had become too narrow, with some only requiring the study of a period of 30–50 years over what was typically a two year period of study. More recently, concern has been expressed about the trend towards many pupils' diet of history being limited post–14 to the study of 'Hitler and the Henries', and repeating the same content at Key Stage 3, Key Stage 4 and GCE A Level. This narrowing of A Level courses had been the major issue emerging from the deliberations of the tribunal of subject experts on the outcomes of the 'Five yearly review of standards in A level history'.

Task 11.8 Preparing to teach GCE A Level history

1   History A Level specifications that are taught in schools are usually selected by the head of department based on three considerations; their personal preference, their expertise and the resources available to them. You no doubt wish to share in the selection but you first need to familiarise yourself with the variety of specifications available. Send for a copy of two separate specifications from two different awarding bodies. You may also send for the examiners' report for that particular specification. After studying each specification comment on the following:

    a   Which publishers produce the appropriate course textbooks? Are they useful?
    b   What assessment arrangements does the awarding body make?
    c   Do the assessment procedures require resources? What are they?
    d   Would the content of the course appeal to both teacher and pupil?
    e   What teaching strategies are necessary for the course?
    f   What skills are demanded from the pupils and how do you prepare them for the examination?
    g   Does the examiners' report help you to decide whether to recommend the specifications?

h   How would the coursework/personal study be marked?

i   Do you need to train the students in new assessment techniques?

j   Is the course 'objectives led'?

2   There is an art to asking questions of documentary sources of the type which are used in the GCE A Level examinations. Pick out some A Level textbooks which have examples of documentary sources and look at the sorts of questions which are asked of them. Look at the document questions from past examination papers and then try setting your own set of questions on a small collection of documents which are appropriate for A Level pupils.

Preparations for teaching a GCE A Level group

Most secondary courses are 11–18 courses so that you find yourself teaching not only Key Stage 3 and GCSE but also some post-16 history classes. Even if you are teaching in an 11–18 school, opportunities to teach whole A Level groups for sustained periods of time are often limited. However accomplished and conscientious you may be, schools have to be careful that involvement in ITE does not compromise the examination preparations of pupils, and have to reassure parents on this point. Because opportunities are limited, you need to take advantage of any offers available to become involved in A Level teaching. This can often include observation, work with small groups, or team and collaborative teaching with the teacher responsible for the group. Often, exposure to A Level classes comes later in your school placement, when you have (hopefully) become more comfortable in the classroom and have had some time to think about the challenges of teaching A Level. Experienced teachers can often make A Level teaching look deceptively easy. Many student teachers find A Level preparation and teaching quite challenging at first, and an illuminating experience. If you do find that it is 'hard going' at first, in terms of both preparation and teaching, remember that many teachers find it to be one of the most enjoyable and rewarding aspects of teaching.

Because you are learning so much with all ages and abilities in such a short space of time, it can be helpful if the topic you are asked to teach is one with which you have considerable familiarity from you own higher education or A Level experience, but as with so many facets of school experience, it is important that you try to fit in with the needs of the department. It may be possible to negotiate A Level experience which ties in with your subject knowledge strengths and the convenience of the department, but if this is not possible, do not eschew the opportunity to get as much experience of A Level as possible. You have to accept that preparation time will be increased if you have to work on subject knowledge in addition to subject application.

Task 11.9 National Curriculum and GCSE as a preparation for A Level teaching

Before considering your preparation for teaching, it may be instructive to consider the extent to which NC history and GCSE might have prepared your A Level pupils for their history course.

1   Ask the head of history for the appropriate documentation related to the A Level course you are to teach. This involves details of the syllabus, the department scheme of

work, the assessment procedures and the examiners' reports. What are the assessment objectives for the A Level course? What are the characteristics of the work of a good A Level candidate?

2   Make a list of the principal characteristics and objectives and then consider the extent to which the study of NC history and the revised GCSE have already developed the pupils' understanding of history in a way that the A Level course can extend. Compare the A Level assessment objectives with the NC Key Concepts and Processes and the revised GCSE assessment objectives.

3   Consider (a) the development of pupils' skills in reading history and (b) their ability to produce extended writing. How much opportunity did pupils have to develop these skills before the A Level course?

Discuss your answers to these questions with the history teachers you work with and ask how such considerations influence their approaches to A Level teaching.

Preparation for A Level teaching can be onerous and time-consuming. Because you are so conscious of the need to do your best for the pupils, knowing from first-hand experience the importance of grades, there may be a danger that you allocate too much time to your A Level preparation at the expense of the younger pupils. To reduce this kind of pressure, if possible, try to ensure that you are given as much prior notice as possible of any A Level teaching commitments. It is often better to begin your A Level teaching a few weeks after the rest of your teaching and very useful to have spent time observing the class for several lessons before you take over. In this way you become more familiar with the prior content and with the teacher's style and approaches. There is a case for undertaking more observation before taking external examination classes.

Your own knowledge of the topic

Your first concern is to gather together background information for yourself. Secure subject knowledge helps you to feel more relaxed and confident about teaching the class, and in responding confidently to pupils' questions. Dig out your own notes if you have them, but be prepared to discuss your preparation with the teachers. They appreciate the pressures on your time and can be very helpful in indicating useful chapters and articles for you to read. Make sure you do not confine your reading too exclusively to the topic you are to teach but read around it as well. In this respect, you should pursue what is also good practice for pupils; that is to read around the subject at several levels, studying general texts, books more specifically related to the topic in question, and also articles and monographs from journals written specifically to support A Level history (see 'Further Reading' at the end of this chapter). You may need to extend your reading as your preparation develops, and as your involvement with A Level classes extends.

Be clear about your objectives

This is just as important as for your teaching of younger pupils. In the same way as your schemes of work covered a variety of objectives and approaches with, say, Key Stage 3, the same applies to A Level teaching. Different lessons will have different purposes. You need to be clear what these are and they could include:

- to contextualise, to present a general framework of the topic;
- to identify the key issues/concepts/attitudes;
- to discuss differing interpretations;
- to develop further the pupils' study skills in communication, oral, written, essay-writing;
- to develop pupils' skills in expressing their opinions with confidence, substantiated by use of knowledge in reading, pursuing enquiries and note-making;
- to develop further the pupils' historical understanding in the analysis, interpretation and evaluation of primary and secondary sources, in the application of key concepts in history, in assessing the significance of events;
- to develop an informed scepticism and an acceptance of uncertainty.

Check the pupils' previous knowledge

As you are taking over a group during the course of the academic year, familiarise yourself with the content they have already covered. This gives you some idea about what the pupils may be expected to contribute and helps you to link your topic to others. You also need to find out about the abilities and attitudes of the pupils. With the great increase in the numbers continuing in full-time education beyond the statutory school-leaving age, you meet a quite wide range of ability in A Level groups with the result that differentiation continues to be a significant factor in your planning and teaching.

Resources

You need to find out what books and other reading materials are in the possession of the pupils and what other books, articles and source material are within easy access to the students. Limitations on resources can be one of the more frustrating aspects of A Level teaching and you need to find out how the department tries to manage, especially if there are large groups. Try as much as you can to resist the temptation to rely on an untransformed version of your own notes from previous study because of the limited availability of books. Your undergraduate notes, however assiduously may well be wildly inappropriate for the purposes of A Level teaching. Find out what scope there is for the pupils to use their own initiative, local libraries and information technology resources such as history CD-ROMS and the internet; whether some purchase their own paperbacks, and the extent to which they co-operate in the effective sharing of resources.

Choice of approaches

As with your teaching of the younger pupils, you need to include a variety of approaches and styles in the planning and delivery of your A Level lessons. Indeed many of the methods recommended elsewhere in this book can be applied with equal effectiveness in the A Level classroom. Your choice of approach is, as ever, determined by your learning objectives for a particular lesson. You still need to think precisely about the outcomes for the pupils and try to avoid the notion that your preparation is only concerned with the historical content.

Teacher presentation

You will find that there are times when you have to do quite a lot of the talking in some lessons. It is useful to think about what aspects of the scheme are most appropriate for teacher presentation. Yet it can be an interesting challenge to try to reduce the amount of teacher talk in teaching A Level history. There is a good case for teacher exposition at the beginning of a topic, to set the framework of the topic in its general context, to draw out the main issues and events and to indicate, where appropriate, the different interpretations that have emerged. Given the range of ability you are likely to encounter there remains a good case for the use of visual aids, charts, diagrams or duplicated handouts to assist your presentation. There is a good case for then presenting the students with task sheets and book references to help them to research the details for themselves rather than you pursuing such detail in a lengthy monologue while the students attempt to transfer your exposition to their notes.

Reading and note-making

Be prepared to allocate time in the classroom for the pupils to do their individual reading and note-making. This could give you time to talk to individuals, review their progress and apply some differentiation. The reading and note-making usually needs to be done within a prescribed framework and time limit with clear indication about the purposes of the reading. *The History Manual* (1985) by J.A. Cloake *et al.* remains one of the best and most detailed guide for A Level students and is particularly helpful on the key activities of reading and note-making. They make the point that often pupils read inefficiently and ineffectively and so much thought needs to be given to helping them to make the most of their reading, especially as reading can be a neglected feature of the learning of history lower down the school. The new entrant to the A Level course needs plenty of help and encouragement. There is a case for spending some time analysing some texts together, deciding what are the key points, what is noteworthy and how one might set out such notes. What pupils decide is noteworthy is often an indicator of their historical understanding. Inspection of pupils' notes can produce a useful dialogue. Cloake, Crinnion and Harrison also emphasise the need for the pupils to be involved in 'active' reading, questioning and consciously assimilating what is being read, with reference to their previous understanding of the topic.

Source skills

The extent to which this might feature in your scheme depends on the topic you have been asked to teach and the syllabus for which you are preparing pupils. With a background of the GCSE pupils have a familiarity with source skills in a way that many former 'O' level candidates did not. This needs to be built upon with more advanced text and language and greater emphasis on the significance of the sources and their relationship to the wider issues. Again it is much better that such source activities are placed in the context of a genuine historical enquiry, debate or problem rather than a rather sterile skills exercise. It can be helpful to use case-studies with the students being given initially a general context and framework, as advocated earlier, and then provided with a selected body of primary sources with which to analyse the historical correctness of a given statement or to discover the solution to a particular problem. Howells (2000) offers practical suggestions for the use of documents with A Level pupils.

Variety of activities

Teaching A Level history can offer plenty of opportunities for pair work and group work. Different groups can be set different tasks, particularly if there are limitations of resources, as a preparation for a plenary feedback. You can try to be imaginative in creating situations where the pupils have to make decisions, e.g. comparing the treatment of a topic by different authors, evaluating interpretations or deciding which of two written responses to a question is the better. Getting the pupils to be able to communicate and discuss *from an informed position* requires thought and preparation, but can be both rewarding and enjoyable to set up properly and implement.

There is a good case for using roleplay in A Level history teaching. It will differ from similar activities with younger pupils in that it is much more firmly rooted in the sources, secondary and primary. Roleplay could be used effectively to draw explanations of why different historians produce different interpretations. The nature of the subject also encourages the use of set debates for which the students need to use their reading to prepare a case. They can be asked to devise and explain charts and diagrams to summarise ideas.

Essay writing

Setting essays, marking them and giving detailed feedback is another important part of A Level teaching, especially as there may have been limited opportunities for extended writing in GCSE. Many students find essay writing to be one of the most difficult features of their study and usually need detailed guidance and feedback, as well as encouragement. Study the examiners' reports for indications of the qualities that should be encouraged. They often give examples of good answers. Pupils can be encouraged to devise, perhaps in pairs, skeleton answers to questions as a basis for discussion.

Reviewing

As indicated above, setting reading and other tasks can free you to talk to individuals and review their progress. With a range of ability you can try to match their individual study to their ability, suggest appropriate reading, check understanding, consider written work, including essays, and set targets. It is useful to keep your own records of such meetings.

Team teaching

There are times when there is much to be gained by team-teaching an A Level topic with the pupils' usual teacher. There are many ways in which together you can present differing viewpoints and stimulate debate. There are other occasions when you and a fellow student can work effectively as a pair in teaching an A Level topic.

The following list is taken from a lecture to student history teachers by Bernadette Josclin of Richmond Tertiary College, which many students found helpful.

Things to try to do

1   Plan your classes carefully within the framework of a topic and then the overall scheme of work. Keep a close eye on *timing*. Know how long you've got for each topic.
2   Ensure that pupils have a clear idea of where they are going in a topic/scheme of work. (Give out a typed scheme, or plan of the topic.)
3   Remember, topics take longer at the start of the course than at the end.
4   Prepare your notes using past papers, syllabuses, key texts, etc.
5   *You* set the agenda in class, i.e. deadlines, work rate, etc.
6   Remember to explain key concepts – particularly at the start of the course.
7   Build in a variety of activities to the sessions.
8   Start from *their* knowledge and work back.
9   Build in study skills sessions – time management, essay writing, etc.
10   Organise some low energy sessions for yourself – sessions where *they* have to do most of the work.
11   Think carefully about how the work which you do in class will translate into effective revision notes for them – clear headings, etc.
12   Set them work which they can bring *to* the lesson, so they know something about the lesson beforehand.
13   Check their notes/files; keeps pupils on their toes and gives you an idea of how they are translating the work you set for them.
14   Build in *regular* checks on understanding – not just essays.
15   Constant reminders of key issues.
16   Recognise and remember that most groups are mixed ability; identify learning difficulties.
17   Be clear about deadlines and stick to them, even if this is unpopular!
18   Use the blackboard (or whatever) to emphasise key words, points, etc.
19   Look in GCSE and Key Stage 3 resources to see if there are good teaching ideas and resources which can be adapted.
20   Use source material wherever possible – try to develop historical skills.
21   Try and create situations where the pupils work/talk rather than you.
22   Be positive in the comments you make in response to pupils' efforts.
23   Give pupils lists of past questions at the end of a topic – useful for revision.
24   Always prepare a fall-back activity in case you run out of material.

Try not to

1   Talk too much: what are the pupils doing?
2   Do all the work – the pupils must do some things for themselves.
3   Always have 'high energy' sessions on your part. They are not always what is educationally best for your pupils.
4   Always prioritise transmission of content at the expense of other learning objectives.
5   Be sloppy in your time keeping – and punctuality to lessons, giving work back – this will only encourage the same traits in them.
6   Assume that all pupils are highly motivated budding historians. Like all other teaching groups, they need motivating and encouraging.
7   Waffle in class – be prepared! Admit mistakes if you don't know.
8   Assume too much about pupils' knowledge and vocabulary.

(Josclin, 1995)

Resources to help with A Level teaching

The major history websites for history teachers (see Figure 9.1 for a list of some of these sites) have been invaluable in enabling student history teachers to quickly develop a wide range of teaching approaches and materials for A Level classes. See for instance:

> www.schoolhistory.co.uk/alevel.shtml
> www.schoolshistory.org.uk/ASLevel_History/index.htm
> www.activehistory.co.uk/Miscellaneous/menus/A_Level/menu.htm
> www.thinkinghistory.co.uk/ActivityKS/ActivityALevel.html

There are also journals specifically targeted at A Level History teaching, such as *Twentieth Century History Review*, and the popular history magazines mentioned in Chapter 9 also contain articles on current historiographical controversies and issues which are appropriate for A Level pupils. *Teaching History* also has regular articles relevant to teaching A Level (see www.uea.ac.uk/~m242/historypgce/exams/as.htm).

SUMMARY AND KEY POINTS

Assessment in history has experienced enormous changes in the last 30 years. Much of what is now established as common practice would be unrecognisable to the history teacher of a generation ago. Such changes in assessment have resulted from the acceptance that what constitutes historical understanding involves a combination of skills, concepts, and attitudes allied to knowledge. Attempts to assess these various elements have led to the use of varied types of assessment and much debate about their validity. The recent moves away from the targeting of a precise skill towards a less compartmentalised and more holistic approach indicates a probable resolution of some of the difficulties surrounding an achievement of balance between historical understanding and knowledge.

REFERENCES

Biddulph, M. and Adey, K. (2003) 'Perceptions v. reality: pupils' experiences of learning in history and geography at key stage 4', *The Curriculum Journal*, Vol. 14, No. 3: 292–303.

Boston, K. (2006) 'QCA awards contract to develop GCSE history pilot', Press Release, London: QCA.

Culpin, C. (2002) 'Why we must change history GCSE', *Teaching History*, No. 109: 6–9.

Dearing, R. (1997) *National Committee of Inquiry into Higher Education*, London: DfEE.

Howells, G. (2000) 'Gladstone spiritual or Gladstone material? A rationale for using documents at AS and A2', *Teaching History*, No. 100: 26–31.

Husbands, C. (1996) *Why teach History?*, Buckingham: Open University Press.

Josclin, B. (1995) Unpublished lecture, Institute of Education, University of London.

OCR (2006) The GCSE History Pilot. Online at: www.ocr.org.uk/qualifications/GCSEHistory-Pilot.html. Last accessed 3 January 2008.

12 Continuing professional development

INTRODUCTION

The final chapter encompasses two elements of teaching history which are not part of the competences outlined in the Standards for QTS (TDA, 2007) which define the capabilities that student teachers must possess if they are to be granted Qualified Teacher Status (QTS). The first is the question of applying for your first post in teaching. It is important to realise that effective preparation for this is a separate area of competence. There is no necessary correlation between teachers' classroom teaching abilities and their skills in self-promotion and preparation for job applications. There are many excellent teachers and student teachers who do not do themselves justice in terms of job applications because they have not applied the same degree of thought and rigour to the process of application as to their classroom competence in teaching history.

The second area returns us to questions which were broached in the first chapter: how do history teachers get better at teaching, and why do some progress to higher levels of competence than others?

What can you do to ensure that you are successful in your applications for teaching posts, and to ensure that your Newly Qualified Teacher (NQT) year marks the start of your progress towards becoming an inspirational history teacher rather than a competent one? You didn't go into teaching with the aspiration of becoming merely 'competent', and your school experience will quickly make you realise that a substantial part of the pleasure to be derived from a career in teaching is knowing that you are getting better at it. It is probably true at least to some extent that the better teachers become at their job, the more they enjoy their work, and in teaching, you can always get better. This is why the job does not lose its interest and challenge.

OBJECTIVES

At the end of this chapter you should be able to:

- draft a letter of application or personal statement for a first post;
- identify a range of questions which might be asked at an interview for a first post in history;
- approach your first teaching post in a manner conducive to assisting your continuing professional development and prospects for career success and job satisfaction.

APPLYING FOR YOUR FIRST TEACHING POST

Advice on job applications and interviews for student teachers for all subjects is provided in Chapter 8 of *Learning to Teach in the Secondary School* (Capel *et al.*, 2005). To a large extent, this chapter confines itself to information relevant to student teachers of history.

The word processor has made it much easier and quicker to adapt personal statements and letters of application to the particular school you are applying to, and the job and person specifications to which you are directing your application. There is a tension here between simply constructing one version and sending it to all the schools you apply for, and 'customising' the content of your letter or statement in order to fit the post advertised. This is a question of judgement. If there has been no effort to direct your response to the post as specified, this might smack of laziness or a casual attitude. There is, however, the danger that if you attempt to tailor your writing to suggest that you have always dreamed of teaching in St Swithin's, Bolton, teaching SHP GCSE syllabuses, and Edexcel 'Syllabus E' A Level, your sincerity might be called into question. Most schools accept the reality that you are applying for a range of schools; there is therefore no need to dissemble your reasons for applying, but it is helpful at interview if it is apparent that you have made some efforts to find out about the school you are hoping to work in. At the very least, you should look at the OFSTED report on the school. Most schools now have a website, and it can be helpful and politic to explore the school and the departmental website. If the departmental website is limited or non-existent, it is an area that you could (diplomatically) declare an interest in and enthusiasm for at interview if you possess the capability to make and maintain a website (see Chapter 8).

The URL for accessing OFSTED school inspection reports is: http://www.ofsted.gov.uk/reports/.

The range of *periods* of history, as well as differences between exam specifications, poses questions about how to approach the issue of subject knowledge which perhaps go beyond those pertaining to other subjects. Very few applicants have expert levels of subject knowledge of all optional elements of the NC, and are familiar with all examination alternatives. You can however, 'do your homework', in terms of studying the information which the school sends to you, to have a look at the exam syllabuses which the school subscribes to, and to consider what you would suggest as your present strengths and developing interests in terms of subject knowledge. As well as being able to talk confidently about areas of history which you think you are particularly well equipped to teach, you should be prepared to talk about the ways in which you have augmented your subject knowledge in the course of your training, and your agenda for developing your subject knowledge further. Capel *et al.* (2005) make the point that there are several ways of developing subject knowledge other than reading. This might include observation in schools, talking to fellow student teachers, watching video recordings, studying history CD-ROMs, and peer or collaborative teaching. Capel also stresses the importance of keeping a record of your developing breadth of competence, in subject knowledge and other areas. If you have kept a thorough record of your experiences in the course of training, it can streamline the process of constructing your letters of application and preparation for interview. If you are well organised, and make the time to record your observations, experiences and evaluations, this can also make your NQT year much easier, and save you from having to redraft lessons from scratch, instead of simply refining and adjusting what you have tried out in the course of your training.

LETTERS OF APPLICATION

Some schools require you to fill in an application form, part of which is a personal statement in support of your application. Other schools simply ask for a letter of application. It is important that you do not repeat yourself and reiterate statements that have been made elsewhere in your response, for instance, in talking about your degree details in the personal statement, when they are appended in a curriculum vitae. The construction of curriculum vitae and letters of application in general are described in depth in Capel *et al.* (2005).

It may be salutary to remind yourself of what schools are looking for when they seek to appoint a new member of staff. Although not all schools send out both a job description and a person specification with the details for a post, it is helpful to keep in mind that there are two ways of looking at what schools want when they advertise a post. One perspective is the audit of various aspects of the job which need to be done: 'What is this person required to do?' Another way of looking at the vacancy is to think of what qualities a person would have to possess in order to do the job effectively. Your letter of application should bear in mind both these considerations. Very few student teachers find writing letters of application an easy or edifying process. How do you indicate that you are good without coming over as bumptious or arrogant? Many applications suffer from an inability to make clear that the candidate has not merely undergone teaching practice, but has done so successfully, and in a way which has developed their teaching skills and reinforced their commitment to entering the profession.

As in writing history, you should attempt to provide supporting evidence for your claims, but in a carefully measured and (if anything) understated manner. One way of doing this is to incorporate brief extracts of summary reports and lesson observation notes which have been produced in the course of your placement. This is a way of avoiding having to rely solely on personal claims about your teaching competence, and can be balanced with statements indicating that you felt or believed that certain aspects of your teaching competence developed and improved as your practice progressed. If you look carefully at all the written comments which have emanated from your school experience, it should be possible to marshal the comments in such a way as to give a clear indication of the ways in which you have done well and proved to be successful, or demonstrated the potential to be a good, or very good history teacher.

There are obvious connections between the competences stipulated by the QTS Standards, and the prerequisites outlined in Figure 12.1, but schools are looking for more than a teacher who can adequately fulfil the demands of the standards. The three domains of competence specified in the QTS Standards are central to teaching competence, but they are a necessary, not sufficient condition of employability – schools are looking for teachers who have reached high levels in these areas of competence, but there are attributes which lie beyond this central core which can often be decisive in interview situations where more than one candidate convinces the interview panel that they possess the fundamental competences of classroom teaching.

The following list may not be comprehensive, but gives some indication of what most heads of history would be looking for when seeking to appoint a new member of staff. The first four criteria are particularly important.

1. Secure a purposeful and controlled atmosphere in the classroom and establish positive working relations with pupils.
2. Arrive at lessons equipped with materials and ideas which provide worthwhile, stimulating and challenging learning experiences for pupils.
3. Work with colleagues in a co-operative and helpful manner and be prepared to play a full part in the life and work of the department.
4. Get good results with their examination groups.
5. Mark pupils' work promptly and thoroughly, with appropriate feedback and comment.
6. Set and mark purposeful and worthwhile homeworks according to school policy.
7. Keep an effective record of pupil attainment and progress.
8. Liaise effectively with parents, heads of year, form teachers, other members of your department and the school's senior management team.
9. Develop and maintain the state of classrooms, prepare display work, etc.
10. Contribute to the department's teaching resources and take care of resources used.
11. Be aware of, and make a positive contribution to school policies and the life of the school in general.

Figure 12.1 What do heads of history want from a prospective member of their department?

There are other facets of classroom teaching to which departments might attach particular importance, in the light of their circumstances: the department may be looking for a new appointment who can provide a lead in the development of ICT, citizenship, or equal opportunities, but the attributes outlined in Figure 12.1 are at the heart of the work of all history departments, and the first four items on the list are of particular importance. Your letter of application, and your performance at interview should bear in mind that these are the considerations which are central to the head of history's concerns. Are you the sort of teacher who can do these things well?

In view of this question, many schools draw up a person specification as well as a job description. Even where this is not the case, in addition to teaching competences, schools are looking for teachers who possess personal and professional qualities which will complement technical classroom competence and subject knowledge. Your letter of application and your performance at interview needs to convince the panel that you are intelligent, conscientious, committed to working with young people, well organised and able to work to deadlines, with a sense of initiative and imagination, and that you are a 'reasonable human being', who has the interpersonal skills to work as part of a team. Probably the most important paragraph of your letter of application, and the one which should be longest, is the one which relates to your performances on school placement, and in composing it, you should attempt to convey these professional attributes, as well as your classroom competence in planning, assessment, and subject knowledge. It is also important to keep in mind the importance which schools attach to the life of the school beyond the classroom. It is not unknown for one of the questions at interview to be about what you could bring to the school in addition to your abilities as a history teacher.

One of the most important things when you start your school experience is to demonstrate your overall professional attitude and approach, and demonstrate to the colleagues you work with that you are conscientious, dependable, quick to learn, a pleasure to work with and keen to do the best for the pupils in your care. A further skill is to prepare and teach a series of good, well planned lessons to the classes you are responsible for, and try to establish a good working atmosphere in your classes.

Once you are (hopefully) established in these ways, you should give some thought to what else you might be able to contribute to the department and the school you are working in. Before the end of the placement, try to make sure that you make at least some contribution (preferably something you are genuinely interested in and have a real enthusiasm for) beyond the history classroom, such as extra curricular activities, ICT or SEN support, clubs, trips, sport, drama, departmental development. As well as being rewarding and worthwhile in its own right, particularly in terms of helping your relations with pupils inside the classroom, it is invaluable for your CV. Most inspirational teachers are 'givers'; they have a generosity of spirit as well as being expert practitioners.

This thought might come at a bad time when you are on your knees with the burdens of preparation, teaching, marking, etc., and crawling towards Easter desperately looking forward to the break, but even if you are feeling pretty tired, give some thought to this for action at some point in your NQT year: what would be the best way (for you as an individual) to contribute to the department or school beyond 'just' being good in the history classroom?

One final point about interview; although you are judged to some extent on the quality of your answers to the specific questions posed by the panel, your general manner and approach can have an important bearing on the outcome. If you come over as sincere, composed, intelligent, personable, and committed, this may outweigh a less than perfect answer to one or more questions. Often student teachers who have been unsuccessful at interview blame their fate on the content of their response to a particular question, and underestimate the importance of their general demeanour. Although you may feel self conscious about the exercise, it can be helpful to tape record your answers to some possible interview questions, and play them back to see whether you are answering at inordinate length, whether your responses come over as glib or ponderous, faltering or garbled, or simply boring.

The following details are an exemplar of a job description for a history post. Read them and then draft a letter of application which attempts to address the demands of this particular post.

In the first instance, the successful candidate will be required to teach across the 11–16 age and ability range, at this mixed, split-site 11–18 high school. Opportunity for A Level work would be considered for candidates with appropriate experience and qualifications. The person appointed would be expected to take responsibility for the teaching and organisation of history in the lower school, under the overall supervision of the head of history. They will also be expected to teach GCSE classes, and contribute to the department's impressive academic record in public examinations. An ability to contribute to extra curricular activities, particularly in the areas of sport and drama would also be welcomed. The ability to promote the development of information technology in the history department would also be helpful. Pupils study modern world history at GCSE, and nineteenth-century British and European history at A Level. History classes are setted according to ability at the end of year 7.

The successful candidate will be expected to possess the following attributes:

- A determination to aspire to the highest academic standards for pupils.
- The ability to take responsibility and initiative in the field of curriculum development.
- Willingness to play a full part in the whole life and activities of the school.
- The ability to contribute effectively to the school's pastoral system by involvement as a form tutor.
- Expertise in information technology and its application to the history curriculum.
- Health, stamina, energy and determination.

Figure 12.2 Composing letters of application

Task 12.1 Adapting letters of application

What changes would you make to your letter of application in the light of the following job specification?

The school is seeking to appoint a candidate who will be able to teach across the age and ability range at this 11–16 inner-city comprehensive school. An ability to teach the subject in a way that will stimulate the interest and enthusiasm of all pupils is an important prerequisite for the post, as is the ability to establish good working relations with pupils. The department enters pupils for Schools Council History syllabus; pupils are in mixed ability groups from year 7 to year 9. The ability to teach some Key Stage 3 Geography or RE would be welcomed, as would a willingness to contribute to the school's extra curricular activities.

The following would be considered to be particularly important attributes for the post in question:

- Liveliness of approach and variety of teaching methodologies.
- Relationships with students and colleagues.
- Commitment to working with pupils of all abilities.
- Contribution to activities outside the classroom.
- Flexibility and resilience.

INTERVIEW QUESTIONS

Although the details of the post which you receive along with the application form may provide some clues as to what questions might be asked, and what are the most urgent concerns and priorities of the school, question spotting is as speculative an activity in the context of interviews as in attempting to predict what questions will be asked in written examinations. There may be general trends underlying which questions are 'fashionable' or prevalent, and it can be helpful to talk to peers to get a feel for the range of questions which seem to be 'current' (ICT, Every Child Matters, Assessment for Learning, Inclusion, Differentiation, 'stretching' able pupils, thinking skills, creativity) but it is probably more helpful to practise answering interview questions in general, rather than rehearse a 'set piece' answer to particular ones in the hope that you can them trot out a pre-rehearsed formula, if one crops up at interview. You should also beware of trying to say what you think the panel wants to hear rather than what you feel. Interviews are not generally a test of political or pedagogical correctness, and you are more likely to talk fluently and convincingly if you believe what you are saying. It is also advisable to be measured and careful in what you claim, rather than lurching beyond what you can plausibly claim from your limited experience. You do not want to come over as dogmatic and inflexible, but neither do you want to be seen as an empty minded opportunist.

The short list for a first appointment in history is unlikely to be fewer than four candidates, and may be as many as ten. Given that part of the day is generally given over to showing candidates round the school, introducing them to the senior management team, and meeting members of the history department, this usually leaves time for an interview of no more than 25 to 45 minutes. The former length would usually leave time for no more than five or six questions; you should be aware of these constraints, not feel the need to talk for the same length on all of them, and keep answers short if you feel you have nothing further of value to say. Another factor which you should keep in mind is that in the course of the day, the head of history will be considering whether you would be a pleasure to work with, and whether you would 'fit in' to the department, both socially and professionally. 'Reasonable human being' qualities are not central to the demands of the QTS Standards, but at this point in the process of entering the teaching profession, they are an important factor.

The following list of questions was drawn up by heads of History who work with student teachers as examples of the sort of questions they have used at interview.

How do you assess pupils' learning in your classes?

Why should we give time and space to history on the school curriculum?

How would you be able to contribute to a collaborative approach to curriculum development?

How would you monitor and assess your own delivery of the curriculum?

What do you feel are the most important issues in history teaching and learning?

Using specific examples, what principles would you apply when designing resources for mixed ability classes?

Describe a lesson that you were responsible for that you feel was particularly successful and explain why?

If appointed to the post, what evidence might you point to in a year's time to show that you had executed the job description successfully?

How can we maximise the achievements of our students?

What are your principal strengths and weaknesses as a teacher? How will you ensure that the effects of your weaknesses are limited?

How do you engage the interest and enthusiasm of the pupils for the study of history? Give some examples of ways in which you have done this.

What can you say to persuade us that you will be successful in securing good results with examination classes?

In what ways might history teachers use ICT successfully in the classroom?

In what ways will pupils have benefited if they have been in your history lessons from year 7 to year 9?

Figure 12.3 Interview questions

Task 12.2 Practising for interview

Together with two fellow student teachers, conduct a practice interview using some of the above questions, or others which you might devise. One of you should act as observer, commenting on what they felt were the strengths and weaknesses of your responses and any idiosyncrasies/habits which might adversely influence performance at interview, such as a tendency to say 'you know' at intervals, scratching the back of your neck, looking too gloomy, or evasive eye contact.

Task 12.3 Finding out about interview procedures and questions

Ask your subject mentor about the general procedures for interview at the school you are working in, what questions are commonly asked at history interviews, what heads of history look for in candidates, what mistakes candidates sometimes make in answering questions, and what advice he or she would give you in terms of preparation for the interview.

TEACHING AT INTERVIEW

It has become increasingly common in recent years to incorporate some element of presentation or teaching into the selection process. Although this introduces an extra hurdle, and possibly an element of pressure and concern into the procedures, in many ways it is easier to prepare for this element of the selection process. Unlike the interview, where you do not know exactly what will be asked of you, it is usual to give candidates a clear brief of what is to be taught, and to what class. It is not likely to be the class from hell on Friday afternoon, and there will usually be someone observing the class, so classroom management should not be a major concern. You are usually told what topic to teach but be given a degree of latitude in how to approach it. In effect, you should have a reasonable amount of time to prepare a single lesson; most applicants find that this can be a comparatively straightforward and surprisingly enjoyable aspect of the selection process, given the extent to which the candidate is informed beforehand what is required (whereas interviewees do not normally know what questions will be asked at interview). You often only have 'half a lesson', and have to plan a lesson for 20–30 minutes rather than an hour or longer, and you should take account of this in your planning rather than try and squeeze too much in and rushing your delivery. In terms of 'components', you need to show that you can teach 'from the front of the class', succinctly explaining the purposes and aims of the session, demonstrating that you have a relaxed, assured and unselfconscious presence in the classroom, that you have good skills of exposition and questioning and can interact with pupils in an accomplished way, even if this is just for a few minutes. There should generally be some 'active learning experience' for pupils, where they 'do the work', and are made to think and learn through some skilfully designed task. It can also be helpful if you can come up with at least one 'impact' resource (see Chapter 8) that evinces the pupils' interest or sticks in their minds. You should also leave at least a couple of minutes to 'construct meaning' from the encounter; to draw things together, summarise what has been learnt (look for a 'golden nugget' for example – see Chapter 3), preferably in a way that makes explicit the purposes and benefits of studying and learning from the past, and a good last line to finish on. All this without rushing it!

THE CAREER ENTRY AND DEVELOPMENT PROFILE

The Career Entry and Development Profile (CEDP) provides a formal plan for mapping your professional career development when you enter the profession. All newly qualified teachers are required to bring with them to their first post an audit of 'strengths and needs' which can serve as a basis to negotiate a programme of continuing support and professional development. You still need to work on weaker areas of your teaching, but you should also give some thought to thinking about which strengths to develop to higher levels, in order to further your career and ensure that you continue to find the business of teaching rewarding.

Some history teachers choose to focus on the consolidation of their subject knowledge, others on progressing to more sophisticated levels of expertise in ICT. Many find that involvement in the mentoring of student teachers is an interesting and helpful area for developing professional expertise. INSET courses, whether accredited and leading to advanced diplomas and masters degrees, or simply one day workshops to develop new schemes of work, do not magic away all your problems and limitations in the classroom, but can serve to sustain your interest and offer some practical ways forward.

The choice of ways forward needs to be negotiated with the school and department you work in, but it is important to be proactive in terms of staff development; initiative and drive are as important after QTS (Qualified Teacher Status) as before. When you start in your first teaching post, your Career Entry Profile should be given to the teacher in charge of staff development. It should be used as a basis for setting short, medium and longer term targets for your professional development. The extent to which you make the most of opportunities for development and advancement as a teacher can depend to some extent on the thought which goes into this process.

The CEDP is important, not least because it says something about you as you start in your new school, but conveys a 'first impression' of your professionalism. Some student teachers produce thoughtful and thorough CEDPs. Others can be rather careless, vague and minimalist. It is interesting to note that in the annual survey of NQTs produced by the Teacher Development Agency (TDA), only 10 per cent of NQTs felt that their preparation for completing the CEDP was 'very good'. This survey can in itself be helpful in thinking about what to put in your CEDP, as it details over 20 aspects of teaching which might be considered as areas for development (use of ICT, using assessment, managing pupil behaviour, working with pupils with SEN or EAL, teaching pupils of differing abilities and so on). The survey is available at www.tda.gov.uk/partners /datasurveys/nqtsurvey.aspx (or do a Google search for 'NQT survey'). One of the key things about the CEDP is not to leave it to the very end of your course of training. It should be formulated in draft form over the latter half of your training, in consultation with the teachers and tutors you work with, and should be based on the feedback you receive from them, as well as on your own ideas and priorities for development.

There should be funding available to support you in your induction year, and it helps to be aware of the range of CPD opportunities available for history teachers (see below). Although support in this area is negotiated rather than dictated with the school you will be working in, it can be helpful to them if you have clear and specific ideas about your priorities for development. This might be in the area of support for your A Level teaching commitments, particular GCSE exam courses, ICT or SEN development, or help with behaviour for learning strategies. It might be as specific as indicating that it would be helpful to have departmental or personal access to *Teaching History*, or a wish to attend the School History Project Annual Conference.

Further information and guidance on the Career Entry Profile can be found at: http://www.tda.gov.uk/teachers/induction/cedp.aspx. (Should the URL change, just type in TDA Career Entry and Development Profile on a Google search.)

GETTING BETTER AT TEACHING HISTORY

In Chapter 1, we posed the question of how people get better at teaching. It is generally accepted that it is not simply a matter of accumulated experience, and that several factors are involved, including learning from doing it, watching it being done, being instructed in it, reading about it and talking about it with fellow practitioners. Matthew Arnold, commenting on a school inspector who boasted of being an inspector of 13 years' experience, remarked that he was an inspector of one year's experience, repeated 13 times over. How can you avoid similar accusations being made of your own teaching career? Although the idea of reflective practice has become an influential one in recent years – the idea that teachers improve through the quality of their reflection on doing it, reading about it and so on – reflection on practice might not *per se* enable teachers to develop to expert levels. (Hamlet was good at reflecting but did not become effective at what he wanted to do.) Part of the definition of being professional is that you want to improve and are determined to do whatever is necessary to effect improvement. Initiative, determination and ambition (to aspire to the highest possible professional standards) are as important as reflection in making progress as a teacher.

Other agendas include the question of developing ownership of your own teaching. Whilst working within the framework of your department, you will hopefully develop your own ideas and style of history teaching, and generate ideas as well as assimilating those of other history teachers and tutors; one of the pleasures of teaching as a profession is that it offers the opportunity for genuinely creative and innovative practice. There is, however, the danger of what MacDonald has termed 'induction into bad practice' (MacDonald, 1984), and of being socialised into a particular brand of professional practice, rather than remaining open to new ideas and suggestions (Calderhead, 1994). This is why it is so important to look for opportunities to meet up with and work with history teachers outside your own department, and become part of a broader 'community of practice'. As well as being useful, this is also one of the most enjoyable facets of being a teacher; teaching tends to attract 'reasonable human beings', and getting to know other history teachers is one of the 'perks' of the job. The Schools History Project Annual Conference is a good example of this (see www.leedstrinity.ac.uk/shp/whatisshp.htm for details).

The demands of your course, and your observations and experiences in the course of your training, will have made you fully aware that however diligent and accomplished you have been, you do not emerge from your training as the perfect, fully equipped 'expert' teacher. As in so many aspects of teaching, the idea of a continuum can be extremely helpful. The best teachers are aware of the continuums involved on the journey towards becoming an expert teacher and are constantly seeking to aspire to the highest possible professional standards. Progression is an issue that pertains to teachers as well as pupils. The Teacher Development Agency's emphasis on the importance of professional development, from NQT, to excellent and advanced skills teacher, and subject and school leadership has focused attention on the need for teachers to continue to be learners who will refine and develop their classroom competences. Figure 12.4 shows the list of qualities which the Teacher Training Agency (now Teacher Development Agency) considered to be desirable in the mentoring of student teachers. It is indicative of the sort of teacher who is likely to be effective, and a good role model, in helping other teachers and student teachers to improve.

The ideal contributor to ITT (Initial Teacher Training) might, amongst other things, be:

- knowledgeable about teaching and learning, and still curious about them;
- knowledgeable about a subject and how to teach it;
- knowledgeable about a range of teaching methods and when and how to use them;
- always ready to reassess teaching methods in the light of research, experience and feedback (a 'reflective practitioner');
- an active listener;
- good at giving clear and constructive feedback;
- a skilful planner;
- a skilful manager of time;
- someone with plenty of enthusiasm, energy and imagination;
- someone who goes on learning throughout their career. (TTA, 1996)

Figure 12.4 Qualities desirable in subject tutors

At one level, this is about continuing to develop and refining your classroom teaching skills, as defined in the specifications for acquiring QTS. You *must* develop to adequate levels of competence in the areas stipulated by the QTS Standards, but you *should* aspire to excellence in all these areas, rather than settling for 'baseline' or minimum levels of competence. The framework of competences outlined for the acquisition of QTS has a continued relevance, but you should now be focusing on expert levels of competence, rather than adequacy. Thus, for instance, with regard to your ability to maintain pupils' interest and motivation, there is the question of the range and percentage of lessons in which you are able to arouse the interest and engagement of pupils, and there is also the degree of interest and engagement which you are able to elicit from your teaching groups. In what percentage of your lessons do pupils leave the room still talking about what they have learnt? As your experience and classroom knowledge increase, there should be more and more historical topics which you are able to present in a way which elicits the engagement and enthusiasm of pupils.

If teaching is to continue to be a rewarding, enjoyable and fulfilling profession, you need to feel that you are getting better at it and learning new skills, or acquiring higher level skills in your teaching. The range of factors involved in developing into the expert teacher, and the 'complete' history person are such that, as in your training, you have to make difficult choices in terms of prioritising some areas of professional development over others; this requires thought, professional dialogue with colleagues, and intelligent judgement.

THE INDUCTION YEAR

All teachers who obtain QTS have to successfully complete an induction period. If you are working part-time, this period could be up to two years. NQTs have a reduced timetable of 90 per cent of the teaching duties of staff without posts of responsibility during this period. Formative assessment of the NQT's progress involves regular observation and monitoring, and targets for progress and development are usually set as part of this process.

In term 1, these will focus on the extent to which you are meeting the Standards for QTS in your teaching post. In term 2, these will move towards the extent to which progress is meeting the Induction Standards, and in term 3, there is a review of whether Induction Standards have been met (see the TDA website for details of these standards: www.tda.gov.uk).

All this is within a professional culture of 'performance management' where the professional performance of all teachers is subject to review and development, with the intention of raising standards in schools, and enabling all teachers to fulfil their professional potential in full.

There are many areas of history teaching where student teachers develop to levels of basic competence, or beyond basic competence in the course of their training, but not to higher levels of competence. The following are 'prompt' questions, which you might consider in thinking about where you stand in terms of the continuum between adequate and expert levels of proficiency in various aspects of teaching history. With all these questions, you might consider both the percentage of lessons in which . . . and the extent to which . . .

How effective are you at explaining to pupils what happened in the past in a way that interests pupils and in a way which they can understand?

How effective are the homeworks which you set in terms of advancing pupils' learning, and reinforcing their motivation to do well in history?

How effective are you in using new technology to enhance the quality of teaching and learning in history?

How effectively do you differentiate your planning for learning in a way that provides both access and challenge for pupils in your history lessons?

> How broad and accomplished is your range of teaching techniques in the history classroom?
>
> How good are you at working co-operatively with colleagues to share ideas and good practice?
>
> How assured is your subject knowledge in the areas you are obliged to teach?

Figure 12.5 Questions to think about in terms of degrees of competence

These are but a handful of many questions/continuums which you should consider in the course of your continuing professional development. As you aspire to subject leadership, there are also agendas such as time management, administrative efficiency, professional relationships and effective communication which complement those of classroom teaching. You also need to continue to develop your subject knowledge, keep abreast of new developments in ICT, keep up to date with new ideas for teaching history, and ensure that you have an up to date knowledge of official documents relating to assessment arrangements and changing syllabuses.

To think about...

Proposition: there are not enough hours in the day to do everything which might be done to become the perfect or complete history teacher (and keep a sliver of life apart from your teaching).

However, if you do at least some of the following things, the improvements in your effectiveness as a teacher will be sufficiently rewarding to justify the time and effort involved.

- They continue to read history books for pleasure and pass on some of the fruits of their reading to pupils.
- They read books, and journal and newspaper articles about current debates about history, history teaching. and the nature and purposes of school history.
- They read review articles about new publications in history.
- They attend INSET courses and history conferences to keep abreast of new ideas and to develop a broader repertoire of teaching skills.
- They talk to other history teachers about their teaching, and exchange ideas and resources.
- They find time to read history journals such as *Teaching History, Modern History Review, History Today*.
- They make changes and refinements to lessons even when they have worked quite well first time with classes.
- They keep abreast of broader educational debates by reading *The Times Educational Supplement*, and the weekly education sections in the newspapers.
- They are familiar with and make regular use of good internet sites for history teachers to improve their practice.
- They continue to try out new ideas and methods in their teaching.
- They display initiative in 'scavenging' for resources which help to make lessons more vivid and enjoyable for pupils.

- Their relations with teaching groups improve as the teaching year progresses.
- They make time to talk to and work with pupils outside formal lesson time.
- They make strenuous efforts to get the best results possible for pupils taking external examinations.
- They enjoy their teaching.
- They learn to balance their personal and professional lives to the advantage of both.

Figure 12.6 Some characteristics of good history teachers

It might also be added that at the end of term, they are tired; but in recent years, intrinsic enjoyment of employment has been increasingly regarded as an important element of job satisfaction. It is much more likely that you will enjoy teaching if you believe you are doing it effectively, and getting better at it.

The areas of competence defined by the regulations for acquiring QTS – professional attributes, professional knowledge and understanding, and professional skills – remain just as central to your development as a teacher after you have gained QTS. There are however other models of competence which might provide insight into which teachers are likely to progress towards mastery of teaching skills and expertise. John Elliott's work on action research as an agent for teacher development has been influential (Elliott, 1991, 2007). Another source of insight might be to study the weekly feature on 'My best teacher', which is now included in both the *Times Educational Supplement,* and *The Guardian's* education section. As well as demonstrating that there are very different types of expert teacher, it is heartening to be reminded of the impact and difference that a good teacher can make.

WHAT FORMS OF CONTINUING PROFESSIONAL DEVELOPMENT (CPD) ARE AVAILABLE TO HISTORY TEACHERS?

OFSTED (2006: 4) recently described opportunities for CPD for history teachers as 'wholly unsatisfactory . . . far more needs to be made available'. Research commissioned by the TDA suggested that although provision was variable, both across and within LEAs, there was a wide range of CPD opportunity for history teachers, some of which was felt to be of high quality. The following list gives some idea of the forms of CPD which history teachers engage in, although they are not universally available:

- Historical Association conferences and residential weekends;
- The Annual Schools History Project conference;
- regional seminars and conferences (London History Forum, Midlands History Forum, etc.);
- local network or 'cluster' meetings of neighbouring schools set up by LEAs;
- LEA History 'county' INSET days;
- meetings of local history teachers run by History Advanced Skills teachers;
- 'in-house' or 'away day' departmental development meetings;
- ITT mentor meetings (often partly, but not wholly focused on CPD issues);
- history specific ICT courses;
- commercial companies (Keynote, SfE, Dragonfly, Lighthouse and others);
- exam board sponsored courses related to particular examination courses;

- action research projects funded by a range of education agencies focused on practitioner research;
- meetings related to the implementation of the 'national strategies' programme;
- reading *Teaching History*;
- E-CPD – a range of electronic/distance learning forums (see Chapter 8);
- Particular Historical Association projects (on, for example, the use of voting technology).

Task 12.4 Finding out about history CPD opportunities

Talk to the teachers you work with about their experience of history CPD; ask them what CPD experiences have been enjoyable and worthwhile, and which less so. Do a Google search on some of the commercial companies, awarding bodies and history organisations which offer CPD for history teachers (see list above) to get a feel for the range of courses which might be possible to enrol on.

SUMMARY AND KEY POINTS

Much of the enjoyment and fulfilment in teaching comes from the knowledge that you are continuing to become more accomplished and effective in various facets of teaching. Don't stop thinking about how to get better, and how to extend your range of teaching abilities. Be proactive in reading, observing, communicating with others, and looking out for valuable experiences.

Your ITE course is the first stage of your development as a history teacher, not the culminating point. Student teachers are not the only ones that sometimes 'plateau' in their development. A large measure of job satisfaction in teaching is derived from the satisfaction of doing the job well and getting better at it. You need to display initiative in your continuing professional development rather than simply waiting passively for professional advancement. Partly this should derive from your own sense of adventure in the classroom, partly from reading, and partly from advice, courses, conferences and guidance from other professionals. The challenge of becoming a comprehensively accomplished history teacher is a very difficult and demanding one, requiring a wide range of knowledge, skills and personal and professional qualities; the nature of this challenge helps to explain why the profession of the history teacher is such an interesting and (potentially) rewarding one.

Some student history teachers develop further than others in the course of their training. Some start well and seem to have the capacity for excellence at an early stage in the course, only to disappoint in terms of their subsequent development. Others start in quite a diffident and hesitant way but then make steady and impressive progress. The same variations in trajectory and progression continue after qualification. Even if you have been an outstandingly successful trainee, there are still many ways in which you can improve as a history teacher. There are two different questions which might be asked of student teachers. One relates to how far into their course it will be before those involved in their supervision and training feel confident that they meet all the Standards for QTS and can be 'passed' to go into teaching. The other is the question of the extent to which the history teacher will continue to develop towards being an inspirational and exceptional teacher, rather than a competent one. The latter question is perhaps the more important one.

FURTHER READING

The conferences of the Historical Association, and the Schools Council History conference are important events in terms of keeping up to date with your subject and keeping abreast of the ideas of leading practitioners, official bodies and recent research into school history. In addition to keynote addresses, a wide choice of workshops, 'drop-in' ICT demonstrations, and publishers' exhibitions, it is generally exhilarating and enjoyable to meet with and talk to fellow history teachers in such a propitious and congenial environment. The conferences demonstrate that it is possible for in-service experience to be useful and enjoyable at the same time.

The main professional journal for history teachers is *Teaching History*, published four times a year by the Historical Association. There has been a conscious attempt to move towards articles which are of use and interest to classroom practitioners. Many of the ideas and suggestions will help you to improve your teaching, and make your teaching more enjoyable and fulfilling. *Teaching History* also contains reviews of new text and topic books and history software. Anyone going into history teaching should regard it as essential reading. Recent improvements to the website, including the archiving of past issues, the monthly newsletter, and reports on recent projects and innovations have made membership of the Historical Association even more essential. Local Education Authorities and some providers of ITT also have courses to support NQTs, but there is some variation in provision.

 The internet address for the Historical Association is www.history.org.uk and for the Schools History Project website is www.leedstrinity.ac.uk/shp.

Some recent texts on the teaching of history are more 'light' and 'user friendly' than others; they are not all easy reading, but as Lawlor (1987) has noted: 'Very many things in life – at school and later – including the acquisition of knowledge, require effort and concentration.' The initial teacher education process, with its taut schedules, frenetic pace and constant demands, does not lend itself to discursive reading, but after qualification, you should at least have some time over the summer break to read some of the important and influential books which have shaped opinion on what school history should be, how it relates to academic history, and now it might best be taught (see Chapter 9 for details).

REFERENCES

Calderhead, J. (1994) 'The reform of initial teacher education and research on learning to teach: contrasting ideas', in P. John and P. Lucas (eds) *Partnership in Progress*, Sheffield: University of Sheffield Department of Education.

Capel, S., Leask, M. and Turner, T. (2005) *Learning to Teach in Secondary School: A Companion to School Experience*, 4th edition, Oxon: RoutledgeFalmer.

Elliott, J. (1991) *Action Research for Educational Change*, Buckingham: Open University Press.

Elliott, J. (2007) *Reflecting Where the Action is*, Oxon: Routledge.

Lawlor, S. (1987) 'Correct core', in B. Moon, P. Murphy and J. Raynor (eds) *Policies for the Curriculum*, Buckingham: Open University Press.

MacDonald, B. (1984) 'Teacher education and curriculum reform – some English errors', paper presented at the symposium 'Theory and practice of teacher education', Madrid, Ministry of Education, February.

OFSTED (2006) *Annual Report of Her Majesty's Chief Inspector of schools, 2005–6*, London: OFSTED.

TDA (2007) *Professional Standards for Teachers: Qualified Teacher Status*, London: TDA.

TTA (1996) *Qualities Desirable in Subject Mentors*, London: TTA.

Index